Rethinking the
Role of the State in Finance

GLOBAL FINANCIAL DEVELOPMENT REPORT 2013

Rethinking the
Role of the State in Finance

THE WORLD BANK
Washington, D.C.

ISBN (paper): 978-0-8213-9503-5
ISBN (electronic): 978-0-8213-9504-2
DOI: 10.1596/978-0-8213-9503-5
ISSN: 2304-957X

Cover photos: Shutterstock
Cover design: Naylor Design

Contents

BOXES

FIGURES

MAPS

TABLES

Foreword

The *Global Financial Development Report* comes at a time when the worldwide financial crisis has starkly highlighted the importance of financial systems and their role in supporting economic development, ensuring stability, and reducing poverty.

Finance matters, both when it functions well and when it functions poorly. Supported by robust policies and systems, finance works quietly in the background, contributing to economic growth and poverty reduction. However, impaired by poor sector policies, unsound markets, and imprudent institutions, finance can lay the foundation for financial crises, destabilizing economies, hindering economic growth, and jeopardizing hard-won development gains among the most vulnerable.

Fostering sustainable financial development and improving the performance of financial systems depends on numerous institutional factors and stakeholders. The policy maker, the regulator, the banker, and the financial consumer must all play their part.

The World Bank Group has been actively engaged in financial sector work for some time, aiming to help various parts of the institutional mosaic—including regulation and supervision, corporate governance, and financial infrastructure—ensure that the financial sector contributes meaningfully to strong and inclusive growth. This report seeks to advance the global financial sector policy debate, highlighting the important perspective of emerging markets and developing economies. It contains a rich array of new financial sector data that are also publicly available as part of our Open Data Agenda.

Sharpening the focus on the central role of finance in socioeconomic development and understanding how financial systems can be strengthened are crucial if we are to realize our goal of boosting prosperity and eradicating poverty. The *Global Financial Development Report* is an important step in this process.

Jim Yong Kim
President
The World Bank Group

Preface

The goal of this inaugural *Global Financial Development Report* is to contribute to the evolving debate on the role of the state in the financial sector, highlighted from the perspective of development. The report is aimed at a broad range of stakeholders, including governments, international financial institutions, nongovernmental organizations, think tanks, academics, private sector participants, donors, and the wider development community. The report offers policy advice based on research and lessons from operational work.

This marriage of research and operational work was possible thanks to the engagement of a diverse set of experts inside and outside the World Bank Group. The report reflects inputs from Bank staff in a broad range of units and collaboration with leading researchers on finance and development. Reflecting the close links between financial development and stability, counterparts at the International Monetary Fund have also provided valuable contributions.

The report benchmarks financial institutions and markets around the world, recognizing the diversity of modern financial systems. In its analysis of the state's role in finance, the report seeks to avoid simplistic, ideological views, instead aiming to develop a more nuanced approach to financial sector policy based on a synthesis of new data, research, and operational experiences.

The report emphasizes that the state has a crucial role in the financial sector—it needs to provide strong prudential supervision, ensure healthy competition, and enhance financial infrastructure. Regarding more direct interventions, such as state ownership of banks, the report presents new evidence that state involvement can help in mitigating adverse effects of a crisis. However, the report cautions that over longer periods, direct state involvement can have important negative effects on the financial sector and the economy. Therefore, as crisis conditions recede, the evidence suggests that it is advisable for governments to shift from direct to indirect interventions.

Because the financial system is dynamic and conditions are constantly changing, regular updates are essential. Hence, this report should be seen as part of an ongoing project aimed at supporting systematic evaluation, improving data, and fostering broader partnerships. Future reports might address financial inclusion, the development of local currency capital markets, the financial sector's role in long-term financing, and the state's role in financing health care and pensions. We hope that this new series of analytical reports will prove useful to all stakeholders in promoting evidence-based decision making and sound financial systems for robust economic performance.

Mahmoud Mohieldin
Managing Director
The World Bank Group

Acknowledgments

The 2013 *Global Financial Development Report* reflects the efforts of a broad and diverse group of experts both inside and outside the World Bank. The report was cosponsored by the World Bank's Financial and Private Sector Development Vice Presidency (FPD) and the Development Economics Vice Presidency (DEC). It reflects inputs from World Bank Group staff across a range of units, including all the regional vice presidencies, the Poverty Reduction and Economic Management Network, and External Affairs, as well as staff of the International Finance Corporation (IFC).

Aslı Demirgüç-Kunt was the director of this project. Martin Čihák led the core team, which included Cesar Calderón, Martin Kanz, Subika Farazi, and Mauricio Pinzon Latorre. Other key contributors were Erik Feyen (chapter 1); Maria Soledad Martínez Pería (chapters 2, 3, and 4); İnci Ötker-Robe, Martín Vázquez Suárez, Miquel Dijkman, Valeria Salomao Garcia, R. Barry Johnston, and Nicolas Véron (chapter 2); Thorsten Beck and Klaus Schaeck (chapter 3); Marcin Piatkowski, Eva Gutierrez, José De Luna Martinez, Carlos Leonardo Vicente (chapter 4); Ouarda Merrouche, Miriam Bruhn, Massimo Cirasino, Marco Nicoli, Maria Teresa Chimienti, Froukelien Wendt, Luchia Marius

Christova, Margaret Miller, Leora Klapper, Shalini Sankaranarayan, Alban Pruthi, and Thilasoni Benjamin Musuku (chapter 5).

The report was prepared under the oversight of Janamitra Devan, Vice President (FPD and IFC); Justin Yifu Lin, Chief Economist and Senior Vice President (DEC); and Martin Ravallion, Acting Chief Economist and Senior Vice President (DEC). World Bank Presidents Robert B. Zoellick and Jim Yong Kim and Managing Director Mahmoud Mohieldin provided overall guidance. The authors received invaluable advice from the FPD Council (Aslı Demirgüç-Kunt, Augusto Lopez-Claros, Gaiv Tata, Gerardo Corrochano, Janamitra Devan, Klaus Tilmes, Loic Chiquier, Marialisa Motta, Pierre Guislain, Sujata Lamba, Tilman Ehrbeck, and Tunc Uyanik) as well as the World Bank–International Monetary Fund Financial Sector Liaison Committee.

Peer reviewers of the report were Stijn Claessens, Augusto de la Torre, Ross Levine, Norman Loayza, Roberto Rocha, and Tunc Uyanik. Luis Servén also reviewed the concept note. Comments on individual chapters were also received from Aart Kraay, Ross Levine, Roberto Rocha, and Sergio Schmukler (chapter 1); Gerard Caprio, Patrick Honohan, Alain Ize, Ross Levine, and Damodaran

Krishnamurti (chapter 2); Franklin Allen, Thorsten Beck, Michael Fuchs, and Martha Martinez Licetti (chapter 3); and Viral Acharya, Charles Calomiris, Heinz Rudolph, and Sergio Schmukler (chapter 4). Aart Kraay reviewed all chapters for consistency and quality multiple times.

The authors also received valuable suggestions and other contributions at various stages of the project from Hormoz Aghadey, Shamshad Akhtar, Deniz Anginer, Madelyn Antoncic, Zsofia Arvai, Steen Byskov, Kevin Carey, Jeffrey Chelsky, Loic Chiquier, Gerardo Corrochano, Mariano Cortes, Robert Cull, Stefano Curto, Mansoor Dailami, Katia D'Hulster, Maya Eden, Tilman Ehrbeck, Matthias Feldmann, Aurora Ferrari, Manuela Ferro, Jose Antonio Garcia, Egbert Gerken, Swati Ghosh, David Gould, Neil Gregory, Mario Guadamillas, Pankaj Gupta, Mary Hallward-Driemeier, Darrin Hartzler, Richard Hinz, Mustafa Zakir Hussain, Sujit Kapadia, Isfandyar Khan, Thomas Kirchmeier, Kalpana Kochhar, Rachel Kyte, Jeffrey Lewis, Samuel Maimbo, Mariem Malouche, Cledan Mandri-Perrott, Claire Louise McGuire, Martin Melecky, Dino Merotto, Sebastian Molineus, Fredesvinda Montes, Cedric Mousset, Nataliya Mylenko, Makoto Nakagawa, Harish Natarajan, Aloysius Uche Ordu, Jorge Patiño, Jean Pesme, Tigran Poghosyan, John Pollner, Daniel Pulido, Haocong Ren, Ivan Rossignol, Heinz Rudolph, Consolate Rusagara, Andre Ryba, David Scott, James Seward, Sophie Sirtaine, Constantinos Stephanou, Mark Stone, Vijay Tata, Marilou Uy, S. Kal Wajid, Juan Zalduendo, Laura Zoratto, and participants in seminars and briefings organized at the World Bank.

The report would not be possible without the production team, including Merrell Tuck-Primdahl and Nicole Frost, as well as Stephen McGroarty, Santiago Pombo, Jose De Buerba, Jane Zhang, Ryan Hahn, Mary Donaldson, and Xenia Zia Morales. Aziz Gokdemir was the production editor, with Debra Naylor as the graphic designer. Roula Yazigi assisted the team with the website and communications. Paul Holtz was the language editor. Excellent administrative assistance was provided by Hedia Arbi, Gracia Sorensen, and Agnes Yaptenco. Other valuable assistance was provided by Benjamin Levine and Vin Nie Ong.

Mauricio Pinzon Latorre and Subika Farazi were instrumental in compiling and updating the databases underlying the report. In so doing, they benefited from the work of the current FinStats database team, which includes Katie Kibuuka and Diego Sourrouille, who in turn relied on key efforts from previous FinStats team members, including Ed Al-Hussainy, Haocong Ren, and Andrea Coppola. Joanna Nasr, Mariana Carvalho, and Zarina Odinaeva helped with the data on the credit information systems used in chapter 5.

The work on the 2011 update of the Banking Regulation and Supervision Survey started with the collaboration of Maria Soledad Martínez Pería, Roberto Rocha, Constantinos Stephanou, and Haocong Ren. The survey benefited from contributions from numerous banking regulation experts in the World Bank, including David Scott, Krishnamurti Damodaran, Katia D'Hulster, Cedric Mousset, and others outside the World Bank, in particular, Michael Andrews and Jan-Willem van der Vossen. Insights and encouragement from Gerard Caprio, Ross Levine, and James Barth, who organized the previous rounds of the survey, are gratefully acknowledged. PKF (UK) and Auxilium helped with compiling and following up on the survey responses. Amin Mohseni provided excellent research assistance on the survey. Catiana Garcia-Killroy (FPD), Dilek Aykut and Eung Ju Kim (both DEC), and Isabella Reuttner (World Economic Forum) provided helpful consultations on data. Tariq Khokhar, Neil Fantom, Ibrahim Levent, and William Prince were instrumental in integrating the report's data with the World Bank's Open Data Initiative.

The authors would also like to thank the many country officials and other experts who participated in the surveys underlying this report, including the Bank Regulation and Supervision Survey and the Financial Development Barometer.

Financial support from State Secretariat for Economic Affairs (Switzerland) is gratefully acknowledged. The latest update of the Bank Regulation and Supervision Survey and related research was financed with financial support from the U.K. Department for International Development. The Knowledge for Change program and the Research Support Budget provided funding for the underlying research program in DEC. Frank Sader had a key role in FPD's fundraising efforts for the *Global Financial Development Report*.

EXTERNAL ADVISERS

Viral Acharya	CV Starr Professor of Economics, New York University Stern School of Business; Program Director for Financial Economics, Centre for Economic Policy Research
Franklin Allen	Nippon Life Professor of Finance and Professor of Economics at the Wharton School of the University of Pennsylvania
Thorsten Beck	Professor of Economics and Chairman of the European Banking Center, Tilburg University, Netherlands
Charles Calomiris	Henry Kaufmann Professor of Financial Institutions, Graduate School of Business, Columbia University
Gerard Caprio	William Brough Professor of Economics and Chair, Center for Development Economics, Williams College
Stijn Claessens	Assistant Director, Research Department, International Monetary Fund
Patrick Honohan	Governor, Central Bank of Ireland
R. Barry Johnston	Former Assistant Director, Monetary and Capital Markets Department, International Monetary Fund
Ross Levine	James and Merryl Tisch Professor of Economics; Director, William R. Rhodes Center for International Economics and Finance, Department of Economics, Brown University
Monica Rubiolo	Head of Macroeconomic Support, State Secretariat for Economic Affairs, Switzerland
Klaus Schaeck	Professor of Empirical Banking, Bangor University
Nicolas Véron	Senior Fellow, Bruegel Institute; Visiting Fellow, The Peterson Institute for International Economics

The report also benefited from suggestions and insights from country officials and other experts participating in the Financial Development Barometer and the other surveys and discussions underlying this report. The findings, interpretations, and conclusions expressed in this report do not necessarily reflect the views of the advisers or institutions with which they are affiliated.

PEER REVIEWERS

Stijn Claessens	Assistant Director, Research Department, International Monetary Fund
Augusto de la Torre	Chief Economist, Latin America and the Caribbean Vice Presidency, World Bank
Ross Levine	James and Merryl Tisch Professor of Economics; Director, William R. Rhodes Center for International Economics and Finance, Department of Economics, Brown University
Norman Loayza	Lead Economist and Director, 2014 *World Development Report: Risks, Vulnerabilities, and the Crisis*, World Bank
Roberto Rocha	Senior Adviser, Financial and Private Sector Vice Presidency, World Bank
Tunc Uyanik	Director, Financial Systems Global Practice and East Asia and Pacific Region, Financial and Private Sector Vice Presidency, World Bank

Abbreviations and Glossary

ATP/TA	after-tax profits to assets
BANSEFI	Banca de Ahorro Nacional y Servicios Financieros
BB	Banco do Brasil
BCB	Banco Central do Brasil
BCBS	Basel Committee for Banking Supervision
BIS	Bank for International Settlements
BNDES	Banco Nacional de Desenvolvimento Econômico e Social (state-owned development bank, Brazil)
BTP/TA	before-tax profits to assets
CCP	central counterparty
CEF	Caixa Econômica Federal
CoCo	contingent capital
CPSIPS	Core Principles for Systemically Important Payment Systems
CPSS	Committee on Payment and Settlement Systems
CR5	concentration ratio (share of the five largest banks in total banking system assets)
DB	development bank
DNS	deferred net settlement
DTAs	deferred tax assets
EAP	East Asia and Pacific
ECA	Europe and Central Asia
EMDEs	emerging markets and developing economies

e-MID	Electronic Market for Interbank Deposit
FIRA	Fideicomisos Instituidos en Relación con la Agricultura, Mexico
FIRST	Financial Sector Reform and Strengthening Initiative
FOGAPE	State-Owned Guarantee Fund for Small Entepreneurs, Chile
FSA	Financial Sector Assessment
FSAP	Financial Sector Assessment Program
FSB	Financial Stability Board
FSSA	Financial System Stability Assessment
GCC	Gulf Cooperation Council
GDP	gross domestic product
GOB	government-owned bank
GTS	global trading system
HHI	Herfindahl-Hirschman index (of market concentration)
IDB	Inter-American Development Bank
IFC	International Finance Corporation
IFRS	International Financial Reporting Standards
IMF	International Monetary Fund
IOSCO	International Organization of Securities Commissions
IRB	international ratings-based

KfW	Kreditanstalt für Wiederaufbau, Germany	PKO BP	PKO Bank Polski
KOTEC	Korean government guarantor	PRISM	Pakistan Real Time Interbank Settlement Mechanism
LAC	Latin America and the Caribbean	PSEFT	Payment System and Electronic Fund Transfer
LIBOR	London interbank offered rate	PwC	Pricewaterhouse Coopers
LLP	loan loss provisioning	RCCP	Recommendations for Central Counterparties
M2	M2 measure of money supply		
MENA	Middle East and North Africa	ROA	return on assets
MFI	microfinance institution	RSSS	Recommendations for Securities Settlement Systems
MIC	Collateralized Interbank Market (Italy)	RTGS	real-time gross settlement
MSR	mortgage servicing rights	RWA	risk-weighted assets
NAFIN	Nacional Financiera, Mexico	SAR	Special Administrative Region
NBFI	nonbank financial institution	SBP	State Bank of Pakistan
NBP	National Bank of Poland	SECO	State Secretariat for Economic Affairs, Switzerland
NI	net interest income		
NII	non-interest income	SELIC	Sistema Especial de Liquidação e de Custódia
NPL	nonperforming loan		
NPS	national payment system	SIFIs	systemically important financial institutions
NSFR	net stable funding ratio		
OECD	Organisation for Economic Co-operation and Development	SME	small and medium enterprise
		SSA	Sub-Saharan Africa
OLS	ordinary least squares	STR	Sistema de Transferência de Reservas
OTC	over the counter		
OV	overhead costs	TA/A	taxes to assets
P/E	price-to-earnings ratio		

GLOSSARY OF KEY TERMS USED THROUGHOUT THE REPORT

The financial system	The financial system in a country is defined to include financial institutions (banks, insurance companies, and other nonbank financial institutions) and financial markets (such as those in stocks, bonds, and financial derivatives). It also includes the financial infrastructure (which includes, for example, credit information–sharing systems and payment and settlement systems).
Financial development	Conceptually, financial development is a process of reducing the costs of acquiring information, enforcing contracts, and making transactions. Empirically, measuring financial development directly is challenging. Instead, the report measures four financial system characteristics (depth, access, efficiency, and stability) for financial institutions and financial markets ("4x2 framework").
The state	The state is defined in a broad economic sense, to include not only the country's government but also autonomous or semiautonomous agencies such as a central bank or a financial supervision agency.
The roles of the state	The roles of the state in the financial sector include those of a promoter, owner, regulator, and overseer. The report focuses on areas that were highlighted by the crisis and are of particular relevance for financial development.
Country	A territorial entity for which statistical data are maintained and provided internationally on a separate and independent basis (not necessarily a state as understood by international law and practice).

Overview

On September 15, 2008, the failure of the U.S. investment banking giant Lehman Brothers marked the onset of the largest global economic meltdown since the Great Depression. The aftershocks have severely affected the livelihoods of millions of people around the world. The crisis triggered policy steps and reforms designed to contain the crisis and to prevent repetition of these events.

Four years later, with banking woes ongoing in various parts of the world (most notably in the euro area), it is a good time to evaluate these reforms and their likely contribution to long-run financial development. The crisis experience is thus an important part of the motivation for this inaugural *Global Financial Development Report*. The crisis has prompted many people to reassess various official interventions in financial systems, from regulation and supervision of financial institutions and markets, to competition policy, to state guarantees and state ownership of banks, and to enhancements in financial infrastructure.

But the crisis does not necessarily negate the considerable body of evidence on these topics accumulated over the past few decades. It is important to use the crisis experience to examine what went wrong and how to fix it.

Which lessons about the connections between finance and economic development should shape policies in coming decades?

On the surface, the main contrast between this global crisis and those in recent decades is that developed economies were affected much more strongly and more directly than were developing economies. But some developed financial systems (such as those of Australia, Canada, and Singapore) have shown remarkable resilience so far, while some developing ones have been brought to the brink of collapse. The bigger point is that the quality of a state's policy for the financial sector matters more than the economy's level of development. This report reassesses the role of the state in finance, based on updated data, ongoing research, and World Bank Group experiences from around the world.

Two building blocks underlie the report's view of the role of the state in finance. First, there are sound economic reasons for the state to play an active role in financial systems. Second, there are practical reasons to be wary of the state playing too active a role in financial systems. The tensions inherent in these two building blocks emphasize the complexity of financial policies. Though economics identifies the social welfare advantages of certain government interventions, practical experience suggests that the state often does not intervene successfully. Furthermore, since economies and the state's capacity to regulate differ across countries and over time, the appropriate involvement of the state in the financial system also varies case by case.

Nevertheless, with ample reservations and cautions, this report teases out broad lessons for policy makers from a variety of experiences and analyses (see box O.1 for a summary of the main messages).

The state tends to play a major role in the modern financial sector, as promoter,

---

BOX O.1 Main Messages of This Report

The report's overall message is cautionary. The global financial crisis has given greater credence to the idea that active state involvement in the financial sector can help maintain economic stability, drive growth, and create jobs. There is evidence that some interventions may have had an impact, at least in the short run. But there is also evidence on potential longer-term negative effects. The evidence also suggests that, as the crisis subsides, there may be a need to adjust the role of the state from direct interventions to less direct involvement. This does not mean that the state should withdraw from overseeing finance. To the contrary, the state has a very important role, especially in providing supervision, ensuring healthy competition, and strengthening financial infrastructure.

Incentives are crucial in the financial sector. The main challenge of financial sector policies is to better align private incentives with public interest without taxing or subsidizing private risk-taking. Design of public policy needs to strike the right balance—promoting development, yet in a sustainable way. This approach leads to challenges and trade-offs.

In regulation and supervision, one of the crisis lessons is the importance of getting the "basics" right first. That means solid and transparent institutional frameworks to promote financial stability. Specifically, it means strong, timely, and anticipatory supervisory action, complemented with market discipline. In many developing economies, that combination of basic ingredients implies a priority on building up supervisory capacity. Here, less can mean more: less complex regulations, for instance, can mean more effective enforcement by supervisors and better monitoring by stakeholders.

The evidence also suggests that the state needs to encourage contestability through healthy entry of well-capitalized institutions and timely exit of insolvent ones. The crisis fueled criticisms of "too much competition" in the financial sector, leading to insta-

bility. However, research presented in this report suggests that, for the most part, factors such as poor regulatory environment and distorted risk-taking incentives promote instability, rather than competition itself. With good regulation and supervision, bank competition can help improve efficiency and enhance access to financial services, without necessarily undermining systemic stability. Rather than restricting competition, it is necessary to address distorted competition, improve the flow of information, and strengthen the contractual environment.

Lending by state-owned banks can play a positive role in stabilizing aggregate credit in a downturn, but it also can lead to resource misallocation and deterioration of the quality of intermediation. The report presents some evidence that lending by state-owned banks tends to be less procyclical and that some state-owned banks even played a countercyclical role during the global financial crisis. However, the track record of state banks in credit allocation remains generally unimpressive, undermining the benefits of using state banks as a countercyclical tool. Policy makers can limit the inefficiencies associated with state bank credit by paying special attention to the governance of these institutions and schemes and ensuring that adequate risk management processes are in place. However, this oversight is challenging, particularly in weak institutional environments.

Experience points to a useful role for the state in promoting transparency of information and reducing counterparty risk. For example, the state can facilitate the inclusion of a broader set of lenders in credit reporting systems and promote the provision of high-quality credit information, particularly when there are significant monopoly rents that discourage information sharing. Also, to reduce the risk of freeze-ups in interbank markets, the state can create the conditions for the evolution of markets in collateralized liabilities.

owner, regulator, and overseer. Indeed, economics provides several good motivations for an active role for the state in finance. These motivations reflect the effects of "market imperfections," such as the costs and uncertainties associated with (a) acquiring and processing information, (b) writing and enforcing contracts, and (c) conducting transactions. These market imperfections often create situations in which the actions of a few people or institutions can adversely influence many other people throughout society. These externalities provide the economic rationale for the government to intervene to improve the functioning of the financial system.

A few examples demonstrate how market imperfections motivate government action. First, when one bank fails, this can cause depositors and creditors of other banks to become nervous and start a run on these other banks. This "contagion"—whereby the weakness in one bank can cause stress for otherwise healthy financial institutions—can reverberate through the economy, causing problems for the individuals and firms that rely on those otherwise healthy institutions. This is the classic bank run.

A second example stresses the externalities associated with risk taking, especially for large financial institutions. For the sake of this illustration, imagine a busy road with cars and trucks. If a car or truck goes faster, it can get to its destination sooner, but there is a chance that it will be involved in a crash. The likelihood of a crash is small but it increases with speed. Crashes involving large vehicles are particularly costly to others involved in the crash and very disruptive to traffic in general. Nobody wants to be involved in a crash, of course. But when deciding on how fast to go, a car or truck driver may not fully consider the costs that a crash might have on others in terms of injuries, damages, time lost in traffic jams, and so on. The state can play a role, for example by imposing and enforcing speed limits, and perhaps imposing stricter regulation of vehicles that pose bigger risks, such as large trucks.

Similarly, financial institutions often do not bear the full risks of their portfolios. When a large bank makes risky investments

that pay off, bank owners reap the profits. But when such gambles fail, the bank may not bear the full cost. For example, bailouts of troubled banks spread the cost of failed bets broadly among others in society who had no connection to the original risky investment decision. This potential for cascading events can be a reason for the state to intervene by imposing "speed limits" on risk taking by banks.

Third, limitations on the ability of people to process information, and the tendency of some people to follow the crowd, can motivate governments to take an active role in financial markets. For example, when people have difficulty fully understanding complex investments or do not appreciate the possibility of rare but extreme events, this can lead investors to make systematic mistakes, which can jeopardize the stability of the economy, with potentially adverse ramifications for people who neither make those investments nor have any influence over those that do.

Governments can limit the adverse repercussions of these market failures. For example, regulation and supervision can limit risk taking by financial institutions to avoid the potential externalities associated with financial fragility. Also, authorities can regulate information disclosure to facilitate sound decisions, and even regulate financial products, similar to how governments regulate the sale of food and drugs. Thus, economics provides many reasons for an active role of the state in finance.

But just because the state can ameliorate market imperfections and improve the operation of financial systems does not mean that it will. Designing and enforcing appropriate policy can be tricky. Returning to the previous analogy with speed limits for cars and trucks, having a single speed limit may not seem very effective, because some vehicles have better safety features, such as braking systems, and therefore are less likely to end up in a crash. If vehicles with better brakes were allowed to go faster, they could spend less time on the road, and traffic could ease up. But brake quality is difficult to monitor in real time. So, differentiated speed limits can be difficult to design and enforce, resulting in more speeding and crashes. The state could also intervene directly by providing government-approved drivers for all cars and trucks. That way, the state can have more control over safety and soundness, but it can become quite expensive for taxpayers. Alternatively, the state could build large speed bumps on the road, so that there are almost no crashes; however, traffic would slow down to a crawl.

The analogy underscores that correcting market imperfections is a complicated task, requiring considerable information and expertise to design, implement, and enforce sound policies. State interventions in finance need to be risk-sensitive, but measuring risk properly and enforcing risk-based regulations is far from straightforward. The state can try to run parts of the financial system directly, but evidence shows that approach to be very costly. And if the state required banks to hold capital as large as their loans, the risk of failures would be minimal, but financial intermediation would grind to a halt since banks would not be able to lend.

An important complicating factor is that the same government policies that ameliorate one market imperfection can create other—sometimes even more problematic—distortions. For example, when the government insures the liabilities of banks to reduce the possibility of bank runs, the insured creditors of the bank may not diligently monitor the bank and scrutinize its management. This can facilitate excessive risk taking by banks. The state can try to limit risk taking by large, interconnected financial institutions. However, such interventions might reduce the incentives of private shareholders to exert strong corporate control over these institutions, because they think the government is already doing it. Thus, state interventions can create even more reliance on the state.

An even deeper issue is whether the state always has sufficient incentives to correct for market imperfections. Governments do not always use their powers to address market imperfections and promote the public interest. Sometimes, government officials use the power of the state to achieve different objectives, including less altruistic ones, such as helping friends, family, cronies, and political constituents. When this happens, the government can do serious harm in the financial system. These arguments suggest a sober wariness concerning the role of the state in finance that will vary according to confidence in the political system's ability to promote the public good.

Determining the proper role of the state in finance is thus as complex as it is important: one size does not fit all when it comes to policy intervention. In less developed economies, there may seem to be more scope for the government's involvement in spearheading financial development. However, less development is often accompanied by a less effective institutional framework, which in turn increases the risk of inappropriate interventions. And the role of the state naturally changes as the financial system creates new products, some of which obviate the need for particular policies while others motivate new government interventions. Reflecting this complexity, country officials and other financial sector experts often hold opposing views and opinions on the pros and cons of various state interventions—a point illustrated by a recent informal global opinion poll carried out by the *Global Financial Development Report* team (box O.2).

The *Global Financial Development Report* provides new insights on financial development and the role of the state in financial systems, building on the experience from the global financial crisis. Varying economic and political circumstances across countries imply that financial sector policies require customization: appropriate policies will differ across countries and over time. But there are common lessons and guidelines. While recognizing the complexity of the issue and the limits of existing knowledge, this report contributes new data and analysis to the policy discussion.

BENCHMARKING FINANCIAL SYSTEMS

A growing body of evidence shows that financial institutions and financial markets

BOX 0.2   Views from Some of the World Bank Clients

As part of its effort to find out more about client country views, the *Global Financial Development Report* team carried out an informal global poll— the 2011/12 Financial Development Barometer. This poll, which covered country officials and financial sector experts from 78 countries (23 developed and 55 developing), provides interesting insights into views about financial development and the role of the state in finance.

Despite the crisis experience, 90 percent of the country officials and experts surveyed in the poll perceive that positive effects of finance (in particular those on economic growth and poverty reduction) outweigh its potential negative effects. A majority of the respondents therefore see that their country's financial sector needs to grow, especially in terms of financial markets and nonbank financial institutions, to better serve its clients and expand to new ones.

As regards the role of the state in the financial sector, the Financial Development Barometer con-firmed various areas of agreement. For example, there is a widespread notion that state-owned financial institutions and government-backed credit guarantees can in principle play a useful role. The poll also shows many respondents seeing potential benefits in more stringent supervision of new financial instruments in light of the crisis. A majority also see a scope for a more active role of the state in promoting technological innovations in financial infrastructure.

Perhaps more interestingly, the poll also indicated many key policy areas where the views for and against are almost evenly split. This split includes, for example, opinions on the need for stringency and greater scope of regulation and supervision, the pros and cons of greater competition in countries' financial systems, the possible countercyclical role of state-owned financial institutions, and the role of the state in promoting information sharing—all topics that are examined in the current *Global Financial Development Report*.

Selected Responses from the 2011/12 Financial Development Barometer

Views were split on important aspects of the state's role . . .	Agree? (%)
"In view of the global financial crisis, more **stringent** financial sector regulation and supervision is needed."	49
"In view of the global financial crisis, there is a need for broadening the **scope** of financial sector regulation and supervision."	54
"More financial sector **competition** would help financial stability in my home country."	58
"State-owned financial institutions played an **effective countercyclical role** during the recent global financial crisis."	48
"Government-backed **credit guarantee schemes** do play an important role in promoting financial stability."	64
"The development of **collateral registries** can be left, fully or mostly, to the private sector."	42

Note: The Financial Development Barometer is an informal global poll covering country officials and financial sector experts from 78 economies (23 developed and 55 developing). The response rate was 65 percent. Results are percentages of total responses received.

exert a powerful influence on economic development, poverty alleviation, and the stability of economies around the world. Yet measuring the functioning of the financial system has important shortcomings. Indeed, empirical work has largely—though not exclusively—relied on measures of the size of the banking industry as a proxy for financial development. However, size is not a measure of quality, efficiency, or stability. Moreover, the banking sector is only one component of financial systems. This report, along with the accompanying public database, assembles and improves cross-country data that can be used to benchmark financial systems. Chapter 1 addresses questions such as: How can one empirically describe different characteristics of financial systems? How can one compare financial systems across countries and regions and through time? How have financial systems been affected by the global financial crisis, and what are the key recent trends?

To measure and benchmark financial systems, the report develops several measures of four characteristics of financial institutions (banks, insurance companies, and so on) and financial markets (stock markets and bond markets): (a) the size of financial institutions and markets (financial depth), (b) the degree to which individuals can and do use financial institutions and markets (access), (c) the efficiency of financial institutions and markets in providing financial services (efficiency), and (d) the stability of financial institutions and markets (stability). These four characteristics are measured both for financial institutions and financial markets, leading to a 4x2 matrix of the characteristics of financial systems. A basic comparison (figure O.1) confirms that although developing-economy financial systems tend to be much

less deep and also somewhat less efficient and to provide less access, their stability has been comparable to developed-country financial systems. These measures are then used to characterize and compare financial systems across countries and over time, highlighting the multidimensional nature of financial development. Country-by-country information on the key financial system characteristics is presented in the Statistical Appendix, with more data available through the report's website.

RETHINKING THE ROLE OF THE STATE IN THE FINANCIAL SECTOR

The report addresses the following key policy questions: (a) What is the early postcrisis thinking on transforming regulatory practices around the world? (b) How should governments promote competition in the financial sector without planting the seeds of the next crisis? (c) When do direct government interventions—such as state ownership and guarantees—help in developing the financial sector, and when do they fail? and (d) What should states do to support robust financial

FIGURE O.1   **Benchmarking Financial Development, 2008–10**

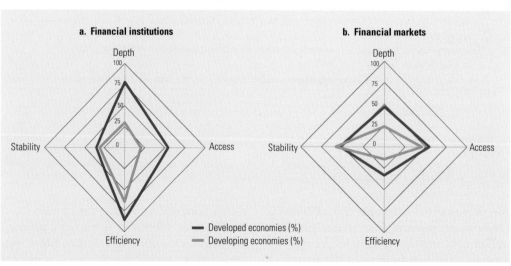

Source: Calculations based on Čihák, Demirgüç-Kunt, Feyen, and Levine 2012.
Note: Average values are shown for 2008–10 with simple (unweighted) averages across country groups. The 0 corresponds to a historical low of the proxy variable, and 100 corresponds to a historical high calculated for all countries over the period 1960–2010. For the explanation of individual proxy variables for financial depth, access, stability, and efficiency, see chapter 1.

BOX 0.3   Navigating This Report

In addition to this Overview, the report has two main parts. The first part (chapter 1) introduces measures of different characteristics of financial systems that are useful in benchmarking financial systems around the world. The second part (chapters 2 through 5) examines various aspects of the state's role in finance.

Chapter 1 describes financial depth, access, efficiency, and stability across countries and regions, especially in developing economies. Chapter 1 introduces a major new database, the Global Financial Development Database, and discusses how subsequent editions of the report will revisit the analysis and benchmarking of financial systems with updated and expanded data.

Chapter 2 examines the role of the state as regulator and supervisor. It presents results from a recently updated and substantially expanded World Bank survey of regulation and supervision around the world, explores how crisis countries were different from noncrisis countries, and tracks changes that governments made after the crisis. The chapter also reviews international regulatory and supervisory reforms and discusses proposals for further reforms.

Chapter 3 focuses on the role of the state in competition policy. After discussing various measures of competition, and presenting trends across countries and over time based on a new worldwide data set, it reviews the evidence on the implications of banking competition for bank efficiency, access to finance, and financial stability. The chapter then analyzes the policy drivers of competition and highlights the role of the state in (a) promoting a contestable banking system and (b) enabling a market-friendly informational and institutional environment. It also analyzes the impact of government actions during crises on bank competition.

Chapter 4 examines direct state interventions, particularly the experience with state-owned banks during the financial crisis. It reviews existing and new research and reexamines the performance of state-owned banks during crises. A large part of the discussion focuses on state-owned commercial banks as opposed to state-owned development banks; nonetheless, the chapter also presents a new data set based on a recent survey of development banks. It also examines the role of credit guarantees.

Chapter 5 relates to the role of the state in financial infrastructure, with a focus on two topics highlighted by the crisis: (a) information sharing in credit markets, and (b) the role of the state in reducing counterparty risk in payments and securities settlement systems.

The accompanying website (http://www.world bank.org/financialdevelopment) contains a wealth of underlying research, additional evidence including country examples, and an extensive database on financial development, providing users with interactive access to information on financial systems. The website is also a place where users participate in an online version of the Financial Development Barometer, provide feedback on this *Global Financial Development Report,* and submit their suggestions for future issues of the report.

The report concentrates on banks. There are some references to and data on financial markets and nonbank financial institutions (for example, in a discussion on the regulatory perimeter and on access by nonbank institutions to financial infrastructure). But to keep the report focused, much of the discussion is devoted to banks. Future issues of the report will cover financial markets and nonbank financial institutions in more depth.

---

infrastructure? Box O.3 provides an overview of the report's chapters.

How should public policy be designed to address these four key questions? The issue of concern in this report is how best to balance the various roles of the state as promoter, owner, regulator, and overseer. The right balance depends on a number of factors, including a country's level of development and the government's capacity. Two themes emerge throughout this report.

The first relates to direct and indirect interventions. During the recent crisis, direct state interventions have increased, and early evidence reveals that some of these interventions worked, at least in the short run.

However, there is also evidence on potential longer-term negative effects. Therefore, as the crisis subsides, there may be a need to rebalance toward less direct state involvement.

The second important theme is the critical role that incentives play in the financial sector. The challenge for the state's involvement is to better align private incentives with public interest, without taxing or subsidizing private risk taking. The design of public policy needs to strike the right balance in order to promote sustainable development. This leads to different challenges and trade-offs in answering each of the four questions below.

What are the best ways to reform regulation and supervision?

The global financial crisis that intensified with the collapse of Lehman Brothers in September 2008 presented a major test of the international architecture developed over many years to safeguard the stability of the global financial system. Although the causes of the crisis are still being debated, there is agreement that the crisis revealed major shortcomings in market discipline, regulation, and supervision. The financial crisis therefore has reopened important policy debates on financial regulation. After the onset of the meltdown, there was much talk about not wasting the crisis, and using it to push through necessary reforms. Indeed, many reforms have been enacted or are in process. Much has been done, but the system was tested further by the more recent euro area crisis, leading to the questions: Are the reforms adequate and will they be sufficient to reduce the likelihood and severity of future financial crises?

Regulation and supervision represent one area in which the role of the state is not in dispute. The crucial role of the state is widely acknowledged and is well established in the economic and financial literature. Hence, the debate is not about whether the state should regulate and supervise the financial sector, but about how best to go about ensuring that regulation and supervision support sound financial development.

Overall, there is broad agreement to address the "basics" first. This means having in place a coherent institutional and legal framework that establishes market discipline complemented by strong, timely, and anticipatory supervisory action. In many developing economies, this also means that building up supervisory capacity needs to be a top priority. Among the important lessons of the global financial crisis are renewed focus on systemic risk and the need to pay greater attention to incentives in the design of regulation and supervision.

Using a new survey of regulation and supervision around the world (figure O.2), chapter 2 confirms that countries where the global financial crisis originated had weaker regulation and supervisory practices (for example, less stringent definitions of capital, less stringent provisioning requirements, and greater reliance on banks' own risk assessment), as well as less scope for market incentives (for example, lower quality of financial information made publicly available, more generous deposit insurance coverage). Tracking changes during the crisis reveals that countries have stepped up efforts in the area of macroprudential policy, as well as on issues such as resolution regimes and consumer protection. However, it is not clear whether incentives for market discipline have improved. Some elements of disclosure and quality of information have improved, but deposit insurance coverage has increased during the crisis. This increased coverage, together with generous support for weak banks, did not improve incentives for monitoring. The survey suggests that there is further scope for improving disclosures and monitoring incentives.

Despite the progress made on regulatory reform, there are still important areas of disagreement. Hence, chapter 2 also presents a number of reform proposals that call for greater emphasis on simplicity and transparency, as well as a focus on incentive-compatible regulations. Importantly, these proposals warn against growing complexity of regulation, which may reduce transparency and accountability, increase regulatory arbitrage

FIGURE 0.2   Selected Features That Distinguish Crisis-Hit Countries

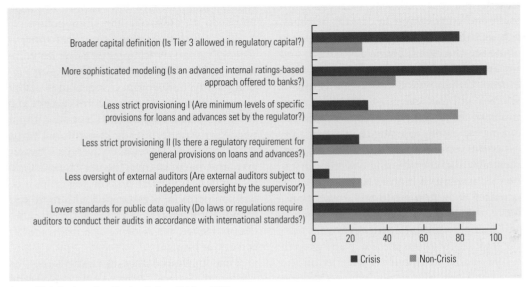

Source: Čihák, Demirgüç-Kunt, Martínez Pería, and Mohseni 2012.
Note: Percentage of countries that responded "yes" to the question in parentheses. Based on the World Bank's 2011 Bank Regulation and Supervision Survey. "Crisis" countries are defined as those that had a banking crisis between 2007 and 2011, as identified in Laeven and Valencia (2012).

opportunities, and significantly strain regulatory resources and capacity. The proposals suggest a regulatory approach that is more focused on proactively identifying and addressing incentive problems and making regulations incentive-compatible. This can help to end the continuous need to eliminate deficiencies and close loopholes that are inevitably present in ever more complex sets of regulations. Other proposals address the incentives that the regulators face and either propose alternative institutional structures or suggest tools to identify incentive issues on an ongoing basis.

In implementing supervisory best practices, emerging markets and developing economies should focus on establishing a basic robust supervisory framework that reflects local financial systems' characteristics, and refraining from incorporating unnecessary (and in several cases inapplicable) complex elements. Referring back to the earlier analogy with speed limits for cars and trucks, it may be appealing to have a complex rule in which each car has its own speed limit, depending on the quality of its brakes and

other risk-mitigating features. However, if the state does not have the capacity to monitor and police such complex rules, the likely result is more speeding and more crashes. Similarly, complex approaches to calculating capital requirements are not appropriate if there is limited capacity to verify the calculations, do robustness checks, and police implementation.

One of the positive developments triggered by the crisis is much greater debate and communication among regulators, policy makers, and academics, who are striving to reach the common goal of designing regulations to minimize the occurrence and cost of future crises. The diverse views and multiple reform proposals in this debate (presented in chapter 2) are likely to inform the regulatory reform process and improve future outcomes.

How should the state promote competition in the financial sector?

The global financial crisis also reignited the interest of policy makers and academics in the impact of bank competition and the role of the state in shaping competition policies. Some believe that increasing financial innovation and competition in certain markets, such as subprime mortgage lending, contributed to the global financial turmoil, and they are calling for policies to restrict competition. Others worry that, as a result of the crisis and the actions of governments in support of the largest banks, concentration in banking increased, reducing the competitiveness of the sector and access to finance, and potentially also contributing to future instability as a result of moral hazard problems associated with "too big to fail" institutions. Hence, the design of competition policy is challenging because it again involves a possible trade-off between efficiency and growth on one hand and stability concerns on the other hand. Another reason why rethinking competition policies is important relates to the changing mandate of central banks and

bank regulatory agencies: survey data reveal that the majority now have explicit responsibilities in the areas of competition policy.

The *Global Financial Development Report*'s analysis (chapter 3) provides guidance on this important issue. Research suggests that bank competition brings about improvements in efficiency across banks and enhances access to financial services, without necessarily undermining systemic stability. A cursory look at trends in average systemic risk and bank market power (figure O.3) indicates that greater market power (that is, less competition) is associated with more systemic risk (chapter 3 examines this in more detail). Hence, the evidence of a real trade-off is weak at best.

This analysis suggests that policies to address the causes of the recent crisis should not unduly restrict competition. The appropriate public policy is (a) to establish a regulatory framework that does not subsidize risk taking through poorly designed exit policies and too-big-to-fail subsidies and (b) to remove barriers to entry of "fit and proper" bankers with well-capitalized financial institutions.

For competition to improve access to finance, the state has an important role to play in enabling a market-friendly informational and institutional environment. Policies that guarantee market contestability, timely flow of adequate credit information, and contract enforceability will enhance competition among banks and improve access. For instance, evidence across business line data in Brazil shows that competition in the corporate segment is higher than in the retail segment. This reflects the existence of a larger pool of credit providers and easier access to information for large corporations. Competition in the retail sector can be fostered by promoting portability of bank accounts, expanding credit information sharing, and increasing payment system interconnection.

In this context, consumer protection laws have been at the forefront of competition policies in many countries. One example is South Africa, where new legislation provided a framework to bolster competition by

FIGURE O.3   **Market Power and Systemic Risk**

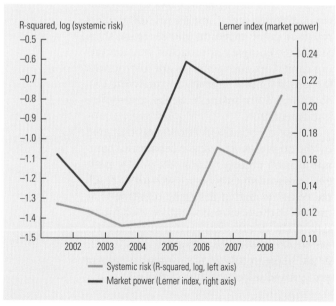

Source: Calculations based on Anginer, Demirgüç-Kunt, and Zhu 2012.
Note: The systemic risk measure follows Anginer and Demirgüç-Kunt (2001) and builds on Merton's (1974) contingent claim pricing. Systemic risk is defined as the correlation in the risk-taking behavior of banks and is captured by the R-squared from a regression of a bank's weekly change in distance to default on country average weekly change in distance to default (excluding the bank itself). Higher R-squared means higher systemic risk. Lerner index is a proxy for profits that accrue to a bank as a result of its pricing power, so higher values mean less competition. The calculations cover 1,872 publicly traded banks in 63 economies (developed and developing).

providing a sound information environment to customers and protecting consumers from unfair credit and credit marketing practices. It established a National Credit Regulator to act as a knowledge platform for credit practices and to ensure compliance with the law.

Competition agencies also play a crucial advocacy role in promoting competition. One example in this regard is Romania's Competition Council, which has extended the European Union Consumer Credit Directive of 2008. The directive establishes common rules on consumer credit over mortgage or real estate guaranteed loans and eliminates (or sets a low threshold for) early repayment fees.

Finally, state interventions during crises may constitute a barrier to exit that permits insolvent and inefficient banks to survive and generate unhealthy competition. Governments should be aware that their interventions during crises may have potentially negative long-term consequences on bank competition and may distort risk-taking incentives.

When do direct government interventions help?

During the global financial crisis, countries pursued a variety of strategies to restart their financial and real sectors. As the balance sheets of private banks deteriorated and they curtailed their lending activities, many countries used state-owned banks to step up their financing to the private sector. Most countries relied heavily on the use of credit guarantee programs. Others adopted a number of unconventional monetary and fiscal measures to prop up credit markets.

Historically, many state-owned banks were created to fulfill long-term development roles by filling market gaps in long-term credit, infrastructure, and agriculture finance, and to promote access to finance to underserved segments of the economy—notably, small and medium enterprises. In practice, however, there is widespread evidence that state banks have generally been very inefficient in allocating credit, more

often than not serving political interests instead. Nevertheless, the global financial crisis underscored the potential countercyclical role of state-owned banks in offsetting the contraction of credit from private banks, leading to arguments that this is an important function that can perhaps better justify their existence.

The crisis and the actions adopted by different countries reignited the debate on the need for direct government intervention in the financial sector. Supporters of state-owned banks argue that they provide the state an additional tool for crisis management and, relative to central banks, may be more capable of providing a safe haven for retail and interbank deposits, creating a fire break in contagion, and stabilizing aggregate credit. On the other hand, those opposing government bank ownership point out that agency problems and politically motivated lending render state-owned banks inefficient and prone to cronyism. Furthermore, past experiences of numerous countries suggest that cronyism in lending may build up large fiscal liabilities and threaten public sector solvency and financial stability, as well as misallocate resources and retard development in the long run.

During the recent crisis, several countries used their public bank infrastructure to prop up the financial sector. For instance, the Brazilian government injected capital into its state-owned development bank and authorized state-owned banks to acquire equity stakes from private banks and loan portfolios from financial institutions with liquidity problems. In China, state-owned banks were instructed to boost credit to specific sectors in order to promote growth. In the Russian Federation, Vnesheconombank, the country's state-owned development bank, received new capital to assist troubled smaller financial institutions and to invest in Russian financial instruments. It also injected money into large state-controlled banks to increase their loans to Russian companies. In Mexico, state-owned development banks extended credit to large companies, participated in loan programs for fragile sectors, and extended guarantees on commercial paper and credit instruments issued by specialized nonbank financial institutions. Similar actions were also taken by some developed economies. For example, Germany's state-owned development bank, Kreditanstalt für Wiederaufbau, increased lending to larger companies with short-term liquidity problems, provided additional financing for infrastructure, and helped recapitalize regional state banks. And in Finland, the government raised the limits on domestic and export financing for the country's state-owned bank to boost lending to small and medium enterprises.

Chapter 4 highlights that not all state-owned banks are alike. They can be classified as state commercial banks, state development banks, and development financial institutions, depending on whether they aim to maximize profits, are deposit takers, or have a clear developmental mandate. State-owned development banks and financial institutions, in turn, can lend to the public either directly or indirectly through private banks. Most of the evidence discussed on the short-term and long-term effects of state-owned banks focuses on commercial banks or does not distinguish between commercial and development banks.

Chapter 4 reviews the historical and new research evidence and concludes that lending by state-owned banks tends to be less procyclical than that of their private counterparts. During the global financial crisis, some state-owned banks have indeed played a countercyclical role by expanding their lending portfolio and restoring favorable conditions in key markets. For instance, the chapter highlights the expansion of the lending portfolio of state-owned commercial banks (for example, PKO Bank Polski in Poland) and state-owned development banks (for example, BNDES in Brazil) in mitigating the effects from the global credit crunch and filling the gap of lower credit from the private sector. Also, Mexican development banks supported the credit channel through the extension of credit guarantees and lending to private financial intermediaries.

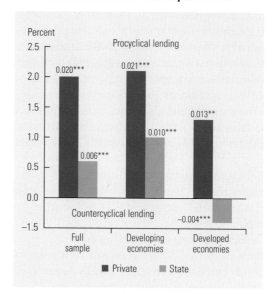

FIGURE O.4 Change in Bank Lending Associated with a 1% Increase in GDP Per Capita Growth

Source: Bertay, Demirgüç-Kunt, and Huizinga 2012.
Note: The figure shows marginal effects from a regression of bank lending on GDP per capita growth and a number of control variables, estimated using a sample of 1,633 banks from 111 countries for the period 1999–2010.
Significance level: ** 5 percent, *** 1 percent.

The mitigating short-term effect of state-owned banks is illustrated in figure O.4. The figure shows the relationship between lending patterns of banks with private and state ownership and economic growth, measured by real GDP per capita growth. Globally, bank lending is procyclical, growing during booms and falling during downturns. Yet the lending pattern of private banks is more procyclical compared with their state-owned counterparts. In high-income countries, state-owned banks even behave in a clearly countercyclical fashion, increasing in downturns.

However, because in many cases lending growth continued even after economic recovery was under way, and loans were not directed to the most constrained borrowers, the countercyclical benefits of state-owned banks came at the cost of resource misallocation and worsened intermediation. This mixed view is supported by evidence from previous crises as well. In other words, a temporary boom in state bank lending has long-term adverse effects by creating a portfolio of bad loans in crises that take a long time to sort out.

Ideally, focusing on the governance of these institutions may help policy makers address the inefficiencies associated with state-owned banks. State banks need a clear mandate to complement (rather than substitute for) private banks, and adopt risk management practices that allow them to guarantee a financially sustainable business. However, these governance reforms are particularly challenging in weak institutional environments, further emphasizing that the trade-off is a serious one for policy makers.

Credit guarantee schemes have also been a popular intervention tool during the recent crisis. However, given their limited scale, they are used not to stabilize aggregate credit but to alleviate the impact of the credit crunch on segments that are most severely affected, such as small and medium enterprises. Unfortunately, rigorous evaluations of these schemes are very few, and existing studies suggest that the benefits of these programs tend to be rather modest, particularly in institutionally underdeveloped settings, and they tend to incur fiscal and economic costs. Nevertheless, best practices can be identified. These include leaving credit assessments and decision making to the private sector; capping coverage ratios and delaying the payout of the guarantee until recovery actions are taken by the lender, so as to minimize moral hazard problems; having pricing guarantees that take into account the need for financial sustainability and risk minimization; and encouraging the use of risk management tools. Success again hinges on overcoming the challenges of getting the design right, particularly in underdeveloped institutional and legal settings.

What is the role for the state in promoting financial infrastructure?

The global financial crisis has highlighted the importance of a resilient financial infrastructure for financial stability. It also has led to a discussion about the role of the state, particularly in promoting the provision of high-quality credit information and in ensuring stable systems for large-value financial transactions. Reflecting the focus on the aftermath of the financial crisis, the report does not examine other components of financial infrastructure, such as retail payment systems and collateral regimes; it leaves these important issues to be covered in future editions.

Chapter 5 emphasizes that the transparent exchange of credit information reduces information asymmetries between borrowers and lenders and is an essential requisite of a well-functioning credit market. However, the financial crisis has shown that there is much room for improvement in this area, especially in the use of existing credit reporting systems for prudential oversight and regulation.

Information sharing in credit markets acts as a public good that improves credit market efficiency, access to finance, and financial stability. Nonetheless, for an individual commercial bank, proprietary credit information is valuable, so it has incentives to collect the information and keep it away from others. Information sharing among private lenders thus may not arise naturally, especially where banking systems are concentrated (figure O.5). This creates an important rationale for state involvement. In addition, the report highlights that information sharing in credit markets has increasing returns to scale: the benefits of credit reporting for financial access and stability are greatest when participation is as wide as possible and includes banks as well as nonbank financial institutions. Therefore, another important role for the state is to create a level playing field for the provision and exchange of credit information, and to facilitate the inclusion of nonregulated lenders into existing credit reporting systems. In many emerging markets, such as China and South Africa, major initiatives are under way to integrate the rapidly growing microfinance and consumer loan markets into the existing credit reporting infrastructure.

Liquidity provision by central banks during the crisis helped prevent major payment system disruptions. However, stress emerged in interbank and over-the-counter derivatives markets. The state can play an important role in mitigating counterparty risks in interbank

FIGURE O.5   Credit Reporting vs. Banking System Concentration

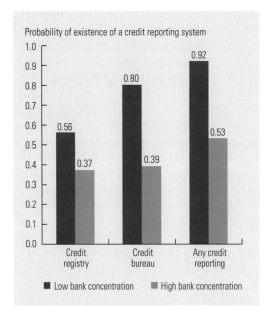

Source: Bruhn, Farazi, and Kanz 2012.
Note: The figure reports the percentage of countries with private (credit bureau), public (credit registry), or any credit reporting institutions for countries with high and low degrees of bank concentration (above and below the sample mean), respectively. It shows that bank concentration (the asset share of a country's three largest banks) is negatively associated with the development of credit reporting. This relationship is also conditional on the level of economic development.

money markets by providing robust and secure infrastructure and, potentially, by promoting the development of collateralized interbank markets. The state can also contribute in the development of a robust infrastructure for security settlement systems and the oversight of securities transactions, particularly for over-the-counter transactions. Increased standardization and transparency of transactions is needed and can be achieved by (a) trading on exchanges or electronic trading platforms; (b) clearing transactions through central counterparties, that is, entities that interpose themselves as counterpart to each trade (examples include the Chicago Mercantile Exchange's CME Clearing in the United States, Eurex Clearing in Germany, and London Clearing House's LCH.Clearnet in the United Kingdom); and (c) reporting transactions to trade repositories, which are entities that store centralized records of transaction data. These policy prescriptions are especially important in many emerging markets, where the development of a modern settlement infrastructure has lagged behind the rapid growth of emerging equity and securities markets.

1

Benchmarking Financial Systems around the World

- *Financial systems are multidimensional. Four characteristics are of particular interest for benchmarking financial systems: financial depth, access, efficiency, and stability. These characteristics need to be measured for financial institutions and markets.*

- *Financial systems come in all shapes and sizes, and differ widely in terms of the four characteristics. As economies develop, services provided by financial markets tend to become more important than those provided by banks.*

- *The global financial crisis was not only about financial instability. In some economies, the crisis was associated with important changes in financial depth and access.*

A growing body of evidence suggests that financial institutions—such as banks and insurance companies—and financial markets—stock markets, bond markets, derivative markets, and so on—exert a powerful influence on economic development, poverty alleviation, and economic stability (Levine 2005). For example, when banks screen borrowers and identify firms with the most promising prospects, this is a key step that helps allocate resources, expand economic opportunities, and foster growth. When banks and securities markets mobilize savings from households to invest in promising projects, this is another crucial step in fostering economic development. When financial institutions monitor their investments and scrutinize

managerial performance, this boosts the efficiency of corporations and reduces waste and fraud by corporate insiders. But that is not all. When equity, bond, and derivative markets enable the diversification of risk, this encourages investment in higher-return projects that might otherwise be shunned. And, when financial systems lower transaction costs, this facilitates trade and specialization—fundamental inputs to technological innovation (Smith 1776).

When financial systems perform these functions poorly, they hinder economic growth, curtail economic opportunities, and destabilize economies. For example, if financial systems collect funds and pass them along to cronies, the wealthy, and the politically connected, it slows economic growth and blocks potential entrepreneurs. And if financial institutions fail to exert sound corporate governance over firms that they fund, that failure makes it easier for managers to pursue projects that benefit themselves rather than the firms and the economy. When financial institutions create complex financial instruments and sell them to unsophisticated investors, it might generate more income for financial engineers and executives associated with marketing the new instruments, distorting the allocation of society's savings and impeding economic prosperity.

Evidence on the financial system's role in shaping economic development is substantial and varied. But there are shortcomings associated with assessing financial systems. There are no good cross-country, cross-time measures of how they (a) enhance information about firms and hence the efficiency of resource allocation; (b) exert sound corporate governance over firms to which they channel those resources; (c) manage, pool, and diversify risk; (d) mobilize savings from savers so that these resources can be allocated to the most promising projects in the economy; and (e) facilitate trade. Instead, researchers have largely focused on the size of the banking industry as a proxy for financial development. But size is not a measure of quality, efficiency, or stability. And the banking sector is only one part of financial systems.

Accordingly, a key contribution of this chapter involves data. In recent years, substantial efforts have been made to improve these data, which this chapter uses. This report is accompanied by the new Global Financial Development Database, an extensive worldwide database that combines and updates several financial data sets (Čihák, Demirgüç-Kunt, Feyen, and Levine 2012). The database is available on the *Global Financial Development Report* Web page (http://www .worldbank.org/financialdevelopment).

But this chapter goes beyond compiling data. It answers some substantive questions using the data, such as how to empirically describe different characteristics of financial systems; how to compare financial systems

across countries and regions and through time; and how financial systems have been affected by the global financial crisis.

To benchmark financial systems, the report measures the following four characteristics of financial institutions and markets: (a) the size of financial institutions and markets (financial depth), (b) the degree to which individuals can and do use financial institutions and markets (access), (c) the efficiency of financial institutions and markets in providing financial services (efficiency), and (d) the stability of financial institutions and markets (stability). These characteristics are measured separately for financial institutions and financial markets (both equity and bond markets), leading to a 4x2 matrix of financial system characteristics. The report uses these measures to characterize and compare financial systems across economies and over time and to assess the relationships between these measures and financial sector policies.

In focusing on these four characteristics of financial institutions and markets, the report gives empirical shape and substance to the complex, multifaceted, and sometimes amorphous concept of the functioning of financial systems. Financial depth, access, efficiency, and stability might not capture all features of financial systems, and the report does not try to construct a composite index of financial development. Instead, it uses these four characteristics to describe, compare, and analyze financial systems and their evolution in recent decades.

This chapter, together with the underlying data and analysis, highlights the multidimensional nature of financial systems. Deep financial systems do not necessarily provide broad financial access, highly efficient financial systems are not necessarily more stable than the less efficient ones, and so on. Each of these characteristics is associated with socioeconomic development, financial sector policies, and other parts of the enabling environment for finance. Financial systems differ widely in terms of the 4x2 characteristics, so it is crucial to measure and evaluate each one.

The chapter also suggests that the global financial crisis resulted in more than financial instability: in some countries, it also caused problems along the other dimensions, such as making people's and firms' access to financial services more difficult. Finance is about more than just stability. Having financial systems channel society's savings to those with the most promising investment opportunities is essential for fostering economic growth, alleviating poverty, and enabling people to pursue their economic goals.

Finally, this chapter is linked to future editions of the *Global Financial Development Report*. The report is envisaged as part of a series, with future reports returning to the analysis of financial systems using updated and extended data. They will use the measurement framework introduced here to examine new topics, such as financial inclusion, capital market development, and others. Future editions might expand or improve on the framework, which is designed to be flexible to accommodate such adjustments if needed—for example, if new types of financial data become available.

THE IMPORTANCE OF FINANCIAL SYSTEMS TO DEVELOPMENT

Finance is central to development. This may seem obvious to financial development experts. It may also seem obvious to bank depositors who just had their entire life savings wiped out by a financial crisis. But financial crises get forgotten after a period of time. And when compared with other factors that are also important—health, the environment, and so on—the case for finance may appear less obvious. Indeed, when panels of the world's leading economists tried to identify "the 10 great global challenges" in both 2004 and 2008 as part of the Copenhagen Consensus Project, the list did not include any financial issues.[1]

This section argues that finance indeed matters. It matters both when it functions well and when it malfunctions. When operating effectively, finance works quietly in the background, contributing to economic growth and poverty reduction. But when things go wrong, the malfunctioning of the financial system can slow growth, throw more people into poverty, and destabilize entire economies. Indeed, financial crises hurt not only those who work in finance or those who access financial systems. When the government undertakes costly bailouts of bankrupt financial institutions, this can lead to increases in public indebtedness, thus undermining governments' ability to support key social objectives, including the funding of education, health, and infrastructure programs. As a result, malfunctioning financial systems can also lay the foundations for enduring economic crises, as illustrated quite dramatically by recent events.

With so much attention focused on stability issues following the recent crisis, the powerful linkages between the functioning of the financial system and economic development have been somewhat underemphasized. Although the focus on stability has been understandable, sound financial sector policies are not only about avoiding crises. Finance is also about the efficient allocation of capital, economic growth, and expanding economic horizons. Therefore, an important goal is to raise awareness of policies to enhance the operation of financial systems, develop a better understanding, and foster debate. To help in framing the debate, this section clarifies the definition of financial development and provides a review of the literature on the linkages between financial sector development, economic growth, and poverty reduction.

What is financial development?

Financial markets are imperfect. Acquiring and processing information about potential investments is costly. There are costs and uncertainties associated with writing, interpreting, and enforcing contracts. And there are costs associated with transacting goods, services, and financial instruments. These market imperfections inhibit the flow of society's savings to those with the best ideas and projects, thus curtailing economic development.

It is the existence of these costs—these market imperfections—that creates incentives for the emergence of financial contracts, markets, and intermediaries. Motivated by profits, people create financial products and institutions to ameliorate the effects of these market imperfections. And governments often provide an array of services—ranging from legal and accounting systems to government-owned banks—with the stated goals of reducing these imperfections and enhancing resource allocation. Some economies are comparatively successful at developing financial systems that reduce these costs. Other economies are considerably less successful, with potentially large effects on economic development.

At the most basic level, therefore, financial development occurs when financial instruments, markets, and intermediaries mitigate—though do not necessarily eliminate—the effects of imperfect information, limited enforcement, and transaction costs. For example, the creation of credit registries tends to improve acquisition and dissemination of information about potential borrowers, improving the allocation of resources with positive effects on economic development. As another example, countries with effective legal and regulatory systems have facilitated the development of equity and bond markets that allow investors to hold more diversified portfolios than they could without efficient securities markets. This greater risk diversification can facilitate the flow of capital to higher return projects, boosting growth and enhancing living standards.

Defining financial development in terms of the degree to which the financial system eases market imperfections, however, is too narrow and does not provide much information on the actual functions provided by the financial system to the overall economy. Thus, Levine (2005) and others have developed broader definitions that focus on what the financial system actually does.[2]

At a broader level, financial development can be defined as improvements in the quality of five key financial functions: (a) producing and processing information about possible investments and allocating capital based on these assessments; (b) monitoring individuals and firms and exerting corporate governance after allocating capital; (c) facilitating the trading, diversification, and management of risk; (d) mobilizing and pooling savings; and (e) easing the exchange of goods, services, and financial instruments. Financial institutions and markets around the world differ markedly in how well they provide these key services. Although this report sometimes focuses on the role of the financial systems in reducing information, contracting, and transaction costs, it primarily adopts a broader view of finance and stresses the key functions provided by the financial system to the overall economy.

Financial development and economic growth

Economists have long debated the financial sector's role in economic growth. Lucas (1988), for example, dismissed finance as an overstressed determinant of economic growth, and Robinson (1952, 86) quipped that "where enterprise leads finance follows." From this perspective, finance responds to demands from the nonfinancial sector: it does not cause economic growth. At the other extreme, Miller (1998, 14) argued that the idea that financial markets contribute to economic growth "is a proposition too obvious for serious discussion." Bagehot (1873) and others rejected the idea that the finance-growth nexus can be ignored without limiting understanding of economic growth.

Recent literature reviews (such as Levine 2005) conclude that evidence suggests a positive, first-order relationship between financial development and economic growth. In other words, well-functioning financial systems play an independent role in promoting long-run economic growth: countries with better-developed financial systems tend to grow faster over long periods of time, and a large body of evidence suggests that this effect is causal (Demirgüç-Kunt and Levine 2008).[3]

Moreover, research sheds light on the mechanisms through which finance affects growth. The financial system influences growth primarily by affecting the allocation of society's savings, not by affecting the aggregate savings rate. Thus, when financial systems do a good job of identifying and funding those firms with the best prospects, not those firms simply with the strongest political connections, this improves the capital allocation and fosters economic growth. Such financial systems promote the entry of new, promising firms and force the exit of less efficient enterprises. Such financial systems also expand economic opportunities, so that the allocation of credit—and hence opportunity—is less closely tied to accumulated wealth and more closely connected to the social value of the project. Furthermore, by improving the governance of firms, well-functioning financial markets and institutions reduce waste and fraud, boosting the efficient use of scarce resources. By facilitating risk management, financial systems can ease the financing of higher return endeavors with positive reverberations on living standards. And, by pooling society's savings, financial systems make it possible to exploit economies of scale—getting the biggest development boost from available resources.

Financial development and poverty reduction

Beyond long-run growth, finance can also shape the gap between the rich and the poor and the degree to which that gap persists across generations (Demirgüç-Kunt and Levine 2009). Financial development may affect to what extent a person's economic opportunities are determined by individual skill and initiative, or whether parental wealth, social status, and political connections largely shape economic horizons. The financial system influences who can start a business and who cannot, who can pay for education and who cannot, who can attempt to realize his or her economic aspirations and who cannot. Furthermore, by affecting the allocation of capital, finance can alter both the rate of economic growth and the demand for labor, with potentially profound implications for poverty and income distribution.

Potentially, finance can have rather complex effects on the income distribution. It could boost returns to high-skilled workers or to low-skilled workers. The mechanisms are complex and could be good or bad for the poor and reduce or increase income inequality.

There is an emerging body of empirical research, however, suggesting that in practice, improvements in financial contracts, markets, and intermediaries actually do tend to expand economic opportunities and reduce persistent income inequality. Figure 1.1 provides a basic empirical illustration of the link between financial development (approximated here in a simplified way by the ratio of private sector credit to gross domestic product) and income inequality (approximated by changes in the Gini coefficient). The graph illustrates that higher levels of financial development are associated with declines in inequality.

More in-depth empirical research is consistent with this basic observation. For example, evidence suggests that access to credit markets increases parental investment in the education of their children and reduces the substitution of children out of schooling and into labor markets when adverse shocks reduce family income (Belley and Lochner 2007). Better-functioning financial systems stimulate new firm formation and help small, promising firms expand as a wider array of firms gain access to the financial system. Moreover, better-functioning financial systems will identify and fund better projects, with less emphasis on collateral and incumbency. Not only do they allow new, efficient firms to enter, they also force old, inefficient firms to leave, as evidenced by data (Kerr and Nanda 2009).

FIGURE 1.1 **Financial Depth and Income Inequality**

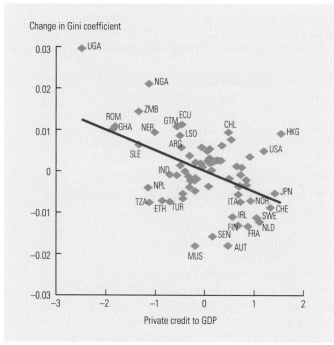

Source: Update of Beck, Demirgüç-Kunt, and Levine 2007.
Note: The Gini coefficient is on a scale from 0 (total equality) to 1 (maximum inequality). The chart is a partial scatter plot, visually representing the regression of changes in the Gini coefficient between 1960 and 2005 on the private sector credit–to-GDP ratio (logarithm, 1960–2005 average), controlling for the initial (1960) Gini coefficient. Variables on both axes are residuals. The abbreviations next to some of the observations are the three-letter country codes as defined by the International Organization for Standardization.

Besides the direct benefits of enhanced access to financial services, finance also reduces inequality, particularly through indirect labor market mechanisms. Specifically, accumulating evidence shows that financial development accelerates economic growth, intensifies competition, and boosts the demand for labor. Importantly, it usually brings relatively bigger benefits to those at the lower end of the income distribution (Beck, Demirgüç-Kunt, and Levine 2007; Beck, Levine, and Levkov 2010). Hence, finance, with good policies, can be both pro-growth and pro–poverty reduction.

Financial development and the enabling environment for finance

Many factors shape the functioning of financial systems and hence their impact on economic growth and poverty alleviation. Legal

and accounting systems influence the costs associated with evaluating firms and writing and enforcing contracts and, hence, in identifying and financing an economy's most promising endeavors. Regulatory, supervisory, and tax systems all affect the incentives facing the executives of financial institutions and participants in securities markets. Thus, these components of the enabling environment for finance also shape the allocation and use of capital. And the state often plays a more direct role in shaping the operation of financial systems, running state-owned banks, subsidizing agriculture or housing, or issuing government securities. Thus, the entire legal, accounting, regulatory, and policy apparatus influences the operation of financial systems.

Given the importance of finance for economic development and poverty alleviation, it is natural to ask: Why does this chapter focus on measuring the functioning of the financial system rather than on examining the direct impact of financial sector policy, regulations, and the rest of the enabling environment on economic growth, poverty alleviation, and the availability of economic opportunities?

The answer is that to provide guidance to policy makers, one needs a detailed understanding of the mechanisms through which the enabling environment for finance influence the functioning of financial systems. It is not enough to assess the associations between financial sector policies and development outcomes because these correlations might reflect reverse causality—in which economic development shapes the types of financial sector policies that a country adopts—or the correlations might simply reflect the impact of some other factor on both economic development and financial sector policies. To provide more accurate assessments about the enabling environment for finance, it is vital to trace through the channels from particular policies and regulations to the operation of financial systems and on to particular economic development outcomes.

This report contributes to this goal of providing more sound advice to policy makers by

FIGURE 1.2   Socioeconomic Development, Financial Development, and Enabling Environment

Socioeconomic Development

Social welfare (sustainable long-term growth, poverty reduction)

Financial Development

Financial sector functions
Producing information about investments and allocate capital; monitoring investments and exerting corporate governance; managing risks; pooling savings; and easing the exchange of goods and services

Financial development outcomes
(empirical proxies, measured separately for financial institutions and markets)
– Depth
– Access
– Efficiency
– Stability

Enabling Environment

Financial sector policies (examples)
– *Regulation* (micro- and macro-prudential, business conduct, etc.)
– *Direct interventions* (state ownership, guarantees, subsidies, liquidity provision)
– *Competition policy* in finance (level playing field, entry/exit, etc.)
– *Promotion of financial infrastructure/ technology*

Other policies and features (examples)
– Macroeconomic policy framework (e.g., exchange rate regime, monetary policy, tax policy, capital controls)
– Legal framework, social capital, etc.
– Concentration in the system
– Internationalization, dollarization

Source: Based on the review of literature in Čihák, Demirgüç-Kunt, Feyen, and Levine 2012.

(a) developing and analyzing measures of the functioning of financial institutions and markets (chapter 1) and (b) assembling databases on regulations, supervision, and institutional structures that shape financial system operations (chapters 2 to 5).

To summarize the discussion in this section, figure 1.2 presents in a visual form the relationships between socioeconomic development, financial development, and the enabling environment. It is important to care about the process of financial development because it has a well-documented association with economic and social development more generally. It improves sustainable long-term growth and reduces poverty, thereby improving social welfare. One can think about these as the ultimate developmental objectives. Figure 1.2 also highlights that financial systems do not exist in a vacuum. Financial system characteristics depend on the enabling environment, which consists of financial sector policies and other relevant policies and features.

THE GLOBAL FINANCIAL DEVELOPMENT DATABASE AND THE 4X2 MEASUREMENT MATRIX

Introducing the Global Financial Development Database

To measure the functioning of financial systems, country officials, researchers, and others would ideally like to have direct measures of how well financial institutions and financial markets (a) produce information ex ante about possible investments and allocate capital; (b) monitor investments and exert corporate governance after providing finance; (c) facilitate the trading, diversification, and management of risk; (d) mobilize and pool savings; and (e) ease the exchange of goods and services. So if data were not an issue, the ideal approach to measurement would involve the following determinations: in terms of producing information about possible investments and allocating capital, the financial sector in Country A, for example, scores 60 on a scale from 0 to 100, while Country B's financial sector scores 75; in terms of monitoring investments and exerting corporate governance after providing finance, Country A scores 90, while Country B scores only 20 on a scale from 0 to 100, and so on.

So, instead of the direct measures, empirical studies have focused on proxy variables, such as various measures of financial depth and access. And despite evidence of the crucial role of finance for economic development, there is a surprising lack of comprehensive data on basic aspects of financial systems across countries and over time. For example, there are major gaps in data on trading volumes in securities markets. Even data on financial institutions become rather patchy when one looks beyond the world's major, publicly listed banks.

Against this background, one of the key contributions of the *Global Financial Development Report* is the launch of a new, comprehensive online database on financial systems—the Global Financial Development Database, which is made available online together with the report. The database, which will be updated on a regular basis, compiles and disseminates data on the characteristics of financial systems in 205 jurisdictions around world. The database has data going back some 50 years (to 1960), although some measures of financial system traits do not go back that far.[4] The data from the Global Financial Development Database are integrated with the World Bank's Open Data initiative. Some of the data are new, and this is the first time such comprehensive data are available. The data are made available in a Web-friendly form, allowing the users of the database to interact with the data, for example, by creating their own country peer groups and their own tables and charts.

The 4x2 measurement framework

This chapter develops and presents four measures of the characteristics of financial systems: depth, access, efficiency, and stability. The focus here is on empirically characterizing financial systems (the middle part of figure 1.2). For completeness, the accompanying database includes some variables that measure social welfare (the upper part of figure 1.2) as well as financial sector policies and the other factors that define the enabling environment for finance (the bottom of figure 1.2). The following subsections introduce each dimension of this measurement framework. The annex to this chapter and Čihák, Demirgüç-Kunt, Feyen, and Levine (2012) provide more detailed information on each component of the measures of the four financial system traits in the matrix.

To obtain a comprehensive characterization of financial systems, one must measure the four categories for the two key components of the financial sector, namely financial institutions (banks and nonbank financial institutions) and financial markets (stock market, bond market, and other markets). Therefore, to be comprehensive, one needs to assemble a 4x2 matrix: four characteristics for two components. Table 1.1 provides a summary representation of such a 4x2 matrix, with examples of variables that can be used to fill in each cell of the matrix. The same structure is used to organize the underlying database. The following subsections go through the individual characteristics in turn. Box 1.1 focuses on the selection of representative variables within the individual characteristics. Box 1.2 discusses the challenges of aggregating across the four dimensions.

Critically, this chapter looks beyond the size of banks and stock markets. Many factors shape the mixture of financial intermediaries and markets operating in an economy. Different types and combinations of information, enforcement, and transaction costs in conjunction with different legal, regulatory, and tax systems have motivated distinct financial contracts, markets, and intermediaries across countries and throughout history. Thus, financial institutions and markets can and do look very different across countries and over time, but these structural differences do not necessarily translate into differences in the quality of the services provided by the financial system to the economy. To measure financial systems, this chapter digs deeper into the functioning of financial

TABLE 1.1   Stylized 4x2 Matrix of Financial System Characteristics (with examples of candidate variables in each category)

	Financial Institutions	Financial Markets
DEPTH	**Private sector credit to GDP** Financial institutions' assets to GDP Money (M2 aggregate) to GDP Deposits to GDP Value-added of the financial sector to GDP	**Stock market capitalization plus outstanding domestic private debt securities to GDP** Private debt securities to GDP Public debt securities to GDP International debt securities to GDP Stock market capitalization to GDP Stocks traded to GDP
ACCESS	**Accounts per thousand adults** (commercial banks) Branches per 100,000 adults (commercial banks) Percent of people with a bank account (from user survey) Percent of firms with line of credit (all firms) Percent of firms with line of credit (small firms)	**Percent of market capitalization outside of top 10 largest companies** Percent of value traded outside of top 10 traded companies Government bond yields (3 month and 10 year) Ratio of domestic to total debt securities Ratio of private to total debt securities (domestic) Ratio of new corporate bond issues to GDP
EFFICIENCY	**Net interest margin** Lending-deposits spread Noninterest income to total income Overhead costs (percent of total assets) Profitability (return on assets, return on equity) Boone indicator (Herfindahl, or H-statistic)	**Turnover ratio** (turnover/capitalization) for stock market Price synchronicity (co-movement) Price impact Liquidity/transaction costs Quoted bid-ask spread for government bonds Turnover of bonds (private, public) on securities exchange Settlement efficiency
STABILITY	**z-score** (or distance to default) Capital adequacy ratios Asset quality ratios Liquidity ratios Other (net foreign exchange position to capital, etc.)	**Volatility** (standard deviation/average) of stock price index, sovereign bond index Skewness of the index (stock price, sovereign bond) Price/earnings (P/E) ratio Duration Ratio of short-term to total bonds (domestic, international) Correlation with major bond returns (German, United States)

Source: Based on the review of literature in Čihák, Demirgüç-Kunt, Feyen, and Levine 2012.
Note: This is a stylized matrix. For details, see Čihák, Demirgüç-Kunt, Feyen, and Levine (2012). Variables that are highlighted in bold are the ones suggested for the benchmarking exercise. Private sector credit to GDP is domestic private credit to the real sector times deposit money banks to GDP. Accounts per thousand adults (commercial banks) is the number of depositors with commercial banks per 1,000 adults. For each type of institution, this figure is calculated as the (reported number of depositors)*1,000/adult population in the reporting country. The net interest margin is the accounting value of the bank's net interest revenue as a share of its average interest-bearing (total earning) assets. The z-score (or distance to default) is (ROA + equity)/assets)/sd(ROA), where ROA is average annual return on end-year assets and sd(ROA) is the standard deviation of ROA. Stock market capitalization plus outstanding domestic private debt securities to GDP is defined as the value of listed shares to GDP plus amount of outstanding domestic private debt securities to GDP. Percent of market capitalization outside of top 10 largest companies is the market capitalization out of the top 10 largest companies to total market capitalization. Turnover ratio (turnover/capitalization) for stock market is the ratio of the value of total shares traded to market capitalization. Volatility (standard deviation/average) of stock price index is the standard deviation of the sovereign bond index divided by the annual average of that index.

systems and does not just look at the size of particular institutions and markets.

First characteristic: Financial depth

The most common way to characterize financial systems is by measuring the size of financial institutions or markets relative to the size of the economy. "Financial depth" is an analytically incomplete, though empirically ubiquitous, measure of the functioning of financial systems.

For financial institutions, the variable that has received much attention in the empirical literature on financial development is private credit, defined as credit to the private sector from deposit money banks, as a percentage of GDP.[5] There is a wide literature demonstrating the link between financial depth, approximated by private sector credit to GDP, on one hand, and long-term economic growth and poverty reduction on the other hand (for example, Demirgüç-Kunt and Levine 2008). Private credit varies widely across countries. For example, averaged over 1980–2010, private credit was less than 10 percent of GDP in Angola, Cambodia, and the Republic of Yemen, while exceeding

---

BOX 1.1   Selecting the Representative Variables for Individual Characteristics

For every category in the 4x2 matrix, several variables could be used as proxies. Which combination of these variables should one choose when trying to compare financial systems?

In some cases, the variables in the same dimension are complementary, and some are even additive. For example, the total assets of banks to GDP and total assets of nonbank financial institutions to GDP are in the same units and complement each other, so they can be added up to obtain a proxy of total assets of financial institutions to GDP. The result will be a good proxy variable, provided that the underlying variables are comprehensive in their coverage and that no double counting occurs between them. Other examples include measures of volatility in the stock market and volatility in the bond market. If these are measured in a similar way (as standard deviations), they can actually be added, using the capitalizations of the two markets, as proxy for their relative weights (as well as the covariance between the two), to approximate the general volatility in the financial markets.

In other cases, the variables "compete" to measure the similar things in slightly different ways. For example, private sector credit to GDP and total assets of financial institutions to GDP are both proxies for financial institutions' size. The two variables differ in terms of their comprehensiveness and country coverage, with private sector credit to GDP covering a smaller set of assets but being available for a large number of countries.

How should one pick among such competing variables? For the purpose of presenting the raw data in the database, it is not necessary to pick. Indeed, the Global Financial Development Database shows the competing variables, so that users can examine the data for themselves. However, for the purpose of characterizing financial systems and for comparisons across the dimensions, it is useful to pick one of the competing variables.

The general approach is to select indicators that are widely available and have a clearly documented link to long-term economic growth or poverty reduction in the literature. When two variables capture the same dimension, and both have a link to economic development, one would select the variable that— even if it is perhaps less sophisticated—has greater country coverage. The more sophisticated variable is still included in the Global Financial Development Database, and relationships between some of these variables are explored in Čihák, Demirgüç-Kunt, Feyen, and Levine (2012). For most of the variables, the competing indicators tend to be highly (although not perfectly) correlated. For example, the correlation coefficient for private sector credit to GDP and total banking assets to GDP is 0.98 (figure 1.3).

The chapter's illustrative comparison of the 4x2 characteristics across countries selects one variable from each dimension. The selected variables are highlighted in bold in table 1.1.

---

85 percent of GDP in Austria, China, and the United Kingdom. The annual average value of private credit across countries was 39 percent, with a standard deviation of 36 percent.

An alternative to private credit is total banking assets to GDP, a variable that is also included in the Global Financial Development Database. Compared to private credit, this variable also includes credit to government and bank assets other than credit. It is arguably a more comprehensive measure of size, but it is available for a smaller number of countries and has been used less extensively

in the literature on financial development. In any case, the two variables are rather closely correlated, with a correlation coefficient of about 0.98 (figure 1.3), so private credit can provide a reasonably close approximation for total banking assets.[6]

Despite the literature's focus on banks, the global financial crisis has highlighted issues in some nonbank financial institutions (NBFIs). Data coverage of NBFIs is less comprehensive than coverage of banks. Nonetheless, recognizing the importance of NBFIs, the Global Financial Development Database includes total assets of NBFIs to GDP, which includes pension fund assets to GDP, mutual fund assets to GDP, insurance company assets to GDP, insurance premiums (life) to GDP, and insurance premiums (non-life) to GDP.

For financial markets, the two main segments for which consistent worldwide data can be collected are stock markets and bond markets (both sovereign and corporate). To approximate the size of stock markets, the most common choice in the literature is stock market capitalization to GDP. For the size of the bond markets, the mostly commonly used proxy for size is the outstanding volume of debt securities (private and public) to GDP.

To measure the depth of stock markets, this report primarily uses the stock value traded indicator, which equals the value of stock market transactions as a share of GDP. This market development indicator incorporates information on the size and activity of the stock market, not simply on the value of listed shares. Earlier work by Levine and Zervos (1998) indicates that the trading of ownership claims on firms in an economy is closely tied to the rate of economic growth. There is substantial variation across countries. Although the mean value of stock value traded is about 29 percent of GDP, the standard deviation is about double this value. In Armenia, Tanzania, and Uruguay, stock value traded annually averaged less than 0.23 percent over the 1980–2008 sample (10th percentile). In contrast, stock value traded averaged over 75 percent in China (both mainland and Hong Kong SAR, China), Saudi Arabia, Switzerland, and the Unites States (90th percentile). Also, this report confirms Levine's and Zervos's results using other market development indicators. In particular, it examines stock market capitalization, which simply measures the value of listed shares on a country's stock exchanges as a share of GDP and securities market capitalization, which equals the capitalization of the stock market plus the capitalization of the private domestic bond markets, divided by GDP.

The relative size of banks and markets—called the financial structure ratio—measures the ratio of private credit to stock market capitalization and provides information

FIGURE 1.3 Correlations between Characteristics in Same Category (example)

Source: Calculations based on the Global Financial Development Database.
Note: Correlation = 0.98. A significant correlation coefficient at the 5% level or better.

on the mixture of financial institutions and markets operating in a financial system.[7] The degree to which the financial system is relatively bank based or market based has been an important topic in the financial development literature. In a recent contribution to this literature, Demirgüç-Kunt, Feyen, and Levine (2012) find that as economies develop, services provided by financial markets tend to become relatively more important than those provided by banks.

Second characteristic: Financial access (inclusion)

But finance is not just about the size of financial institutions and securities; finance is also about the ability of individuals and firms in an economy to access financial services. Measures of financial access are indeed strongly associated with economic development, a relationship that is separate from the association between financial depth and economic development. Besides the direct benefits of enhanced access to financial services, finance also reduces inequality, particularly through indirect labor market mechanisms. Specifically, accumulated evidence shows that financial access accelerates economic growth, intensifies competition, and boosts the demand for labor—and it usually brings bigger benefits to those at the lower end of the income distribution (see, for instance, Beck, Demirgüç-Kunt, and Levine 2007, and Beck, Levine, and Levkov 2010). It is important to emphasize that the issue is not only access to any form of finance, but also the quality of financial services available to people. In other words, having a bank account is nice, but it is also important to have a competitive interest rate, reliable payment services, and so on.

A well-functioning financial system offers savings, payments, and risk-management products to as large a set of participants as possible. It seeks out and finances good growth opportunities wherever they may be. Without inclusive financial systems, poor individuals and small enterprises need to rely on their personal wealth or internal resources to invest in their education, become entrepreneurs, or take advantage of promising growth opportunities. Though still far from conclusive, the existing body of evidence suggests that developing the financial sector and improving access to finance are likely not only to accelerate economic growth but also to reduce income inequality and poverty.

Access to financial services—financial inclusion—implies an absence of obstacles to the use of these services, whether the obstacles are price or nonprice barriers to finance. It is important to distinguish between access to—the possibility to use—and actual use of financial services. In some cases, a person or business has access to services but decides not to use them. But in other cases, price barriers or discrimination, for example, bar access. Failure to make this distinction can complicate efforts to define and measure access. Financial market imperfections, such as information asymmetries and transaction costs, are likely to be especially binding on the talented poor and on micro- and small enterprises that lack collateral, credit histories, and connections. Without inclusive

financial systems, these individuals and enterprises with promising opportunities are limited to their own savings and earnings. Financial access has been overlooked in traditional literature on financial system characteristics, mostly because of serious data gaps on who has access to which financial services and a lack of systematic information on the barriers to broader access. The Global Financial Development Database contains both variables that measure the use of financial services (which reflects both supply and demand) as well as variables that focus more closely on the supply of financial services.

The main proxy variable in the financial access category for financial institutions is the number of bank accounts per 1,000 adults. Other variables in this category include the number of bank branches per 100,000 adults (commercial banks), the percentage of firms with line of credit (all firms), and the percentage of firms with line of credit (small firms). When using these proxies, one needs to be mindful of their weaknesses. For example, the number of bank branches is becoming increasingly misleading with the move toward branchless banking. The number of bank accounts does not suffer from the same issue, but it has its own limitations (in particular, it focuses on banks only).

The measure of access in financial markets relies on various measures of concentration in the market, the idea being that a high degree of concentration reflects difficulties for access for newer or smaller issuers. The variables in this category include the percentage of market capitalization outside of the top 10 largest companies, the percentage of value traded outside of the top 10 traded companies, government bond yields (3 month and 10 year), ratio of domestic to total debt securities, ratio of private to total debt securities (domestic), and ratio of new corporate bond issues to GDP.

The data for the financial access dimension of the Global Financial Development Database came largely from the IMF's recently established Access to Finance database, based on earlier work by Beck, Demirgüç-Kunt, and Martínez Pería (2007).[8] In addition, a part of the financial access data is based on the Global Financial Inclusion Indicators database (Global Findex) that is being built at the World Bank (Demirgüç-Kunt and Klapper 2012). The Global Findex is the first public database of indicators that consistently measures individuals' usage of financial products across countries and over time. It can be used to track the effect of financial inclusion policies and facilitate a deeper and more nuanced understanding of how adults around the world save, borrow, and make payments. The data will be based on interviews with at least 1,000 people per country in up to 150 countries about their financial behavior through the Gallup World Poll survey. The survey was rolled out in January 2011. The first data set was made available to the public in April 2012, and the full database will be updated every three years, with headline indicators of the use of bank accounts and formal credit, which are collected on an annual basis.

Third characteristic: Financial efficiency

To perform its functions well, a financial sector should be efficient. It should perform its intermediating functions in the least costly way possible. If intermediation is costly, the higher costs may get passed on to households, firms, and governments. (In)efficiency measures for institutions include indicators such as overhead costs to total assets, net interest margin, lending-deposits spread, noninterest income to total income, and cost to income ratio (table 1.1). Closely related variables include measures such as return on assets and return on equity. While efficient financial institutions also tend to be more profitable, the relationship is not very close (for example, an inefficient financial system can post relatively high profitability if it operates in an economic upswing, while an otherwise efficient system hit by an adverse shock may generate losses).

As with the other dimensions, these are relatively crude measures of (in)efficiency. For a subset of countries, it is possible to calculate efficiency indices based on data envelopment

analysis and other more sophisticated measures; for example, Angelidis and Lyroudi (2006) apply data envelopment analysis and neural networks to calculate efficiency indexes using bank-by-bank data for the Italian banking industry. But the data required for this type of analysis are available only for a small subsample of countries, and therefore much additional data-collection work would be needed to compile a comprehensive cross-country database. The background paper by Čihák, Demirgüç-Kunt, Feyen, and Levine (2012) contains a discussion on data envelopment analysis and other examples of more sophisticated measures.

For financial markets, the basic measure of efficiency in the stock market is the turnover ratio, that is, the ratio of turnover to capitalization in the stock market. The rationale of using this variable is that the higher turnover relative to capitalization means relatively higher volumes of trading in the market and more liquidity. This in turn means more scope for price discovery, better transmission of information in the price, and greater efficiency of the market. In the bond market, the most commonly used variable is the tightness of the bid-ask spread (with the U.S. and Western European markets showing low spreads, and the Dominican Republic, Pakistan, Peru, Qatar, and Vietnam reporting high spreads) and the turnover ratio (although the measurement of the latter often suffers from incomplete data).

A range of other proxies for efficiency in financial markets have been used in empirical literature (table 1.1). One of them is price synchronicity, calculated as a degree of co-movement of individual stock returns in an equity market. The variable aims to capture the information content of daily stock prices. It is based on the notion that a market operates efficiently when prices are informative about the performance of individual firms. When their movements are highly synchronized, they are less likely to provide such individualized information (although one also needs to control for common shocks to economywide fundamentals to establish a benchmark for this variable). Also, efficiency can be approximated by the real transaction cost. Based on daily return data of the listed stocks, this variable attempts to approximate the transaction costs associated with trading a particular security. This variable helps determine the barriers to efficiency in the market. All these indicators are constructed by compiling and statistically processing firm-level data from a variety of market sources.

Fourth characteristic: Financial stability

Last, but not least, the degree of financial stability is an important feature of the financial sector. There is a vast literature specifically on measuring systemic risk. Because of the importance of financial stability for broader macroeconomic stability, the topic is sometimes treated as separate from the other three dimensions.[9] But financial stability is an important feature of financial systems, and it is closely interlinked with the broader process of financial development. To illustrate this, imagine a country where banks' lending standards become very loose, with banks providing loans left and right, without proper risk management and loan monitoring. On the surface, one could observe the rapid growth as a sign of deepening and increased access to finance. Also on the surface, the financial sector can seem efficient, for some period of time: without the loan approval process, such banks would be able to lower their costs, at least until the loans turned bad. And this is the problem, of course: the system would be unstable and likely would end in a crisis. For more on the complex linkages between financial development, financial fragility, and growth, see, for example, Loayza and Ranciere (2006).

The key variable used here to measure financial stability is the z-score, defined as the sum of capital to assets and return on assets, divided by the standard deviation of return on assets. This variable explicitly compares buffers (capitalization and returns) with the potential for risk (volatility of returns). The z-score has a direct link with the probability of default, and for this reason the variable

has been used extensively in the empirical literature. For other indicators, such as the regulatory capital to risk-weighted assets and nonperforming loans to total gross loans, the Global Financial Development Database cross-references the Financial Soundness Indicators database available on the IMF website (http://fsi.imf.org). Variables such as the nonperforming loan ratios may be better known than the z-score, but they are also known to be lagging indicators of soundness (Čihák and Schaeck 2010).

One of the few reliable forward-looking indicators of financial instability is excessive credit growth. The focus here is on *excessive* credit growth. A well-developing financial sector is likely to report expansion in credit growth. Without credit growth, financial sectors would lack depth or would not be able to provide good access to financial services. Credit growth is important, and indeed may be necessary, even if it is connected with some instability.[10] But a very rapid growth in credit is one of the most robust common factors associated with banking crises (Demirgüç-Kunt and Detragiache 1997; Kaminsky and Reinhart 1999). IMF (2004), for example, estimated that about 75 percent of credit booms in emerging markets end in banking crises. Typically, credit expansions are fueled by overly optimistic expectations of future income and asset prices, often combined with capital inflows. Over time, households and firms accumulate substantial debt while income does not keep pace. A decline in income or asset prices then leads to an increase in nonperforming loans and defaults. If the problem is severe, the country experiences a banking crisis. Drehmann, Borio, and Tsatsaronis (2011) examine the performance of different variables as anchors for setting the level of the countercyclical regulatory capital buffer requirements for banks, finding that the gap between the ratio of credit to GDP and its long-term backward-looking trend performs best as an indicator for the accumulation of capital, because this variable captures the build-up of systemwide vulnerabilities that typically lead to banking crises.

BOX 1.2   **To Aggregate or Not**

To provide a rough sense of how financial systems stack up across the 4x2 dimensions, it is helpful to convert the individual characteristics to the same scale. To prepare for this, the 95th and 5th percentile for each variable for the entire pooled country-year data set are calculated, and the top and bottom 5 percent of observations are truncated. Specifically, all observations from the 5th percentile to the minimum are replaced by the value corresponding to the 5th percentile, and all observations from the 95th percentile to the maximum are replaced by the value corresponding to the 95th percentile. In effect, the 5th and 95th percentile become the minimum and maximum of the new (truncated) data set. The main reason for truncating the "tails" of the distribution is that sometimes the best and worst scores are very extreme and may reflect some peculiar (idiosyncratic) features of a single jurisdiction. However, the top and bottom 5 percent of observations are not dropped from the sample completely. If they were dropped, the calculations would lose too much of the potentially valuable information. Replacing the top and bottom 5 percent of observations with the 95th and 5th percentile value, respectively, ensures that much of the original information is still retained. This so-called winsorizing is consistent with approaches used in earlier literature.

To convert the representative indicator in each of the 4x2 characteristics to a 0–100 scale, each score is rescaled by the maximum for each indicator and the minimum for each indicator. The rescaled indicator can be interpreted as the percent distance between the worst (0) and the best (100) outcome, defined by the 5th and 95th percentile of the original distribution. These winsorized and rescaled variables are the core of much of the analysis presented in this chapter.

To arrive at a more condensed aggregate indicator, it may be useful to examine the average across the various characteristics; however, a strong caveat applies. An ongoing and rather active debate on multidimensional indices (such as the Multidimensional Poverty Index, Human Development Index, and various Unsatisfied Basic Needs indices long used in many countries) has focused much criticism on the difficulty of the choice of weights for such an index (for example, Ravallion 2011). Mindful of the debate and the shortcomings associated with creating such mash-up indices, this report does not explicitly present such a formal mash-up index. Nonetheless, the data made available on this report's website allow interested users to assign different weights to the various characteristics and calculate their own aggregate indices.

The advantage of the credit growth variable is that it is relatively easy to observe and monitor. Also, unlike some of the other measures (for instance, those that include nonperforming loan ratios), it is a forward-looking measure of instability. A disadvantage is that the definition of "excessive" credit growth is not trivial. Also, this measure does not, by itself, capture situations where financial sector problems have already crystallized in a full-blown crisis. In such situations, credit is declining in real terms rather than growing. It is therefore important to amend the excessive credit growth indicator, as an ex ante measure of financial instability, by including credit declines as ex post proxies for situations of financial instability.

For financial markets, the most commonly used proxy variable for (in)stability is market volatility, although other proxies are also included in the database (table 1.1). One of these variables is the skewness, the reason being that a market with a more negative skewed distribution of stock returns is likely to deliver large negative returns, and likely to be prone to instability.

Other variables approximating (in)stability in the stock market are the price-to-earnings ratio (P/E ratio) and duration (a refined version of the P/E ratio that takes into account factors such as long-term growth and interest rates). These variables are based on the empirical fact that market prices contain expectations of future cash flows and growth instead of current fundamentals only, and therefore stock prices may be more volatile and negatively skewed in the future.

Measuring the enabling environment for finance: A start and an important area for further data work

The focus of the 4x2 matrix is on characterizing financial systems (the middle part of figure 1.2). It does not explicitly include variables capturing financial sector policy, such as features of financial sector regulation and supervision (the bottom of figure 1.2). The reason for focusing on measures of the functioning of financial systems is that those indicators bridge the gap between policy measures and final objectives, such as growth, poverty alleviation, and the expansion of economic opportunities. Financial depth, access, efficiency, and stability function as "intermediate" indicators and targets. To some extent, this is an analogy with monetary policy, where intermediate targets have a relatively clear link to the policy variable (such as a central bank's interest rate) and an impact on the policy target (such as future inflation rate).

This report, however, has started the process of assembling comprehensive data on the enabling environment for finance: financial sector policies, regulations, supervisory practices, legal and accounting systems, and so forth. As part of the work underlying chapter 2 of this report, a comprehensive and updated data set on bank regulation and supervision around the world was put together, building on earlier work by Barth, Caprio, and Levine (2004). The database also covers policies and issues that go beyond the narrow concept of banking regulation and supervision, such as deposit protection systems and resolution issues. Also, the World Bank has recently published a comprehensive update on payment systems and the related policies around the world— some of these results are featured in chapter 5. As part of chapter 4, new data are presented on development financial institutions and some other forms of direct government

interventions. Finally, another group of indicators relates to the features of the underlying financial infrastructure. This includes basic indicators on information disclosure, contract enforcement, and other quantitative characteristics of financial infrastructure (for example, public registry coverage in percent of adults, private bureau coverage in percent of adults, procedures to enforce contracts, time to enforce contract, and cost to enforce contracts). Several other traits of the enabling environment for finance are included in the Global Financial Development Database and listed in this chapter's annex.

But this is just a start. For policy evaluation and policy design purposes, it is important to start collecting more consistent and more comprehensive information on government policies in the financial sector (for example, on supervision of nonbank financial institutions and financial markets). This is an important gap in the globally available data; future reports hope to go in more depth into how this gap might be filled.

SELECTED FINDINGS

Financial system multidimensionality

One basic, yet important, observation derived from the Global Financial Development Database is that the four characteristics of financial systems are far from closely correlated across countries (figure 1.4). Each characteristic captures a different, separate facet of financial systems. Capturing only financial institutions and not financial markets would be insufficient. Also, looking only at financial depth as the only proxy would not be sufficient. And similarly, focusing only on financial stability or on access or on efficiency would be insufficient. Stability has particularly low correlation with the other three characteristics.

Important differences across regions and income groups

A regional comparison shows major differences in the four characteristics of financial

FIGURE 1.4   Correlations among Financial System Characteristics

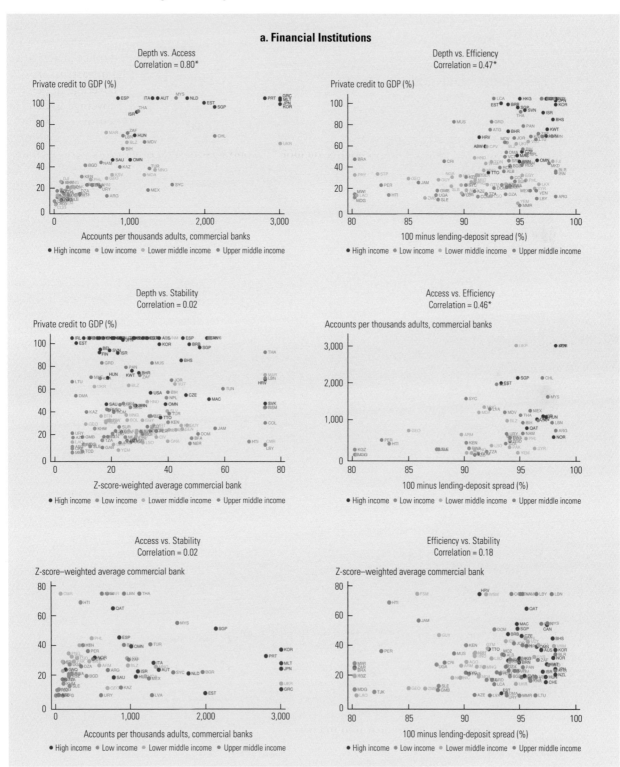

(figure continues next page)

FIGURE 1.4   **Correlations among Financial System Characteristics** *(continued)*

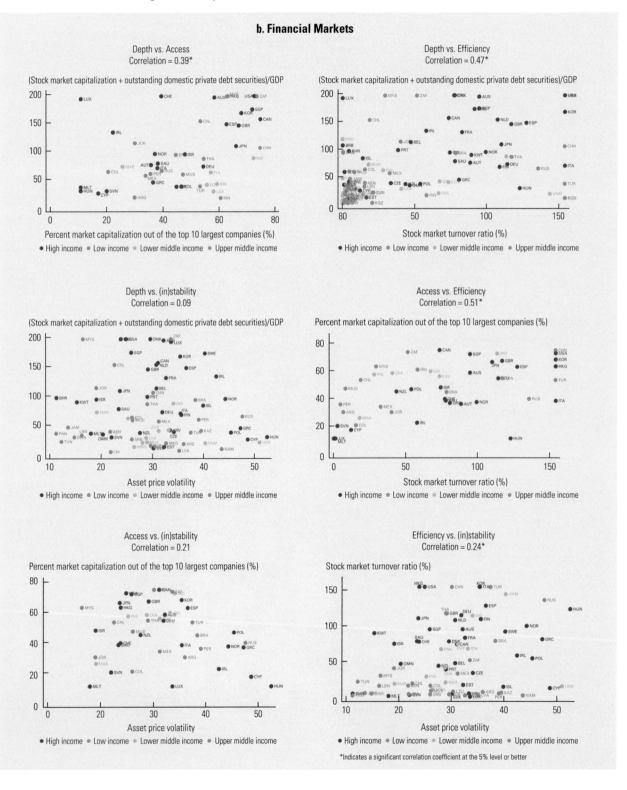

FIGURE 1.4   **Correlations among Financial System Characteristics** *(continued)*

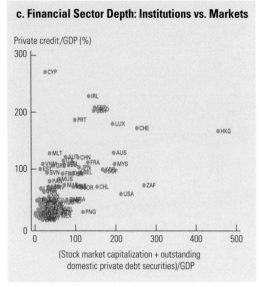

c. Financial Sector Depth: Institutions vs. Markets

Private credit/GDP (%)

(Stock market capitalization + outstanding domestic private debt securities)/GDP

Source: Calculations based on the Global Financial Development Database.
Note: See table 1.2.

systems across the key regions as of 2010 (table 1.2). The results are by and large in line with what one would expect, with Sub-Saharan Africa scoring the lowest on average on most of the characteristics, and high-income countries scoring the highest on most dimensions. A remarkable number is the relatively low score of Middle East and North

Africa on access to finance (table 1.2). This number resonates with the complaints heard during the unrest in the region in 2011.[11]

Much of the differences among regions are correlated with differences in income levels. Countries that have lower income tend to also show lower values on the 0–100 scale in the 4x2 framework (table 1.2 and figure 1.5). However, the stability indicator is not very correlated with income level—a point highlighted quite dramatically by the global financial crisis.

Large disparities in financial systems across countries

Behind these regional and peer group averages are vast differences among individual countries, and in some cases also major differences among different parts of each country's financial sector. The data from the Global Financial Development Database demonstrate rather strikingly the large differences in financial systems around the globe. For example, the largest financial system in the sample is more than 34,500 times the smallest one. Even if the financial systems are rescaled by the size of the corresponding economies (that is, by their GDP), the largest (deepest) financial system is still some 110 times the smallest (least deep) one. And even if the top and bottom 5 percent of this

TABLE 1.2   **Financial System Characteristics: Summary**

Financial Institutions (Mean)	High income	East Asia and Pacific	Europe and Central Asia	Latin America and the Caribbean	Middle East and North Africa	South Asia	Sub-Saharan Africa
Depth	69	43	37	37	33	32	17
Access	43	23	35	30	14	16	10
Efficiency	80	70	65	62	83	81	51
Stability	42	52	20	35	57	38	32

Financial Markets (Mean)	High income	East Asia and Pacific	Europe and Central Asia	Latin America and the Caribbean	Middle East and North Africa	South Asia	Sub-Saharan Africa
Depth	43	38	12	21	24	17	20
Access	46	80	56	40	50	85	77
Efficiency	29	40	17	8	24	49	7
Stability	66	60	43	64	81	56	54

(table continues next page)

TABLE 1.2   **Financial System Characteristics: Summary (continued)**

Financial Institutions (Mean)	High income	Upper middle income	Lower middle income	Low income
Depth	84	44	28	13
Access	55	32	19	5
Efficiency	86	75	61	42
Stability	35	38	40	35

Financial Markets (Mean)	High income	Upper middle income	Lower middle income	Low income
Depth	51	27	16	10
Access	53	58	69	29
Efficiency	45	19	20	21
Stability	53	60	53	44

Source: Calculations based on the Global Financial Development Database.
Note: The summary statistics refer to the winsorized and rescaled variables (0–100), as described in the text. Financial Institutions—Depth: Private Credit/GDP (%); Access: Number of Accounts Per 1,000 Adults, Commercial Banks; Efficiency: Net Interest Margin; Stability: z-score. Under Financial Markets—Depth: (Stock Market Capitalization + Outstanding Domestic Private Debt Securities)/GDP; Access: Percent Market Capitalization Out of the Top 10 Largest Companies (%); Efficiency: Stock Market Turnover Ratio (%); Stability: Asset Price Volatility.

FIGURE 1.5   **Financial System Characteristics, by Income Group, 2010**

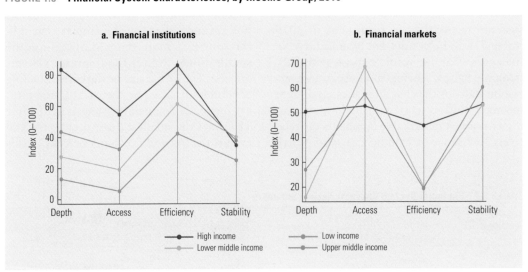

Source: Calculations based on the Global Financial Development Database.
Note: The summary statistics refer to the winsorized and rescaled variables (0–100), as described in the text. See also table 1.2.

distribution are taken out, the ratio of the largest to the smallest is about 28—a large degree of disparity, considering that these are not raw figures but ratios relative to the size of the economy. Similar orders of magnitude are obtained for the other characteristics of financial systems.[12] In other words, when one examines country-level data, one finds vast differences in financial sector depth, as well as in the other characteristics.

The cross-country differentiation along the key characteristics of financial systems can be seen from the scatter plots in figure 1.4 as well as from cartograms such as the one shown for illustration in figure 1.6. The scatter plots and the cartogram underscore the large cross-country differences. The measurement framework underscores that financial sectors in jurisdictions such as the Republic of Korea and the United States exhibit a relatively great financial market depth, as one would expect. The United States has less deep financial institutions, reflecting the less bank-centric (and more market-based) nature of the U.S. financial system. Several European countries exhibit relatively great financial depth.

Financial systems have changed. As illustrated in figures 1.7 and 1.8, the most visible change is the observed declines in stability, which in turn reflects the increased volatility in returns by financial institutions in some countries and in most financial markets.

Overall, the data from the Global Financial Development Database suggest that the key disparities among countries in terms of the nature of their financial systems have somewhat subsided in the aftermath of the recent crisis, as financial sectors in many medium- and low-income countries were relatively more isolated from the global turmoil, and therefore less affected by the global

liquidity shocks. In addition, financial institutions on average rebounded faster than markets, showing improvements in depth and efficiency after the crisis. This improvement seems to have been the case so far, for example, for Brazil and other Latin American countries (de la Torre, Ize, and Schmukler 2011), China (box 1.3), and many Sub-Saharan African countries (see, for example, World Bank 2012). However, the medium-term effect of the crisis on financial systems still remains to be seen, and will be examined further in future issues of the *Global Financial Development Report*.

Increased importance of securities markets at higher income levels

The Global Financial Development Database allows for an examination of the relative size of financial institutions and financial markets around the world. The issue of financial structure—usually approximated by the relative size of bank credit and stock market capitalization—has been an important topic in the policy debate.

In a recent paper that used data that are part of the Global Financial Development

FIGURE 1.6   The Uneven Nature of Financial Systems (Illustration)

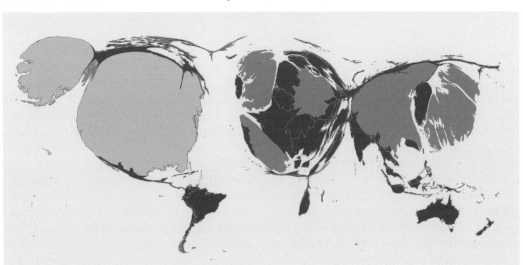

Source: Calculations based on the Global Financial Development Database.
Note: The map is for illustration purposes only. Country sizes are adjusted to reflect the volume of financial sector assets in the jurisdiction, measured in U.S. dollars at the end of 2010. The image was created with the help of the MapWindow 4 and ScapeToad software.

FIGURE 1.7   **Financial Systems: 2008–10 versus 2000–07 (Financial Institutions)**

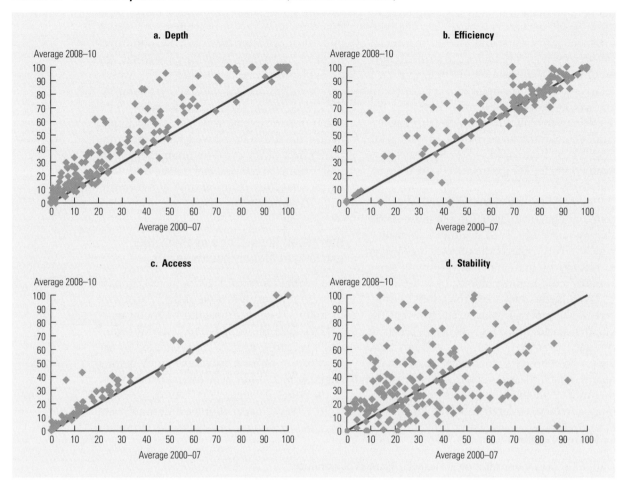

Source: Calculations based on the Global Financial Development Database.

Database, Demirgüç-Kunt, Feyen, and Levine (2012) examine empirically the issue of financial structure and find that, as economies develop, use of services provided by securities markets increases relative to those provided by banks. This work suggests that policies and institutions should adapt as countries develop in order to allow financial structure to evolve.

The existing research and policy work do not provide enough guidance to justify targeting a particular financial structure for a particular country. However, if market or bank development is too skewed compared to what one could expect given their level of economic development, the above research findings provide a reason to dig deeper: one

would need to find out if taxes, regulations, legal impediments, or other distortions are leading to excessive reliance on banks or markets. Using policy to facilitate a shift from a bank-centric system to a more market-based system is never an easy task. Actively intervening to develop markets is likely to be problematic. Interventions should be more along the lines of fostering an enabling environment and reducing impediments. Even in systems with a relatively strong state role in the economy, shifts in the financial sector structure do not occur overnight. China (box 1.3) is a case in point: despite policy intentions and reforms aimed at promoting nonbank financial institutions and markets, the financial system remains very much

FIGURE 1.8   **Financial Systems: 2008–10 versus 2000–07 (Financial Markets)**

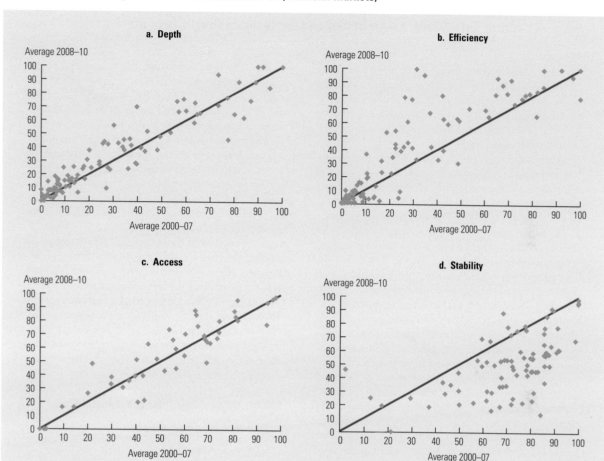

Source: Calculations based on the Global Financial Development Database.

dominated by large banks, and in some ways has become even more bank-centric during the recent period of rapid credit growth.

The "bright" and "dark" sides of financial systems

The data from the Global Financial Development Database can be used to examine the notion that growth of financial systems may seem explosive. To some extent, this notion reflects the inadequacy of some of the available proxies for financial systems. For instance, in the case of the United Kingdom, the nominal value-added of the financial sector (as measured in the System of National Accounts) grew at the fastest pace on record

in the fourth quarter of 2008, around the Lehman failure. On the surface, it may seem as if the U.K. financial sector underwent a "productivity miracle" from the 1980s onward, as finance appeared to rise as a share of GDP despite a declining labor and capital share. However, a decomposition of returns to banking suggests that much of the growth reflected the effects of higher risk taking (Haldane, Brennan, and Madouros 2010). Leverage, higher trading profits, and investments in deep-out-of-the-money options were the risk-taking strategies that generated excess returns to bank shareholders and staff. Subsequently, as these risks materialized, the "miracle" turned into a mirage.

BOX 1.3   Large Banks and the Need to Diversify to Markets

China Case Study:

The 4x2 measurement framework allows country officials and analysts to examine financial systems across borders and to put them in a broader international perspective. The rapid and somewhat uneven development of China's financial system provides for an interesting case study.

Over the past three decades, China's economy has maintained high growth rates. Since the start of reforms in 1978, productivity growth has been rapid and capacity has been expanded by very high levels of investment.

China has made progress in moving toward a more commercially oriented financial system and toward strengthening of its banks (World Bank 2011c). This progress has been underpinned by reforms that included recapitalizing the banking system, upgrading the prudential regulatory regime, opening the financial system following accession to the World Trade Organization, and taking steps to reform interest rate and exchange rate policies. Reform of the joint-stock banks has boosted the commercial orientation of the banking system, and reform of the rural credit cooperatives has yielded some initial results.

The commercial banking sector has grown very rapidly in the past decade. In terms of the 4x2 framework, the Chinese banking sector was already rather large, being close to or at the 100 score in terms of the depth indicator (see figure B1.3.1). In this sense, China may seem already "developed" in terms of the size of its financial institutions. However, the rapid credit growth of the 2000s may have been too rapid and contributed to a somewhat reduced stability score. Perhaps greater increase in depth of the financial markets may have been more warranted.

The 4x2 framework underscores that one of the challenges for the Chinese financial sector is to increase its diversification. Banks, particularly the largest ones, still dominate financial intermediation. Recognizing this challenge, the country authorities have taken steps to diversify the financial sector. In the securities sector, key companies have been

restructured, and a resolution mechanism and investor protection scheme have been set up. Pension sector reform has also progressed, with the establishment of a National Social Security Fund in 2000. The fixed income market has grown as an alternative funding channel, but it remains heavily concentrated in public sector securities. The equity market mainly meets the needs of large enterprises, in spite of recent progress in establishing a multilayer equity market to facilitate funding to small and medium enterprises (SMEs). Assets under management by the insurance sector corresponded to less than 11 percent of household bank deposits. Trust, financial leasing, and finance companies have all been growing rapidly but remain small relative to banks. China also has a flourishing informal financial sector, parts of which provide funding to SMEs and small retail investors. Nonetheless, the large commercial banks make up almost two-thirds of commercial bank assets, with the assets of the four largest banks each exceeding 25 percent of GDP (and ranking among the largest banks in the world).

FIGURE B1.3.1   The Chinese Financial Sector

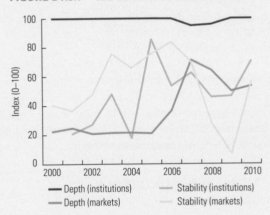

Source: Calculations based on World Bank 2011c.
Note: For simplicity, the figure shows only four out of the eight variables in the 4x2 framework. See also the note to table 1.2.

More examples of the explosive growth of financial systems using the data from the Global Financial Development Database can be found in de la Torre, Ize, and Schmukler (2011) and de la Torre, Feyen, and Ize (2011).

They observe that financial systems development paths exhibit "convexities," as rising participation and interconnectedness generate positive externalities that promote further participation and interconnectedness. Thus, much of financial system growth may be explosive. According to the authors, a counterpart of such explosiveness is that the association between financial development (approximated, for example, as private credit to GDP) and real development (output growth) exhibits decreasing returns. In other words, the association between finance and growth levels off at some point. This result is consistent with findings of recent papers that regress output growth against financial depth indicators.[13]

A different aspect of this convexity has been brought up recently by Čihák, Muñoz, and Scuzzarella (2011). Using a subset of data from the Global Financial Development Database, and building on an earlier theoretical paper by Nier and others (2007), they examine the "bright" and "dark" sides of cross-border financial interlinkages. They ask whether making a country's banking sector more linked to the global banking network renders that country more or less prone to banking crises. Their answer, interestingly, is that it depends on how connected the country's banking sector already is. For banking sectors that are not very connected to the global banking network, increases in interconnectedness are associated with a reduced probability of a banking crisis. Once interconnectedness reaches a certain value (estimated to be about the 95th percentile of the distribution of countries in terms of interconnectedness), further increases in interconnectedness can increase the probability of a banking crisis. Also, the analysis suggests that it is important to distinguish whether the cross-border interlinkages are stemming primarily from banks' asset side or from their liabilities side: increasing interconnectedness on the liabilities (borrowing) side is more likely to become detrimental to banking stability than increasing interconnectedness on the asset (creditor) side.

Analysis of the crisis: Increased instability in the run-up, decreased access in the aftermath

The rich data set in the Global Financial Development Database allows one to examine in more depth the developments in the run-up

to the crisis. For example, the financial stability indicators for many countries show deterioration several years prior to the crisis (see figure B1.3.1 in box 1.3 for an illustration for China). This finding is consistent with the observation by Anginer and Demirgüç-Kunt (2011), who construct a default risk measure for publicly traded banks using the Merton contingent claim model, and examine the evolution of the correlation structure of default risk for some 1,800 banks in over 60 countries. Based on their measure, which is a more sophisticated analogue of the z-score used in this chapter, they find a significant increase in default risk codependence over the three-year period leading to the financial crisis. They also find that countries that are more integrated, and that have liberalized financial systems and weak banking supervision, have higher codependence in their banking sector. The results support an increase in scope for international supervisory cooperation, as well as capital charges for "too-connected-to-fail" institutions that can impose significant externalities.

The 4x2 framework also allows examining the effects of the global financial crisis. Box 1.4 illustrates this in the case of Romania, a country whose financial sector seemed relatively sound based on conventional ratios (such as capital adequacy and nonperforming loan ratios) but that was subjected to rather large shocks during the crisis. Figures 1.7 and 1.8 examine the crisis effect in a cross-section of countries.

CONCLUSION

The 4x2 framework presented in this chapter puts a spotlight on the multifaceted nature of modern financial systems. Focusing only on one dimension—say, financial depth or financial stability—would be shortsighted. Also, focusing only on financial institutions, or just on banks, is too much of a simplification and can lead to distorted results and biased policy conclusions.

This chapter illustrates that financial sectors come in different shapes and sizes, and they differ widely in terms of the 4x2

BOX 1.4   Romania Case Study: Rapid Growth Enabled by Foreign Funding

In the run-up to the global financial crisis, Romania's financial sector has gone through a period of rapid growth, reflected in an increase in the measured financial depth. Similarly to many other countries in the region, the rapid growth of domestic credit was fueled by ample funding provided by parents of foreign-owned banks to their subsidiaries in Romania. In terms of the 4x2 framework, Romania's score for financial institutions' depth grew from only 3 in 2000 to 28 in 2007, and its score for financial markets' depth grew from 1 to 13 over the same period.

The Romanian banking system, which dominates the financial sector, entered the crisis with relatively high reported capitalization and liquidity ratios (IMF 2009). Also, the ratios of nonperforming loans to total loans reported before the crisis were rather low; however, this finding was mostly just a reflection of the high credit growth that masked to some extent the underlying weaknesses in the system. The z-score, that is, the proxy for stability used in the 4x2 framework, suggested that the soundness of Romanian banks was far from perfect in the run-up to the crisis.

A rapid deterioration in market confidence in the Romanian economy has led to bouts of downward pressure on the exchange rate, upward pressure on interest rates, and a large decline in equity values (some 80 percent between 2008 and 2009). These effects led to sharp increases in nonperforming loans, putting strains on bank capital positions. Stress-testing analysis performed during the recent Financial Sector Assessment Program (FSAP) (IMF 2009) suggested that some banks were at risk of

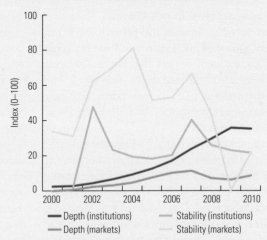

FIGURE B1.4.1   Romania's Financial Sector

- Depth (institutions)
- Depth (markets)
- Stability (institutions)
- Stability (markets)

Source: Calculations based on World Bank; IMF 2009.
Note: For simplicity, the figure shows only four of the eight variables in the 4x2 framework. See also the note to table 1.2

becoming undercapitalized as the downturn continues. The FSAP therefore called for strengthening of capital positions of some banks and for maintaining by parents of foreign-owned banks those lines of credit to their subsidiaries and corporate borrowers in Romania. In terms of the 4x2 framework, these stability challenges are reflected in major declines of the stability indicators, both for financial institutions and financial markets, in 2008 and 2009. Also, the framework highlights that the crisis has halted, at least temporarily, Romania's increases in financial depth.

dimensions. More specifically, the chapter also documents developments during the global financial crisis, not only in terms of financial instability, but also in terms of financial depth, access, and efficiency.

Despite the remarkable progress in gathering data and information on financial systems around the world in recent years, researchers' and practitioners' ability to properly measure financial systems has been constrained by lack of comprehensive data. The data that are being made publicly available, together

with this report, should help country officials, researchers, and anybody else with interest in the matter to better benchmark financial systems. The Statistical Appendix to the report includes country tables with select indicators, as well as aggregates across regions and income groups. A pocket edition of the database is also made available as *Little Data Book on Financial Development*. Finally, readers are encouraged to go online and explore this large and interesting source of data by themselves.

Future versions of the *Global Financial Development Report* will revisit issues of measurement of financial systems around the world. They will also report on substantial new trends or observations, and they will focus on the relevant theme at hand, such as financial inclusion or capital market development, or other issues of policy relevance.

Chapter 1 Annex: Overview of the Data Sources Underlying the Global Financial Development Database

This annex is a summary. For more on the Global Financial Development Database, including the individual country data and metadata, see this report's Statistical Appendix and the *Global Financial Development Report* website at http://www.worldbank.org/financialdevelopment.

Database on Financial Development and Structure (updated November 2010). This database was used a starting point for many of the basic indicators of size, activity, and efficiency of financial intermediaries and markets. Beck, Demirgüç-Kunt, and Levine (2010) describe the sources and construction of, and the intuition behind, different indicators and present descriptive statistics.

Bankscope (Bureau van Dijk, http://www.bvdinfo.com/Products/Company-Information/International/BANKSCOPE.aspx) was used to obtain and update data on banks. Bankscope combines widely sourced data with flexible software for searching and analyzing banks. Bankscope contains comprehensive information on banks across the globe. It can be used to research individual banks and find banks with specific profiles and analyze them. Bankscope has up to 16 years of detailed accounts for each bank.

Bloomberg (http://www.bloomberg.com/), **Dealogic** (http://www.dealogic.com/), and **Thomson Reuters Datastream** (http://thomsonreuters.com/products_services/financial/financial_products/a-z/datastream/) were used to obtain higher frequency data on stock exchange and bond markets that were aggregate on a country level.

The **Doing Business** database (http://www.doingbusiness.org/data), a part of the *Doing Business* project, offers an expansive array of economic data in 183 countries, covering the period from 2003 to the present. The data cover various aspects of business regulations, including those relevant to financial sector development issues, such as enforcing contracts and obtaining credit.

IMF's Access to Finance database (http://fas.imf.org/) aims to systematically measure access to and use of financial services. Following Beck, Demirgüç-Kunt, and Martínez Pería (2007), the database measures the reach of financial services by bank branch network, and availability of automated teller machines, and does so by using four key financial instruments: deposits, loans, debt securities issued, and insurance. The website contains annual data from about 140 respondents for the six-year period, including data for all G-20 countries.

The **Global Financial Inclusion Index (Global Findex)** is a new database of demand-side data on financial inclusion, which documents financial usage across gender, age, education, geographic regions, and national income levels. The core set of indicators and subindicators of financial inclusion, based on the Global Findex database, includes *Use of bank accounts* (% of adults with an account at a formal financial institution, purpose of accounts, frequency of transactions; % of adults with an active account at a formal financial institution, mode of access); *Savings* (% of adults who saved in the past 12 months using a formal financial institution, % of adults who saved in the past 12 months using an informal savings club or a person outside the family, % of adults who otherwise saved in the past 12 months); *Borrowing* (% of adults who borrowed in the past 12 months from a formal financial institution, % of adults who borrowed in the past 12 months from informal sources, % of adults with an outstanding loan to purchase a home or an apartment); *Payments* (% of adults who used a formal account to receive wages or government payments in the past 12 months, % of adults who used a formal account to receive or send money to family members living elsewhere in the past 12 months, % of adults who used a mobile phone to pay bills or send or receive money in the past 12 months); *Insurance* (% of adults who personally purchased private health insurance, % of adults who work in farming, forestry, or fishing and personally paid for crop, rainfall, or livestock insurance).

Financial Soundness Indicators database (http://fsi.imf.org/), hosted by the IMF, disseminates data and metadata on selected financial soundness indicators provided by participating countries.

World Development Indicators (http://data.worldbank.org/data-catalog/world-development-indicators) is the primary World Bank collection of development indicators, compiled from officially recognized international sources. It presents the most current and accurate global development data available, and includes national, regional, and global estimates.

International Financial Statistics (http://elibrary-data.imf.org/FindDataReports.aspx?d=33061&e=169393), from the IMF, provides is a standard source of international statistics on all aspects of international and domestic finance. It reports, for most countries of the world, basic financial and economic data on international banking, money and banking, interest rates, prices, production, international transactions, international liquidity, government accounts, exchange rates, and national accounts.

Bank for International Settlements (BIS) (http://www.bis.org/) statistics were used for the aggregate data on bond statistics, including domestic debt securities by residence and type of instrument (bonds and notes vs. money market instruments, issued by financial and nonfinancial corporations; based on publicly available or country-reported data). Domestic debt securities (Quarterly Review Table 16) for a given country comprise issues by residents in domestic currency targeted at resident investors, whereas international debt securities (Quarterly Review Table 11) are the ones targeted at nonresidents (a) in domestic currency on the domestic market, (b) in domestic and foreign currency on the international market, plus (c) the issues in foreign currency in the domestic market (further information can be found in the Guide to the International Financial Statistics, http://www.bis.org/publ/bppdf/bispap14.htm).

Two different collection systems are used (s-b-s for international debt securities and aggregated data for domestic debt securities), resulting in some possible overlap (between domestic debt securities and international debt securities) and inconsistencies (classification of issuers).

Country authorities' websites were used to reconfirm and fill in some of the gaps in the data.

NOTES

1. See http://www.copenhagenconsensus.com. Among the top 30 solutions, microfinance was considered as a way to improve livelihoods of poor women, but this topic did not make it to the top 10.
2. This is not the only approach to classifying the functions provided by the financial system, but it is not dramatically different from other approaches (such as Merton 1992; Merton and Bodie 2004), and it is an approach that fits rather well with the large finance literature, including recent research.
3. In the empirical literature, identifying the impact of finance has sometimes proved challenging. Some of the early literature on the subject requires the problematic iden-

tifying assumption that legal origins matter for development only through their impacts on finance. But subsequent papers have tried more nuanced and more persuasive approaches to identification (such as Rajan and Zingales 1998).

4. The database builds on previous work within the World Bank Group, in particular the relevant papers by Beck, Demirgüç-Kunt, and Levine (2000, 2010) and Beck and others (2006). The database also builds on Financial Soundness Indicators database (http://fsi.imf.org/) and the Financial Access Survey (http://fas.imf.org/). There are several major sets of data. Chapter 1 annex provides a basic description of the data sources. The Statistical Appendix at the end of the report shows country-by-country data for 2008–10.

5. The data source is IMF's International Financial Statistics (see annex). Private credit isolates credit issued to the private sector and therefore excludes credit issued to governments, government agencies, and public enterprises. Private credit also excludes credit issued by central banks.

6. This report includes other measures as well. Also relevant are indicators of structure within the individual financial segments, such as the concentration ratios (Herfindahl index, shares of various types of financial institutions in total assets and in GDP, and shares of individual markets in total market capitalization). Some of these measures (for example, the percentage of assets of the three or five largest financial institutions in GDP) are important for the stability dimension, because they provide a rough approximation for the potential for impact in the case of a major financial disruption.

7. Financial structure differs markedly across economies. Over the full sample period, the annual average value of the financial structure ratio is 279. Countries such as Australia, India, Singapore, and Sweden have this ratio at or below 2.35 (10th percentile), while Bolivia, Bulgaria, Serbia, and Uganda are examples of countries where this ratio is over 356 (90th percentile).

8. See annex.

9. For example, many central banks around the world publish reports focused almost exclusively on financial stability (Čihák, Muñoz, Teh Sharifuddin, and Tintchev 2012). Similarly, the IMF's Global Financial Stability Report has a clear stability focus. There are, however, many complementarities between financial stability, depth, access, and efficiency, as emphasized for instance in the World Bank–IMF's Financial Sector Assessment Program.

10. Ranciere, Tornell, and Westermann (2008), for example, find that countries that have experienced occasional financial crises have, on average, grown faster than countries with stable financial conditions.

11. In contrast, efficiency seems surprisingly relatively high in Middle East and North Africa, as well as in South Asia. This is in part because an important part of bank lending goes to large companies and to the public sector, leading to relatively lower reported margins.

12. To put this in a more anthropomorphic perspective, the tallest adult person on earth is less than 5 times taller than the smallest person (http://www.guinessworldrecords.com).

13. For example, Rioja and Valev (2004) find (a) no statistically significant relationship between finance and growth at low levels of financial development, (b) a strong positive relationship at intermediate levels of financial development, and (c) a weaker but still positive effect at higher levels of financial development. Arcand, Berkes, and Panizza (2011) find that finance actually starts having a negative effect on output growth when credit to the private sector exceeds 110 percent of GDP. Similarly, Cecchetti and Kharroubi (2012) find that the aggregate productivity growth in an economy increases with private sector credit to GDP, but only up to a point; after that point, increases in private sector credit to GDP are associated with lower aggregate productivity growth.

2

The State as Regulator and Supervisor

- *Financial sector regulation and supervision are areas where the role of the state is not in dispute; the debate is about how to ensure that the role is carried out well.*

- *A key challenge of regulation is to better align private incentives with public interest, without taxing or subsidizing private risk taking. Supervision is meant to ensure the implementation of rules and regulations. It needs to harness the power of market discipline and address its limitations.*

- *The financial crisis underscored limitations in supervisory enforcement and market discipline. It emphasized the importance of combining strong, timely, anticipatory supervisory enforcement with better use of market discipline. It also highlighted the importance of basics—solid and transparent legal and institutional frameworks to promote financial stability. In many developing economies that means that building supervisory capacity needs to be a priority.*

- *Useful lessons can be learned by analyzing regulation and supervision in economies that were at the epicenter of the global financial crisis and those that were not. A new World Bank global survey, presented in this chapter, suggests that economies that suffered from the crisis had weaker regulation and supervision practices as well as less scope for market incentives than the rest.*

- *This chapter reviews progress on regulatory reforms at the global and national levels, and identifies advances made so far. Tracking changes during the crisis reveals that countries have stepped up efforts in the area of macroprudential policy, as well as on issues such as resolution regimes and consumer protection. However, the survey suggests that there is further scope for improving market discipline, namely disclosures and monitoring incentives.*

- *The financial crisis has triggered a healthy debate on approaches to regulation and supervision among regulators, policy makers, and academics, leading to multiple proposals for further reforms. These proposals aim to limit regulatory arbitrage and make better use of regulatory resources. Common themes of these proposals are calls for more transparency and simpler regulation to enhance accountability, as well as for more proactive efforts to identify and address incentive problems.*

For years, developed economies enjoyed stable macroeconomic conditions—often referred to as the Great Moderation—where developments in the financial sector were often considered major contributors to financial stability and thus to economic growth.[1] This has been followed by a phase of deep instability, in which major financial institutions collapsed and financial markets malfunctioned.

Because of the central role that financial sectors play in market economies, governments and major central banks intervened to avoid the collapse of the economic system. Massive rescue packages and unorthodox monetary measures were used to lower market participants' risk aversion to tolerable levels and to avert the worst scenarios. This frantic activity presented a striking contrast with the sanguine attitude of investors and supervisors in the years before the crisis, when the excesses of financial institutions were allowed to grow unhampered.

The global financial crisis that began in 2007 and intensified with the collapse of Lehman Brothers in 2008 presented a major test of the international architecture developed to safeguard the stability of the global financial system—and the architecture largely failed.

Although there is some consensus on attributing to financial markets an important component of procyclicality, the reasons behind the absence of decisive preemptive supervisory action in the run–up to the crisis are still a subject of debate. Some analysts emphasize the weaknesses in policy making. Others blame the trend toward deregulation. Yet others emphasize problems with incentives in the financial markets and the regulatory and supervisory framework.

Whatever the relative importance of these factors, the crisis has thrust into the spotlight major shortcomings in regulation and supervision, in the capacity of market discipline to promote financial stability, and in the soundness of national and international arrangements for crisis management and surveillance, reopening debates and analyses in all these areas. The results of these debates and analyses can provide insight to policy makers and regulators designing reforms aimed at making financial systems more resilient and efficient.

After the onset of the crisis, there was much talk about using the crisis to push through needed reforms. At the global level, the G-20 has mandated the Financial Stability Board (FSB), after its transformation in 2009, to promote the coordinated development and implementation of effective regulatory, supervisory, and other financial sector policies.[2] As part of this regulatory reform agenda, the Basel Committee has prepared new capital and liquidity requirements for banks under the third Basel framework, Basel III. On the national level, many economies have enacted or are considering new laws and regulations in response to the lessons from the crisis. The crisis has also led to an active policy debate among regulators, policy makers, and academics, giving rise to multiple reform proposals.

Much has been done, but is it appropriate? And will it be sufficient to reduce the likelihood and severity of future financial crises? The key questions addressed in this chapter are: What is the early thinking on transforming regulatory practices around the world? What are the specific issues for emerging markets and developing economies (EMDEs)? What should be the role of the state as regulator and supervisor of the financial sector?[3] This chapter reviews some of the lessons from the crisis and the responses proposed to address them, including those reflected in the World Bank's updated survey of bank regulation and supervision practices around the globe. The chapter summarizes the progress made through recent regulatory reforms, as well as some promising new ideas and reform proposals.

There is no major debate on whether the state should be in regulation and supervision. Though the benefits of, for example, direct state ownership of financial institutions are often disputed, the importance of the state regulating and supervising the financial sector is well established in the economic and financial literature. The case for financial sector regulation has been built around the following market failures:[4] (a) anticompetitive behavior, (b) market misconduct, (c) information asymmetries, and (d) systemic instability. These failures can impair the capacity of financial markets to deliver efficient outcomes and justify regulatory intervention if the benefits outweigh the costs. The first two market failures give rise to inefficiencies that need to be resolved through market regulation, while the last two underpin the case for prudential regulation. Regulation aimed at curbing anticompetitive behavior is needed to foster an efficient allocation of resources and intermediation of funds. Market misconduct regulation is needed to ensure that participants act with integrity and that sufficient information is available to make informed decisions. Information asymmetries have traditionally served as the main justification for prudential regulation, but experiences in the financial crisis have raised the importance attributed to prudential regulation in preventing systemic instability.

States' regulation and supervision (usually done via autonomous or semiautonomous agencies) can improve welfare by providing the monitoring functions that dispersed counterparts (in particular, depositors, shareholders, and bondholders) are unable or unwilling to perform (Barth, Caprio, and Levine 2006). For example, Dewatripont and Tirole (1994) develop a model of banks' capital structure, showing how optimal regulation can be achieved using a combination of basic capital adequacy requirements with external intervention when those are violated, with elements of market discipline being an important complement (though not a substitute) to this regulation. Dewatripont and Tirole, as well as other authors, see the key challenge for regulation as providing the right incentives to managers of financial intermediaries. Regulation is seen as a "speed bump"—a term coined by Joseph Stiglitz—mitigating managers' incentives to generate profits by rapid growth. Politicians and regulators are often subject to intense pressure from regulated firms to modify regulations, resulting in suboptimal regulation and

supervision (Laffont and Tirole 1993; Stigler 1971). According to some authors, that has contributed to the financial crisis (Johnson and Kwak 2010). So the real question is how best to ensure that regulation and supervision support sound financial development.

Shortcomings in private and public institutions have to be addressed in a comprehensive way, focusing on the roots of the crisis, instead of its consequences. This approach entails correcting weaknesses prevalent before the crisis in many financial markets and institutions, including their supervisory bodies (such as deep information asymmetries, distorted incentives, defective governance arrangements, and defective accountability). Doing so would improve market discipline by providing information to market participants and supervisory bodies if inefficient risk taking is sufficiently and timely penalized before the correction of excesses entails prohibitive costs for the whole economic system. But it also implies that, given the limits of market discipline (due to, for example, coordination problems, fallacy of composition, and herd behavior), a complementary and equally necessary role is reserved for well-designed regulatory and supervisory action.

Because of the crisis, much focus has been placed on regulating and monitoring systemic risk. Indeed, using the latest round of the World Bank's survey of regulatory and supervisory practices around the world, this chapter confirms that countries have stepped up efforts on macroprudential policy, as well as on resolution regimes and financial consumer protection. All these efforts place more demands on supervisors, which introduces greater burden in smaller and lower-income economies where supervisory capacity is already constrained.

Breakdowns in incentives are a unifying theme when discussing the roots of the crisis (see Calomiris 2011; Demirgüç-Kunt and Servén 2010; Levine 2010, 2011; Rajan 2010). Misaligned incentives in the financial markets and in the regulatory and supervisory framework were among the key factors contributing to the crisis. Incentive conflicts help explain how securitization went wrong, why credit ratings proved inaccurate, and why the crisis cannot be blamed on mark-to-market accounting or an unexpected loss of liquidity. Contradictory market, bureaucratic, and political incentives undermined financial regulation and supervision (Caprio, Demirgüç-Kunt, and Kane 2010). Insufficient incentives to enforce the existing rules (Barth, Caprio, and Levine 2012a), combined with a lack of capacity, resulted in regulations that were not applied and supervisory powers that were not used in the years leading to the crisis. Reducing the likelihood of future crises therefore requires addressing these incentive issues; along these lines the chapter discusses reform proposals that emphasize greater transparency and disclosure, importance of incentive compatibility in reforms, and simple regulation.

Transparency and disclosure of good information, coupled with the right incentives, help make market participants behave in ways consistent with the public interest. Complicated regulation is not desirable, since it is harder to implement and supervise, particularly in smaller and less developed economies with lower supervisory capacity. In most middle-income and nearly all low-income economies, basic regulations, combined with strong supervision and enforcement of transparency, are a better approach. Market discipline is not a panacea, but it is an important ingredient in the regulatory and supervisory mix. When regulation is ineffective, market discipline often breaks down, as illustrated in the recent crisis.

This chapter acknowledges the progress made by recent global regulatory reforms, which include measures to address moral hazard in too-big-to-fail institutions, abusive compensation policies, undue activity with over-the-counter derivatives, and biased credit ratings. It also discusses reform proposals that argue for taking these reforms further, as well as new approaches to regulation and supervision.[5]

The challenge of financial sector regulation is to align private incentives with the public interest without taxing or subsidizing private risk taking. Threats of market entry

and exit, healthy competition, and disclosure of quality information, combined with strong and timely supervisory action, are essential in getting this balance right. But by revealing limits of market and regulatory discipline, the crisis has led to a policy debate on the right approach to regulation and supervision. This ongoing debate continues to inform regulatory reforms.

SOME LESSONS FROM THE GLOBAL FINANCIAL CRISIS

The global financial crisis—which began in 2007 and intensified with the collapse of Lehman Brothers in September 2008—provided a fundamental test of the international architecture, developed to safeguard the global financial system (Rajan 2010). Besides macroeconomic factors, the main contributing factors identified by scholars and policy makers include major regulatory and supervisory failures, together with failures in other parts of the financial system, such as governance of private institutions, rating agencies, accounting practices, and transparency.[6] This section concentrates on the shortcomings identified by the crisis in microprudential regulation and supervision and market discipline.

The chapter's focus on shortcomings and areas for improvement does not mean that *all* precrisis regulation failed, or that all supervisors performed uniformly badly. Supervision in many jurisdictions has actually performed well. Within advanced economies, Australia, Canada, and Singapore have been mentioned among examples of countries that withstood the global crisis rather well, in part as a result of their prudent supervisory approaches (Palmer and Cerrutti 2009). Also, many emerging markets and developing economies had limited exposure to the risky behaviors that precipitated the crisis, and most of these countries averted outright distress in the financial system partly because of their conservative prudential and supervisory practices. Malaysia and Peru are just two countries that have been praised for their prudential policies.[7] Nonetheless, some emerging market countries suffered direct impacts of the crisis, especially in Europe and Central Asia, which need to be seen against a background of a heavy reliance on parent bank funding and a buildup of funding imbalances in the run-up to the crisis.

Weaknesses in regulation and supervision

A major weakness in the precrisis approach to regulation and supervision was that it focused on risks to individual institutions and did not sufficiently take into account what a confluence of risks implies for the financial system as a whole (systemic risk). Thus the crisis raised questions about the effectiveness of narrowly focused microprudential policy in preventing systemic risk. Such approaches seek financial stability by focusing on the safety and soundness of individual financial institutions, with emphasis on institutions accepting retail deposits. Because questions have been raised on whether this amounts to financial stability, many supervisory bodies, in their risk evaluations, take into consideration systemwide developments to assess their potential repercussions for individual institutions and for the whole system.

If an institution or market fails, the impact on the financial system and economy can exceed the losses sustained by individual institutions or markets. A microprudential approach that sets regulations and conducts supervision to limit the risk in an individual institution does not necessarily limit the risk to the financial system. For example, the push for Basel II implementation led in some jurisdictions to increased emphasis on banks' internal models and on credit rating agencies to evaluate risk. But the implementation of banks' internal models focused on the risks in the banks' own balance sheets (private risks), and did not adequately take into account the risks posed by individual banks to the financial system as a whole (systemic risk, or public risk). In addition to this regulatory issue, many financial institutions also suffered from poor risk management surrounding the models that they used for their own internal risk

management purposes. These risks were especially great in the case of large and interconnected banks.[8] Similarly, many of the credit ratings produced in the run-up to the crisis failed to properly reflect systemic risk, raising questions about the role for credit ratings in the regulatory framework. These examples underscore the broader point: supervising the safety and soundness of individual financial institutions, though very important, does not necessarily lead to a financial system that is robust and stable, thus demonstrating the importance of following the example of those supervisory bodies that have been traditionally incorporating systemwide considerations in their supervisory evaluations.

The second weakness was that the prudential approach suffered from regulatory "silos" along functional and national lines. The approach focused on the risks in individual institutions and in their legal form, with separate approaches for regulation and supervision of banks, insurance, and securities not complemented by strong oversight at the financial group level and systemic level. This approach allowed transactions to be channeled through the entities that were subject to weaker regulation, and for transactions to be conducted in the gaps between the regulatory silos to avoid regulation altogether. The rapid growth of the shadow banking system was a case in point. The emergence of the shadow banking system in the United States needs to be seen against the background of different regulatory approaches toward deposit-taking banks and other less-regulated segments of the financial system. By drawing a "line in the sand" and separating deposit-taking banks from other entities (including investment banks), and by placing risky activities in separate legal entities such as special-purpose vehicles, policy makers expected that the prudentially regulated segment—primarily the deposit-taking banking sector—would be isolated from difficulties in the unregulated segment of the financial system that was populated by well-informed professional investors. In addition to these functional silos, there are also national silos: whereas the regulated entities have become increasingly global, financial regulation is national, and cross-border regulatory cooperation—despite some progress—still faces serious incentive problems and broke down in the face of crisis pressures (box 2.1).

Third, some microprudential regulations were poorly designed, contributing to systemic risk. The Basel capital adequacy measures considerably misrepresented the solvency of banks. There were various reasons for this, including the use of risk weights that underestimated the riskiness of assets such as mortgages and sovereign debts, the different treatment under the Basel rules of assets held in banking books and those in trading books, and the definition of capital.[9] The regulatory framework has also struggled to

adequately capture lending concentration, excessive maturity transformation, and—especially in small, open developing economies—the indirect credit risk associated with foreign exchange exposures of unhedged borrowers. Moreover, the rules encouraged risk transfers to entities that were legally separate but not separately capitalized. When market sentiment with regard to complex, structured products started to deteriorate, parent banks felt compelled for reputational reasons to shoulder the losses in those entities.[10] Risk was also transferred in nontransparent ways owing to the rapidly increasing trade in complex, structured financial products, which often underwent successive repackaging and sale. Because of these layers of opacity, the

---

BOX 2.1   Distorted Incentives: Subprime Crisis and Cross-Border Supervision

Distorted incentives at various levels were a main cause of the financial crisis. For example, the policies to promote home ownership in the United States created perverse incentives within official and quasi-official agencies, contributing to the buildup of exposures in subprime mortgages, and to forbearance in regulation and supervisory oversight (Calomiris 2011; Wallison and Calomiris 2009). Regulation also played a role in distorting incentives for rating organizations to conduct appropriate due diligence. Other issues included moral hazard associated with too-big-to-fail policies (Ötker-Robe and others 2011), adverse selection associated with the rules for assessing the creditworthiness of borrowers, and the principle or agent problems within financial institutions, related to the nature of ownership and the structure of executive compensation that favored risk taking and higher short-term returns to the longer-term detriment of shareholders.

Levine (2010) finds that the design, implementation, and maintenance of financial policies in 1996–2006 were primary causes of the financial system's demise. He rejects the view that the collapse was only due to the popping of the housing bubble and the herding behavior of financiers selling increasingly complex and questionable financial products. Rather, the evidence indicates that regulatory agen-

cies were aware of the growing fragility of the financial system associated with their policies during the decade before the crisis, yet they chose (under pressure from the industry and politicians) not to modify those policies.

Distorted incentives have also played an important role in regulation and supervision of financial institutions across several jurisdictions. Supervisory memorandums of understanding and supervisory colleges have been used to strengthen cross-border supervision. And some of the colleges have been useful in good times. But in times of crisis, cross-border cooperation almost always breaks down, as during the Fortis failure in 2008. This and many other examples confirm that the supervisory task sharing anchored in the Basel Concordat of 1983 is not crisis-proof, reflecting misalignments in underlying incentives (D'Hulster 2011). Without an agreed resolution and burden-sharing mechanism and with deteriorating health of the bank, incentive conflicts escalate and supervisory cooperation breaks down. Thus, good practices for cooperation among supervisors are insufficient to address the incentive conflicts. D'Hulster (2011) calls for rigorous analysis and review of the supervisory task sharing, so that the right incentives are secured during all stages of supervision extent to which individual financial institutions were exposed to these toxic assets became increasingly nontransparent. So though individual banks' regulatory capital positions appeared sound, some were not, and the capital adequacy of the financial system was weakened, increasing systemic risk.

Fourth, implementation of the rules was constrained by the capacity and incentives of regulators and supervisors. Supervisory resources became stressed as financial institutions, instruments, and regulation grew more complex. Information on exposure and risk became harder to compile as financial groups became more complex and interconnected, with operations both locally and overseas, and spanned many business lines. The regulators also faced conflicts of interest, with some mandated to promote financial system development as well as supervise it.[11] Some regulators lacked independence, and even supervisors that were legally independent found it difficult to withstand pressures from the industry.[12] The "revolving door" moving staff between supervisory authorities and the financial industry—though hard to avoid completely because having an industry background and familiarity with financial instruments helps in understanding risks— resulted in perceptions of conflicts of interest for some supervisors (Kane 2007). It has also been suggested that supervisors exercised regulatory forbearance on the treatment of subprime mortgages because of political considerations. Across borders, misalignments in incentives between home and host supervisors impede cross-border sharing of supervisory information (box 2.1).

Finally, shortcomings in crisis management and surveillance compounded several of the problems identified above. In particular, information gaps and asymmetries limited the capacity of financial stability assessors to monitor exposures, risk transfers, and threats to systemic stability. It was difficult to know how the failure of one institution would affect others. Systemically important segments of the financial system were not covered by surveillance and crisis management arrangements. The political and economic climate dampened incentives for analysts of financial stability to dig deeper and question the adequacy of the information and the underlying benign assumptions on which their analysis was based. The crisis also revealed severe shortcomings in resolution frameworks, especially for large financial institutions active in multiple jurisdictions.

Capacity constraints in regulation and supervision

In many developing economies and emerging markets, weak supervisory capacity and a lack of regulatory independence are at least as important as gaps in the regulatory framework in explaining fragility. Nearly all assessments of developing economies under the Financial Sector Assessment Program (FSAP) find capacity constraints in regulation and supervision. In many of these economies, licensing and closure decisions are still vested with ministries of finance rather than bank regulators, which gives rise to a risk of political interference in these critical decisions, as well as delays in early intervention in the case of fragile and weak banks. In many countries in Sub-Saharan Africa, for example, supervisory resources are limited, including qualified staff and the availability of analytical tools and skills. Supervisory processes focus on compliance with regulatory standards but are not set up to identify and manage the changing risks in banking systems. In addition, the ability to monitor risk at the institutional and systemic level is hampered by insufficient quality in data and reporting processes.

The West African Economic and Monetary Union Banking Commission, for example, lacks sufficient power to enforce corrective measures in cases of noncompliance with regulations, a situation that has only recently begun to be addressed by political authorities (Beck and others 2011). Ill-suited regulations, such as on preapproval of loan applications, are often ignored, undermining supervisory discipline. To ensure certainty and supervisory discipline, such outdated regulations should be dropped and the focus shifted to enforcing meaningful ones. Suggestions to

TABLE 2.1 **Examples of Weak Supervisory Capacity Identified in the FSAP**

Bangladesh FSA 2010	"Although the government has improved the prudential regulatory and supervisory framework for banks, further improvement would be needed to bring the system up to international standards. Loan classification, provisioning, rescheduling, and even capital in banks appears uneven and needs strengthening to be brought to international standards."
Barbados FSA 2009	"To assure continued financial stability and competitiveness, important regulatory and remaining supervisory weaknesses in the financial system also should be addressed. The prudential oversight of the banking sector could be strengthened by enhancing supervisory capabilities, accelerating the transition to risk-based banking supervision, tightening supervision of large exposures and exposures to related parties, improving the criteria for asset classification and provisioning, improving consolidated supervision for banking groups and regional financial conglomerates, and establishing more active home-host supervisory cooperation arrangements."
Burundi FSA 2009	"The supervisory approach adopted by the [central bank] BRB is still largely based on monitoring compliance with laws and regulations, despite the fact that the international trend favors the risk-based approach. The level of supervision could also be stepped up by developing closer surveillance methods so as to have greater visibility with respect to the major risk areas and fragilities of each establishment."
Haiti FSSA 2008	"Supervisory procedures appear largely adequate, but the capacity of the supervisory function should be improved. Its operational autonomy can be strengthened in the context of greater central bank independence. The current staffing of the DBS seems insufficient, and its budget needs to be increased in a sustained manner, while supervisory staff skills should be upgraded through training focused on banking and risk management."
Lithuania FSA 2008	"Resolving these issues requires an urgent review of supervisory arrangements for Lithuanian financial markets. Future supervisory arrangements should be designed with the objectives to (i) strengthen capacity to supervise the interactions of banks with their related entities; . . ."
Mozambique FSA 2009	"(ii) increase capacity of BM's supervisory staff, especially in the areas of on-site inspections and risk management"
Papua New Guinea FSSA 2011	"Enhance the capacity of the supervisory staff through training, so that the BPNG can move to full risk-based supervision. The BPNG should assert itself more rigorously to ensure full compliance with the supervisory regime. It is good to seek consensus but less desirable to leave necessary prudential statements in draft for over five years (as has happened with the revised large exposures prudential standard). With new tools and the complete suite of regulations recommended above, the BPNG will be in a position to ensure good risk management practices are followed and move to risk-based supervision. It will need further assistance to build capacity to achieve this, so that its committed and professional staff can work in partnership with financial businesses to focus on identifying and managing the key risks in the sector."

Source: World Bank FSAP website (http://worldbank.org/fsap).

improve supervisory capacity are among the most common recommendations in FSAPs. For example, the 2011 FSAP assessment on El Salvador noted that, despite an ambitious project to move toward risk-based supervision, "it is essential to further upgrade supervisory capacity, both in quantitative and in qualitative terms" and that "the existing regulatory framework has significant gaps." In another recent example, the 2011 FSAP assessment on Rwanda warns that the ambitious agenda to improve access to finance and provide more long-term financing to the

economy poses significant risks if steps are taken too fast or not sequenced appropriately, given "considerable capacity constraints for qualified personnel in financial institutions and in financial sector supervision." (For additional examples, see table 2.1.)

These deficiencies weigh increasingly in a globalized world that is moving toward more complex regulations. The survey results show that a move toward Basel II and Basel III and the increased complexity of postcrisis regulations are adding pressures on resource requirements. In line with these observations, a recent joint report by FSB, International Monetary Fund (IMF), and World Bank (2011), endorsed by G-20 leaders in the Cannes Summit, calls for countries that have less internationally integrated financial systems or substantial constraints in supervisory capacity to focus on reforms to ensure compliance with the more basic principles of sound regulation before considering a move to the Basel II and Basel III standards. The same report also calls for further development of supervisory capacity in developing economies through targeted and well-coordinated technical assistance and other capacity-building activities. These efforts need to be part of a broader, sustainable strategy to overcome capacity constraints in regulation and supervision in developing economies.

Strengthening of supervisory capacity and improvements in regulations are areas where donors can provide help. One of the tools in this regard is the Financial Sector Reform and Strengthening (FIRST) Initiative, a multidonor grant facility managed by the World Bank. Strengthening supervisory capacity and improving regulations account for more than a half of FIRST's recent projects. Individual donors have also provided support directly to various projects aimed at strengthening capacity in regulatory agencies. For example, the State Secretariat for Economic Affairs (SECO) in Switzerland has an extensive program of banking sector training in Vietnam, which includes practical training for the regulatory body, complemented by a train-the-trainer project for Vietnam's two largest universities, management training for bank managers, and technical assistance in modernizing the central bank and its strategy to develop the banking sector. (For information on SECO's programs in the area of capacity building, see the relevant background materials at http://www.worldbank.org/financialdevelopment.)

Weaknesses in market discipline and the role of incentives

Before the crisis, financial systems in many jurisdictions (especially advanced economies,

but also some emerging markets) relied on market discipline to safeguard financial soundness and stability. Market discipline requires that markets objectively assess the risks and value of financial instruments and financial institutions, and price them accordingly.

The crisis has made it clear that such objective market valuation does not always occur. For example, in the first half of 2007, the stock market valuation of Irish banks was at or close to their long-term maximum. Also, spreads between Greek debt and German bund were very small for years, as were the spreads of other euro area countries, not providing much indication of what was to take place. Similarly, credit default swap spreads for southern European countries were negligible for many years compared to their peers in Northern Europe, which allowed some countries to go on a lending binge for many years. It was only through the economic slowdown during the crisis and escalation of events in Greece that market perceptions started to change substantially and credit default swap spreads on government paper shot up (and became more closely correlated with bank risk measures).

These observations are reminders of the tendency of economic agents and the financial system to be overly tolerant of risk in credit cycle upswings and excessively risk averse in downswings. Put differently, the failure of market discipline needs to be seen against the collective tendency of financial markets to underestimate risks in boom times and overestimate it in times of bust.

Still, the failures of market discipline in the run-up to and during the crisis do not mean that financial markets did not provide useful signals. As shown for example by Haldane (2011), equity markets were differentiating between banks in trouble and those that were not several years before the financial crisis, when intervention could have vastly reduced the subsequent costs. Papers that examined previous crises find similar relationships. Markets can provide useful signals, but the real question is, when do they provide such signals? And how can these signals be caught by market agents and supervisors?

The idea of market discipline rests on the notion that, given the right incentives and information, rational market participants would penalize institutions that take on excessive risk. The Basel II capital framework sought to expand the role of market discipline in the regulatory framework. Rating agencies were given a role in the evaluation of the risks in the portfolio under so-called Pillar I (Minimum Capital Requirements), and an explicit role for market discipline was introduced under so-called Pillar III (Market Discipline). Reliance on markets to safeguard financial stability was also evident well beyond the Basel rules. It was reflected, for example, in the limited attention by officials to the risks posed by unregulated entities in the shadow banking system or to the lack of information on risk transfers.[13] The assumption was that the regulated financial institutions have incentives to be prudent in managing exposures to their counterparties.

But market discipline in the run-up to the crisis did not work well—mainly because incentives of market players were distorted and they did not have access to the needed information. Many institutions and instruments were allowed to grow highly complex and nontransparent. Information on interconnections and exposures of financial institutions was lacking. The increasing use of over-the-counter financial derivatives enabled financial institutions to transfer or to take on risk in nontransparent ways, rapidly and without the necessary capital for ultimate risk-taking institutions to be able to withstand losses when they became apparent. In many cases, assessment of the entities and instruments was outsourced to specialized institutions, such as rating agencies and auditing firms, while the incentives of these agencies to conduct due diligence were often compromised by conflicts of interest. As a result, effective market discipline could not function.

The lack of effective market discipline also resulted from moral hazard. There is ample evidence that large financial institutions enjoyed an implicit market subsidy prior to the crisis, consistent with the moral hazard associated with too-big-to-fail policies (Goldstein and Véron 2011; Ötker-Robe and others 2011). They could take on more risk and expand their balance sheets rapidly to boost short-term profits without having to increase their capital. Indeed, one long-known problem that came to the fore during the crisis was the too-big-to-fail problem (Rajan 2010), in which institutions that are too large or too interconnected to be allowed to fail are given more favorable treatment during crises. This condition severely distorts their risk-taking incentives during normal times by undermining market discipline to be exercised by their unsecured debtors and transaction counterparts. The implicit assumption is that given the prohibitive consequences of failure of these large and highly interconnected financial institutions, policy makers will do whatever it takes to prevent these institutions from collapsing. This expectation translates into a funding advantage and skews incentives toward leveraging and risk taking.[14] The problems associated with the too-big-to-fail condition are often exacerbated by shortcomings in the resolution framework for failing financial institutions, especially when they operate across borders. In most cases, these weaknesses originate in insolvency frameworks that do not distinguish between financial companies—especially banks—and nonfinancial corporations. Part of the answer is to strengthen bank resolution frameworks and to put greater emphasis on resolvability in the context of ongoing supervision, also by demanding that banks establish their resolution plans (also called living wills).[15]

Executive compensation is one aspect of these inadequate governance structures that attracted close attention during the crisis. Before the crisis, compensation was generally a no-go area for supervisors. Supervisors rarely had adequate powers to address issues related to risk and compensation structures. The collapse of banks with executives who were allegedly paid for performance clearly raised many questions about the link between executive pay and risk taking. Philippon and Reshef (2009) show that, whereas in 1980 bankers made no more than their counterparts in other parts of the economy, by 2000 wages for employees in the financial sector were 40 percent higher than for those with the same formal qualifications in other sectors. The last time such a discrepancy was observed was just prior to the Great Depression—an irony that has not been lost on critics of bank compensation, who range from regulators to the Occupy Wall Street protesters. But the level of compensation alone may not be the real problem. Leading economists, such as Alan Blinder and Raghuram Rajan, have emphasized that a much more important (and difficult) question to answer is how the structure of performance pay may encourage excessive risk taking at all levels of the institution, from traders and underwriters right up to the firm's chief executive officer and the board of directors.

But how exactly the structure of executive pay affects risk taking is still a topic of heated debate. Some have argued—even before the crisis—that executive compensation at banks must have several features to discourage short-term and excessive risk taking: paying bankers with equity or stock options, for instance, should ensure that if the firm's market value gets wiped out, the same fate awaits the paycheck of its senior management. But matters may be more complex. Incentive schemes may unduly emphasize immediate revenue generation over a prudent long-term assessment of credit risk (as was likely the case in mortgage lending); and bonuses awarded to managers today may entail risks for the institution that do not become apparent until much later. Both aspects of bank compensation have become the focus of increased regulation intended to discourage bank executives from excessive risk taking. But policy makers' understanding of how incentives at banks translated into actual risk-taking behavior is still limited, and regulators struggle to come up with rules that can rein in reckless risk taking without extinguishing banks' ability to reward actual performance.[16] A recent study by Ellul and Yerramilli (2010) find that commercial banks with a strong commitment to risk management—as proxied by the ratio of the compensation of the chief risk officer relative to the compensation received by the chief executive officer—fared much better during the subprime crisis than those with weaker commitments to risk management. Although risk managers, acting in the interest of their stockholders, are the first line of defense against imprudent investing, prudential regulation and supervision are the second line of defense.[17]

REGULATION AND SUPERVISION IN CRISIS VERSUS NONCRISIS COUNTRIES

How do regulatory and supervisory practices in countries at the epicenter of the global financial crisis differ from the rest of the world? What can one learn from those differences? And how have the actual national regulatory and supervisory practices changed in recent years as a result of Basel II and other initiatives and in response to the global financial crisis and its aftermath? To answer these questions, this section provides a status update and analysis of the regulatory and supervisory practices around the world. The section relies on the recently updated data from the World Bank's Bank Regulation and Supervision Survey (see box 2.2 for an introduction to the survey; all the country-level data are publicly available at http://www .worldbank.org/financialdevelopment).

To examine the regulatory and supervisory differences between crisis and noncrisis countries, this section and the paper by Čihák, Demirgüç-Kunt, Martínez Pería, and Mohseni (2012) compare country officials' inputs from the World Bank's Bank Regulation and Supervision Survey and juxtapose them with the countries' experience during the crisis. Specifically, to distinguish crisis and noncrisis countries, this chapter uses an existing and often-used database of banking sector crises, last updated in Laeven and Valencia (2012). Laeven and Valencia use a set of well-defined criteria to assess the 143

BOX 2.2   What Is in the World Bank's Bank Regulation and Supervision Survey?

An important input into this chapter was the update of the World Bank's Bank Regulation and Supervision Survey. The survey is a unique dataset of bank regulation and supervision around the world. In the early 2000s, the World Bank created a database of bank regulation and supervision around the globe (Barth, Caprio, and Levine 2001). The second, updated iteration of the database was issued in 2003, and the third version was issued in 2007. The survey has been widely used in research and policy work.

The current round of the survey provides comprehensive information on the state of regulation and supervision around the world as of 2011. It is the first comprehensive look at regulation since 2007. Some of the questions have been kept unchanged from the 2007 survey, for reasons of comparability. Other questions have been reformulated to result in more precise answers. Several questions were added, in particular on consumer protection and macroprudential regulation. The survey involved a major effort to ensure the consistency of responses across countries. Its design involved expertise of both

supervisors and researchers, and detailed guidelines were drafted by a senior banking regulator to make the questions more specific and clearer.

Data for 143 jurisdictions (see map B2.2.1) for 2010–11 allow comparisons across countries and with the previous three rounds. The survey consists of information from over 730 questions and subquestions in 14 sections. About half of the questions are the same as in the previous three survey rounds (for reasons of comparability), and about half are new (mostly on macroprudential issues, consumer protection, and Basel II implementation).

The survey contains questions in the following 14 sections: 1. Entry into banking; 2. Ownership; 3. Capital; 4. Activities; 5. External auditing requirements; 6. Bank governance; 7. Liquidity and diversification requirements; 8. Depositor (savings) protection schemes; 9. Asset classification, provisioning, and write-offs; 10. Accounting/information disclosure; 11. Discipline/problem institution exit; 12. Supervision; 13. Banking sector characteristics; 14. Consumer protection.

MAP B2.2.1   Coverage of the 2011 Bank Regulation and Supervision Survey

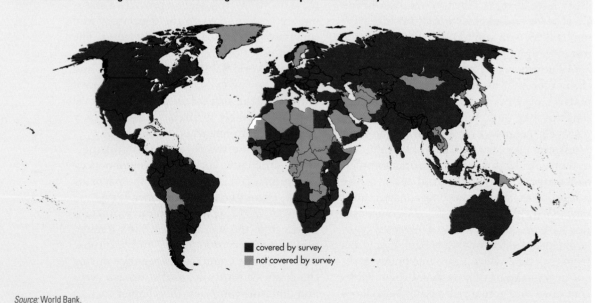

■ covered by survey
■ not covered by survey

Source: World Bank.

TABLE 2.2   **Differences between Crisis and Noncrisis Countries**
(percent, unless indicated otherwise)

Question (Yes/No)	Noncrisis % Yes	Crisis % Yes	Difference P-value[a]
Is tier 2 allowed in regulatory capital?	85.3	100.0	0.07
Is tier 3 allowed in regulatory capital?	27.5	80.0	0.00
Was advanced internal ratings-based approach offered to banks in calculating capital requirements for credit risk?	44.7	94.7	0.00
Are there minimum levels of specific provisions for loans and advances that are set by the regulator?	78.8	30.0	0.00
Can the supervisory agency require commitment/action from controlling shareholder(s) to support the bank with new equity?	83.2	65.0	0.06
Are asset/risk diversification requirements employed to oversee more closely and/or limit the activities of large/interconnected institutions?	39.1	13.3	0.07
Is there a regulatory requirement for general provisions on loans and advances?	69.9	25.0	0.00
Do you have an asset classification system under which banks have to report the quality of their loans and advances using a common regulatory scale?	89.3	65.0	0.00
Does accrued, though unpaid, interest/principal enter the bank's income statement while the loan is classified as nonperforming?	23.9	50.0	0.02
Is there a regulatory limit on related party exposures?	97.3	84.2	0.01
Are external auditors subject to independent oversight by banking supervisory agency?	25.9	9.5	0.10
In cases where the supervisor identifies that the bank has received an inadequate audit, does the supervisor have the powers to take actions against the bank?	93.6	75.0	0.01

Question (Quantitative)	Median	Median	P-value[b]
Risk-based capital ratio of banking system (end of 2008)	14.9	12.8	< .01
Risk-based capital ratio of banking system (end of 2009)	16.5	14.6	< .01
Risk-based capital ratio of banking system (end of 2010)	16.5	15.9	< .05
Tier 1 capital ratio of banking system (end of 2008)	12.9	9.8	< .01
Tier 1 capital ratio of banking system (end of 2009)	14.0	11.6	< .01
Tier 1 capital ratio of banking system (end of 2010)	14.6	12.0	< .01

Source: World Bank's Bank Regulation and Supervision Survey (database), 2011 data. See also www.worldbank.org/financialdevelopment.
Note: The following countries included in the Bank Regulation and Supervision Survey had a systemic banking crisis between 2007 and 2011 according to Laeven and Valencia (2012): Austria, Belgium, Denmark, Germany, Greece, Iceland, Ireland, Kazakhstan, Latvia, Luxembourg, Netherlands, Nigeria, Spain, Ukraine, United Kingdom, and United States. The following countries had borderline systemic crises: France, Hungary, Italy, Portugal, the Russian Federation, Slovenia, and Switzerland.
a. For questions with yes or/no responses, Student's t-test was used to test for the equality of the means (percentage of "yes" responses) between crisis and noncrisis.
b. For quantitative questions, Stata's cendif utility was used to test for the equality of the medians between crisis and noncrisis. See Newson (2002) for more on this utility.

countries covered by the World Bank's Bank Regulation and Supervision Survey. Of those, they identify 16 countries—mostly advanced economies, but also some EMDEs—that experienced a systemic banking crisis between 2007 and 2011 and 7 countries that experienced a borderline systemic crisis in the same period (see table 2.2 for a list). All the other countries in the database are treated as noncrisis countries.

When one uses the data from the survey to compare regulation and supervision in crisis countries to the rest of the world (table 2.2), the following differences stand out:[18]

- The crisis countries allowed for less stringent definitions of capital and had lower actual tier 1 capital. Whereas 80 percent of crisis countries allowed tier 3 in regulatory capital and 100 percent allowed tier 2, only some 28 percent among noncrisis countries allowed tier 3 and 85 percent allowed tier 2.
- The median level of tier 1 capital to assets was 13 percent for noncrisis countries in 2008, compared to 10 percent among crisis countries.
- The share of crisis countries that allow banks to calculate their capital require-

ment for credit risk based on the banks' internal ratings models is 95 percent, about twice as a large as in the rest of the world (45 percent).

- Regulators and supervisors in crisis countries were less able to require bank shareholders to support the bank with new equity. Although the regulator had this power in 83 percent of noncrisis countries, this was true in only 65 percent of crisis countries.
- Although almost 70 percent of noncrisis countries had a regulatory requirement for general provisions on loans and advances, only 25 percent of crisis countries had such provisions in place. Close to 90 percent of noncrisis countries had an asset classification system under which banks had to report the quality of their loans using a common regulatory scale, while 65 percent of crisis countries had such systems in place. Half of crisis countries allowed accrued though unpaid interest and principal to enter the bank income statement when loans are nonperforming, but only 24 percent of noncrisis countries allowed this.
- Crisis countries have relatively less strict limited party exposure limits and audit procedures.
- Finally, crisis countries also had less scope for market discipline, in terms both of providing incentives to monitor and of ensuring quality of information to enable accurate monitoring; for example, they had more generous deposit insurance coverage and lower quality of financial information made publicly available.

GLOBAL REGULATORY REFORMS[19]

In response to the deficiencies in financial regulation revealed by the global financial crisis, leaders of the world's major economies designated the G-20 to be the premier forum for international economic cooperation. They also established the FSB to include major emerging economies and welcomed its efforts to coordinate and monitor progress in strengthening financial regulation.[20]

The expansion of the Financial Stability Forum and its reestablishment as the FSB, with a broader mandate in the area of financial stability and the coordination of the global financial sector reform, is the most important development in the international architecture of financial regulation in recent years.

As part of the regulatory reform package coordinated by the FSB, the Basel Committee on Banking Supervision (BCBS) introduced a new global regulatory framework for bank capital adequacy and liquidity. This new framework, called Basel III, aims to strengthen bank capital requirements and introduces new regulatory requirements on bank liquidity, while limiting bank leverage. This proposal (summarized in table 2.3) contains many useful steps that help to address the problems highlighted by the crisis. For example, the elimination of tier 3 and most of tier 2 capital and other measures should help in raising the quality of banks' capital, while the significantly more stringent regulatory treatment of securitizations would result in more capital to be held against the credit risk of these positions.

In addition to the steps taken by the Basel Committee, the FSB has come up with a broad range of proposals that, in some cases, are meant to address certain failures in market discipline that became strikingly apparent during the crisis. In particular, the FSB has specifically addressed issues relating to compensation practices, credit rating agencies, filling of information gaps, and methods to deal with the too-big-to-fail issue.

As regards compensation practices, compensation at significant financial institutions was recognized by FSB as one factor among many that contributed to the financial crisis that began in 2007. A part of the official response was the issuance of FSB's Principles for Sound Compensation Practices (FSB 2009b) and the related Implementation Standards (FSB 2009c). The stated aim of these principles and standards is to enhance the stability and robustness of the financial

TABLE 2.3   **Summary of the Basel III Framework**

Proposed changes	Specific steps
Raising quality, consistency, and transparency of the capital base	The predominant form of tier 1 capital must be common shares and retained earnings.
	Tier 2 capital instruments will be harmonized.
	Tier 3 capital will be eliminated.
Strengthening risk coverage of the capital framework	Promote more integrated management of market and counterparty credit risk.
	Add the credit valuation adjustment risk due to deterioration in counterparty's credit rating.
	Strengthen the capital requirements for counterparty credit exposures arising from banks' derivatives, repo and securities financing transactions.
	Raise the capital buffers backing these exposures.
	Reduce procyclicality.
	Provide additional incentives to move over-the-counter derivative contracts to central counterparties.
	Provide incentives to strengthen the risk management of counterparty credit exposures.
	Raise counterparty credit risk management standards by including wrong-way risk.
Introducing a leverage ratio as a supplementary measure to the Basel II risk-based framework	The committee therefore is introducing a leverage ratio requirement that is intended to put a floor under the buildup of leverage in the banking sector.
	Introduce additional safeguards against model risk and measurement error by supplementing the risk-based measure with a simpler measure that is based on gross exposures.
Reducing procyclicality and promoting countercyclical buffers	Dampen any excess cyclicality of the minimum capital requirement.
	Promote more forward-looking provisions.
	Conserve capital to build buffers at individual banks and the banking sector that can be used in stress.
Protecting the banking sector from periods of excess credit growth.	Requirement to use long-term data horizons to estimate probabilities of default.
	Downturn loss-given-default estimates, recommended in Basel II, to become mandatory.
	Improved calibration of the risk functions, which convert loss estimates into regulatory capital requirements.
	Banks must conduct stress tests that include widening credit spreads in recessionary scenarios.
Promoting stronger provisioning practices (forward looking provisioning)	Advocate a change in the accounting standards toward an expected loss approach.
Introducing a global minimum liquidity standard for internationally active banks	A 30-day liquidity coverage ratio requirement underpinned by a longer-term structural liquidity ratio called the net stable funding ratio.

Source: Based on Basel Committee on Banking Supervision 2011a.

system. They are not to be used as a pretext to prevent or impede market entry or market access.

The reform of credit rating agencies is another important part of the FSB agenda. In an effort to reduce the financial stability–threatening herding effects that currently arise from credit rating thresholds being hardwired into laws, regulations, and market practices, the FSB has drawn up principles to reduce reliance on credit ratings in standards, laws, and regulations (FSB 2010b). The

BOX 2.3   Reforming Credit Rating Agencies

Credit rating agencies have not met the expectations placed on them by investors and policy makers. For example, empirical evidence suggests that ratings have often been lagging indicators that show at best only information already known by the market (see, for example, Afonso, Furceri, and Gomes 2011; Arezki, Candelon, and Sy 2011).

Much of the postcrisis debate on credit rating agencies has revolved around conflicting interests because of the commingling of rating and advisory services. The issue is that many larger credit rating agencies offer "credit rating advisory services" that essentially advise an issuer on how to structure its bond offerings and "special purpose entities" so as to achieve a given credit rating for a certain debt tranche. This creates potential conflicts of interest, of course, because credit rating agencies may feel obligated to provide issuers with those ratings if issuers followed their advice on structuring the offering. Some credit rating agencies avoid this conflict by refusing to rate debt offerings for which its advisory services were sought. This was an important reason why many of the risky, complex structured financial products had very favorable ratings.

Credit rating agencies derive some of their importance from the fact that the regulatory system relies on their assessments. This reliance is observed in bank regulation, which in some circumstances sets banks' capital requirements in relation to asset risks as assessed by the rating agencies. Similar regulations exist for insurance and other financial market participants. Following failures of ratings in the U.S. subprime mortgage-based securities market, work has been undertaken to reduce regulatory reliance on credit ratings. However, this is proving difficult at times, not least because it complicates the adoption of global supervisory standards that do refer to ratings. At the global level, a review of this issue by the Financial Stability Board has concluded that it may take a number of years for market participants to develop enhanced risk management capability to enable reduced reliance on credit rating agencies (FSB 2010b).

Though references to risk ratings in regulations are undesirable, the alternatives have drawbacks. In particular, bank models of risk assessment have proved even less reliable than credit ratings, including in the largest banks where risk management was widely believed to be most advanced (see, for instance, UBS 2008). Replacing references to ratings with references to market-based risk indicators could sharply increase procyclicality because such indicators are typically much more volatile than credit ratings. As a result, it is to be expected that ratings will be complemented with other measures of risk. But eliminating references to credit ratings in regulations is impractical and undesirable given the lack of proper alternatives. Moreover, contemplating such steps given the current period of market stress could increase short-term volatility.

Véron and Wolff (2012) argue that the role of credit ratings in regulation should be reduced—but that eliminating it entirely would have important downsides, at least in the short term. Transferring the responsibility for ratings to public authorities is unlikely to be a good alternative because of inherent conflicts of interest. Goodhart (2008) and Caprio, Demirgüç-Kunt, and Kane (2010) suggest that credit rating agencies need to bond the quality of their work by subjecting it to effective independent review and setting aside some of their fees in a fund from which third-party special masters of expedited civil judgments could indemnify investors for provable harm.

Reform of credit rating agencies is not just an issue for advanced economies. Many EMDEs have adopted or have been adopting regulatory frameworks that are similar to those of the advanced economies, including the reliance on credit ratings. For illustration, data from the 2011 Bank Regulation and Supervision Survey show that 17 percent of EMDE regulators require their commercial banks to have external credit ratings; the comparable number for advanced economy regulators is 8 percent.

principles aim to trigger a significant change in existing practices that would end mechanistic reliance by market participants on credit ratings and establish stronger internal credit

risk assessment practices instead. They set out broad objectives for standard setters and regulators to follow by defining the more specific actions that will be needed to implement the changes over time. For a discussion on credit rating agencies, see box 2.3.

Much work at the FSB level has been devoted to filling information gaps. In 2009, the G-20 finance ministers and central bank governors endorsed recommendations to address information gaps identified by the FSB Secretariat and IMF staff. The FSB, in cooperation with the IMF and others, has launched a major initiative to fill existing information gaps (FSB and IMF 2010).

To deal with the too-big-to-fail issue, the FSB has developed, in response to requests from G-20 leaders, a set of policies to address the systemic and moral hazard risks associated with systemically important financial institutions (SIFIs).[21] The policies—to be implemented from 2012, with full implementation from 2019—basically consist of the following:[22]

- A new international standard, titled "FSB Key Attributes of Effective Resolution Regimes," setting out the responsibilities, instruments, and powers that national resolution regimes should have to enable authorities to resolve failing financial firms in an orderly manner and without exposing taxpayers to the risk of loss
- Requirements for resolvability assessments and for recovery and resolution planning for global SIFIs, and for the development of institution-specific cross-border cooperation agreements so that home and host authorities of the global SIFIs are better prepared for dealing with crises and have clarity on how to cooperate in a crisis
- Requirements for banks determined to be globally systemically important to have additional loss absorption capacity tailored to the impact of their failure, rising from 1.0 percent to 2.5 percent of risk-weighted assets, to be met with common equity
- More intensive and effective supervision of SIFIs, including through stronger supervisory mandates, resources, and powers, and higher supervisory expectations for risk management functions, data aggregation capabilities, risk governance, and internal controls

The FSB, in coordination with the Basel Committee, has come up with a list of 29 banks considered global SIFIs. These banks will need to meet the resolution planning requirements by the end of 2012. National authorities may decide to extend these requirements to other institutions in their jurisdictions. The group of global SIFIs will be updated annually and published by the FSB each November. The methodology and data used by the FSB will be publicly available so that markets and institutions can replicate the authorities' determination.[23]

The FSB acknowledged that consistent implementation will be critical to the effectiveness of these measures. Legislative changes will be required in many jurisdictions to implement the FSB Key Attributes of Effective Resolution Regimes and to strengthen supervisory mandates and capabilities. Other requirements will demand a high degree of cooperation among authorities, and firms will have to review and change their structures and operations.

NATIONAL REGULATION AND SUPERVISION IN RESPONSE TO THE CRISIS[24]

What is the effect of the global regulatory reforms so far at the national level? The World Bank survey of bank regulation and supervision is useful in answering this question. The results from the survey underscore the evolutionary nature of the regulatory and supervisory changes at the national level. To illustrate this point, for the qualitative questions in the survey, 85 percent of yes or no responses were unchanged between 2007 and 2011. Similarly, most of the quantitative indicators showed relatively little overall movement throughout the crisis.

This relatively slow evolution notwithstanding, the World Bank survey shows notable changes in individual countries in several areas. For example, in an attempt to respond to the crisis, countries introduced a

FIGURE 2.1   **Introduction of Bank Governance Frameworks**

(In response to the global financial crisis,
have you introduced new regulations in the following areas?)

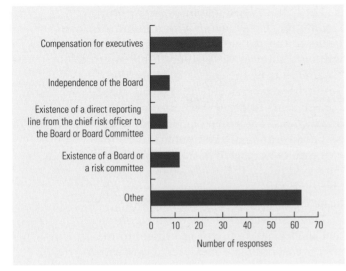

Number of responses

Source: World Bank's Bank Regulation and Supervision Survey (database), 2011.
Note: The figure shows the number of positive responses in each area. A country could respond positively in several areas.

FIGURE 2.2   **New Insolvency Frameworks**

(Have you introduced significant changes to the bank resolution
framework in your country as a result of the global financial crisis?)

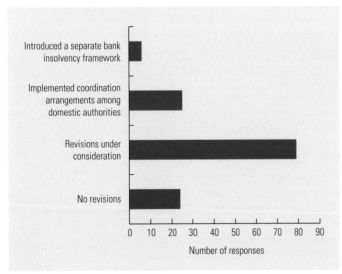

Number of responses

Source: World Bank's Bank Regulation and Supervision Survey (database), 2011.

plethora of new requirements on bank governance frameworks (figure 2.1), and they have sought or are seeking to strengthen bank insolvency frameworks (figure 2.2).

The survey also indicates that many jurisdictions resorted to increasing the amount covered by deposit protection systems as a means to avert the systemic consequences of a widespread mistrust in banking institutions (figure 2.3).

The crisis experience and the survey also provide a unique opportunity to reexamine the broader framework for regulation and supervision. One of the most visible developments in financial sector regulation in the past 20 years has been a shift from the traditional sector-by-sector approach to supervision toward a greater cross-sector integration of financial supervision Čihák and Podpiera 2008). This shift, which was to a large extent in response to the growing integration of the banking, securities, and insurance markets, has an important impact on the practice of supervision and regulation around the globe. Box 2.4 discusses the crisis experience with the regulatory frameworks.

The World Bank's Bank Regulation and Supervision Survey confirms that macroprudential policies received renewed impetus after the crisis, with many new macroprudential bodies involved (such as the Financial Stability Oversight Council in the United States and the European Systemic Risk Board in the European Union). This involvement led to rapid growth in new financial stability reports, with India, Italy, and the United States being some of the recent entrants, and it also encouraged a trend toward increased publication of financial sector stress tests (figure 2.4).

Most developing economy supervisory authorities still use the Basel I capital regime, though the majority plan on implementing the Basel II capital requirements soon (figure 2.5a). In the survey, some 75 percent of responding jurisdictions, including many developing economies, indicated their intention to implement Basel II. Basel II allows for several approaches, some relatively simple and similar to Basel I, so in principle, for developing economies, especially those facing important supervisory capacity constraints, a simplified version of the standardized approach is probably the most appropriate option. Yet many are aiming to adopt more complex approaches (figure 2.5b), sometimes without justification in terms of the complexity of the institutions that are to be supervised or the types of transactions in which they are involved. Indeed, experience from World Bank country work indicates that in some small or lower-income countries, the full range of options proposed by the BCBS is not properly thought through, resulting in the adoption of overly complex regulations for the level of economic development and complexity of the financial system. The survey indicates that introducing Basel II already had substantial impacts in many countries (figure 2.6), with the implementation being more challenging for the developing economies than for developed economies.

Developing-economy regulators offer a variety of reasons why they want to adopt Basel II, although adoption is not mandatory outside the member states of the BCBS. Specifically, some are concerned that Basel I is beginning to be perceived as an inferior standard by international investors and that developing-economy financial institutions and markets may be penalized by international market participants or that their domestic banks may eventually be denied access to foreign markets if they do not comply with the latest Basel standards. According to Financial Stability Institute (2004), the main driver among nonmember countries of the BCBS to move toward Basel II is the fact that foreign-controlled banks or local subsidiaries of foreign banks operating under Basel II expect regulators in low-income countries to adopt the framework as well. Whether or not these concerns are justified, they have accelerated the diffusion of the Basel frameworks across the developing world, as documented by the World Bank survey.

The survey results suggest a somewhat increased emphasis on higher-quality capital in regulatory capital relative to earlier surveys. For example, respondents in the more recent survey were less likely to include subordinated debt in regulatory capital (figure 2.7). Also, since the 2007 survey, seven countries have added basic leverage ratios (with

FIGURE 2.3   Introduction of Deposit Protection Schemes

(Have you introduced changes to your deposit protection system as a result of the global financial crisis?)

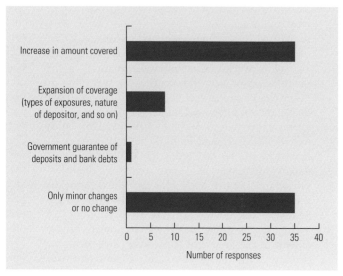

Source: World Bank's Bank Regulation and Supervision Survey (database), 2011.

narrow definitions of capital and without risk weighting) to their minimum requirements. This trend is likely to continue as countries move toward Basel III.

As for the impact of Basel III, recent calculations (such as Majnoni 2012) suggest that Basel III implementation may, in contrast to Basel II, be relatively easier for developing economies than for developed ones, given that the former have built relatively higher capital buffers. Indeed, minimum required as well as actual risk-based capital ratios of banking systems tend to be relatively higher in developing economies (figure 2.8). However, higher capital (and liquidity) buffers may also be warranted, considering that emerging-market and developing-economy banks operate in a more volatile economic environment. Also, a common observation from assessments under the World Bank/IMF's Financial Sector Assessment Program and other diagnostic work is that high reported capital buffers overstate the true resilience of financial institutions in light of deficiencies in accounting and regulatory frameworks, especially as regards loan classification, provisioning, and consolidated supervision. To examine the likely impact

BOX 2.4   Institutional Structures for Regulation and Supervision

Regarding the broader architecture for regulation and supervision, three broad models are being used around the world: a three-pillar or "sectoral" model (banking, insurance, and securities); a two-pillar or "twin peak" model (prudential and business conduct); and an integrated model (all types of supervision under one roof). One of the arguably most remarkable developments of the past 10 years, confirmed by the World Bank's Bank Regulation and Supervision Survey, has been a trend from the three-pillar model toward either the two-pillar model or the integrated model (with the twin peak model gaining traction in the early 2000s).

In a recent study, Melecky and Podpiera (2012) examined the drivers of supervisory structures for prudential and business conduct supervision over the past decade in 98 countries, finding among other things that countries advancing to a higher stage of economic development tend to integrate their supervisory structures, small open economies tend to opt for more integrated supervisory structures, financial deepening makes countries integrate supervision progressively more, and the lobbying power of the concentrated and highly profitable banking sector acts as a negative force against business conduct integration. (The related data on the structure of supervision are available on the website accompanying this report, http://www.worldbank.org/financialdevelopment.)

How do these various institutional structures compare in terms of crisis frequency and the limiting of the crisis impact? Cross-country regressions using data for a wide set of developing and developed economies provide some evidence in favor of

the twin peak model and against the sectoral model (Čihák and Podpiera 2008). Indeed, during the global financial crisis, some of the twin peak jurisdictions (particularly Australia and Canada) have been relatively unaffected, while the United States, a jurisdiction with a fractionalized sectoral approach to supervision, has been at the crisis epicenter. However, the crisis experience is far from black and white, with the Netherlands, one of the examples of the twin peaks model, being involved in the Fortis failure, one of the major European bank failures. It is still early to make a firm overall conclusion, and isolating the effects of supervisory architecture from other effects is notoriously hard.

There is one area where the postcrisis policy consensus is rather clear, though, and that relates to the role of the central bank in the supervisory framework. Recent policy papers on the subject (such as Nier and others 2011) emphasize the importance of central banks playing an important role in macroprudential policy. Indeed, the World Bank's bank regulation survey underscores the growing role of central banks in the supervisory framework and the growing emphasis on macroprudential policy. The emphasis here is on *macro*prudential, as views differ on the appropriate involvement of central banks in microprudential supervision. In a recent study on the subject, Masciandaro, Pansini, and Quintyn (2011) used empirical evidence from the crisis to make a case for keeping macro- and microprudential supervision institutionally separate to allow for more checks and balances and thus reduce the probability of supervisory failure.

of Basel III on developing economies, World Bank staff have undertaken in-depth analysis of individual bank data. The results (box 2.5) suggest that the impact of the new capital regulations may be broadly manageable, whereas the liquidity regulations may be more challenging, given the difficult external funding environment, as well as the relatively undeveloped local financial markets. However, there are important differences across regions, as well as within each region and across financial institutions.

Finally, the survey suggests there is further scope for improving disclosures and incentives for stakeholders to monitor financial institutions, hence the need to address market discipline. The findings in this area are somewhat mixed. Deposit insurance coverage has increased during the crisis and, coupled with too-big-to-fail policies, is further eroding incentives to monitor. Although the survey suggests that some elements of disclosure and quality of information have improved, it is not clear whether market discipline has been strengthened overall.

HOW TO STRENGTHEN THE CRISIS RESPONSE

Are the global and national regulatory and supervisory responses sufficient to address the issues highlighted by the crisis? Is anything missing in the crisis response so far? As illustrated in this chapter, the financial crisis has triggered much discussion and many regulatory reform initiatives on the global level as well as on the national level. Economists have been following this reform process, and have voiced concerns that the reforms are only going halfway (Beck 2011; Shadow Regulatory Financial Committee 2011; Squam Lake Group 2010; London School of Economics 2010). Economists, regulators, and policy makers agree that the challenge is to design regulations to minimize the occurrence and cost of future crises; however, there is less agreement on the proposed approaches to regulation and supervision. Table 2.4 provides a summary of selected proposals.

One common theme emerging from these studies involves concerns about the effectiveness and efficiency of the regulatory approach adopted by the official sector. The concerns

FIGURE 2.4   Financial Stability Reporting and Stress Test Publication, 1995–2011

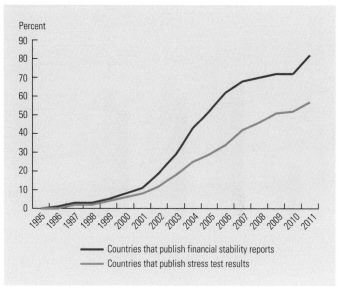

Source: Čihák, Muñoz, Teh Sharifuddin, and Tintchev 2012.

reflect issues of regulatory complexity as well as the capacity of the regulatory approach to address systemic risk that can lead to financial crises. The trend toward regulating more and the growing complexity of regulation distorts

FIGURE 2.5   Push to Implement New Basel Rules

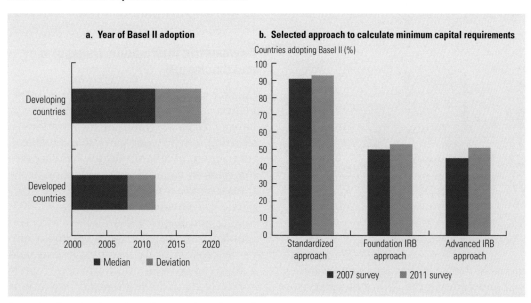

Source: World Bank's Bank Regulation and Supervision Survey (database).
Note: IRB = international ratings-based.

FIGURE 2.6   **Impact of the Move to Basel II**

(What was the impact of moving to Basel II on the overall regulatory capital level in the banking system?)

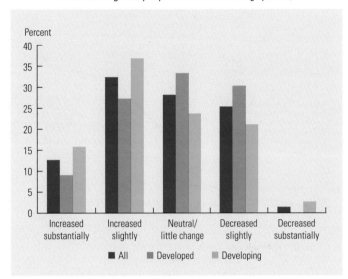

Source: World Bank's Bank Regulation and Supervision Survey (database), 2011.
Note: Percentage of countries responding in each category (of all countries that implemented Basel II).

FIGURE 2.7   **Quality of Capital**

(Is subordinated debt included in regulatory capital?)

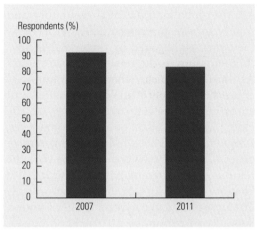

Source: World Bank 's Bank Regulation and Supervision Survey (database), 2011.

FIGURE 2.8   **Capital Adequacy Ratios: Minimum and Actual**

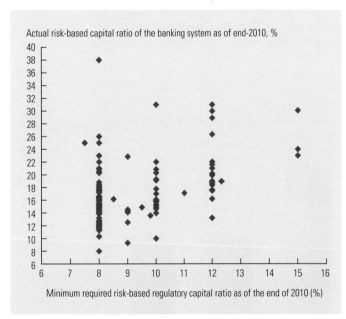

Source: World Bank's Bank Regulation and Supervision Survey (database), 2011.

incentives by facilitating regulatory arbitrage and undermining the ability of supervisors to monitor and enforce these regulations. The concerns also reflect the risk of excessive regulation that may limit innovation and hinder the ability of the financial system to perform its role in supporting growth and development. Overall, these reforms emphasize (a) the importance of greater transparency and disclosure, (b) closer attention to incentives, so that regulations are "incentive-robust," and (c) simplicity, that is, keeping regulatory rules as simple as possible to make it more difficult for market participants to circumvent rules and easier for supervisors to monitor and enforce them.

Asymmetric information, transparency, and disclosure

Further enhancing the disclosure of information should be a key component of regulatory reform. Asymmetric information—a situation in which one party to the financial transaction, usually the debtor, has access to information material to the valuation of the transaction that is not available to the other party, usually the creditor (Bebczuk 2003; Stiglitz and Rothschild 1976)—is a central problem in financial systems because it limits the capacity of the investors, lenders, and analysts to monitor effectively and to price correctly the risks in financial institutions and instruments. The problems of asymmetric information have increased as financial

BOX 2.5   Impact of the Basel III Implementation in Developing Economies

This box examines implications of the Basel III regulatory measures for developing economies. The analysis, which closely follows Ötker-Robe, Pazarbasioglu, and others (2010), focuses on the impact of Basel III capital requirements for banks to have higher and better quality capital with greater loss absorption characteristics, taking into account the Basel Committee on Banking Supervision (BCBS) rules on capital deductions and the market risk framework agreed to in July 2010. It also covers the impact of the new liquidity requirements in the form of the so-called net stable funding ratio (NSFR). Because of data constraints, this analysis does not include the short-term liquidity coverage ratio and the leverage ratio. The sample covers 127 banks in 42 countries over six regions.

The calculations are based, in large part, on company reports and data from the Bankscope database. An array of assumptions common to all banks are made, given the lack of access to more granular country-specific data on the various components of banks' capital bases on a consistent basis. The findings should hence be interpreted with caution. Since regional averages are affected by the sample, they may not fully represent the actual vulnerability of a given region to the new requirements.

According to the new capital standards, banks will be required to deduct most of their assets with less loss-absorbing characteristics—such as minority interests, goodwill, net deferred tax assets (DTAs), investment in unconsolidated subsidiaries, and mortgage servicing rights (MSRs)—from the common equity component of capital. The definition of capital will contain only a limited amount of certain intangibles and qualified assets (for example, banks can count up to 10 percent of DTAs resulting from timing differences, MSRs, and significant investments in unconsolidated subsidiaries, capped at 15 percent for the sum of DTAs, MSRs, and significant investments in unconsolidated subsidiaries). Analysis follows the BCBS indication that market risk capital requirements will increase by an estimated average of three to four times for large, internationally active banks.

Overall, the analysis suggests that the share of assets with less loss-absorbing characteristics to be deducted from core tier 1 capital is relatively small on average for EMDE banks, except in the Latin America and Caribbean region (figure B2.5.1). The proportion of core tier 1 capital to be deducted varies greatly across banks, reflecting their business characteristics and differences in tax systems; hence, the needed increase in capital to meet the new requirements can be large for some banks. Other intangible assets form the core of items to be deducted (more than 30 percent), followed by net DTAs due to loss carry forwards (23 percent) and investments in unconsolidated subsidiaries (20 percent). Net DTAs seem particularly important for Latin America and the Caribbean (LAC), East Asia and Pacific (EAP), and Southern Africa, and investment in unconsolidated subsidiaries is relatively high in Europe and Central Asia (ECA) and EAP. If applied immediately, the proposed deductions and market

FIGURE B2.5.1   EMDEs: The Impact of Basel III Capital and Liquidity Requirements

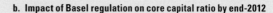

a. % of core tier 1 to be deducted

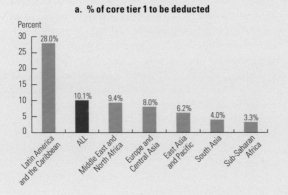

b. Impact of Basel regulation on core capital ratio by end-2012

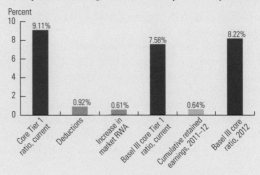

(box continued next page)

BOX 2.5   **Impact of the Basel III Implementation in Developing Economies**   *(continued)*

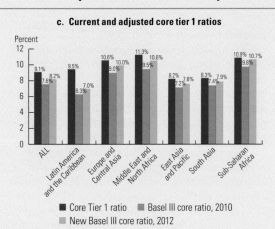

c. **Current and adjusted core tier 1 ratios**

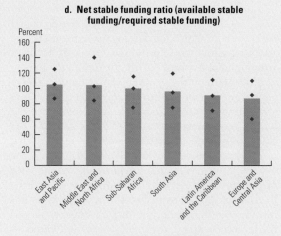

d. **Net stable funding ratio (available stable funding/required stable funding)**

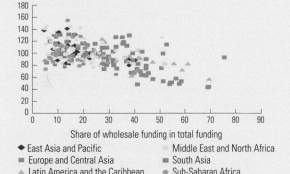

e. **NSFR vs. share of wholesale funding**

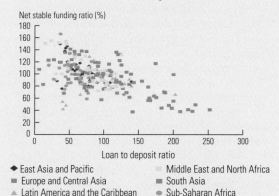

f. **NSFR vs. loan to deposit ratio**

risk adjustments would lower the core tier 1 ratio by about 1–3 percentage points on average. The overall impact on the core tier 1 ratio is the largest for LAC, Middle East and North Africa (MENA), and ECA regions, but most banks in the latter two regions still pass the required 7 percent level comfortably after the adjustments.

There is also wide variation in banks' ability to meet the required 100 percent level for the net stable funding ratio (NSFR). The calculations suggest that the NSFR may have varying degrees of impact on EMDEs across regions, with wide variations within a given region. The ECA and LAC regions seem to be the most vulnerable to the NSFR, where dependence on wholesale funding (ECA, given the high

dependence on parent funding and underdeveloped local capital markets) or loan-to-deposit ratios are high (ECA and some LAC countries). However, other factors may also affect the level of NSFR (for example, low levels of government securities in asset portfolios may result in low NSFRs). Moreover, further challenges may be ahead in meeting the NSFR requirement: for example, upcoming rollover needs of European banks and sovereigns may raise the cost of term funding that may spill over to EMDEs and result in competition for deposits. There are also challenges associated with holding high levels of (liquid) government securities; this would help in meeting the NSFR target but expose the bank to higher sovereign risk.

Source: World Bank staff calculations based on Bankscope data for 127 banks in 42 countries.

TABLE 2.4   Summary of Selected Proposals for Regulatory Reform

Proposal by	Specific Steps
Admati and Hellwig 2012; Hellwig 2010	Replace risk-weighted capital ratios by (significantly higher) leverage ratios, combined with strong disclosures about risk exposures.
Barth, Caprio and Levine 2012a	Rather than focusing on the regulations themselves, focuses on how to better oversee the regulators. Establishment of a "sentinel" agency, watching over the regulators on behalf of the taxpayers.
Bartlett 2012	Redesign bank disclosures to facilitate credit modeling by market participants. (Illustrates that basic credit risk modeling, combined with appropriate bank disclosures, could have enhanced investors' ability to detect the portfolio risk leading to recent banking crises, without revealing sensitive position-level data.)
Brunnemeier and others 2009	Develop more "prompt corrective action"-types of rules to facilitate "leaning against the wind."
Calomiris 2011	Proposes "incentive-robust" reform proposals to address mortgage risk subsidization, regulators' inability to measure risks ex ante and losses ex post, the too-big-to-fail problem, liquidity risk, macroprudential regulations that vary over the cycle, prudential regulations to encourage the greater use of clearinghouses in clearing over-the-counter transactions, and design of appropriate guidelines to constrain government assistance to banks during crises.
Caprio, Demirgüç-Kunt, and Kane 2010	Make oversight more adaptive to changes (innovations) and hold supervisors accountable for their adaptiveness. Regulators should disclose information on the value and measurement of potential claims that institutions make on the government's safety net. Establishing the right incentive structure for supervisors requires a chain of reforms.
Čihák, Demirgüç-Kunt, and Johnston 2012a	Reorient the approach to financial regulation to have at its core the objective of addressing incentives on an ongoing basis. As part of this, consider conducting regular "incentive audits."
Claessens and others 2010	Recognize mitigation of systemic risks as an explicit objective of all agencies involved in supervision, to enhance accountability: Clear mandates and tools commensurate with these mandates to preserve financial stability; sufficient resources; clear allocation of responsibilities among agencies; Clear communication among agencies.
de la Torre and Ize 2011	Establish strong and independent supervisory agencies, populated by highly skilled civil servants.
Demirgüç-Kunt 2011; Rajan 2010	Scale back explicit deposit insurance from large banks as an additional measure to claw back implicit guarantees and remove the too-big-to-fail subsidies.
Enriques and Hertig 2010	Strengthen internal and external governance of supervisors: (a) strong CEOs with boards' and commissions' powers limited to basic policy-making decisions and monitoring, (b) increased line responsibilities for staff, (c) requirement subjecting supervisors to stronger disclosure requirements.
FSA (The Turner Review) 2009	Address the need for more intrusive supervision, more outcomes-oriented supervision, and more risk-based supervision, more systemic supervision, and international coordination of supervision.
Masciandaro, Pansini, Quintyn 2011	Make a clearer organizational distinction between macro- and microprudential supervision to allow for more checks and balances to improve supervisory governance.

(table continues next page)

TABLE 2.4 **Summary of Selected Proposals for Regulatory Reform** *(continued)*

Proposal by	Specific Steps
Palmer and Cerutti 2009	Summon the "will to act" by (a) leaning more against the wind; (b) strengthening the context of supervision (independence, leadership, accountability); (c) strengthening supervisory processes by making them more intensive, result-oriented, risk-based, and proactive; (d) strengthening macroprudential surveillance and mitigating procyclicality; and (e) improving cross-border supervisory cooperation.
Viñals and others 2010	Implement more intrusive supervision—"skeptical but proactive supervision" that is comprehensive, adaptive, and conclusive. Achieve changes through (a) enabling legislation and budgetary resources; (b) clear strategy; (c) robust internal organization; and (d) effective coordination with other agencies. Create revisions through (a) clear mandate, (b) independence and accountability, (c) skilled staff, (d) healthy relationship with industry, and (e) partnership with board.
Weder di Mauro 2009	Establish more independence and accountability for supervisors to address time-inconsistency issues; offer higher compensation levels for supervisors; and set up supervision at supranational levels (Europe) to eliminate local industry capture.
Wellink 2011	Address the need for "intrusive supervision."

instruments, structures and interconnections, regulatory and accounting rules, and institutions' risk control and assessment techniques have become more complex.

Asymmetries of information and principal-agent issues abound between buyers and sellers of financial services and products, as evidenced by the malpractices in the U.S. mortgage sector in the run-up to the crisis. Professional bankers possess expert knowledge, and obtaining such knowledge is time-consuming and costly. This puts the client at a disadvantage, notably when monitoring compliance with contractual arrangements. In principle, disgruntled consumers can seek legal recourse, but the legal process is time-consuming, costly, and uncertain. These conditions highlight the general case for detailed disclosure requirements and conduct of business regulation. Moreover, information asymmetries are an important rationale for *prudential* regulation and supervision of banks accepting deposits from retail clients, as these nonprofessional consumers are ill-equipped to evaluate the safety and soundness of banks.

As part of the crisis response, the FSB and others have launched useful initiatives on data and information gaps. At the national level, many regulators have started collecting additional data to allow for strengthened supervision. These initiatives, which focus primarily on ensuring better information for supervisory purposes, go some way toward addressing the weaknesses highlighted by the crisis.

The focus on collecting better data for supervision should not detract from the need for much better public disclosure of information. The value of transparency and disclosure has been emphasized by many observers as well as by recent research (Bartlett 2012; Demirgüç-Kunt, Detragiache, and Tressel 2008). Greater disclosure would allow creditors, investors, and analysts to assess directly the solvency of the financial institutions. The financial crisis illustrated that financial institutions are rather opaque organizations for investors in capital markets. Although bank regulatory policy has long sought to promote market discipline of banks through enhanced public disclosure, bank regulatory disclosures are notoriously lacking in granular, position-level information concerning their credit investments, largely because of conflicting concerns about protecting the confidentiality of a bank's proprietary investment strategies and customer information.

When particular market sectors experience distress, investors are thus forced to speculate as to which institutions might be exposed, potentially causing significant disruptions in credit markets and contributing to systemic risk. Bartlett (2012) argues that redesigning bank disclosures to facilitate credit modeling by market participants has the potential to meaningfully increase market discipline while minimizing the disclosure of sensitive bank data. He illustrates how even basic credit risk modeling, when combined with appropriate bank disclosures, could have significantly enhanced investors' ability to detect the portfolio risk leading to two recent severe banking crises. Moreover, because such an approach leverages the same aggregate metrics banks themselves use to monitor their risk exposure, the proposed disclosure regime would impose a limited disclosure burden on banks while avoiding the need to reveal sensitive position-level data.

It would be naive, of course, to think that all creditors, investors, and analysts have the resources and capacity to understand, assess, and identify these increasingly more complex structures, institutions, and instruments. Indeed, the collective tendency of financial firms, nonfinancial corporations, and households to overexpose themselves to risk in the upswing of a credit cycle, and to become overly risk-averse in a downswing, has been well documented. These tendencies raise some questions about the capacity of financial markets and investors to instill discipline on the behavior of financial entities, and they underscore the importance of having *both* strong supervision and market discipline.

One of the important advantages of complementing strong supervision with market discipline is that, with sufficient disclosures and proper incentives, investors and analysts would be more likely to develop their own assessments of capital adequacy and liquidity, and there could be scope for competition and evolution in the design of the most appropriate measures. This approach would limit the likelihood of "groupthink" and focusing too much on a single and possibly flawed proxy or rating system. Ultimately, the approach would help in limiting the buildup of risk that occurred prior to the financial crisis.

Further improvements in transparency and disclosures are seriously needed, both on the systemwide level and on the level of individual financial institutions. As regards the disclosures on systemic risks, many countries have been publishing so-called financial stability reports. Recent research on the subject suggests that simply publishing a financial stability report seems to have no impact on financial stability (Čihák, Muñoz, Teh Sharifuddin, and Tintchev 2012). The effectiveness of such reports in signaling and addressing systemic risk has, however, been affected by a number of factors. In the absence of a unifying analytical framework for assessing systemic risk, most financial stability reports were rather descriptive and refrained from explicit statements about the level of systemic risk present in the financial system. Data gaps, particularly in the nonbank sector, led many reports to focus on the banking sector, impeding a true systemwide perspective. Also, the articulation of financial stability analysis into remedial policies, aimed at curbing the buildup of systemic risk, was problematic. There is thus substantial scope for improving such reports (as well as the associated information on systemic-level risks) in terms of clarity, consistency over time, and coverage. The ongoing work on good practices in macroprudential surveillance (such as Nier and others 2011) could usefully address transparency and disclosures of systemic risk.

At the level of individual financial institutions, further reforms are needed to ensure a higher quality of disclosures. Much reliance has been placed on the external auditors, a sector that came to be dominated by the "Big Four" (KPMG, PwC, Ernst & Young, and Deloitte). In the run-up to the financial crisis, many financial institutions were given a clean bill of health by the external auditors, only to be bailed out a few months later as the financial crisis unfolded. In the wake of the crisis, the European Union has proposed a draft law to tighten supervision of the external auditors. At the global level, the FSB has requested action from several global bodies to ensure greater international consistency in audit practices, and to provide more specific guidance for external audits. The focus of these reforms is on ensuring higher-quality information for supervisors, but it is important to use the momentum also for improving the quality of information that investors get from the audits.

Finally, a further push is needed to strengthen global accounting standards. Many observers have recently awakened to the importance of accounting because of the controversy over the mark-to-market principle (or more appropriately, "fair value accounting") and its impact during the financial crisis. In late 2007 and early 2008, several prominent financiers and analysts protested that the rapid decreases in the market prices of U.S. mortgage-based securities and other assets were meaningless and caused by liquidity shortfalls. According to them, marking these assets to reduced amounts in balance sheets would precipitate an unnecessary crisis. With hindsight, this analysis was not completely correct. It is widely accepted that financial markets can overshoot in their corrections, which in a mark-to-market environment could create contagion effects; however, for the most part, the reason for the reduced market prices was a permanent loss of value rather than a temporary effect resulting from lack of liquidity in the markets. In this case, the transparency that fair value accounting provided played a key role in pushing these institutions' management through the recognition of losses. Box 2.6 provides a viewpoint on this topic.

Greater transparency and better information would not have the desired positive effect on sustainable financial development if market participants did not have incentives to monitor performance. The next section therefore turns to the issue of incentives.

Incentive issues

The identification and correction of incentive problems that create systemic risk should be at the center of any framework that seeks to maintain financial stability. Many economists believe incentive problems are perhaps the most important

source of financial instability in financial systems. Modern financial systems with limited liability encourage risk-taking incentives in financial institutions,[25] and these incentives can be exacerbated by badly designed regulations and safety nets. The literature has identified a number of market failures that are relevant to financial stability and that result from incentive problems.[26]

Of course, most regulations affect incentives in one way or another, and the importance of designing regulations in a way that is incentive-compatible is being increasingly recognized in international forums. The recent regulatory reforms at the global level, as well as at the country level, have included measures on systemically important financial institutions, compensation policies, a reduced role of credit ratings, initiatives on data, and information gaps, all of which go some way toward addressing the weaknesses highlighted by the crisis.

Reconciling private incentives with public interest by regulation is key, but far from trivial. Addressing one incentive issue by a new or amended regulation often only leads to creating incentive breakdowns elsewhere. And some of the existing incentive issues (for example, lack of incentives of supervisors from different jurisdictions to share relevant information in situations of stress) have not really been fully addressed, in spite of the efforts made at the international level under the coordination of the FSB. As demonstrated, for example, in Barth, Caprio, and Levine (2012a), regulators have often failed to implement the regulations and exercise the powers that they already had. They point out that among other factors, psychological bias in favor of the industry—similar to that prevailing in sports, where referees regularly call games in favor of home teams—also operates in finance. In the authors' view, therefore, the key issue to address is not necessarily more regulations (although some additional regulations may be appropriate), but it is how to get regulators to enforce the rules. So, how are governments to ensure that addressing the incentive breakdowns is indeed central to the

BOX 2.6   Accounting Standards (Viewpoint by Nicolas Véron)

Sometimes it takes a narrow lens to distinguish the true features of big objects. The future of financial globalization, whatever one's perspective on its dangers or merits, is one of the biggest questions of the moment. By contrast, accounting has often been perceived as boring. But the policy debate on accounting, and especially on International Financial Reporting Standards (IFRS), entails large stakes and important lessons for global financial integration.

As is so often the case, the policy debate is obscured by the weight of special interests. Most notably, financial industry executives and their lobbyists were able to convince many policy makers and non–accounting experts that fair value accounting had been a major aggravating factor in the initial phase of the crisis, in late 2007 and early 2008, even as later developments clearly demonstrated that there had been no excessive undershooting of market prices during that period. A similar sequence had happened a few years earlier in the United States, when corporate advocates managed to delay the accounting recognition of the cost of stock options for nearly a decade. In accounting, as in most other areas of financial regulation, the issues are technical and jargon-ridden, and the potential financial consequences are large, so that public debates and policy decisions are easily captured. Therefore, governance arrangements are crucial.

The governance of accounting standard setting has widely varied over time and across countries. The general trend of the past few decades has been toward standard setters that are more independent vis-à-vis governments and special industry interests. But the challenges related to the IFRS are unprecedented because these standards are set at the global level. There is no global government to oversee the IFRS Foundation, the organization that sets the standards, or to enforce consistent IFRS implementation across countries. Nor is there any coherent global representation of investors, whose information needs the standards are primarily meant to serve.

Answers may lie in the IFRS Foundation making more efforts to organize the global investor community, and setting incentives for individual jurisdictions to adopt and enforce standards to foster genuine cross-border comparability of financial statements. At this point, it is still too early to judge whether the attempt to make IFRS the dominant global accounting language can succeed on an enduring basis. But there are already important lessons that have wide significance beyond the community of accounting professionals.

First, global financial rules are not a utopian vision but a reality. The initial success of IFRS has been remarkable. Their adoption has been smooth and has generally improved financial reporting quality, starting in the European Union in 2005 but increasingly now in other countries as well. Given the right conditions, financial regulatory harmonization can work across continents.

Second, the crisis has increased the need for public oversight of financial rules, but it is not yet clear how this can be done effectively and consistently. A monitoring board of public entities was created in 2009 to oversee the IFRS Foundation, but its construction is awkward and raises concerns about its legitimacy and future effectiveness. For the foreseeable future we will have to rely on trial-and-error experimentation for international financial regulatory bodies, which in most cases cannot take existing national arrangements as a direct model.

Third, those global bodies that exist have yet to adapt to the ongoing rebalancing of the financial world. The IFRS Foundation is registered in the United States; its staff is in London; its monitoring board gives permanent seats only to the United States, European Union, and Japan; and it still caters largely to audiences in the developed world, even as large emerging economies represent a rapidly increasing share of global finance. We don't know whether or how China, India, and others will take responsibility at the global level for transparency and integrity in financial reporting. But if efforts to empower them in formal global institutions are not accelerated, it is hard to see how such institutions can fulfill their potential.

regulatory framework? One suggestion, proposed by Barth, Caprio, and Levine (2012a), instead of focusing on the regulations themselves, focuses on how to better oversee the regulators. Specifically, they propose a sentinel agency, which would watch the regulators on behalf of taxpayers. The agency would have no regulatory powers, but it would have the ability to obtain all the information available to regulatory agencies, along with the duty to report on the key systemic risks and on what the regulators are doing to address those risks.

Going in a similar direction, Masciandaro, Pansini, and Quintyn (2011) emphasize the distinction between macro- and microprudential supervision. Using empirical evidence from the crisis, they make a case for keeping macroprudential supervision institutionally separate from microprudential supervision. In other words, it seems better for macroprudential supervisors not to have direct microprudential supervisory powers, as long as they have the ability to obtain all the relevant information to assess the key systemic risks and the steps to address those risks. Such an arrangement allows for more checks and balances and thus reduces the probability of supervisory failure.

Many countries have recently been putting in place committees or new agencies to carry out macroprudential regulation and supervision. In some cases, these agencies or bodies maintain a clear separation between macro- and microprudential supervision. In other countries, however, macroprudential committees or agencies are also involved in microprudential supervision. This is different from the sentinel agency, which cannot have any direct regulatory or supervisory powers, to limit the risk of conflicts of interest.

How are governments and agencies to increase the focus on incentives in practice? Čihák, Demirgüç-Kunt, and Johnston (2012a, 2012b) propose that the identification of incentive problems be based on a specific analysis of incentives, an "incentive audit" (box 2.7). Such audits, building on a methodology proposed in an earlier paper by Johnston, Chai, and Schumacher (2000), could be used to complement other approaches to assessing financial stability, in particular, stress testing and use of supervisory codes and standards. The incentive audit would focus on the key elements that motivate and guide financial decision making.

A focus on correcting incentive issues and putting them front and center does not mean discarding the existing regulatory and supervisory frameworks. In other words, what is needed is an evolutionary change, not a revolution. The effort would involve a reorientation toward a regulatory and supervisory framework that is more focused on the sufficiency of information disclosures, factors that influence the incentives to monitor activities within financial firms, corporate governance and compensation practices, conflicts of interest, and explicit and implicit guarantees. A greater focus on incentives, which could be achieved by extending or improving existing efforts, would support the regulatory approaches by identifying the underlying distortions that can give rise to systemic risk, including in the design and application of the regulations themselves. The effort would also help to prioritize the regulatory response on a systemwide basis and increase the attention on bolstering effective market discipline in support of regulation.

Keeping regulatory rules as simple as possible, and promoting strong enforcement

It is important to keep the rules as simple as needed for their effective monitoring, and to promote strong enforcement.[27] This point relates closely to the previous two points on asymmetric information and incentive problems: complexity can make it difficult for supervisors, investors, and others to distill the relevant information about soundness of financial institutions and about systemic risk. Also, combined with bad incentives for financial institutions' managers, complexity can make it easier for financial institutions to bypass regulatory rules and use obfuscation to their advantage.

However, finance is not a simple business. Imposing simplicity through draconian measures would be either too costly or not

BOX 2.7   Incentive Audits (Viewpoint by Martin Čihák, Asli Demirgüç-Kunt, and R. Barry Johnston)

Introducing incentive audits could strengthen financial sector policy. The basic idea of such audits is to more regularly and systemically evaluate structural factors that affect incentives for risk taking in the financial sector. The key issues that audits would need to cover include contract design, banking powers, banking relationships, structure of ownership and liabilities, industrial organizations, existence of guarantees, and the adequacy of safety nets.

How would incentive audits look in practice? To get a clearer idea, one can take a 2010 report by a parliamentary commission examining the roots of the 2007 financial crisis in Iceland. The report notes the overly rapid growth of the three major Icelandic banks as a major contributor of the crisis, and documents the underlying "strong incentives for growth," which included the banks' incentive schemes as well as the high leverage of the major owners (Special Investigation Commission 2010). The report maps out the network of conflicting interests of key bank owners, who were also the largest debtors of these banks.

This illustration captures the basic notion of an incentive audit. There are other examples (such as Calomiris 2011, who uses an incentive-based approach to propose a reform of the U.S. regulatory framework). Čihák, Demirgüç-Kunt, and Johnston (2012b) provide a more detailed description of the audit, going from a top-level examination of the key elements of the financial environment in an economy—market structure and financial instruments, government safety net, legal framework, and quality of enforcement—to a more detailed and prioritized assessment of incentives, mindful of the likely effect on the behavior of the main agents in the system. The checklist of key features would be accompanied by guidance with evaluation methodology for consistent application across countries.

To be effective, incentive audits would have to be performed regularly, and their outcome used to address incentive issues by adapting regulation, supervision, and other measures. In Iceland, the analysis was done as a postmortem, benefiting from hindsight. But it is feasible to do such analysis ex ante. Indeed, much of the information used in the commission's report was available (readily, or with moderate data-gathering effort) even before the crisis. Also, the commission had relatively modest resources (three members and small support staff), illustrating that incentive audits need not be very costly or overly complicated to perform. As the commission's report points out, "it should have been clear to the supervisory authorities that such incentives existed and that there was reason for concern," but supervisors "did not keep up with the rapid changes in the banks' practices," and instead of examining the underlying reasons for the changes, they took comfort in the banks' capital ratios exceeding a statutory minimum and appearing robust in narrowly defined stress tests (Čihák and Ong 2010).

Existing approaches do not entirely overlook issues related to incentives. Many reports on financial stability focus very narrowly on a quantitative description and analysis of trends (Čihák, Muñoz, Teh Sharifuddin, and Tintchev 2012), but some do mention the misalignments between private sector incentives and public interests. So this area could be usefully extended and made a more permanent feature of the reporting. Also, in the context of the World Bank/IMF Financial Sector Assessment Program, when assessments collect information on ownership of financial institutions, they look into issues such as safety nets. The idea of incentive audits, therefore, is not to build a new assessment from scratch, but to raise the profile of incentive-related issues and bring more structure to the assessments. Incentive audits should be seen not as a replacement of other parts of the overall assessment of vulnerabilities, but as a complement.

feasible. For example, requiring all banks to move from limited to unlimited liability could bring banks' size down substantially, but it would not be feasible in contemporary financial systems.[28] Other proposals that have been circulated—for example, those that suggest directly constraining financial institutions' size or substantially narrowing the range of permissible activities—would potentially have serious side effects and weaknesses, such that their implementation should be subject to careful analysis before their actual adoption. One possible way to keep institutions from becoming systemically important, as noted, for example, in Rajan (2010), may not be through crude prohibitions on size or activity, but through collecting and monitoring of information about exposures among institutions and risk concentrations in the system.

An important aspect of the debate on complexity relates to issues of capital adequacy and leverage. Empirical evidence suggests that when faced with uncertainty, markets tend to pay more attention to more basic indicators that are more difficult to bypass. For example, Demirgüç-Kunt, Detragiache, and Merrouche (2012) used a multicountry panel of banks to study whether better-capitalized banks experienced higher stock returns during the financial crisis. They found that a stronger capital position was associated with better stock market performance, and that the relationship is stronger when capital is measured by the leverage ratio rather than the risk-adjusted capital ratio, and that higher-quality forms of capital, such as tier 1 capital and tangible common equity, were more relevant. These empirical findings, of course, do not imply that using leverage as the only tool is a complete solution; nonetheless, the authors use these results to make a case for relatively greater reliance on simpler capital ratios, such as the leverage ratio, that are more difficult to circumvent.

Of course, a sole reliance on the leverage ratio, which is not risk-sensitive, could become problematic, as it could give banks an incentive to shift to riskier activities to boost returns. Therefore, it is important to take into account the relative riskiness of the various assets; however, views differ as to who should do it and how. Basel III has recognized the usefulness of basic leverage ratios and narrower (high-quality) measures of capital and has combined them with the risk-based ratios.

Several authors have proposed to move even further. For example, Hellwig (2010) and Admati and Hellwig (2012) have been critical of the risk-weighted asset concept as a proxy for actual exposures, and suggested replacing risk-weighted capital ratios with (significantly higher) leverage ratios, combined with strong disclosures about risk exposures. Their argument is based on the observation that the system of risk-calibrated capital requirements, in particular under the model-based approach, played a key role in allowing banks to be undercapitalized prior to the crisis, with strong systemic effects for deleveraging multipliers and for the functioning of interbank markets. The issue is not trivial, of course, partly because of the short- and medium-term adverse effects such high ratios could have on financial intermediation and financial development.

Another alternative approach to current risk-based capital regulation would be to have a simple leverage ratio (which is simple enough to monitor and enforce) adjusted upward by the loan spreads banks charge their customers. As discussed in Calomiris (2011), using loan spreads to measure loan default risk is desirable because these spreads are accurate forecasters of the probability that a loan will become nonperforming (Ashcraft and Morgan 2003). This would be an example not only of a simple regulation but also of an incentive-robust one, since banks clearly would not have an incentive to lower their interest rates just to reduce their capital budgeting against a loan, because doing so would reduce their income and defeat the purpose of circumventing the regulation.[29] An added advantage of this approach would be that monitoring interest rates is fairly uncomplicated even in the least developed of emerging markets.

Other approaches focus on complementing basic capital ratios (such as a common equity requirement) by so-called contingent capital (CoCo) requirements. These authors provide evidence that seems to imply that a CoCo requirement, complementing common equity, would be an effective prudential tool. CoCos can help the prompt recapitalization of banks after significant losses of equity but before the bank has run out of options to access the equity market. That dynamic

---

BOX 2.8   Regulatory Discipline and Market Discipline: Opposites or Complements?

In a major precrisis study of banking regulation around the world, Barth, Caprio, and Levine (2006) have used the data from the earlier versions of the World Bank's Bank Regulation and Supervision Survey to examine the various regulatory approaches and compare them to the outcomes that countries care about. They concluded that the standard features of banking supervision and regulation do not reduce—and may even increase—the chance that countries experience banking crises. Nor do these rules and regulations lead to more developed banking sectors or more efficient banks. These findings are, according to the authors, consistent with private interest views and the fact that "few countries have highly developed democratic institutions" (13). In contrast, policies that enable private markets to better monitor banks and that encourage private actors to "discipline" banks are associated with desirable outcomes. But critically, they found no link between market monitoring and the likelihood of a bank crisis.

The global financial crisis has highlighted failures both in regulatory and supervisory discipline as well as in market discipline. It has thrown a particularly unflattering light on market discipline, highlighting its intrinsic limitations, especially when key assumptions are not met. At the same time, the crisis has also highlighted the serious regulatory and supervisory failures that contributed to the crisis.

In a recent paper, Barth, Caprio, and Levine (2012b) follow up on this analysis, using the crisis observations as well as data from the 2011 Bank Regulation and Supervision Survey database. The results of their analysis support a complementary role for regulation and market discipline, as highlighted recently by Haldane (2011). Market discipline and state-imposed regulatory and supervisory discipline are complementary, since each has its own limitations, and market failures often have their roots in regulatory failures.

---

incentive feature of a properly designed CoCo requirement would encourage effective risk governance by banks, provide a more effective solution to the too-big-to-fail problem, reduce forbearance risk (supervisory reluctance to recognize losses), and address uncertainty about the appropriate amount of capital banks need to hold (and the changes in that amount over time). Calomiris and Herring (2011) examine this proposal in detail, concluding that if a proper CoCo requirement had been in place in 2007, the disruptive failures of large financial institutions, and the systemic meltdown after September 2008, could have been avoided. They note that, to be effective, (a) a large amount of CoCos relative to common equity should be required, (b) CoCo conversion should be based on a market value trigger, (c) all CoCos should convert if conversion is triggered, and (d) the conversion ratio should be dilutive of preexisting equity holders. However, how these untested instruments would actually perform in case of need remains to be seen.

The debate on these proposals is still ongoing, so this is unlikely to be the last word. But most proposals argue that the regulatory framework should include well-defined capital and liquidity measures that are monitored and enforced by a strong supervisory body, which should be held accountable for its activities. This need for strong enforcement of regulatory rules should also include transparency and disclosure requirements (as pointed out, for example, by the Shadow Financial Regulatory Committee 2011). In other words, proposals suggest market discipline should become an important complement to the supervisory discipline provided by an independent but accountable supervisory body (box 2.8).

The issue of regulatory complexity is, of course, much broader than the capital requirements and the issue of risk weighting. The U.S. Shadow Regulatory Committee has long advocated simpler and more transparent regulations (Shadow Financial Regulatory Committee 2011). However, the broader trend, confirmed also by the Bank Regulation and Supervision Survey, is toward more complex regulations, not only in developed economies but also in developing economies. Various observers have pointed out the burden of this new complexity for the industry;[30] but in many countries, especially the smaller and lower-income ones, this also adds substantially to the already existing capacity constraints. This complexity makes it more difficult for supervisors to ensure that regulations are actually and effectively implemented and, importantly, for taxpayers to see what is being done to keep the system safe and to hold supervisors accountable.

CONCLUSION

Although the overall role of the state in finance is an open question, there is clearly an important role for the state in financial sector regulation and supervision. This is the one area where the role of the state is not in dispute; the real debate is over how to ensure that the role is performed well.

Good regulation needs to better align private incentives with public interest, without taxing or subsidizing private risk taking. Supervision is meant to ensure implementation of rules and regulations and to address limitations of market discipline.

The global financial crisis underscored limitations in both regulatory and market discipline. It emphasized the importance of combining strong, timely, and anticipatory supervisory enforcement with a better use of market discipline. It also highlighted the importance of the basics, that is, solid and transparent legal and institutional frameworks to promote financial stability. In many developing economies, the conclusion is that building up supervisory capacity needs to be a top priority.

Lessons can be learned by analyzing regulation and supervision in economies that were at the epicenter of the global financial crisis and those that were not. The World Bank's new global survey, presented in this chapter, suggests that noncrisis countries—those

that did not have a banking crisis in 2007 through 2009—had more stringent definitions of capital, higher capital levels, and less complex regulatory frameworks. They had stricter audit procedures, limits on related party exposures, and asset classification standards; and their supervisors were more likely to require shareholders to support distressed banks with new equity. Noncrisis countries were also characterized by better quality of financial information and greater incentives to use that information—among other reasons, because they have relatively less generous deposit insurance coverage.

The global financial crisis has also triggered a healthy policy debate on approaches to regulation and supervision. This ongoing debate among regulators, policy makers, and academics has led to multiple reform proposals, highlighting the diversity of views. This is likely to inform the regulatory reform process and improve future outcomes.

This chapter reviewed the progress with regulatory reforms at the global level as well as in individual countries, and identified the advances made so far in many areas. It also recognized a number of reform proposals that suggest improvements on the current approaches to regulation and supervision. These proposals aim to limit regulatory arbitrage opportunities and better employ regulatory resources and capacity. Among the common themes of these proposals are calls for greater regulatory simplicity and transparency as a way to enhance accountability, as well as for more proactive identifying and addressing of incentive problems.

NOTES

1. For example, Greenspan (2005, para. 17–19) remarked that "regulatory reform, coupled with innovative technologies, has stimulated the development of financial products, such as asset-backed securities, collateral loan obligations, and credit default swaps that facilitate the dispersion of risk. . . . These increasingly complex financial instruments have contributed to the development of a far more flexible, efficient, and hence resilient

financial system than the one that existed just a quarter-century ago."

2. See FSB Charter, article 1.

3. This report uses a broad concept of "the state" that includes not only government but also autonomous or semiautonomous agencies such as a central bank or financial supervision agency.

4. For example, Carmichel and Pomerleano (2002) and de la Torre, Ize, and Schmukler (2011).

5. In addition to regulation, another state intervention that can also have an impact on financial sector risk taking is financial taxation. It has received some policy attention during the crisis (see, for example, IMF 2010c). Nonetheless, the regulatory approach is likely to remain central for practical policy in the foreseeable future, and is therefore the focus of this chapter (for a discussion of the pros and cons of regulation and taxation, see Keen 2011).

6. Masciandaro, Pansini, and Quintyn (2011) provide an overview of the literature on the causes on the crisis, focusing on supervisory and regulatory failures.

7. See the respective IMF country reports (IMF 2010a; IMF 2012).

8. Data on larger and more interconnected financial institutions show that they have been taking on more risk and have been more likely to experience financial stress than others (Ötker-Robe and others 2011).

9. Many banks, especially in advanced economies, held a relatively small part of capital as equity, with the remainder being in capital with weak loss-absorbing characteristics that had little value during the crisis. Given the large differences and lack of transparency in the definition of capital, it was hard to assess and compare the adequacy of capital across institutions.

10. Banks could reduce their risk capital requirements through shifts in assets to legally remote entities excluded from asset definitions, through credit default swaps that reduced the regulatory risks in their portfolio, or through credit enhancements that improved the ratings of assets and thus the need to hold regulatory capital.

11. For example, the mandates of the United Kingdom's Financial Services Authority and Switzerland's Federal Banking Commission.

12. Even supervisors that are independent in principle can be overruled for political purposes. For example, U.S. supervisors did raise alarms about the risks of subprime lending, but a significant tightening of the prudential practices did not occur before the crisis, reflecting pressures from the industry and lawmakers (Levine 2010). Reviews of compliance with the Basel Core Principles find that some of the weakest areas relate to the operational independence of the regulators, and that—despite some progress in recent years—this is still an issue in many developing economies (Čihák and Tieman 2011).

13. For more on shadow banking and FSB-related response see FSB (2012).

14. Demirgüç-Kunt and Huizinga (2011), using a wide international sample of banks, present evidence that casts doubts on the need for systemically large banks even from the narrower perspective of bank shareholders. It suggests that bank growth has not been in the interest of bank shareholders in small economies, and it is not clear whether those in larger economies have benefited. Inadequate corporate governance structures in financial institutions have enabled managers to pursue high-growth strategies at the expense of shareholders, providing support for greater government regulation (as also argued, for example, in Barth, Caprio, and Levine 2012a).

15. The work of the FSB in this area is meant to make credible to all counterparts of a financial institution the possibility of its failure, so they exercise due monitoring on management and control of shareholders.

16. Another related, although less explored, facet of market discipline is the forced departure of managers from underperforming financial institutions. Schaeck and others (2011) find that when banks take on too much risk and get into trouble, their managers do get forced out. But it is often too late for the banks, which tend to remain in trouble for years after the turnover.

17. For more on this subject, see also a recent debate between Rene Stulz of Ohio State University and Lucian Bebchuk of Harvard Law School and others at the "All About Finance" blog on the World Bank's website. (http://blogs.worldbank.org/allaboutfinance/the-aaf-virtual-debates).

18. Gaps and weaknesses in regulation and supervision were not the only factors contributing to the crisis, as discussed earlier in this chapter, though they are expected to have

played an important role. Also, although systemic crisis prevention is not the only objective of regulation and supervision (for example, some regulations focus on customer protection, anti–money laundering, and so on), crisis prevention is usually seen as a key objective, so juxtaposing regulation and supervision in crisis and noncrisis countries does offer interesting insights. Nevertheless, users should note that these findings are correlations, and do not imply causality.

19. This section does not aspire to be an all-inclusive compendium of all reforms. More work is ongoing or contemplated, for instance on accounting standards, shadow banking, financial supervision, and market infrastructures. For more on these, see http://www.financialstabilityboard.org/publications/r_111104.pdf.

20. See the Leaders' statement after the Pittsburgh Summit in September 2009 (G-20 Leaders, 2009).

21. See FSB (2011b). SIFIs are financial institutions whose distress or disorderly failure, because of their size, complexity, and interconnectedness, would cause significant disruption to the wider financial system and economic activity.

22. In addition to the four steps listed here, stronger international standards for core financial market infrastructures are to be finalized in early 2012, aiming to reduce contagion risks when failures occur.

23. On May 31, 2012, the International Association of Insurance Supervisors released for public consultation its assessment methodology for identifying globally systemically important insurers (see http://www.iaisweb.org/view/element_href.cfm?src=1/15384.pdf).

24. This report focuses on global trends. Recent regional reports of the World Bank provide related updates on regulatory and supervisory trends in individual regions, such as Latin America and the Caribbean (de la Torre, Ize, and Schmukler 2011) and Middle East and North Africa (Rocha, Arvai, and Farazi 2011).

25. Banks have not always operated with limited liability, pre-19th-century England being a case in point. Several authors have discussed the pros and cons of returning to unlimited liability for banks. Although such a move would almost certainly bring banks' size down "with a bang" (as noted by Charles Goodhart in his March 1, 2012, debate with Robert Pringle at centralbanking.com), it would not be feasible in a contemporary financial system.

26. For a broad overview of the underlying factors of financial crises, see de la Torre and Ize (2011). In addition to incentive breakdowns and asymmetric information, they also mention issues of collective cognition ("nobody really understands what is going on") and costly enforcement ("crises are a natural part of the financial landscape").

27. The long-running debate on rules versus principles in supervision (Mersch 2007) has been intensified by the crisis. In the context of this debate, for example, the incentive audits proposal calls for a greater emphasis on well-defined principles. Specifically, the principles need to address the various misalignments in incentives, both among market participants and among regulators. But emphasizing well-defined principles does not mean that one can do away with rules. Similarly, the proposal to focus on incentives does not mean abolishing microprudential supervision. Effective rules and efficient principles are both essential to promote financial integration and reinforce financial stability. It would be naive to think that principles applied on a stand-alone basis can eliminate the need for rules.

28. The intrinsic desirability of such a measure for financial stability purposes is far from undisputed, since the solvency analysis that creditors are expected to make would shift its focus from the bank per se to the personal wealth of the bank proprietors, which would probably prove to be a quite challenging task.

29. Interest rates on deposits could also be used because these too are associated with bank risk (Acharya and Mora 2012). However, deposit rates tend to be sensitive to bank risk only very close in time to bank insolvency because of explicit and implicit deposit insurance.

30. For the United States, see for example, the *Economist* 2012; for the European Union, see, for example, *Wall Street Journal* 2011.

3

The Role of the State in Promoting Bank Competition

- *Competition in the banking sector promotes efficiency and financial inclusion, without necessarily undermining financial stability.*

- *Even if the recent crisis is perceived as an episode where competition exacerbated private risk taking and helped destabilize the system, the correct public policy is not to restrict competition. What is needed is a regulatory framework that ensures that private incentives are aligned with public interest.*

- *The state can play a role in enhancing banking competition by designing policies that guarantee market contestability through healthy entry of well-capitalized institutions and timely exit of insolvent ones and by creating a market-friendly informational and institutional framework.*

- *Governments should be mindful of the consequences of their intervention during crises and limit negative consequences on bank competition and risk taking.*

The recent crisis reignited the interest of policy makers and academics in assessing bank competition and rethinking the role of the state in shaping competition policies (that is, policies and laws that affect the extent to which banks compete).[1,2] Some believe that increases in competition and financial innovation in markets such as subprime lending contributed to the recent financial turmoil. Others worry that the crisis and government support of the largest banks increased banking concentration, reducing competition and access to finance, and potentially contributing to future instability as a result of moral hazard problems associated with too-big-to-fail institutions. Box 3.1 presents a recent debate on the relationship between competition and financial stability.

Another reason why competition matters is related to the changing mandate of central banks and bank regulatory agencies. Although traditionally the primary goal of bank regulators has been to ensure bank stability, this is changing. According to the World Bank's Bank Regulation and Supervision Survey, updated in 2011, 71 percent of

---

BOX 3.1   Two Views on the Link between Competition and Stability

In a recent debate held by *The Economist* magazine, two banking professors expressed contrasting views about the role of bank competition in promoting stability.

According to Franklin Allen, Nippon Life Professor of Finance and Economics, Wharton School, University of Pennsylvania, "more competition does make banking more dangerous." But he also cautions that "competition is only one of the factors contributing to instability." He goes on to say that "the experience of a number of countries in the past and during the recent crisis provides some insights into the relevant issues. Historically, the comparison that has often been made is between the stability of the Canadian banking system compared to the United States' experience. In the late 19th and early 20th century, the United States had many banking crises, while Canada did not. The standard explanation for this is that Canada had a few large banks, while the United States had many small banks. In the recent crisis, the banking system in Canada and also that in Australia were very resilient. Six banks dominate the Canadian financial system, while there are four major banks together with a few small domestic banks in Australia. However, the United Kingdom, whose banking system has a broadly similar structure to Australia's, with four major banks and a few other small domestic and foreign banks, had a very different experience. The lesson of this comparison is that competition is only one of the many factors that are important. In addition to the competitive nature of the industry, funding structure and the institutional and regulatory environments are important. These factors are well illustrated by the recent experience of Canada, Australia, and the United Kingdom. Canadian and Australian banks mainly relied on depositary funding. This funding source proved stable through the crisis. In contrast, British banks increasingly used wholesale funding from financial markets. Canada and Australia also have much more conservative regulatory environments than the UK. For example, in Canada, capital regulation is stricter than the Basel agreements require. Banks' foreign and wholesale activities are limited. The mortgage market is also conservative in terms of the products offered, with less than 3 percent being subprime and less than 30 percent being securitized. In the UK a 'light touch' regulatory framework was implemented. An illustration is that capital ratios were weakened by banks' off balance sheet vehicles, which were used to hold securitized assets."

On the other hand, Thorsten Beck, Professor of Economics and Chairman of the European Banking Center at Tilburg University, argues that "competition in banking is not dangerous per se; it is the regulatory framework in which banks operate and which sets their risk-taking incentives that drives stability or fragility of banking. Competition can be a powerful source of useful innovation and efficiency, ultimately benefitting enterprises and households; competition can also foster stability through improved lending technologies; competition, however, can also endanger stability if mixed with the wrong kind of regulation."

"Risks and dangers in banking arise primarily from a regulatory framework that is not adapted to the market structure. Large financial institutions turn too-big-to-fail because the regulator does not have any means to properly discipline and resolve them. Similarly, competition results in herding and increased fragility risk in the absence of macro-prudential tools to counter asset price and credit booms and take into account co-variation between banks' risk profiles. The experience from the last crisis has led to reform attempts exactly in these two areas: resolution, especially of systemically important financial institutions, and macro-prudential regulation. It is thus not market structure or competition per se, that drives fragility, but a regulatory framework that sets the wrong incentives."

"The challenge is to maintain competition in the market to the benefit of the real economy, while at the same time creating a regulatory framework that minimizes the negative implications that competition can have for stability. Such a framework would include additional capital charges for size, complexity and systemic importance of banks, macro-prudential regulations that take into account the interaction between financial institutions, and—most critically—a resolution framework that allows resolving even the largest financial institutions, thus reducing the perverse incentives stemming from a too-big-to-fail status."

This discussion suggests that both sides share more in common than they disagree with, but see *Economist* 2012 http://www.economist.com/debate/days/view/706 for more.

Source: The Economist 2012 (reprinted with permission).

bank regulators report that their mandate also includes promoting financial inclusion and economic development. Also, 65 percent mention issues of market conduct, and nearly 25 percent mention competition policy. Hence, either directly or indirectly—because competition influences market conduct and access to finance—competition is an important issue for regulators.[3]

This chapter presents measures of bank competition and describes basic trends across economies and over time. By illustrating various approaches to measuring competition and discussing factors that drive it, the chapter seeks to provide guidance to policy makers.

The chapter conveys four main messages:

- Bank competition improves efficiency across banks and enhances access to financial services, while not necessarily eroding the stability of the financial system.
- Policies to address the causes of the recent crisis should not restrict competition. The correct public policy should establish a regulatory framework that supervises and ensures the alignment of private incentives with public interest.
- The state should promote competition both as a regulator and as an enabler of a market-friendly informational and institutional environment. Policies that improve market contestability—through healthy entry of well-capitalized institutions and timely exit of insolvent ones, opportune flow of adequate credit information, and contract enforceability—will enhance competition among banks.
- State interventions during crises may create barriers to exit that permit insolvent and inefficient banks to survive and generate unhealthy competition. Governments should take steps to eliminate distortions in risk taking and limit their negative consequences on bank competition.

The chapter first discusses alternative measures of competition and presents trends across economies and over time, using measures of market concentration, contestability,

and bank pricing behavior. It then reviews the evidence on the implications of banking competition for bank efficiency, access to finance, and financial stability. After that, the chapter analyzes the policy drivers of competition and highlights the role of the state as a regulator and enabler of a market-friendly informational and institutional environment. It also examines the impact on competition of government actions during crises. The chapter concludes by summarizing the policy implications.

BANK COMPETITION: MEASUREMENT AND STYLIZED FACTS

There are three main approaches to assessing bank competition: measures of bank concentration under the "structure-conduct-performance" paradigm, regulatory indicators that measure the contestability of the banking sector, and direct measures of bank pricing behavior or market power based on the "new empirical industrial organization" literature.

An alternative approach used by some studies to analyze bank competition is based on interest spread decomposition (box 3.2). But spreads are outcome measures of efficiency, and in addition to the competition environment, cross-country differences in spreads can reflect macroeconomic performance, the extent of taxation on financial intermediation, the quality of the contractual and judicial environment, and bank-specific factors such as scale and risk preferences. So this chapter instead presents direct measures such as the Panzar-Rosse H-statistic, the Lerner index, and the so-called Boone indicator. Box 3.3 summarizes these measures.[4]

Competition may vary within economies and across products (for example, by type of loan, such as corporate or consumer). Ideally, competition should be measured by business line for different markets (box 3.4). But such disaggregated data are often not available, and most measures cannot be computed separately for these submarkets. Accordingly, in what follows, country and regional measures

---

BOX 3.2   **Decomposing Bank Spreads to Make Inferences about Bank Competition**

Bank interest spreads are frequently used as an indicator of the efficiency of the banking system (Beck and Fuchs 2004; Demirgüç-Kunt and Huizinga 1999; Demirgüç-Kunt, Laeven, and Levine 2004). An accounting decomposition of bank spreads or of interest margins (the value of a bank's net interest income divided by assets) can be derived from a straightforward accounting identity:

Before-tax profits to assets (BTP/TA) = After-tax profits to assets (ATP/TA) + taxes to assets (TA/A)

From a bank's income statement, before-tax profits must satisfy the accounting identity:

$$BTP/TA = NI/TA + NII/TA - OV/TA - LLP/TA$$

where NI is net interest income, NII refers to non-interest income, OV stands for overhead costs, and LLP refers to loan loss provisioning. The identities above allow for a decomposition of net interest margins (NI/TA) into its components:

$$NI/TA = ATP/TA + TA/A - NII/TA + OV/TA + LLP/TA$$

Demirgüç-Kunt and Huizinga (1999) and Beck and Fuchs (2004) follow the identities above to conduct an accounting decomposition and an economic analysis of the determinants of bank net interest margins using data for 80 countries between 1988–95, in the first case, and focusing on 38 banks in Kenya for the year 2002, in the second case.

To the extent that high spreads are explained by high profit margins, these studies infer that lack of competition could be a factor. In the economic analysis of spreads, Demirgüç-Kunt and Huizinga (1999) regress spreads and profits on measures of concentration (as an indicator of competition) and conclude that, aside from other factors, lack of bank competition drives bank spreads and profits across countries. Similarly, Beck and Fuchs (2004) conclude that the high profit margins that explain part of the high spreads in Kenya are due to lack of competition in the banking sector.

---

are used to illustrate different approaches to assessing bank competition.

The structure-conduct-performance paradigm assumes that there is a stable, causal relationship between the structure of the banking industry, firm conduct, and performance. It suggests that fewer and larger firms are more likely to engage in anticompetitive behavior. In this framework, competition is negatively related to measures of concentration, such as the share of assets held by the top three or five largest banks and the Herfindahl index.

Figure 3.1 depicts the asset share of the five largest banks (CR5) in developed and developing economies, showing that banking systems are more concentrated in developing than developed economies. Across regions, banking systems in Sub-Saharan Africa and the Gulf Cooperation Council (GCC) countries of the Middle East and North Africa region have the largest CR5 concentration ratios (figure 3.2).

Concentration measures are not good predictors of competition.[5] The predictive accuracy of concentration measures on banking competition is challenged by the concept of market contestability. The behavior of banks in contestable markets is determined by threat of entry and exit. Banks are pressured to behave competitively in an industry with low entry restrictions on new banks and easy exit conditions for unprofitable institutions— even if the market is concentrated.

Figure 3.3 depicts two (admittedly imperfect) proxies of regulatory indicators that capture entry conditions into the banking industry: an index of barriers to entry and the share of banking licenses denied. These two indicators are from the World Bank's Bank Regulation and Supervision Survey, and they capture entry restrictions into the

BOX 3.3   Measuring Banking Sector Concentration and Competition

Banking concentration can be approximated by the concentration ratio—the share of assets held by the k largest banks (typically three or five) in a given economy—or the Herfindahl-Hirschman index (HHI), the sum of the squared market share of each bank in the system. The HHI accounts for the market share of all banks in the system and assigns a larger weight to the biggest banks. Instead, concentration ratios completely ignore the smaller banks in the system. The concentration ratio varies between nearly 0 and 100. The HHI has values up to 10,000. If there is only a single bank that has 100 percent of the market share, the HHI would be 10,000. If there were a large number of market participants with each bank having a market share of almost 0 percent, the HHI would be close to zero.

The Panzar and Rosse (1982, 1987) H-statistic captures the elasticity of bank interest revenues to input prices. The H-statistic is calculated in two steps:

1. Running a regression of the log of gross total revenues (or the log of interest revenues) on log measures of banks' input prices.
2. Adding the estimated coefficients for each input price. Input prices include the price of deposits (commonly measured as the ratio of interest expenses to total deposits), the price of personnel (as captured by the ratio of personnel expenses to assets), and the price of equipment and fixed capital (approximated by the ratio of other operating and administrative expenses to total assets).

Higher values of the H-statistic are associated with more competitive banking systems. Under a monopoly, an increase in input prices results in a rise in marginal costs, a fall in output, and a decline in revenues (because the demand curve is downward sloping), leading to an H-statistic less than or equal to 0. Under perfect competition, an increase in input prices raises both marginal costs and total revenues by the same amount (since the demand curve is perfectly elastic); hence, the H-statistic will equal 1.

A frequently used measure of markups in banking is the Lerner index, defined as the difference between output prices and marginal costs (relative to prices). Prices are calculated as total bank revenue over assets, whereas marginal costs are obtained from an estimated translog cost function with respect to output. Higher values of the Lerner index signal less bank competition.

The Boone indicator measures the effect of efficiency on performance in terms of profits. It is calculated as the elasticity of profits to marginal costs. To calculate this elasticity, the log of a measure of profits (such as return on assets) is regressed against a log measure of marginal costs. The elasticity is captured by the coefficient on log marginal costs, which are typically calculated from the first derivative of a translog cost function. The main idea of the Boone indicator is that more-efficient banks achieve higher profits. The more negative the Boone indicator is, the higher the level of competition is in the market, because the effect of reallocation is stronger.

banking industry. The first indicator, an overall index of barriers to entry, summarizes the information needed to obtain a banking license. Higher index values indicate more stringent requirements for bank entry. The second indicator of contestability is the share of applications for bank licenses that were denied. Regulations concerning entry to the banking sector are, on average, more stringent in developing economies than in developed ones. Between 2001 and 2010, the share of denied banking licenses declined for both groups of countries.

The competitive environment of the banking system can also be affected by the strategic reactions of banks. The new empirical industrial organization literature provides three indicators of banks' pricing behavior.[6]

First, the H-statistic measures the elasticity of banks' revenues relative to input prices (Panzar and Rosse 1982, 1987). Under perfect competition, an increase in input prices raises both marginal costs and total revenues by the same amount, and hence the H-statistic equals 1. Under a monopoly, an increase

---

BOX 3.4   Analyzing Bank Competition Using Disaggregated Business Line Data: Evidence from Brazil

Urdapilleta and Stephanou (2009) use disaggregated business data for banks in Brazil to analyze the drivers of bank revenues, costs, and risks in the retail and corporate segments. The study allocates revenues, costs, and all other line items in the financial statements of the banking system into different business lines. This approach results in financial statements and ratios by business line. Other public data sources were used and assumptions made to estimate notional financial statements for each business line. Interviews with senior management served as a consistency check on the overall methodology.

A key finding of the analysis is that the retail banking segment has significantly higher returns (39 percent) than the corporate segment (16 percent), despite being riskier and costlier. In particular, higher lending rates and fees more than compensate for additional expenses.

The study argues that one of the reasons for lower profitability in the corporate sector is the higher degree of competition among providers in the segment. In particular, the study mentions how the existence of more substitute providers (like capital markets or overseas banks) in the corporate sector keeps loan rates and fees lower. Similarly, the study cites easier access to credit information for large corporations as another reason why competition in this segment is higher.

Among the policies that can foster competition in the retail segment, the study mentions promoting the portability of bank accounts, permitting positive credit information sharing, and expanding payment system interconnection. All these allow customers to switch banks more easily and, therefore, force banks to compete more actively.

The study illustrates how differences across market segments, which tend to be averaged out in an aggregate analysis, need to be taken into account when designing public policy in banking. The study also highlights that a great deal of in-depth knowledge of the banking sector is required to be able to use the practitioner approach to obtaining profitability measures by business line and to be able to assess bank competition across market segments.

FIGURE 3.1   **Five Bank Concentration Ratio (CR5): Developed and Developing Economies**

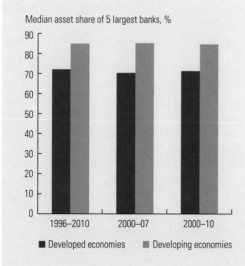

Median asset share of 5 largest banks, %

■ Developed economies   ■ Developing economies

Source: Calculations based on Bankscope (database).

in input prices results in a rise in marginal costs, a fall in output, and a decline in revenues, leading to an H-statistic less than or equal to 0. Panzar and Rosse (1987) show that when H is between 0 and 1, the system operates under monopolistic competition. In general, the H-statistic is interpreted as a measure of the degree of competition in the banking market.[7]

Second, the Lerner index captures the difference between output prices and marginal costs of production—that is, the markup of output prices over marginal costs (Lerner 1934).[8]

Finally, the Boone indicator is based on the association between firm performance and efficiency (Boone 2001; Boone, Griffith, and Harrison 2005; Hay and Liu 1997). See box 3.3 for further details on the calculation

FIGURE 3.2   Five Bank Concentration Ratio (CR5): Developing Regions, Median Values, 1996–2010

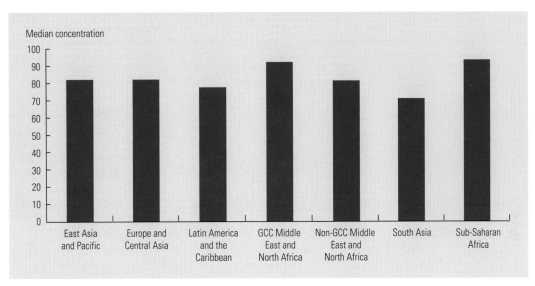

Source: Calculations based on Bankscope (database).

of these pricing indicators of banking competition.

Figure 3.4 depicts the H-statistic for developed and developing economies. Bank pricing behavior was more sensitive to changes in the price of inputs among developed compared with developing economies in 1996–2007, indicating that banking systems in developed economies behave more competitively. But bank competition declined in 2008–10 for developed economies, while it improved for developing economies. It can be argued that the declining trend in developed economies may be attributed to the implications on industry structure and competitive conduct of the recent systemic banking crisis and its associated large-scale policy responses.

Figure 3.5 examines the competitive behavior of banking systems across developing regions. Latin America has the systems with the highest sensitivity of output to input prices, whereas those in the Middle East and North Africa appear to be the least competitive (see box 3.5 for further details).

Figure 3.6 shows the evolution of the Lerner index, a measure of market power that compares output pricing and marginal costs (that is, markup), as well as the Boone

indicator, a measure of the effect of efficiency on performance in terms of profits. An increase in the Lerner index or the Boone indicator indicates a deterioration of the competitive conduct of financial intermediaries. Banking competition in developed economies deteriorated initially (1996–2003), increased in the run-up to the global financial crisis (2004–08), and worsened afterward (2009–10). The initial deterioration could be associated with the drop in competition observed in the euro area after the adoption of the European Monetary Union (Sun 2011) and in line with findings of less competitive behavior of banks in large and integrated financial markets (Bikker and Spierdijk 2008).[9]

It is important to note that the simple observation that competition increased before the crisis does not necessarily suggest that greater competition in itself spurred the crisis. Recent studies suggest the problem was that the increase in competition occurred in an environment where regulation and supervision were too lax and incentives for adequate risk management were missing (Barth, Caprio, and Levine 2012; Caprio, Demirgüç-Kunt, and Kane 2010).

On the other hand, the financial crisis—and the subsequent policy responses by

FIGURE 3.3   **Regulatory Indicators of Market Contestability**

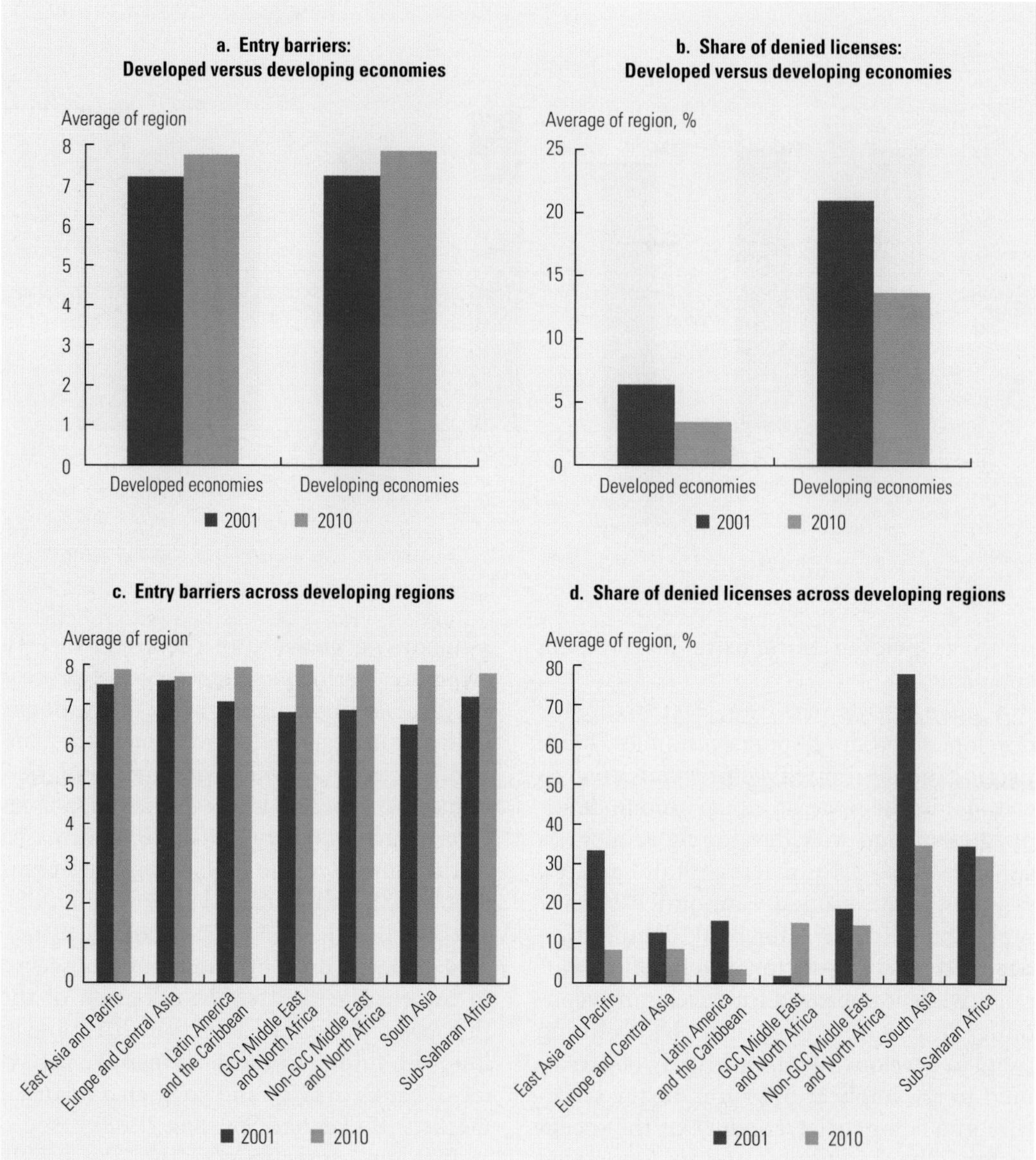

a. Entry barriers:
Developed versus developing economies

Average of region

b. Share of denied licenses:
Developed versus developing economies

Average of region, %

c. Entry barriers across developing regions

Average of region

d. Share of denied licenses across developing regions

Average of region, %

■ 2001   ■ 2010

Sources: Calculations based on Bank Regulation and Supervision Survey (database), World Bank, 2007 data; Barth, Caprio, and Levine 2001, 2004, 2006; Čihák and others 2012.
Note: The index of entry into banking requirements captures whether various types of legal submissions are required to obtain a banking license. Higher scores indicate greater restrictions on entry into banking. On the other hand, the share of denied licenses is the ratio of denied to total license requests.

governments—may have affected the competitive conduct of financial intermediaries in developed economies.[10] Sun (2011) finds that bank competition in developed economies deteriorated during this period, especially in countries that had large credit and housing booms (such as the United States and Spain). The Lerner index and the Boone indicator for developing economies evolve in a similar fashion, with a smoother trend in the Boone indicator than the Lerner index. Deterioration of bank competition may have taken place in spite of financial reforms across developing economies—especially in

FIGURE 3.4   Bank Competition: Developed vs. Developing Economies

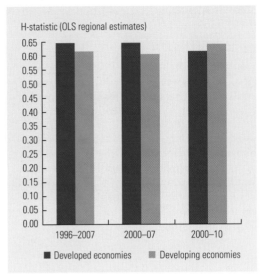

Source: World Bank staff, based on Bankscope (database).
Note: OLS = ordinary least squares.

countries with weak institutions (low bureaucratic quality and low transparency) and low levels of economic development (Delis 2012).

The Lerner index and Boone indicator in developing country regions mimic the average for developing economies—although

with variability across geographical regions (figure 3.7). Though GCC countries in the Middle East and North Africa display the least competitive banking systems, Latin American banking systems have the most competitive systems in developing regions.

THE IMPACT OF COMPETITION ON THE BANKING SYSTEM

Competition affects the banking industry along three dimensions: efficiency, access to finance, and stability.

Competition and banking efficiency

There are two views on the direction of causality between competition and efficiency. The "quiet life" hypothesis argues that monopoly power allows banks to relax their efforts and increases their costs, predicting a positive link from competition to efficiency (Hicks 1935). Alternatively, the "efficient structure" hypothesis predicts a negative relationship between competition and efficiency, where causality runs from efficiency to competition (Demsetz 1973). According to this view, better managed, more efficient firms can secure the largest market shares,

FIGURE 3.5   Bank Competition across Developing Regions, 1996–2007

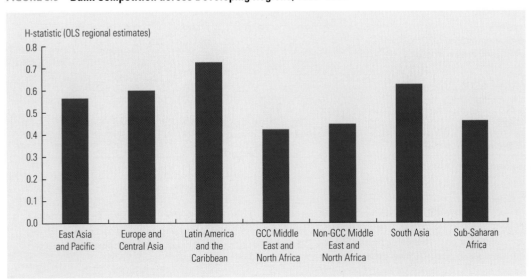

Source: Calculations based on Bankscope (database).
Note: H-statistic figures are calculated following the methodology described in Demirgüç-Kunt and Martínez Pería 2010.

BOX 3.5   Banking Competition in the Middle East and North Africa

Banking sectors in the Middle East and North Africa region (MENA) are among the deepest in the developing world (see table B3.5), but are they competitive?

Anzoategui, Martínez Pería, and Rocha (2010) analyze bank competition in the region in four different ways. First, the study analyzes two distinct measures of competition, the H-statistic and the Lerner index, over a longer period of time, 1994–2008. Second, the paper examines the behavior of competition in the region and tests for differences across two subperiods: 1994–2001 and 2002–08.

Third, the paper compares the extent of banking sector competition in the region to that observed in other regions of the developing world. Finally, the paper analyzes the factors that explain differences in competition between MENA and other regions.

The estimations of the H-statistic and the Lerner index show that banking sectors in MENA operate under monopolistic competition. Comparisons over time indicate that competition within MENA, both among Gulf Cooperation Council (GCC) countries and non-GCC economies, has not improved and, in many cases, worsened.

TABLE B3.5.1   **Competition in MENA and across Regions**

Regions	H-statistics		Lerner index	
	(1994–2008)	(2002–08)	(1994–2008)	(2002–08)
Middle East and North Africa	0.520	0.482	0.320	0.373
GCC countries	0.497	0.470	0.360	0.435
Non-GCC countries	0.528	0.508	0.241	0.258
p-value GCC = non-GCC	0.640	0.640	0.050	0.010
East Asia and Pacific	0.614	0.584	0.230	0.265
p-value East Asia and Pacific = GCC	0.070	0.120	0	0
p-value East Asia and Pacific = non-GCC	0.020	0.140	0.810	0.890
Eastern Europe	0.685	0.694	0.182	0.196
p-value Eastern Europe = GCC	0	0	0	0
p-value Eastern Europe = non-GCC	0	0	0.240	0.240
Latin America and the Caribbean	0.743	0.765	0.215	0.234
p-value Latin America and the Caribbean = GCC	0	0	0	0
p-value Latin America and the Caribbean = non-GCC	0	0	0.580	0.630
Former Soviet Union	0.659	0.669	0.271	0.266
p-value Former Soviet Union = GCC	0.010	0	0	0
p-value Former Soviet Union = non-GCC	0	0	0.520	0.860
South Asia	0.710	0.677	0.244	0.272
p-value South Asia = GCC	0	0.010	0.020	0
p-value South Asia = non-GCC	0	0	0.970	0.800
Sub-Saharan Africa	0.521	0.518	0.223	0.169
p-value Sub-Saharan Africa = GCC	0.700	0.510	0.040	0.020
p-value Sub-Saharan Africa = non-GCC	0.830	0.850	0.810	0.450

Note: GCC = Gulf Cooperation Council, MENA = Middle East and North Africa.

Relative to other regions, MENA is lagging behind in terms of bank competition. The evaluation of the factors explaining differences in banking sector competition between MENA and other regions suggests that a worse credit information environment and stricter regulations and practices governing bank entry are at least partly to blame.

leading to more concentration and less competition.

Although studies that examine the link between concentration and efficiency find mixed results,[11] the overwhelming majority of recent empirical studies conclude that competition brings about improvements in efficiency in both developed and developing economies. Using data for more than 14,000 banks operating in Europe and the United States, Schaeck and Čihák (2008) find a positive effect of competition on profit and cost efficiency. Similarly, using a technique to obtain joint estimates of efficiency and market power among banks in the European Monetary Union, Delis and Tsionas (2009) find a negative relationship, which is in line with the quiet life hypothesis.

Comparable findings are obtained when the sample of economies is extended to include developing economies. Using data on net interest margins and overhead costs for over 1,400 banks in 72 developed and developing economies, Demirgüç-Kunt, Laeven, and Levine (2004) find that tighter regulations on bank entry and bank activities lead to higher costs of financial intermediation. Lin, Ma, and Song (2010) find a similar result for 2,500 banks operating in 74 economies. Finally, focusing on 60 developing economies, Turk-Ariss (2010) finds a significant negative association between bank market power (as measured by the Lerner index) and cost efficiency.[12]

Overall, the literature examining the link between direct measures of competition and efficiency suggests that more bank competition increases bank efficiency in both developed and developing economies.

Competition and access to finance

Theory makes ambiguous predictions regarding the effect of competition on access to finance. The conventional market power hypothesis argues that competition in the banking market reduces the cost of finance and increases the availability of credit. On the other hand, the information hypothesis posits that in the presence of information

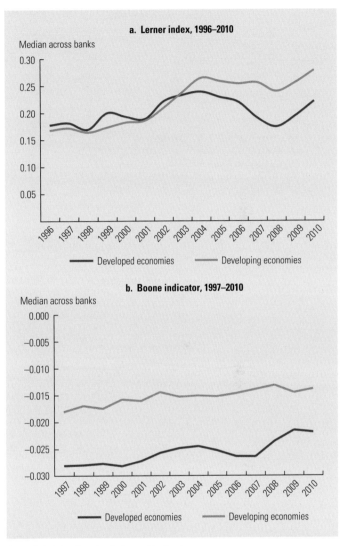

FIGURE 3.6   **Bank Competition: Developed vs. Developing Economies**

a. Lerner index, 1996–2010
Median across banks

— Developed economies   — Developing economies

b. Boone indicator, 1997–2010
Median across banks

— Developed economies   — Developing economies

Source: Calculations based on Bankscope (database).
Note: Lerner index estimations follow the methodology described in Demirgüç-Kunt and Martínez Pería (2010). The regional estimates for the Lerner index are based on the median of bank estimates within the region. Boone indicator estimations follow the methodology used by Schaeck and Čihák (2010a) with a modification to use marginal costs instead of average costs. Data are pooled by region in order to estimate the regional Boone indicator. Boone indicator data are not shown for Sub-Saharan Africa because of a lack of adequate data

asymmetries and agency costs, competition can reduce access by making it more difficult for banks to internalize the returns from investing in lending, in particular, with opaque clients.[13]

Most of the empirical studies on this question used concentration as a measure

FIGURE 3.7   **Bank Competition across Developing Regions**

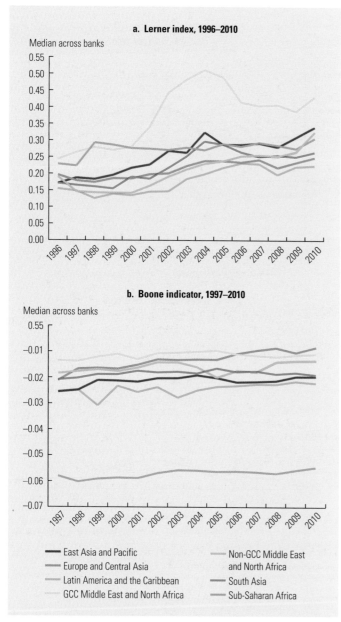

a. Lerner index, 1996–2010

Median across banks

b. Boone indicator, 1997–2010

Median across banks

— East Asia and Pacific
— Europe and Central Asia
— Latin America and the Caribbean
— GCC Middle East and North Africa
— Non-GCC Middle East and North Africa
— South Asia
— Sub-Saharan Africa

Source: Calculations based on Bankscope (database).
Note: Lerner index estimations follow the methodology described in Demirgüç-Kunt and Martínez Pería (2010). The regional estimates for the Lerner index are based on the median of bank estimates within the region. Boone indicator estimations follow the methodology used by Schaeck and Čihák (2010a) with a modification to use marginal costs instead of average costs. Data are pooled by region in order to estimate the regional Boone indicator. Boone indicator data are not shown for Sub-Saharan Africa because of a lack of adequate data.

of competition, obtaining mixed results.[14] But studies that focus on direct measures of competition and contestability show that access to finance is easier in more competitive

banking sectors.[15] Using data on growth in value added from 1980–90 for 16 countries, and measuring competition at the country-level (using the Panzar and Rosse H-statistic), Claessens and Laeven (2005) find that competition is positively associated with industrial growth. They suggest that competitive banking sectors are better at providing financing to financially dependent firms.

Exploiting a rich dataset on small and medium-sized enterprises in Spain, Carbó-Valverde, Rodríguez-Fernández, and Udell (2009) also find evidence that competition promotes access to finance, using the Lerner index.[16] In sum, similar to the findings on the link between competition and efficiency, the evidence that measures bank competition directly suggests that competition is beneficial for the banking sector. In particular, bank competition enhances access to credit.

Competition and banking stability

Competing theories explain the link between competition and stability.[17] The traditional view predicts that competitive banking systems are less stable because competition reduces bank profits and erodes the charter value of banks, consequently increasing incentives for excessive risk taking (Chan, Greenbaum, and Thakor 1986; Keeley 1990; Marcus 1984). Furthermore, in more competitive environments, banks earn lower informational rents from their relationship with borrowers, reducing their incentives to properly screen borrowers, again increasing the risk of fragility (Allen and Gale 2000, 2004; Boot and Greenbaum 1993). Competition can also destabilize the banking sector through its impact on the interbank market and the payments system.

For example, if all banks are price-takers in a competitive market, banks have no incentives to provide liquidity to a troubled bank, leading to bank failure, and creating negative repercussions for the entire sector (Allen and Gale 2000). A somewhat different argument in support of the competition-fragility view is that more concentrated banking systems have larger banks, which in turn allow them to diversify their portfolios better. A final argument refers to the number of banks to be supervised. Given that a more concentrated banking system typically implies a smaller number of banks, this might reduce the supervisory burden and enhance the overall stability of the banking system.

The competition-stability view argues that market power in banking boosts profits and stability, yet ignores the potential impact of market power on borrower behavior (Boyd and de Nicoló 2005). Because banks in less competitive sectors can charge higher interest rates, this may induce firms to assume greater risk—resulting in a higher probability that loans become non-performing. Similarly, higher interest rates might attract riskier borrowers through the adverse selection effect. Thus, in contrast to the charter-value hypothesis, the competition-stability view predicts that bank actions will result in more risk taking and greater fragility in more concentrated and less competitive banking systems. Advocates of the competition-stability view also disagree with the notion that concentrated banking systems are easier to monitor than less concentrated banking systems with many banks, since larger banks can be more complex and, hence, harder to supervise.

The early empirical literature on the link between competition and stability is mixed. Some country studies have shown that increasing competition leads to greater individual bank risk taking.[18] In the context of the U.S. subprime crisis, Dell'Ariccia, Igan, and Laeven (2012) document that the rapid growth of credit in U.S. mortgage markets in the run-up to the crisis was accompanied by a reduction in lending standards (lower loan application denial rates), which they argue was in part explained by the entry of new and large lending institutions. However, some previous studies failed to find that larger banks are less likely to fail as would be predicted by the competition-fragility view (Boyd and Graham 1991, 1996; Boyd and Runkle 1993; De Nicoló 2000).

On the other hand, studies using cross-country, time-series data sets offer evidence supporting the competition-stability view. Beck, Demirgüç-Kunt, and Levine (2006,

2007a) find that more competitive banking systems (defined as those with fewer regulatory restrictions on bank entry and activities) are less likely to suffer systemic banking distress. This finding is confirmed by Schaeck, Čihák, and Wolfe (2009), who find a negative relationship between bank competition and systemic bank fragility using the H-statistic to measure competition. Schaeck and Čihák (2010b) identify bank capitalization as one of the channels through which competition fosters stability. Using data for more than 2,600 European banks, they show that banks have higher capital ratios in more competitive environments. This is consistent with Berger, Klapper, and Turk-Ariss (2009), who find that banks in more competitive banking systems take greater lending risks, but compensate with a higher capital-asset ratio, resulting in an overall lower level of bank risk, as measured by the z-score.

Measures of bank risk, such as the z-score, ignore systemic stability, but regulators are concerned with systemic stability much more than the absolute level of risk of individual banks. In a recent paper, Anginer, Demirgüç-Kunt, and Zhu (2012) introduce a new measure of systemic risk taking by banks. Using Merton's 1973 contingent claim pricing framework, they calculate the default probability for each bank in the system. They measure systemic risk as the codependence in default probability across banks. After controlling for various bank- and country-level variables, Anginer, Demirgüç-Kunt, and Zhu (2012) find a positive relationship between competition and systemic stability. They also show that lack of competition (as measured by the Lerner index) has a more adverse effect on systemic stability in countries with low levels of foreign ownership, weak investor protection, generous safety nets, and weak regulation and supervision.

The advantages of competition in an efficient and inclusive financial system are significant. Recent studies provide evidence questioning the conventional view that competition is bad for stability. Importantly, policy bodies such as the OECD Competition Committee have suggested that to promote banking stability, policy makers should design and apply better regulations and supervisory practices rather than limit bank competition (OECD 2010).

DRIVERS OF BANK COMPETITION

The main drivers of competition are entry and exit policies, underlying information and institutional environment, and competitive pressures in the financial sector.[19] The state can directly influence all three. The state can also affect bank competition by owning banks. Box 3.6 analyzes the determinants of banking competition across economies.

Entry and exit policies in banking are important for competition because they keep incumbents on their toes. The threat of entry and exit to the industry forces banks to worry about providing good, affordable products and limits their ability to exercise market power. Entry policies include regulations on licensing, as well as the practice by regulators of approving new licenses. Exit policies refer to regulations as well as the measures taken by regulators to close insolvent banks. The state can directly affect bank competition by promoting policies and practices that facilitate bank entry and exit. A delicate balance needs to be struck where regulators foster contestability (to streamline requirements for bank licensing, speed up the licensing process, and implement efficient bank resolution) without jeopardizing bank stability (that is, maintaining a licensing process that keeps out unfit bankers).

Access to credit history information about potential borrowers also facilitates competition in the banking sector. Dell'Ariccia, Friedman, and Marquez (1999) show that to the extent that access to credit information is restricted, incumbent banks are better able to exercise market power and limit competition. At the same time, greater disclosure of information regarding the terms of banking products will generate greater awareness by bank clients and promote bank competition. By promoting the establishment and operation of credit bureaus and by having in place consumer protection regulations and practices, the state can shape the information environment and influence the extent of bank competition.

The institutional environment can also have an impact on bank competition. For example, to the extent that corruption is rampant in the economy, there will be less scope for a level playing field in the financial sector, and competition will suffer as a result. Similarly, to the degree that creditor rights are not protected, there will be less incentive for new banks to enter the banking sector. The state directly influences the institutional environment by the laws that it promotes and the extent to which it upholds compliance.

All else being equal, the entry of foreign banks and the presence of nonbank intermediaries are likely to affect bank competition. Foreign banks often bring new technologies and new products to banking sectors, creating an incentive for local banks to compete. Similarly, the presence of a liquid stock market or other financial intermediaries that can provide financing to firms is likely to foster competition in the banking sector, because banks will have to compete to provide financial services to firms. Once again, the state has a role to play here by introducing regulations and practices that foster the entry and operation of nonbank competitors.

Finally, government ownership of banks can also affect bank competition. On the one hand, government banks can spur competition if (because they typically do not maximize profits) they push other banks to lower prices. On the other hand, if government banks dominate the system and other banks are crowded out, competition falls. Box 3.6 shows that banking systems are more competitive in countries with lower entry barriers, greater foreign bank participation, and more developed capital markets (which are also associated with greater development of nonbank financial intermediaries).[20] Greater information disclosure, as captured by depth of credit information, also promotes competition. Box 3.7, on the other hand, highlights the importance of consumer protection measures to enhance banking competition.

BOX 3.6   An Econometric Analysis of Drivers of Bank Competition

The Lerner index is used as the summary measure of competition across 83 countries and is regressed against variables capturing the following:

1. Entry and exit policies in the banking sector.
2. The information and institutional environments.
3. Competitive pressures from within and outside the banking sector. Bank-level Bankscope data for the period 2000–10 are used to compute the Lerner index for all countries with at least five banks.

The first group of barriers to entry comprise measures such as the number of documents and procedures required to obtain a banking license, the percentage of denied applications for banking licenses, and the minimum entry capital required for banks. The second group includes a synthetic indicator of activity restrictions that captures a bank's ability to engage in activities other than banking (say, securities, insurance, or real estate). Higher values of this index represent greater restrictions. Both indexes are constructed with data from the World Bank 2006 Bank Regulation and Supervision Survey.

The availability of credit history information is captured by the depth of credit information index gathered from Doing Business (see http://www.doingbusiness.org). This index takes values from 0 to 6, and higher values indicate greater availability of information. The extent to which the government requires that financial institutions disclose information about financial contracts to potential users of this service is measured by an index on the strictness of financial contract disclosure requirements, which was constructed based on questions from the World Bank Regulation and Supervision Survey. This contract disclosure index is also a measure of consumer protection. The quality of the overall

institutional framework is measured by the index of control of corruption, which measures the degree to which public power is exercised for private benefit—such as state capture by elites and private interests (Kaufmann, Kraay, and Mastruzzi 2009).

Competitive pressures from within and outside the banking sector are captured by indicators of market structure, presence of foreign banks, liquidity of the stock market, and importance of nonbank intermediaries such as insurance companies and pension funds. Market structure is measured by the share of assets held by the top five banks in the system. To the extent that there is some validity to the structure-conduct-performance paradigm, this variable is expected to be positive and significant. Cross-border banking as captured by the share of banking assets held by foreign banks may reflect a greater degree of market contestability. To the extent that this is the case, promoting foreign bank participation may increase competition in the industry. On the other hand, if foreign bank entry is associated with mergers and acquisitions, it might not enhance competition. Finally, a more competitive banking system may arise from greater interindustry competition. In short, the development of nonbank financial intermediaries may affect the market power of the banking sector. The relative importance of such intermediaries is approximated by the value of shares traded to gross domestic product (GDP), the value of life insurance premiums to GDP, and the share of pension fund assets to GDP.

The table below suggests that the banking sector is more competitive (the Lerner index is lower) in countries with greater contestability (lower entry barriers), greater information disclosure, better institutions, more foreign bank participation, and more liquid stock markets.

(Continued on next page)

STATE INTERVENTIONS DURING CRISES AND BANKING COMPETITION

During crises, governments, central banks, and other authorities in charge of the supervision and regulation of financial institutions introduce deposit freezes, declare bank

holidays, provide blanket guarantees, inject capital, increase deposit insurance coverage limits, and extend liquidity support to banks on an unprecedented scale (Laeven and Valencia 2008, 2010). During tranquil periods, the competitive effects of rescue operations on individual banks (such as capital injections,

BOX 3.6 **An Econometric Analysis of Drivers of Bank Competition** *(continued)*

TABLE B3.6.1 **Cross-Country Determinants of Banking Competition**[a]

Variable	[1]	[2]	[3]	[4]	[5]	[6]
State as regulator: Market contestability						
Entry barriers	0.0401*	0.0376	0.013	0.0279	0.0242	0.0537**
	[0.024]	[0.023]	[0.028]	[0.021]	[0.019]	[0.021]
Share of bank licenses denied	−0.0025	0.0229	−0.0616	−0.0132	−0.0589	
	[0.038]	[0.037]	[0.049]	[0.042]	[0.043]	
Restrictions on bank activities	−0.0074	−0.0049	−0.01	−0.0087	−0.009	
	[0.005]	[0.005]	[0.008]	[0.006]	[0.006]	
Minimum entry capital required (ln)	0.0025**	0.0022*	0.0011	0.0006	0.0005	0.0031**
	[0.001]	[0.001]	[0.001]	[0.001]	[0.001]	[0.001]
State as enabler of market-friendly environments						
Depth of credit information					−0.0110*	−0.0130**
					[0.006]	[0.006]
Strictness of financial contract disclosure requirements (0-4)						−0.0074
						[0.010]
Control of corruption	−0.0291**	−0.0172	−0.0299*	−0.0318***	−0.0235*	−0.0193
	[0.011]	[0.013]	[0.017]	[0.011]	[0.012]	[0.015]
State as bank owner						
Government bank participation	−0.0417	−0.0793*	−0.0854	−0.044	−0.0394	−0.0734
	[0.046]	[0.044]	[0.064]	[0.047]	[0.047]	[0.048]
Competitive pressures within the banking sector and from other parts of the financial sector						
Foreign bank participation	−0.0594**	−0.0677	−0.0614	−0.0859***	−0.0715**	−0.0822**
	[0.028]	[0.034]	[0.050]	[0.029]	[0.030]	[0.034]
Concentration (CR5)				0.1119**	0.0816	0.0191
				[0.055]	[0.063]	[0.065]
Stock market value traded (ratio to GDP)		−0.0371*	−0.0616**			
		[0.020]	[0.023]			
Life insurance premium (ratio to GDP)		0.3105				
		[0.445]				
Pension fund assets (ratio to GDP)			0.0448			
			[0.031]			
Constant	0.0178	0.0195	0.2706	0.0503	0.1403	−0.0858
	[0.191]	[0.189]	[0.221]	[0.176]	[0.152]	[0.158]
Observations	83	71	38	72	64	42
R-squared	0.189	0.231	0.369	0.273	0.355	0.399

Note: GDP = gross domestic product.
a. A country's Lerner index is the median estimate across banks over the period 2000–10. Robust standard errors are in brackets.
***$p < 0.01$ **$p < 0.05$ *$p < 0.1$

emergency liquidity facilities, and assisted mergers) tend to be relevant only for a limited number of distressed institutions and their competitors (Gropp and others 2011; Hakenes and Schnabel 2010). However, episodes of systemic banking crises frequently result in large-scale, repeated policy responses that affect large numbers of institutions, with potential implications for industry structure and competitive conduct in financial systems over longer periods of time.

An emerging body of research examines the effects of bank bailouts and other policy responses on risk taking at the bank

---

BOX 3.7   Consumer Protection and Competition in South Africa

Among emerging markets, South Africa has a well-developed financial sector and one of the largest capital markets. In 2010, the outreach of the banking sector, as measured by its credit to the private sector, totaled 145 percent of GDP, while stock market capitalization to GDP amounted to 278 percent of GDP. In recent years, major South African banks have also expanded throughout the region—notably, Absa and Standard Bank (Beck and others 2011). However, the banking sector is heavily concentrated, with the five largest banks accounting for over 90 percent of total assets and deposits in the system in 2010. Estimates of market power in the South African banking industry show that there is evidence of monopolistic competition (Greenberg and Simbanegavi 2009; Mlambo and Ncube 2011), which is consistent with the fact that large banks tend to avoid competition among themselves, as reported by the Competition Commission on Banking (OECD 2008).

The lack of competition in the South African banking sector has been documented in several reports prepared for the National Treasury and the South African Reserve Bank (Falkena and others 2004; Competition Commission of South Africa 2006). As manifested by high prices and poor quality of financial services, low rates of innovation, and financial exclusion, the lack of competition was attributed partly to high concentration and profitability in retail banking and payments (OECD 2010). This led to the Banking Enquiry launched by the Competition Commission in August 2006. The result of this inquiry led to several recommendations to address problems of restrictive interbank arrangements and barriers to entry in the payments systems, but the inquiry put special emphasis on measures of consumer protection.

Advances in consumer protection are justified on the grounds that they can promote competition and depth. Providing better information to customers can lead to rising price and product competition among banking intermediaries. In this context, South Africa established a series of mechanisms and institutions that promoted a more sound information environment. The National Credit Act 34 (enacted in 2005), for instance, provides a general framework to promote responsible lending practices, protect South African consumers from unfair credit and credit marketing practices and, more generally, establish norms and standards on consumer credit. It also created the National Credit Regulator to ensure the law's compliance, investigate complaints, promote financial literacy, and provide a knowledge platform on credit practices. On the other hand, cases of noncompliance and appeals to decisions of the regulators were allowed to be presented and solved by the National Consumer Tribunal.

In spite of the advances on abusive lending practices, the mechanisms established by the National Credit Act to restructure consumer debt have been slow. For instance, Beck and others (2011) point out that as few as 5 percent of the 150,000 applications made by overly indebted consumers have been finalized by courts. Finally, better use of consumer protection networks requires financially aware consumers. Efforts to raise the effectiveness of financial literacy programs are required.

Sources: Beck and others 2011; Greenberg and Simbanegavi 2009; Mlambo and Ncube 2011; OECD 2010.

---

level (Berger and others 2010; Duchin and Sosyura 2011; Farhi and Tirole 2012; Gropp, Hakenes, and Schnabel 2011; Hakenes and Schnabel 2010; Hoshi and Kashyap 2010; Richardson and Troost 2009). However, how these actions affect competition has received less attention. This issue is of vital importance because of the unintended (and possibly detrimental) effects for consumer welfare. For example, guarantees can result in entrenchment of the supported institutions; assisted mergers of large financial institutions increase concentration, presumably reducing competition in retail markets and reinforcing the perception that these banks are too big to fail (Beck and others 2010; Hakenes and Schnabel 2010).

More research is clearly needed in this area, though a number of studies suggest that state interventions that favor some bank services (such as guarantees, liquidity support, recapitalizations, and nationalizations) force competitors to behave more aggressively, leading to decreased margins and increased competition (Gropp, Hakenes, and Schnabel 2011; Hovakimian and Kane 2000; Kane 1989). Using data for 138 countries that witnessed a variety of policy responses during 46 banking crises, Calderón and Schaeck (2012) find that Lerner indexes and net interest margins drop as a result of state interventions such as guarantees, liquidity support, recapitalizations, and nationalizations.

This apparent increase in competition should be interpreted with caution—especially if the type of state intervention under consideration delays the exit of inefficient and insolvent banks. Kane (2000) argues that some state interventions can constitute a barrier to exit by allowing these banks to survive beyond their "natural death." State support to these zombie banks—a term coined by Kane (1989)—would allow these institutions to bid up deposit rates and accept low interest rates on high-risk loans and investments, thus reducing profit margins in the industry (Kane 2000; Kane and Rice 2001). In sum, states can create zombie banks by distorting risk-taking incentives of the system and generating unhealthy competition. Calderón and Schaeck (2012) show that the increase in competition that might result from state interventions during crises is also accompanied by other negative consequences. Despite the evidence that the cost of borrowing is reduced and credit is restored as a result of these state interventions, access to credit by opaque borrowers such as small and medium enterprises is reduced.

To avoid the distorting effects of state interventions, sunset clauses and exit plans are important (Beck, Coyle, and others 2010). By providing credible signals that interventions are temporary, governments can reduce the negative repercussion for competition. Similarly, addressing governance deficiencies in the supported institutions can also be important in reducing incentives for excessive risk taking. Finally, measures such as government-sponsored mergers that reduce the

number of banks in the system can easily lead to lower levels of bank competition (OECD 2009). In that case, governments should promote the entry of deserving institutions to mitigate the negative impact of mergers.

Overall, it is clear that state interventions during crises can have an impact on bank competition and potentially on future banking stability. Governments should avoid insolvency resolution policies that not only distort risk-taking incentives and jeopardize future stability, but also have implications for the level of competition in the banking sector.

IMPLICATIONS FOR THE DESIGN OF COMPETITION POLICIES

Bank competition increases efficiency and financial inclusion. Recent evidence suggests that bank competition can even enhance systemic financial stability. Hence, bank competition should not be restricted with the hope of promoting stability. Instead, the state should design and enforce regulations that create the right incentives to safeguard stability, while at the same time promote competition and efficiency.

The state can shape bank competition through its actions as a regulator and an enabler of a market-friendly and information-rich environment. In particular, banking sectors are more competitive in economies where the state designs, implements, and enforces regulatory frameworks that ensure greater contestability. More specifically, policies designed to ease the entry of deserving institutions (those that can pass fit and proper tests) and promote timely exit may prevent incumbent banks from exercising market power and lead to a more competitive environment. Related to the less stringent barriers to entry, foreign bank penetration may also be conducive to greater competition.

The state can also promote competition in the banking sector by ensuring banks' and consumers' access to information as well as by building up a sound institutional framework that levels the playing field. Free flow of credit information among banks and transparency of financial products offered by banks to potential consumers should be ensured by the state. A sound institutional framework that ensures the enforcement of contracts, property rights, and the rule of law that limits the exercise of public power for private benefit is conducive to greater competition in the banking sector. Finally, policies to promote deeper and more diversified financial markets—especially the development of nonbanking financial institutions—also appear to increase the level of competition in the banking sector.

Government interventions during crises that prevent the exit of insolvent institutions and increase market power through mergers can also affect competition and bank risk taking. In trying to mitigate the impact of financial crises, governments should be aware of the potentially negative consequences of their actions on bank competition and future bank stability.

Finally, implementation of competition policies depends on the institutional arrangement in place. The increased integration across different parts of the financial industry has led to a shift in financial supervision from a sector-based approach to more integrated approaches, including (a) a fully integrated supervisory model with one agency (a Financial Supervision Authority) carrying out all supervisory roles (such as microprudential, business conduct, and competition policy), or (b) a so-called functional or objective-based approach in which sectorally integrated agencies undertake different supervisory roles.[21]

An example of the latter is the twin peaks model. One agency is responsible for prudential supervision in the financial system, and another one oversees market conduct, consumer protection, and corporate governance in all sectors.[22] The effectiveness of the twin peaks approach, as argued by its advocates, is guaranteed by having a clear focus and division of roles, to minimize turf battles between agencies, as well as strong collaboration, to work together in overlapping areas (Kremers and Schoenmaker 2008, 2010). Evidence so far suggests that regulatory quality is stronger in systems with objectives-based supervision—in favor of the twin peaks model

and full integration—as opposed to different types of partial integration supervisory models.

Competition can bring important benefits to the financial sector and should not be sacrificed for the sake of stability. Instead governments should implement the measures discussed in this chapter to monitor competition and strengthen the information and institutional frameworks to promote competition, while ensuring that regulations and supervisory practices are in place that safeguard banking stability.

NOTES

1. The chapter focuses on competition in the banking sector rather than the broader financial sector. But it does touch on the impact of nonbank intermediaries on bank competition. See Motta (2004) for a broader discussion on the theory and practice of competition policy.
2. For example, in February 2010, the OECD Competition Committee held a discussion on competition, concentration, and stability in the banking sector.
3. Several developed and developing economies have competition agencies that have mandates or that can influence market outcomes in banking. Competition agencies enforce antitrust laws (for example, assess the competitive harm of mergers, deter anticompetitive behavior, and minimize distortions from state aid) and promote measures to enable firm entry and rivalry (that is, competition advocacy).
4. In general terms, the view of competition presented here and discussed in the literature is based on the notion that banks primarily compete in deposit and loan markets. However, in practice, especially in developed economies, banks offer a variety of services (such as market making, asset management, and underwriting) where market power may arise. Payment systems are another area in which there might be significant deviations from marginal cost pricing.
5. See Cetorelli (1999), Claessens and Laeven (2004), and Demirgüç-Kunt, Laeven, and Levine (2004), among others. Nevertheless, concentration measures are presented first because they are the most widely used and easiest to compute of measures of competition.

6. There is a growing literature on measuring and explaining bank competition using direct measures of competition: Anzoategui, Martínez Pería and Melecký (2010); Anzoategui, Martínez Pería, and Rocha (2010); Beck, de Jonghe, and Schepens (2011); Berger, Klapper, and Turk-Ariss (2009); and Delis (2012); Demirgüç-Kunt and Martínez Pería (2010); Schaeck and Čihák (2008, 2010a, 2010b); Schaeck, Čihák, and Wolfe (2009); Turk-Ariss (2010), among others.

7. Note that the H-statistic can only be used to test the hypothesis of perfect competition if the market is in long-run equilibrium (returns on bank assets are not related to input prices). However, tests using the H-statistic for the null of monopoly are still valid, since the long-run profit condition does not apply in the case of a monopoly.

8. Measuring marginal costs is difficult and requires certain assumptions about the cost function of banks. Typically, studies that calculate the Lerner index assume a translog cost function.

9. Bikker and Spierdijk (2008) argue that banks in large and integrated financial markets (such as in Europe after establishing the European Monetary Union) are pushed by rising capital market competition and tend to shift from traditional intermediation to more sophisticated and complex products associated with less price competition.

10. In recent work, Calderon and Schaeck (2012) use data for 138 countries, of which 43 experienced banking crises. Their analyses show that government interventions (such as blanket guarantees, liquidity support by the central bank, recapitalizations, and nationalization of banks) during crises significantly increase competition in banking systems, and the distortionary effects cannot be reversed easily.

11. See Berger (1995), Goldberg and Rai (1996), and Berger and Hannan (1998), among others.

12. One exception is Casu and Girardone (2009), who find a positive causation between market power and efficiency for 2,701 banks operating in France, Germany, Italy, Spain, and the United Kingdom from 2000 to 2005.

13. See Petersen and Rajan (1995) and Marquez (2002).

14. Using U.S. data, Petersen and Rajan (1995) and Zarutskie (2006) find that bank concentration facilitates access credit, whereas Beck, Demirgüç-Kunt, and Maksimovic (2004) and Chong, Lu, and Ongena (2012) find the opposite result using data for 74 countries and for Chinese small and medium enterprises, respectively.

15. At the same time, using bank-level data, Beck, Demirgüç-Kunt, and Martínez Pería (2008) find that barriers to banking (minimum balances to open deposit accounts and to obtain loans, as well as documentation requirements to access financial services) are higher in countries with greater entry restrictions for banks.

16. At the same time, the authors find that their results for the Lerner index are not consistent with results using concentration as a measure of competition. They conclude that "researchers and policymakers need to be very careful in drawing strong conclusions about market power and credit availability based on analyses that rely exclusively on concentration as a measure of market power."

17. See Beck (2008) for a thorough review of the theoretical and empirical literature on bank competition and stability.

18. See, for example, Keeley (1990) and Dick (2006), in the case of the United States; Jimenez, Lopez, and Saurina (2007) in the case of Spain.

19. See Anzoategui, Martínez Pería, and Rocha 2010; Claessens and Laeven 2004; Delis 2012; Demirgüç-Kunt and Martínez Pería 2010.

20. Rocha, Arvai, and Farazi (2011) find that the lack of competition in the Middle East and North Africa banking sectors is the outcome of barriers to entry and lack of competition from nonbanking financial intermediaries, among other factors.

21. Čihák and Podpiera (2008) discuss the different types of supervisory arrangements.

22. Countries with a twin peaks supervisory structure are Australia (Australia Prudential Regulation Authority and the Australian Securities and Investments Commission) and the Netherlands—with the Netherlands Bank (DNB) in charge of prudential supervision and the Authority for the Financial Markets supervising market conduct (Čihák and Podpiera 2008; Kremers and Schoenmaker 2008).

4

Direct State Interventions

- *Lending by state-owned banks is less procyclical than lending by private banks, and some state banks played a countercyclical role during the global financial crisis. However, this lending did not always target the most constrained borrowers and continued even after economic recovery ensued, questioning the effectiveness of the policy. Furthermore, the evidence based on previous episodes of downturns and recoveries is mixed.*

- *Moreover, research finds that efforts to stabilize aggregate credit by state-owned banks come at a cost, particularly through the deterioration of the quality of intermediation and resource misallocation. This effect undermines the benefits of using state banks as a countercyclical tool.*

- *The empirical evidence largely suggests that government bank ownership is associated with lower levels of financial development and slower economic growth. Policy makers need to avoid the inefficiencies associated with government bank ownership by paying special attention to the governance of these institutions and ensuring, among other things, that adequate risk management processes are in place, which is particularly challenging in weak institutional environments.*

- *Another popular form of intervention during the recent crisis was through credit guarantee programs. Rigorous evaluations of these programs are rare, but existing studies suggest that the benefits are modest and costs are often significant. Success hinges on overcoming the challenges of getting the design right, particularly in underdeveloped institutional and legal settings.*

State-owned banks were typically created to fulfill long-term development roles by filling market gaps in long-term credit, infrastructure, and agriculture finance, and to promote access to finance for underserved segments of the economy—notably, small and medium enterprises (SMEs).[1] In practice, however, widespread evidence shows that state banks have generally been very inefficient in allocating credit, more often than not serving political interests. Nevertheless, the recent global financial crisis underscored the countercyclical role of state-owned banks in offsetting the contraction of credit from private banks, leading to arguments that this function is an important one that can potentially better justify their existence.

During the recent global financial crisis, countries pursued a variety of strategies to restart their financial and real sectors. As the balance sheets of private banks deteriorated and they curtailed their lending activities, many countries used state-owned banks to step up their financing to the private sector (for example, Brazil, China, and Germany).[2] Some economies relied heavily on the use of credit guarantee programs. For example, Canada, Chile, Finland, Germany, the Republic of Korea, Malaysia, and the Netherlands extended new and special schemes or refueled existing ones to alleviate the impact of the credit crunch on SMEs. Finally, other countries, such as the United States, United Kingdom, and those of the euro area, adopted a number of unconventional monetary and fiscal measures to prop up credit markets.[3]

The crisis and the actions adopted by different countries reignited the debate on whether there is a need for direct government intervention in the financial sector. Supporters of state-owned banks argue that these institutions provide the state an additional tool for crisis management and, relative to central banks, they may be more capable of undertaking the role of safe haven for retail and interbank deposits, creating a fire break to mitigate contagion, and stabilizing aggregate credit.

On the other hand, those who oppose government bank ownership point out that agency problems and politically motivated lending render state-owned banks breeding grounds for corruption. Furthermore, rewarding political cronyism may build up large fiscal liabilities and threaten public sector solvency and financial fragility, as well as misallocate resources and retard development.

This chapter reevaluates the merits of government bank ownership in the wake of the global financial crisis.[4] The chapter also discusses public credit guarantees that were also widely used to offset the credit crunch and mentions other policies adopted by central banks to deal with the recent crisis. The main messages from this chapter are as follows.

First, lending by state-owned banks is less procyclical. During the recent global financial crisis, state-owned banks in some countries expanded their lending portfolios and were credited with assisting in the economic recovery. However, it is unclear that the recent crisis illustrates that state-owned banks can effectively play a countercyclical role. Lending growth continued even after economic recovery was under way, and loans were not directed to the most constrained borrowers. Furthermore, the evidence from previous crises on this issue is also mixed. Any benefits of credit stabilization that may arise from countercyclical lending by state-owned banks come at a cost. The state faces a direct cost to the extent that outlays to the financial sector (such as state treasury purchases of securities, recapitalization, and so forth) and public debt burdens are piling up.[5] Perhaps more important, financial intermediation by state-owned banks is subject to the risk of political capture and often leads to a deterioration of the quality of loans and misallocation of resources in the medium to long term. The bulk of the empirical evidence suggests that state ownership of banks tends to be associated with lower financial development, greater financial instability, and slower rates of economic growth. Hence, the trade-off between the potential benefits of a countercyclical role of state banks and the long-term adverse impact on credit allocation requires careful consideration.

Second, focusing on the governance of state-owned banks ideally may help policy makers address the inefficiencies associated with these institutions. Policy makers need to design a clear mandate, allow the institutions to work as a complement to (rather than a substitute for) the private banks, and adopt risk management practices that allow them to guarantee a financially sustainable business. However, these governance reforms are particularly challenging in weak institutional environments.

Third, credit guarantee schemes were also a popular intervention tool used during the recent crisis. However, because these programs are small scale, they are not likely to have a large macroeconomic impact. Furthermore, research suggests that the benefits of these programs in terms of financial and economic "additionality" are rather modest, and they may bring along significant fiscal and economic costs.[6] The effectiveness of these programs relies on their design. Best practices include (a) leaving credit assessments and decision making to the private sector, (b) capping coverage ratios and delaying the payout of the guarantee until recovery actions are taken by the lender so as to minimize moral hazard problems, (c) pricing guarantees so they take into account the need for financial sustainability and risk minimization, and (d) encouraging the use of risk management tools.

The rest of the chapter is organized as follows. It first presents data on bank ownership structure worldwide, highlighting the regions where state-owned bank presence is significant. Next, it analyzes the countercyclical nature of government bank lending during the recent crisis and in previous episodes. It also discusses the evidence on the longer-term implications of government bank ownership and then turns to credit guarantee schemes.

OWNERSHIP STRUCTURES AROUND THE WORLD

State-owned banks account for less than 10 percent of banking system assets in developed economies and double that share in developing economies (figure 4.1). In a comparison of the periods 2001–07 and 2008–10, the recent global crisis brought about a small surge in government bank ownership in developed countries (6.7 percent to 8 percent, respectively), while the opposite is true in developing economies (government bank ownership declined from 20.5 to 17.3 percent). The uptick in the share of state-owned banks in developed countries may

FIGURE 4.1   Trends in Government Ownership of Banks

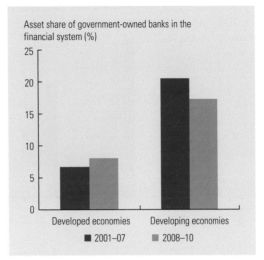

Sources: Calculations based on Farazi, Feyen, and Rocha 2011; Bank Regulation and Supervision Survey (database), World Bank 2003, 2007, 2011; Barth, Caprio, and Levine 2001, 2004, 2008).

be attributed to the recent bailouts, mergers, recapitalizations, and nationalization of distressed financial institutions that were more common among developed economies than developing economies.

Though government bank ownership is more prevalent in the developing world, it has declined considerably over time (figure 4.2). Since the 1970s, the share of state-owned banks relative to the total assets of the banking system declined sharply in all emerging regions, from an average of 67 percent in 1970 to 22 percent in 2009. The retrenchment of government participation has been dramatic in the Eastern European and Central Asian region. The massive privatization program in transition economies launched in the early 1990s reduced the government stake in the banking system from almost full ownership (88 percent in 1985) to intermediate levels of government participation (20 percent in 2009).[7] Finally, the World Bank report *Financing Africa* illustrates the dramatic transformation of the ownership structure in African banks over the last 50 years (Beck and others 2011). From a system mostly dominated by state-owned banks, the region now has the second highest share of

FIGURE 4.2   **Government Ownership across Developing Regions, 1970–2009**

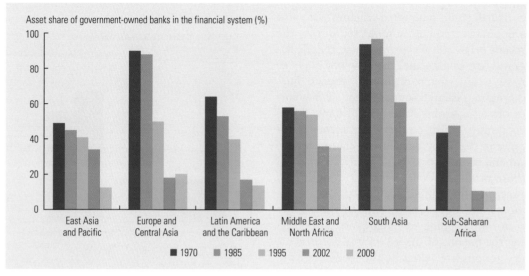

Sources: Calculations based on Farazi, Feyen, and Rocha 2011; Bank Regulation and Supervision Survey (database), World Bank 2003, 2007, 2011; Barth, Caprio, and Levine 2001, 2004, 2008.

foreign-owned banks—trailing only the transition economies of Eastern Europe and Central Asia.[8]

The retrenchment of state-owned banks in the financial sector can be attributed to their poor financial performance as well as their less than stellar contribution to financial and economic development—especially in countries where they dominated the banking system. This trend also reflects retrenchment of the public sector and fiscal consolidation in some countries.[9]

Despite the fact that the activity and importance of state-owned banks declined sharply over time, they still play a substantive role in some countries. For instance, state-owned banks still dominate the process of financial intermediation in Algeria, Belarus, China, the Arab Republic of Egypt, India, and the Syrian Arab Republic, where the asset market share of these banks exceeded half the assets of the banking system in 2010. In other countries, state-owned banks do not lead the process of credit creation but still play an important role. For example, state-owned banks in Argentina, Brazil, Indonesia, Korea, Poland, the Russian Federation, and Turkey

have an asset market share between 20 and 50 percent. While the average market share of government-owned banks is negligible in Eastern European nations, it is still large among countries in Central Asia.[10] Almost half of the countries that responded to the latest round of the World Bank's Bank Regulation and Supervision Survey report a market share for state-owned banks below 5 percent.

ROLE OF GOVERNMENT BANK LENDING IN MITIGATING ECONOMIC CYCLES AND CRISES

The recent global financial crisis has brought to the fore the potential role of state-owned banks in stabilizing aggregate credit.[11] Historical evidence shows that the failure of credit flows to recover may drag down the recovery of real economic activity (Biggs, Mayer, and Pick 2010). In other words, a precondition for the recovery of the corporate sector may be the recovery of the financial sector.[12] Though a strand of the empirical literature argues that recoveries in real output without a recovery in credit flows—creditless recoveries or "Phoenix miracles"—are not rare events, and become more frequent after a banking crisis or credit boom (Abiad, Dell'Ariccia, and Li 2011; Bijsterbosch and Dahlhaus 2011; Calvo, Izquierdo, and Talvi 2006a, 2006b), the evidence at the macro-economic level is far from conclusive and displays a great deal of heterogeneity. Furthermore, firm-level evidence (Ayyagari, Demirgüç-Kunt, and Maksimovic 2011a) shows that real sector recoveries are not creditless, and that firms substitute short-term credit with long-term external finance, either through long-term borrowing or capital issuance. In sum, Phoenix miracles are not supported by firm-level data either in the United States or among emerging markets.

The global recession in 2008–09 involved unprecedented conditions: real output fell sharply and in a synchronized fashion across the world (with more than 80 percent of the countries sharing a recessionary phase in the period from the third quarter of 2008 to the first quarter of 2009). In addition, real credit also fell in a synchronized manner across countries. Aisen and Franken (2010) show that 95 percent of countries experienced a contraction in bank credit in at least one month between September 2008 and May 2009. The dire financial conditions in the world economy reignited the debate on the countercyclical role of government banks.

The fact that recoveries may not take place without credit growth may be reason enough for the state to use their government bank infrastructure in order to keep the credit flowing. State-owned banks may facilitate credit stabilization for several reasons. First, stabilization of credit markets may be a part of state-owned banks' mandate. In this context, state-owned banks may fill the gap of credit caused by underprovision by their private counterparts in times of crisis (Rudolph 2009, 2010). Second, state-owned banks could be perceived as safer during recessions or crises, and their more stable deposit base could allow them to have more stable lending activity during crises (Micco and Panizza 2006).

During the recent crisis, many countries deployed their state-owned banks to counteract the credit contraction by privately owned

banks. Governments injected capital into their state-owned banks to roll over existing loans or provided new credit to SMEs or exporting firms (this has been the case, for example, in Canada, Chile, Korea, and Tunisia), raised credit ceilings of their state-owned banks (in Finland and Korea, among others), and established credit facilities for banks (for example, in India and Tunisia). In Brazil, a state-owned development bank (Banco Nacional de Desenvolvimento Econômico e Social, BNDES) played an important role in expanding credit during the recent crisis. However, the fact that most loans seem to have gone to large firms and that credit continued to expand even after the economy recovered in 2010–11 calls into question the ability of this bank to behave countercyclically (box 4.1). State-owned development banks in Mexico expanded their loan portfolios and also supported key markets through special guarantee programs (box 4.2). Nonperforming loans (NPLs) and profitability seem stable so far, perhaps because most of the lending was through tier II operations in which credit decisions are left to private intermediaries.[13] However, because credit kept growing even after the economy recovered, it is still unclear whether state-owned development banks in Mexico will be able to play an effective countercyclical role rather than crowd out private banks.

In Poland, state-owned bank PKO Bank Polski has played a role in credit stabilization by lending to the corporate and SME sectors (box 4.3). Though so far the bank has remained profitable and NPLs have not changed dramatically, time will tell whether the bank's credit allocation was efficient. The case of Poland is not representative of all countries in Eastern Europe. Research comparing the behavior of state-owned and foreign-owned banks in relation to private domestic banks in Eastern Europe and Latin America before and after the 2007–09 crises (box 4.4) shows that in Eastern Europe, state-owned banks in general did not play a countercyclical role. On the other hand, state-owned banks in Latin America increased loan growth during the crisis relative to their

BOX 4.1   Intervention Using State-Owned Banks in Brazil

The Brazilian government actively used its state bank infrastructure to engineer a rapid countercyclical response to mitigate the contagion effects from the global financial crisis. New liquidity assistance lines were created by the Central Bank of Brazil (BCB) to enable the country's state commercial banks, Banco do Brasil (BB) and Caixa Econômica Federal (CEF), to acquire ownership interest in private and public financial institutions—including insurance companies, social welfare institutions, and capitalization companies—with or without the acquisition of the capital stock control. Moreover, the government used its public bank infrastructure—BB, CEF, and Banco Nacional de Desenvolvimento Econômico e Social (BNDES), the state-owned development bank—to play a countercyclical role in credit markets during this period of global financial turmoil. Figure B4.1.1 illustrates the expansion of credit by Brazilian state-owned banks from 13.4 percent of GDP in September 2008 to 18.1 percent of GDP by end-2009. As of December 2011, credit extended by public banks represented 21.4 percent of GDP, while overall credit operations in the financial system totaled 49.1 per-

cent of GDP. The continued expansion of credit by public banks, and especially BNDES, in 2010 and 2011 illustrates the difficulties of behaving counter-cyclically during upswings in real economic activity.

BNDES played an important role: it extended special credit facilities thanks to a generous capital injection by the government (R$100 billion in 2009). Loans from BNDES were extended at a subsidized rate—the long-term interest rate was set at 6 percent, which is 7.5 percentage points lower than the market rate (Lazzarini and others 2011). In fact, credit by BNDES surged from R$160 billion (at 2005 prices) in September 2008 to R$277 billion in December 2010. The fact that most of this credit is being extended to large firms that are likely to get loans elsewhere (Lazzarini and others 2011) indicates that private banks are crowded out in credit markets.

The portfolio expansion of BNDES was accompanied by a shift in the composition of its funding. Figure B4.1.2 shows that resources channeled from the national treasury rather than those coming from the Workers' Assistance Fund became the main source of funding beginning in 2009. The transfer from Trea-

FIGURE B4.1.1   Ownership and Credit in Brazil

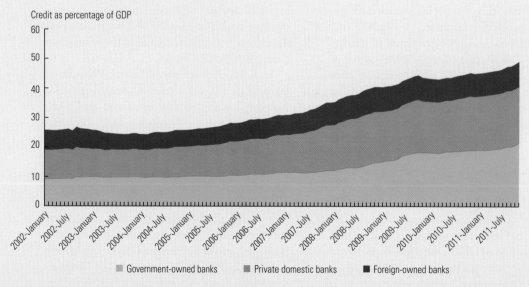

Source: Central Bank of Brazil.
Note: Government-owned banks refer to institutions in which federal, state, or municipal governments hold more than 50 percent of the voting capital. Private domestic banks include those institutions in which individuals or corporate entities domiciled and resident in the country hold more than 50 percent of the voting capital. Foreign-owned banks include those institutions that have—under external control and either directly or indirectly—the majority of voting capital. They also include those banks established and headquartered abroad with agencies or branches in the country.

BOX 4.1   Intervention Using State-Owned Banks in Brazil   *(continued)*

FIGURE B4.1.2   BNDES: Sources of Funding

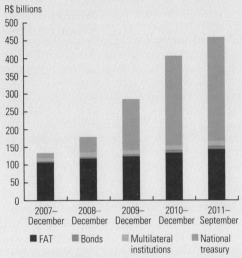

R$ billions

FAT ■ Bonds ■ Multilateral institutions ■ National treasury

Source: Central Bank of Brazil.
Note: FAT = Workers' Assistance Fund.

sury through bond issuances may crowd out private credit, keep interest rates at high levels, and thus reduce the provision of credit in the overall economy. The transfers also involve a fiscal cost that reduces the scope of direct public investment.

As pointed out in the report, state-owned bank interventions in credit markets also carry economic

consequences. Figure B4.1.3 breaks down BNDES disbursements by firm size: 85 percent of disbursements by BNDES went to large firms in 2009 (R$115.9 billion)—the worst year of the crisis. In the midst of a strong postcrisis recovery, BNDES continued lending at the same pace of the crisis years (R$139.7 billion in 2011 from R$136.4 billion in 2009). Large firms still represented a big share of BNDES disbursements in 2011 (64 percent); however, the participation of micro and small firms as well as individuals has increased to 26 percent (R$36.3 billion).

Recent research also shows that loan activities deployed by BNDES are consistent with the political view of public lending: an increasing amount of funds are typically channeled to firms in regions where allied incumbents are facing political competition (Carvalho 2010), or to firms that donate to candidates that won an election (Claessens, Feyen, and Laeven 2008; Lazzarini and others 2011). Economically, employment expands among (manufacturing) firms that are eligible to BNDES loans in regions where allied incumbents face political competition (Carvalho 2010). However, profitability, market valuation and investment appear to remain unchanged in firms that received funding from BNDES—either through loans or equity provision. Only their financial expenses were reduced considerably (Lazzarini and others 2011).

FIGURE B4.1.3   Distribution of BNDES Disbursements by Company Size (percentage)

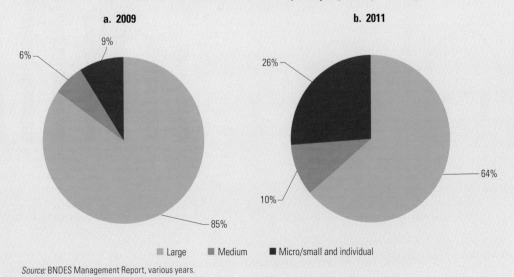

a. 2009

b. 2011

■ Large ■ Medium ■ Micro/small and individual

Source: BNDES Management Report, various years.

BOX 4.2   The Recent Global Crisis and Government Bank Lending in Mexico

Mexican development banks (DBs) rapidly expanded operations during the critical moments of the global financial crisis by providing short-term credit to well-established private sector firms and nonbank financial institutions with problems, both to refinance their debt and to mitigate the sharp deceleration in private bank lending (figure B4.2.1).[a] Credit to the private sector (instead of public sector) expanded fastest, and overall credit stabilized or began declining after fourth quarter 2009. Despite the DBs' strong lending expansion, the portfolio share of DBs relative to that of private banks remained below the 2006 level, as its share in total lending had been contracting prior to the crisis.

Mexican DBs were credited with restoring operations in key markets such as commercial paper through special guarantee programs—with most of these programs being temporary. Overall, DBs have extended Mex\$71 billion (approximately US\$6.1 billion) in guarantees as of June 2011—about 20 percent of the total loan portfolio balance—and each guaranteed peso induced 2.8 pesos in credit (figure B4.2.2).

Nonperforming loans have remained at reasonable levels—1.1 percent compared to 3.0 percent for private banks as of November 2011—and provisions

cover about 200 percent of NPLs. Profitability has remained stable or even improved in some cases. Preliminary estimates of the fiscal costs (in terms of capital allocations to DBs) appear modest because banks were adequately capitalized before the crisis and did not need additional funds to increase their lending portfolios. Moreover, the bulk of total interventions took place through credit guarantees and tier II operations, in which credit decisions are left to private intermediaries. Tier I lending expanded, but to a large extent (especially loans by Bancomext) those loans carried high rates and were highly collateralized, providing firms with incentives for early repayment as market conditions stabilized (which many firms have done). However, it is still early to assess the full impact on the quality of intermediation.

Overall, Mexican DBs played an important countercyclical role during the downturn. However, the portfolio of credit and, especially, guarantees has decreased very slowly during the upturn. Expanded operations have so far not compromised the financial position of DBs. Going forward, it may be useful to establish mechanisms to facilitate the expansion and contraction of the DBs' balance sheet—and, in particular, of capital—to mitigate incentives to compete with the private sector during the upswing.

FIGURE B4.2.1   Gross Loan Portfolio Growth

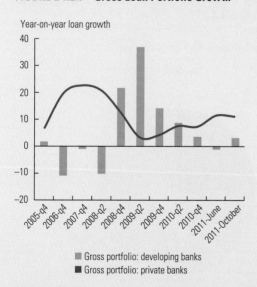

Year-on-year loan growth

- Gross portfolio: developing banks
- Gross portfolio: private banks

FIGURE B4.2.2   Partial Credit Guarantees

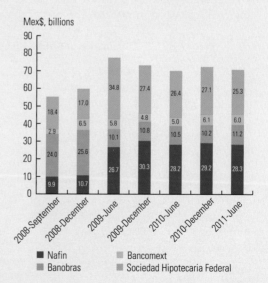

Mex\$, billions

- Nafin
- Banobras
- Bancomext
- Sociedad Hipotecaria Federal

Source: Calculations based on data from the Mexican Banking and Securities Commission.

a. The Mexican financial system has six development banks along with several trust funds and development institutions that provide credit. DBs provide tier I and tier II financing and guarantees and undertake loan portfolio sales and special development programs besides administrative functions, such as technical assistance and training. Banobras and Nafin account for about a third of total development bank assets each, while Banobras alone accounts for 44 percent of total development banks loans.

BOX 4.3   State Commercial Banks in Action during the Crisis: The Case of Poland

Poland was the only economy in the European Union that avoided a recession in 2009 thanks to timely fiscal stimulus and growth in lending, which were supported by policy measures undertaken by the Polish Financial Supervisory Authority and the National Bank of Poland (NBP), as well as by an expansion of the loan portfolio by the country's state-owned commercial bank, PKO Bank Polski (PKO BP).

PKO BP expanded credit at a faster pace during the crisis than Polish subsidiaries of foreign banks, which control almost three-fourths of the total assets of the system. Despite high credit spreads, credit by PKO BP grew by more than 1 percent of GDP per year during 2009–11. PKO BP's share in total lending increased from 15.6 percent of GDP in 2008 Q3 to 17.2 percent in 2010 Q4 (figure B4.3.1). In turn, its loan portfolio increased for all market segments, including, most important, the corporate and SME sectors—in which the value of new loans that were extended to those sectors throughout the crisis totaled 0.5 percent of nominal GDP in 2011.

Rapid credit expansion by PKO BP relative to that of foreign-owned banks is attributed to four major drivers. First, PKO BP's management made an arm's-length commercial decision to capitalize on the decreased participation of foreign-owned banks in loan markets and to create attractive business opportunities for households and corporations. Second, the government supported PKO BP's lending activities during the crisis through public announcements by its supervisory board. Third, PKO BP's conservative funding structure reduced the bank's dependence on wholesale financing (domestically and abroad), as opposed to foreign banks that relied partly on external funding from parent banks. Finally, PKO BP's capital adequacy ratio—above the regulatory minimum of 8 percent—was further raised following a 5 billion Polish zlotys rights and new share issuance in late 2009.

So far, PKO BP's nonperforming loans have increased at a roughly similar pace to that of the average of the largest foreign-owned banks, despite the substantial increase in lending during the crisis (figure B4.3.2). Credit overdue by more than 90 days amounted to 4.2 percent for PKO BP (as opposed to the 5.8 percent market average). Moreover, PKO BP remained profitable during the crisis period,

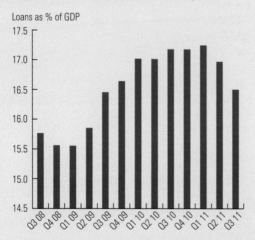

FIGURE B4.3.1   **PKO BP's Loan Share, 2008–11**

Loans as % of GDP

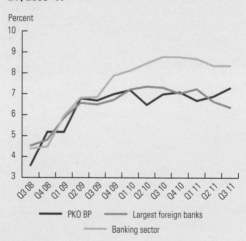

FIGURE B4.3.2   **Nonperforming Loans for PKO BP, 2008–11**

Percent

PKO BP   Largest foreign banks
Banking sector

Sources: PKO BP, Polish Financial Supervisory Authority, and publicly available data on large foreign banks.

as reflected by its high return on equity. However, these indicators are largely backward looking, and more time will be needed to assess the full impact of increased lending on loan quality.

Overall, PKO BP played a countercyclical role during the crisis, partly offsetting the decline in the available credit from foreign-owned bank subsidiar-ies. Its relative success in propping up credit may be tied to the fact that it is a commercially oriented bank, open to free-market competition, and with conservative lending and funding policies. Stock market–induced transparency, market discipline, formidable budget constraints, and professional management have also played a role.

Source: Piatkowski 2012.

BOX 4.4   Bank Ownership and Credit Growth during the 2008–09 Crisis: Evidence from Eastern Europe and Latin America

Using bank-level data from 2004 to 2009, Cull and Martínez Pería (2012) examined the impact of bank ownership on credit growth in developing economies before and during the crisis (table B4.4.1). They analyzed the growth of banks' overall loan portfolios, as well as changes in corporate, consumer, and residential mortgage loans. They compared the determinants of credit growth for banks in eight countries in Eastern Europe (Bulgaria, Croatia, the Czech Republic, Hungary, Poland, Romania, the Slovak Republic, and Slovenia) and six countries in Latin America (Argentina, Brazil, Chile, Colombia, Mexico, and Peru). They found that the decline of credit growth among foreign banks in Eastern Europe was larger than that of their domestic private counterparts during the crisis. In Latin America, foreign banks did not fuel loan growth prior to the crisis and did

not contract their credit flow at a faster pace than their domestic counterparts. On the other hand, the behavior of state-owned banks in Eastern Europe (in terms of credit growth) did not differ from that of private domestic banks. In general, state-owned banks in Eastern Europe did not mitigate the impact of the crisis on aggregate credit in the economy. The opposite is true in Latin America. Lending by state-owned banks grew during the crisis at a faster pace than domestic and foreign banks (figure B4.4.1).

Complementary evidence by de Haas and others (2012) from 1,294 banks for 30 Eastern European countries over the period 1999–2009 shows that foreign bank credit grew at a faster pace than domestic (public and private) banks before the crisis, and it sharply decelerated in 2008. On the other hand, credit extended by both state and private domestic

TABLE B4.4.1   **Determinants of the Growth of Total Gross Loans**

Variables	Latin America			Eastern Europe		
Foreign banks (Fgn)	−11.098***	−10.403***	−9.320***	2.651	3.83	4.04
	[−6.293]	[−6.014]	[−4.705]	[0.558]	[0.986]	[0.956]
Government banks (Govt)	−8.66	−8.576	−9.833	−1.338	0.174	1.207
	[−1.779]	[−1.694]	[−1.765]	[−0.248]	[0.030]	[0.203]
Crisis2008 (dummy)	−39.508**			−22.540**		
	[−3.102]			[−3.360]		
Crisis2009 (dummy)	−11.75			−19.179*		
	[−0.867]			[−2.063]		
Fgn × Crisis2008	11.431*	11.375*	8.793	2.499	1.909	1.83
	[2.267]	[2.091]	[1.450]	[0.574]	[0.384]	[0.377]
Fgn × Crisis2009	−7.336	−10.269	−10.006	−14.394**	−13.504*	−15.562**
	[−0.508]	[−0.754]	[−0.994]	[−3.048]	[−2.120]	[−2.648]
Govt × Crisis2008	27.569***	27.648***	27.926***	4.677	2.303	0.318
	[8.882]	[5.441]	[4.778]	[0.605]	[0.302]	[0.057]
Govt × Crisis2009	14.954	14.831*	20.421	−1.249	−3.244	−4.989
	[1.411]	[2.222]	[1.945]	[−0.153]	[−0.386]	[−0.599]
Constant	53.932***	48.121***	70.439***	47.285***	17.877**	20.015
	[13.125]	[11.527]	[15.072]	[7.362]	[2.372]	[1.606]
Country–time interactions	No	Yes	Yes	No	Yes	Yes
Bank characteristics	Yes	Yes	Yes	Yes	Yes	Yes
Bank characteristics interacted with crisis	No	No	Yes	No	No	Yes
Observations	878	878	878	770	770	770
R-squared	0.17	0.311	0.326	0.21	0.54	0.544
Number of countries	6	6	6	8	8	8

Source: Cull and Martínez Pería 2012.
Note: The dependent variabloe is the annual percentage in total gross loans. t-statistics are in brackets.
Significance level: * = 10 percent, ** = 5 percent, *** = 1 percent

---

BOX 4.4 **Bank Ownership and Credit Growth during the 2008–09 Crisis: Evidence from Eastern Europe and Latin America**   *(continued)*

---

banks declined in 2009. However, the behavior of state banks was less procyclical than that of (domestic and foreign) private banks. Hence, state-owned banks in some Eastern European countries may have partly mitigated the contraction of credit when private banks began to deleverage.

FIGURE B4.4.1 **Growth of Gross Loans and Bank Ownership in Latin America and Eastern Europe, 2004–2009**

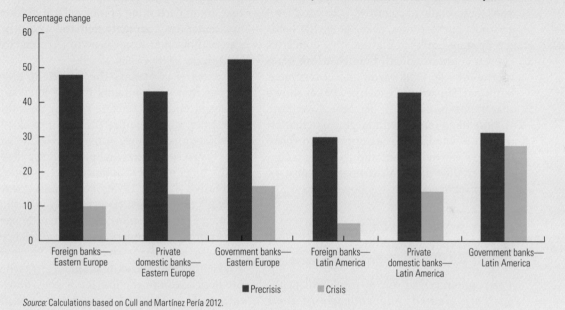

Source: Calculations based on Cull and Martínez Pería 2012.

---

private counterparts (box 4.4 and Cull and Martínez Pería 2012).

In sum, the experiences mentioned above regarding the role of state-owned banks during the recent crisis show that they played a countercyclical role in some instances but not others. Furthermore, although it is too early to assess the quality of intermediation based on information on NPLs, there is evidence, in some cases, of (a) difficulty unwinding the expanded portfolios of development banks; (b) politically motivated lending; and (c) negligible effects on revenues, investment, and employment for eligible firms.

The evidence is also mixed regarding the cyclicality of lending by government banks in previous crises and economic cycles. Using bank-level data for 119 countries over the 1995–2002 period, Micco and Panizza

(2006) find that state-owned bank lending is less procyclical than lending by private domestic banks. However, one important caveat is that their paper does not analyze the general equilibrium effect of the smoothing activity of state-owned banks. State-owned bank lending may merely crowd out lending from private banks; hence, the presence of state-owned banks would not affect aggregate lending during the business cycle. Comparing the lending behavior of Western European state-owned and private banks during 2000–09, Iannotta, Nocera, and Sironi (2011) find no difference in the behavior of both types of banks across the business cycle. Nonetheless, unlike private banks, loan growth of state-owned banks is significantly more sensitive to the election cycle, thus indicating the political role of the government as a bank's owner.

In a recent paper, Bertay, Demirgüç-Kunt, and Huizinga (2012) use an approach similar to Micco and Panizza (2006) and Iannotta, Nocera, and Sironi (2011), but unlike these studies they control for the endogeneity of GDP growth to credit growth by using the system-generalized method of moments estimation. Using a large worldwide sample of banks for the recent period from 1999 to 2010, they also show that state bank lending is less procyclical than lending by private banks, especially in countries with good governance. Furthermore, they show that lending by state banks in high-income countries is even countercyclical. Finally, using macrolevel data on bank credit and government bank participation, Calderón (2012) shows that cycles in real credit per capita are more volatile in countries with large participation of state-owned banks (as opposed to those with low participation) and that the recovery of credit—although stronger because of a larger rebound effect—is slower (box 4.5).

LONG-RUN IMPACT OF GOVERNMENT BANK OWNERSHIP

The countercyclical role of state banks cannot be evaluated independently of their long-term performance in credit allocation. In theory, economists hold different views about the merits of government bank ownership for long-run financial development and economic growth.[14] Box 4.6 summarizes competing views on the role of state-owned banks in promoting financial development and access.

Advocates of state presence argue that government ownership in banking is justified by market failures and development goals. They point out that financial markets are different from other markets and that government intervention can remedy market failures (such as the underprovision of information or the undersupply of capital in the case of projects that have externalities). The *development view,* associated with Alexander Gerschenkron (1962), argues that in countries where economic institutions are not developed,

capital is scarce, and public distrust is significant, government banks can play a significant role in jump-starting financial and economic development.[15] According to this view, governments have adequate information and incentives to promote socially desirable projects, and ownership of banks enables the government both to collect savings and to direct them toward strategic longer-term projects. Through such project finance, the government overcomes institutional failures that are undermining private capital markets and generates aggregate demand and other externalities that foster growth (Armendáriz de Aghion 1999; Bruck 1998).

In stark contrast, the *political view* argues that governments do not have sufficient incentives to ensure socially desirable investments and acquire control of banks to provide employment, subsidies, and other benefits to supporters, who return the favor in the form of votes, political contributions, and bribes (Kornai 1979; Shleifer and Vishny 1998).[16] In this view, government ownership politicizes resource allocation, softens budget constraints, and hinders economic efficiency.

The development and political views of government ownership make contrasting predictions about the impact of government ownership on financial development. According to the development view, government ownership should result in deeper, more efficient, inclusive, and stable credit markets. On the other hand, the political view predicts that government ownership of banks will result in inefficient, noninclusive, underdeveloped, and unstable credit markets. While the development view predicts that government ownership will enhance economic growth through its positive impact on financial sector development, the political view maintains that government ownership could be pernicious for the real economy because it leads to credit misallocation.

Theoretical arguments notwithstanding, the bulk of the empirical evidence suggests that government bank ownership in developing economies has had negative consequences for long-run financial and economic development. A large number of cross-country

BOX 4.5   Macroeconomic Evidence on the Impact of Government Banks on Credit and Output Cycles

Calderón (2012) studies the impact of government bank participation on credit and output cyclicality using a country-level quarterly database of 66 countries over 1980–2010. Aggregate credit cycles are deeper in financial systems of countries with high participation of government-owned banks (GOBs), especially during times of banking crises. In fact, credit contractions are almost twice as deep in countries with high GOB participation when compared with those with a low participation—14.3 versus 7.7 percent, respectively (table B4.5.1). Credit recoveries are faster and have a stronger rebound effect in countries with high GOB participation (8.4 percent) than those with low participation (5.1 percent).

During financial crises, credit contractions tend to be shorter but deeper in developing economies with high GOB share relative to those with low share. Calderón (2012) shows that credit dropped at an annualized rate of 6.4 percent per quarter over a

9-quarter period in countries with high GOB share, while it declined at 2.9 percent per quarter over an 11-quarter period in those with low GOB share. Credit recoveries following the banking crises were shorter: it took approximately 5 quarters for the trough in real credit to reach the previous peak in developing economies with high GOB share compared with the 9 quarters that it took a country with low GOB share. Also, credit recoveries after crises occurred at a slightly faster pace in high-GOB-share developing economies (3.2 percent per quarter).

When looking at upswings in real economic activity, credit appears to behave procyclically. Figure B4.5.1 shows that credit grows in tandem with real GDP as real economic activity starts its recovery (period T), and the recovery in real output and credit in countries with high GOB share appears to be stronger because of a larger rebound effect. However, credit growth is above trend after 10 quarters of

TABLE B4.5.1   Credit Cycles and Government Ownership of Banks

Region	GOB Share[a]	Main feature of credit contractions and recoveries								
		All episodes			Episodes coinciding with crisis			Episodes with no crisis		
		Duration	Amplitude	Slope	Duration	Amplitude	Slope	Duration	Amplitude	Slope
1. *Credit contractions*										
All economies	Low	6.7	−7.7%	−1.7%	9.3	−16.2%	−2.0%	6.4	−6.9%	−1.6%
	High	6.8	−14.3%	−2.3%	9.2	−37.4%	−5.3%	6.3	−11.8%	−2.1%
Developed economies	Low	6.7	−4.9%	−1.1%	18.0	−25.1%	−1.4%	6.4	−4.6%	−1.1%
	High	6.2	−6.7%	−1.6%	7.3	−6.7%	−1.7%	6.0	−6.6%	−1.3%
Developing economies	Low	7.0	−11.3%	−2.0%	11.1	−22.8%	−2.9%	6.6	−10.0%	−2.0%
	High	6.7	−15.4%	−2.8%	8.6	−45.0%	−6.4%	6.0	−13.6%	−2.5%
2. *Credit recoveries*										
All countries	Low	4.9	5.1%	1.2%	8.8	9.2%	1.3%	4.6	4.9%	1.2%
	High	4.5	8.4%	2.0%	5.8	9.4%	2.8%	4.3	8.0%	1.8%
Developed economies	Low	5.3	4.4%	0.9%	30.0	4.5%	0.8%	4.9	4.4%	0.9%
	High	4.6	4.4%	0.6%	6.6	1.8%	0.4%	4.3	4.8%	0.6%
Developing economies	Low	4.7	5.7%	1.5%	9.2	19.5%	2.9%	4.4	5.5%	1.5%
	High	4.5	9.6%	2.5%	4.9	9.6%	3.2%	4.4	9.3%	2.3%

Source: Calderón 2012.
Note: The duration of contractions is defined as the period (in quarters) between the peak in real credit per capita and its subsequent trough. Recoveries, on the other hand, are defined as the early stages of expansion. Duration of contractions elapses the time that the corresponding variable goes from its trough to the previous peak level. The table reports the average duration of the different cyclical phases (downturns and upturns) for real credit per capita. The statistics for amplitude and slope refer to sample median across episodes. The amplitude of the downturn is the distance between the peak in real output and its subsequent trough, and that of the upturn is computed as the four-quarter cumulative variation in real output following the trough. The slope of the downturn is the ratio of the peak-to-trough (trough-to-peak) phase of the cycle to its duration. These calculations were made using a quarterly database of 66 countries over the period 1980–2010 (21 developed economies and 45 developing economies).
a. The financial system of a country with high (low) participation of state-owned banks is defined as the system with an asset share of government-owned banks that is above the median sample.

(Continued on next page)

BOX 4.5 **Macroeconomic Evidence on the Impact of Government Banks on Credit and Output Cycles** *(continued)*

the start of the recovery in countries with low GOB share, while it is still converging to trend growth in high-GOB-share countries.[a]

In general, credit starts to recover in the period following the start of the upswing in real GDP—period T + 1—regardless of the magnitude of the shock that led the economy to a recession. Figure B4.5.2 shows that the dynamics of credit around real economic recoveries is similar among countries

with low GOB share when comparing crisis-related upturns with other upturns. It can be inferred from this finding that countries may not be equipped with government infrastructure or may find ways other than government banking to prop up financial conditions. For instance, they may choose to expand the balance sheet of their central bank. In countries with high GOB share, real credit per capita fluctuates more intensely in recoveries that follow crisis-related

FIGURE B4.5.1 **Evolution of Real GDP and Credit around Recoveries in Economic Activity**

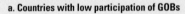

a. Countries with low participation of GOBs

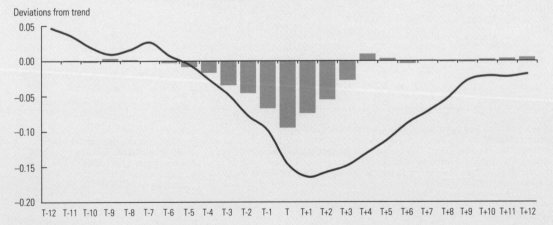

b. Countries with high participation of GOBs

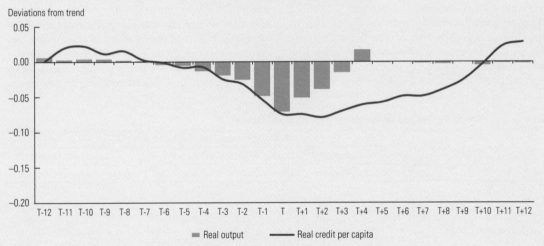

Source: Calderón 2012.
Note: T represents the trough in real GDP (start of the recovery period).

BOX 4.5   Macroeconomic Evidence on the Impact of Government Banks on Credit and Output Cycles *(continued)*

recessions when compared with regular upswings in economic activity. Following a crisis-related recession, credit takes more time to hit a trough and start

its own recovery. Also, the stronger surge in credit in countries with GOB share is related to a greater rebound effect from the crisis.

FIGURE B4.5.2   Evolution of Real GDP and Credit around Recoveries in Economic Activity

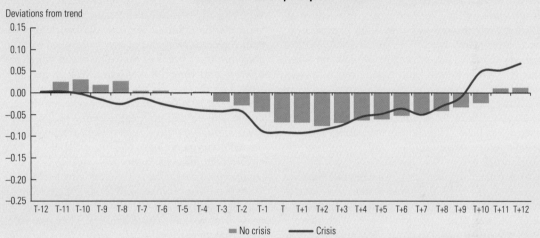

a. Countries with low participation of GOBs

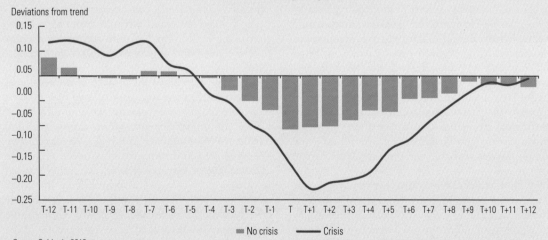

b. Countries with high participation of GOBs

Source: Calderón 2012.
Note: T represents the trough in real GDP (start of the recovery period), and the dating of the banking crisis corresponds to that of Laeven and Valencia (2010).

a. The analysis conducted in figure B4.5.1 and B4.5.2 follows Beck, Levine, and Levkov (2010). It consists of regressing the (year-on-year) growth in real credit on a 25-quarter window (12 quarters before and after the peak or trough in real GDP) centered on a dummy variable at time T that takes the value of 1 when there is a trough in real GDP at quarter T (that is, the starting period of a recovery). The remaining variables are leads and lags of the trough taking place at time T. These regressions also include dummy variables to control for other country-specific characteristics. The plot of the time evolution of credit along this window shows deviations of credit relative to the average credit growth in tranquil times.

BOX 4.6 Two Views on the Role of State-Owned Banks

In a recent debate published in the World Bank's *All About Finance* blog, two academics expressed contrasting views about the role of state-owned banks in promoting financial stability and access.

Franklin Allen, Nippon Life Professor of Finance and Economics, Wharton School, University of Pennsylvania, argues that, despite being outperformed by their private counterparts in terms of long-term resource allocation, "public banks may enjoy an advantage over private banks in times of crisis and, hence, their merits need to be reassessed." He goes on to say that "the real advantage would come when there is a crisis. Rather than having central banks intervene in commercial credit markets, where they have little expertise, the state-owned commercial bank can temporarily expand its role both in terms of assets and loans. This should considerably improve the functioning of the economy and overcome credit crunch problems."

"The financial system can be safeguarded during times of crisis through a *mixed* system with mostly private banks but one or two are state-owned commercial banks. They would compete with private banks in normal times to ensure a competitive cost structure and prevent corruption, and they would provide useful information to regulators by signaling excess risk-taking or exercise of monopoly power by private banks. However, their real advantage would become evident during a financial crisis. State-owned commercial banks would be a safe haven for retail and interbank deposits, act as a fire break in the process of contagion, and provide loans to businesses—particularly small and medium size enterprises—through the crisis. They could expand and take up the slack in the banking business left by private banks. Listing such banks will ensure full information on them is available and their stock prices will indicate how well they are performing."

"Public banks can play another important role in increasing access to financial services. If the government wishes it to pursue this agenda then it may be helpful to subsidize this kind of activity. In many European countries in the nineteenth and twentieth centuries, the post office provided access to savings accounts and other kinds of financial services that many customers would not otherwise have had. A good example of a public bank that plays these roles is Chile's Banco del Estado, which is entirely owned by the Chilean Government. It is the country's third largest lender and operates in all major segments of the banking market. The fact that it has to compete with private banks ensures it is well run. Banco del Estado also has a long history of promoting access in all parts of the country and to all people. Many other countries might benefit from this type of bank."

In contrast, Charles Calomiris, Henry Kaufman Professor of Financial Institutions at Columbia University, argues that academic work "indicates powerfully the negative effects of state-controlled banks on the banking systems of the countries in which they operate and that the winding down of state-controlled banks was rightly celebrated in many countries in the 1990s as creating new potential for economic growth and political reform." He goes on to say that there are three main reasons that explain the dismal performance of state-controlled banks. "First, government officials do not face incentives that are conducive to operating well-functioning banks. They are typically not incentivized to maximize economic effectiveness and they tend not to be trained in credit analysis as well as private bankers. They face incentives that reward politically rather than economically motivated allocations of credit. Second, the politically motivated allocation of funds to crony capitalists has adverse consequences for the political and social system of a region or country. State-controlled banks are a breeding ground for corruption of elected and appointed government officials, the financial regulatory authorities, and the courts. Not only do they stunt the growth of the economy, they also weaken the core political and bureaucratic institutions on which democracy and adherence to the rule of law depend. Third, state-controlled banks are *'loss-making machines.'* Because they are not geared toward profitability or the aggressive enforcement of loan repayment, but rather toward rewarding political cronies with funding, the losses of state-controlled banks pose a major fiscal cost for governments. Those fiscal costs crowd out desirable government initiatives, and given the large size of the losses, can be a threat to the solvency of government and a source of inflationary deficit financing."

"The crisis has only reconfirmed the extreme damage that politically motivated lending can inflict. The quasi-state-controlled U.S. entities Fannie Mae and Freddie Mac accounted for more than half of the

---

BOX 4.6   **Two Views on the Role of State-Owned Banks**   *(continued)*

---

funding of subprime and Alt-A mortgages leading up to the crisis. There is evidence that political motivations drove the intentional risk taking and deterioration of underwriting standards at those institutions after 2003—a crucial ingredient in the subprime boom of 2004–2007. Government quotas dramatically increased the funding that Fannie and Freddie had to supply to low-income and underserved borrowers, but the supply of creditworthy low-income and underserved borrowers was limited. Inevitably, lending standards were relaxed. The U.S. experience is not unique. Political motivations drove Spanish *cajas* to support a real-estate boom that ended in a massive bust. In Germany, state-controlled banks also made horrible investment decisions, thus reflecting incompetence more than corruption or political motives for channeling funds. Looking back historically, it is clear that state-controlled lending has been a major contributor to unwise and politically motivated risk taking that has ended badly over and over again."

Source: All About Finance (blog), World Bank.

"The huge crisis-related losses of equity capital in the banking system and the subsequent stepping up of regulatory oversight over banks have resulted in a short-term contraction in the supply of credit. This credit crunch magnified the decline of GDP during the recession, and slowed the pace of the recovery. In such an environment, it may seem appealing to pass a law creating a state-owned bank with the goal of re-starting the rapid flow of loanable funds. But such an initiative would be short-sighted. Rather than promoting sustainable growth, it would slow growth over the medium or long run, as funds would be channeled to low-productivity users. A move to support state-controlled banks would also raise systemic risk (as Fannie and Freddie, and the Spanish cajas clearly show), promote corruption of government officials and institutions, and lead to fiscal losses that could threaten the solvency of government and lead to high inflation."

---

studies show that greater government participation in bank ownership is associated with lower levels of financial development (Barth, Caprio, and Levine 2001, 2004; La Porta, López-de-Silanes, and Shleifer 2002), more politically motivated lending (Dinç 2005; Micco, Panizza, and Yañez 2007), lower banking-sector outreach (Beck, Demirgüç-Kunt, and Martínez Pería 2007), wider intermediation spreads and slower economic growth (La Porta, López-de-Silanes, and Shleifer 2002), and greater financial instability (Caprio and Martínez Pería 2002; La Porta, López-de-Silanes, and Shleifer 2002).[17] The evidence also suggests that state-owned commercial banks operating in developing economies have lower profitability than comparable private banks, as well as lower interest margins, higher overhead costs, and a higher fraction of nonperforming loans (Berger, Hasan, and Zhou 2009; Farazi, Feyen, and Rocha 2011; Iannotta, Nocera, and Sironi 2007; IDB 2005; Micco, Panizza,

and Yañez 2007).[18] State-owned banks also tend to display lower z-scores, thus showing greater instability than their private counterparts (Ianotta, Nocera, and Sironi 2007).

Interpreting cross-country evidence is difficult because of the potential for endogeneity biases resulting from reverse causation and omitted factors.[19] In other words, it is feasible that the negative association of government bank ownership with the different dimensions of financial development and with economic growth could arise from the need for more government intervention in countries with lower financial and economic development or from some omitted factor. Similarly, analyzing differences in the profitability of state-owned versus private banks does not necessarily provide conclusive evidence regarding their impact and performance. State-owned banks may exhibit lower profitability because they maximize broader social objectives, investing in financially unprofitable projects with positive externalities.

However, detailed within-country studies that are less susceptible to endogeneity concerns and are better able to identify the impact of government ownership provide evidence consistent with the bulk of the cross-country studies. For instance, Cole (2009a) analyzes the expansion of government bank ownership through nationalization in India and finds that, although areas with more nationalized banks showed a large increase in credit to rural borrowers, this increase did not result in improved agricultural outcomes. Moreover, his results suggest that government bank ownership was associated with a lower quality of financial intermediation and a misallocation of resources. Using detailed loan-level data from Pakistan, Khwaja and Mian (2005) find that politically connected firms were able to obtain larger and cheaper loans from state-owned banks (but not from private ones) and defaulted on these loans more frequently than nonconnected borrowers. They estimate that the economy-wide costs of the resulting misallocation of resources could be as high as 1.9 percent of GDP every year. Cole (2009b) also presents evidence of political manipulation of lending in India, with state-owned banks increasing agricultural lending substantially in tightly contested districts during election years.[20] The election-year increase in government lending is associated with higher default rates and does not have a measurable effect on agricultural output.

Carvalho (2010) provides support for the view that politicians use government bank lending to influence the real behavior of firms using plant-level data for the universe of Brazilian manufacturing firms with at least 50 employees. He shows that firms eligible for government bank lending expand employment in regions with allied incumbents near reelection years. The effects represent persistent and economically important increases in the local employment of firms and are associated with greater borrowing from government banks. However, they are not associated with persistent expansions of the overall employment and capital of firms. The analysis suggests that politicians use bank lending to target rents to voters by subsidizing multilocation firms to shift employment and capital toward politically attractive regions and away from nonattractive regions. Political manipulation of public bank lending does not seem to be restricted to developing economies, as shown by Sapienza (2004), who presents evidence that state-owned banks serve as a mechanism to provide political patronage in Italy.

Not only are state-owned banks more likely to be engaged in political lending, but they also do not serve firms that require more active participation of the state—that is, firms with deeper asymmetric information problems, such as SMEs. In a study of bank lending relationships in India, using firm-level and bank-level data during the late 1990s, Berger and others (2008) find that state-owned banks have tighter relations with state-owned enterprises than with SMEs. Similarly, Ongena and Sendeniz-Yuncu (2011) find that Turkish state banks fail to engage small opaque firms.

State-owned banks can also exist for populist reasons. Acharya (2011) demonstrates that the government can threaten the stability of the financial system with the formulation and implementation of financial policies that focus on short-term populist goals. So-called short-termist governments may extend guarantees, weaken capital requirements, provide direct lending, and encourage competition to generate greater entry into the financial sector and expand economic activity. Excess risk-taking arising from these policies may fuel credit booms and threaten the stability of the financial system down the line. The boom-bust cycle of U.S. housing prices in the run-up to the 2007–09 financial crisis is an illustration of this type of policies.[21]

Not all state-owned banks are alike, however. Depending on whether they aim for profit maximization, take deposits, or have a clear mandate, state-owned banks can be classified as state commercial banks, state development banks, and development financial institutions (Scott 2007). State-owned commercial banks are institutions that behave similarly to private commercial banks: they are deposit-taking institutions that may have a profit-maximizing objective. State development banks can take deposits and have a clear mandate, while development financial institutions are state-owned financial institutions that have a specific mandate and are not funded through deposits. State-owned development banks and financial institutions further distinguish between tier 1 and tier 2 institutions—those that lend directly to the public and those that lend to private banks that in turn lend to the public. A large part of the evidence on the impact of state-owned banks either focuses entirely on commercial banks or does not distinguish between commercial and development banks.

De Luna and Vicente (2012) have recently undertaken a global survey of development banks, which include state development banks and development financial institutions. They find large differences in the way these institutions are run and perform. The authors show that although there are some bright spots, in general, most development banks and institutions need institutional reform (box 4.7). The literature identifies a set of good practices to follow so that state-owned banks institutions are well-run (Gutiérrez and others 2011; Rudolph 2009; Scott 2007). To avoid the problems of credit misallocation discussed earlier, state-owned banks need a clear and sustainable mandate. To fulfill their mandate, state-owned banks should target strategic sectors and work as complements to rather than substitutes for private sector efforts to allocate resources. They also require adequate risk management systems to guarantee financially sustainable business and to obtain funding from markets without explicit guarantees from the government. Sound corporate governance plays a key role in explaining good performance of state-owned banks. It requires the transparent nomination of board members and the selection of senior management by the board. Drafting an ownership policy is recommended, with principles associated with sound commercial practices, good corporate governance, and competitive neutrality (Scott 2007). Unfortunately, getting these design

features right tends to be most challenging in weak institutional environments, where the potential benefits of these institutions are likely to be the greatest.

Few success stories can be found for the role of state-owned banks in promoting financial development when these institutions are engaged directly in the allocation and pricing of credit. However, some examples of targeted government interventions in the financial sector show positive results. Development banks in Mexico have played a positive role in the provision of more complex (noncredit) financial services despite heavy setup costs and uncertainty on financial returns. Partnership of state-owned financial intermediaries with their private counterparts has allowed them to overcome first-mover disincentives, coordination failures, and obstacles to risk sharing and distribution (Demirgüç-Kunt, Beck, and Honohan 2008). For instance, NAFIN (Nacional Financiera) developed an online platform called Cadenas Productivas to provide reverse factoring services to SMEs. This framework allows small suppliers to use their accounts receivable from large creditworthy firms to get working capital financing (Klapper 2006). BANSEFI (Banca de Ahorro Nacional y Servicios Financieros) implemented an electronic platform to help semiformal and informal financial institutions reduce their operating costs by providing centralized back-office operations (for example, clearinghouse services and liquidity management, among others). Finally, FIRA (Fideicomisos Instituidos en Relación con la Agricultura) has brokered structured financial products to align incentives and curtail adverse selection problems between financial intermediaries and firms in different parts of the supply chain of several industries. For example, FIRA has arranged collateralized loan obligations for shrimp producers and asset-backed securities for sugar mills (de la Torre, Gozzi, and Schmukler 2007).[22] These examples suggest that the government has a role, to be directly involved in the financial sector through short-run interventions that address specific market failures and that seek to complement private financial

BOX 4.7 Development Banks: What Do We Know? What Do We Need to Know?

The world economy has witnessed a revival of interest in development banks (DBs) in recent years. New DBs have been formed in low- and middle-income countries (for example, Bosnia and Herzegovina, India, Malawi, Mexico, Mongolia, Mozambique, Serbia, and Thailand) as well as in some high-income countries (for example, the U.K.'s Green Investment Bank). DBs, along with other state-owned financial institutions, account for one-quarter of banking assets in developing economies—and this share is even larger among Brazil, Russia, India, and China.

The renewed debate and interest in DBs has been fueled by their potential countercyclical role in times of crisis. Typically, DBs have fulfilled long-term development roles by filling market gaps in long-term credit and agriculture finance and by promoting access to finance for SMEs. More recently, in light of the global financial crisis, DBs are now being perceived by national authorities as an important part of the policy toolkit to mitigate contractions in aggregate credit during crises. In fact, the loan portfolio of DBs grew by 36 percent globally during the period 2007–09—that is, four times as fast as the growth in credit provided by private commercial banks. However, there is historical evidence that the benefits from DBs' intervention in credit markets may come with potentially large costs, if these institutions have unsound operating practices—that is, if they have neither appropriate risk management practices nor sound corporate governance.

A global survey conducted by De Luna-Martínez and Vicente (2012) aims at building new knowledge on activities, funding, business models, lending instruments, government arrangements, and challenges faced by development banks. The survey, which defines development banks as financial institutions with more than 30 percent of their shares owned by the state and with a public mandate, covers 90 DBs from 61 countries—with their combined assets and their loan portfolio as of December 2009 being approximately US$2 trillion and US$1.6 trillion, respectively.

The global survey suggests that the performance of most DBs still needs substantial improvement. Although one can identify some bright spots among development banks (for example, Mexico's NAFIN and Germany's Kreditanstalt fuer Wiederaufbau [KfW]), many DBs still are far from adopting best practices in governance and risk management. For instance, DBs remain vulnerable to undue political interference and capture by interest groups because about 75 percent of them do not have independent members on their boards. In addition, several DBs have not adopted criteria with regard to the minimum qualifications that their board members and senior management should meet. There is concern about the real financial situation of DBs—about one-quarter of the surveyed institutions are not supervised with the same accounting and prudential standards applicable to private commercial banks.

Financial performance of DBs is mixed. Although 15 percent of DBs report nonperforming loans exceeding 30 percent of their total loan portfolio, 78 percent of them admit the need to improve their risk management framework. Going forward, DBs' major challenges include the need to reduce their reliance on government budget transfers and to improve their own profitability: 59 percent of them indicate that self-sustainability is a major challenge. Success of DBs would also require major improvement in corporate governance and transparency, with one out of two institutions surveyed responding that they are still far from having best practices in these areas.

Successful stories of government bank ownership are not abundant. However, some DBs have proved more effective than others in achieving their goals while ensuring financial sustainability. The more effective DBs have defined a clear and sustainable mandate and have adopted better corporate governance practices. A clear mandate (including a target sector, positioning with regard to the private sector and other DBs, and financial sustainability objectives) helps to focus the activity of the DBs and avoids the tendency to engage DBs in business where the private sector has a comparative advantage. A clear mandate also complements the accountability of the board of directors and management and facilitates performance monitoring.

Good practices in DB governance call for clear definition of the roles of shareholders, the board of directors, and management, as well as a separation of their functions to avoid conflicts of interest. The shareholder representative should be clearly identified (for example, the minister of finance), provide broad policy guidelines, and appoint the board of directors, but it is advisable to avoid the presence of

---

BOX 4.7   Development Banks: What Do We Know? What Do We Need to Know? *(continued)*

---

ministers on the board of DBs. The board should be professional and independent. The board provides a strategic vision to ensure compliance with the policy objectives and establishes indicators to monitor performance. It should also ensure that the financial sustainability of the institution is preserved and should appoint and dismiss the chief executive officer. Finally, more effective DBs are supervised and regulated as any other bank by the financial supervisory authorities.

The survey found that innovative procedures have been put in place to help DBs operate effectively in various jurisdictions. For instance, some DBs are legally obliged to achieve a minimum return on capital, measured in terms of the inflation rate or the government's cost of borrowing. Moreover, certain DBs have been partially privatized, and the management has been transferred to the private sector under management contracts. Certain governments

have also adopted legislation that prevents them from bailing out DBs in case of failure. In other jurisdictions, DBs lend only through tier II operations and share with the private sector the risk of lending to underserved segments of the market. Some DBs are also governed by boards with only independent members. It is worth exploring all these innovations because they may be part of the solutions needed to strengthen the weak institutions covered in the survey, in particular those operating in difficult institutional environments.

Good practice recommendations are particularly difficult to apply in countries with weak institutional settings. Development banks could add most value in financially underdeveloped countries where there are significant market failures, but it is in those environments in particular that the design can go bad. That is why, in practice, many DBs tend to underperform.

Source: De Luna-Martínez and Vicente 2012.

---

intermediation, not replace it. Of course, once again the design and governance of such interventions are key factors.

GOVERNMENT INTERVENTION IN CREDIT MARKETS BEYOND BANK OWNERSHIP

Credit guarantee schemes are a popular intervention tool during crises. For example, during the 2007–08 crisis, many governments (for example, Canada, Chile, Finland, France, Germany, Greece, Japan, Korea, Malaysia, the Netherlands, the United Kingdom, and the United States) extended new and special schemes or refueled existing ones to alleviate the impact of the credit crunch on SMEs.[23] Credit guarantee schemes typically serve as risk transfer and risk diversification mechanisms. By replacing part or all the risk of the borrower with that of the issuer of the guarantee (depending on the coverage ratio), they tend to lower the lender's risk. They

can also diversify risk by guaranteeing loans across different sectors or geographic areas. Credit guarantee schemes are designed to enable lenders to learn about the creditworthiness of constrained borrowers without incurring the initial risks involved and to allow these borrowers to establish a repayment reputation and in time graduate to nonguarantee loans. Public guarantee schemes refer to those funded or managed with government resources.

Even before the crisis, credit guarantee schemes have become one of the most popular mechanisms of intervention to expand the use of financial services for credit-constrained firms, such as SMEs. According to Green (2003), there are over 2,000 such schemes in place in almost 100 countries. As discussed by Honohan (2010), credit guarantee schemes can emerge for three main reasons: to mitigate asymmetric information problems between lenders and borrowers that can result in credit rationing, as a means of spreading and diversifying risk, and to exploit regulatory arbitrage if the guarantor is not subject to the same regulatory requirement as the lender. None of these three reasons per se imply government involvement in guarantee schemes.

Government involvement in guarantee schemes can be primarily justified on the grounds of coordination failures among private parties.[24] *Coordination failure* among private parties and first mover disadvantage can prevent private providers from entering the market for credit guarantees or prevent lenders from pooling resources for such a scheme. As Green (2003) argues, because banks cannot exclude the free riding of other financial institutions, they have little incentive to produce information on constrained borrowers such as SMEs. A similar reluctance applies to developing lending technologies suitable for such borrowers. Anginer, de la Torre, and Ize (2011) argue that government guarantees may have an edge over private guarantees because the government is better at solving collective action frictions or coordinating failures among private parties—rather than solving agency frictions (such as informational asymmetries or adverse selection).

Political factors also justify the existence of public guarantee schemes (for example, Beck and others 2010). Theory shows that guarantee funds are more effective and less costly in expanding access than directed lending schemes (Arping, Lóránth, and Morrison 2010). Also, guarantee schemes might be easier to justify politically because they resemble market-friendly instruments, in which the lending decision typically stays with the lender, and because they imply small initial costs of funding (losses accumulate over time as defaults materialize).

Rigorous evaluations of the total costs and benefits of these schemes are rare. Guarantee schemes strive to attain financial and, ultimately, economic additionality. *Financial additionality* refers to greater provision of credit to credible clients for whom credit was previously rationed. *Economic additionality*, by comparison, refers to improvements in the income and quality of life of the borrowers and, in general, an increase in the amount of commercial and economic activity in the country, as measured in terms of employment and economic growth.

Measuring the benefits of credit guarantees through financial and economic additionality is far from easy, and most of the existing evidence examines the ability of credit guarantees to overcome problems in access to credit—that is, financial additionality. For instance, Riding, Madill, and Haines (2007) found that 75 percent of guarantees generated additional loans thanks to the implementation of a credit scoring methodology on loan applications to Canadian banks. In Chile, there is evidence that microenterprises are more likely to get a bank loan using the State-Owned Guarantee Fund for Small Entepreneurs, or FOGAPE (Larraín and Quiroz 2006), and credit guarantees have helped expand lending to insurance-intensive sectors (Cowan, Drexler, and Yañez 2009). There is also evidence of financial additionality among G-7 countries. For example, firms that participated in the Italian credit guarantee scheme during 1999–2004 benefited from an increase in credit and a reduction in borrowing costs (Zecchini and Ventura 2006). In Japan, SMEs using the Special Credit Guarantee Program for financial stability received more credit than nonusers (Uesugi, Sakai, and Yamashiro 2010; Wilcox and Yasuda 2008). Finally, guaranteed loans by the U.S. Small Business Administration were less affected by economic shocks than nonguaranteed loans—thus providing some evidence of countercyclicality of guarantee schemes (Hancock, Peek, and Wilcox 2007).

There is also some evidence—although rather scant—of economic additionality. For instance, the rate of employment was higher in U.S. districts that received more guaranteed lending (Craig, Jackson, and Thompson 2007). In addition, sales performance and productivity improved among firms financed by KOTEC, a Korean government guarantor that provides credit guarantees to new technology-based enterprises (Kang and Heshmati 2008; Roper 2009).

Credit guarantees can generate financial and economic benefits; however, because the programs are generally targeted to specific sectors, they are unlikely to have large macroeconomic effects. Also, they are not truly countercyclical tools since they do not tend to contract during periods of economic booms. At the same time, they can bring about sizable displacements and deadweight losses. For instance, there is evidence that a large and growing share of guarantees granted by FOGAPE have been allocated to the same firms (Benavente, Galetovic, and Sanhueza 2006). In addition, approximately half of the guaranteed loans in the Philippines went to borrowers with sufficient collateral, thus generating significant deadweight loss (Saldana 2000). In Pakistan, half of the subsidized credit for exporters went to financially unconstrained firms that did not need the funds, and the diversion in unneeded credit to beneficiary firms could have held GDP below its potential by 0.75 percent (Zia 2008).

There is also evidence of significant costs in credit guarantee schemes among developed nations. The massive credit guarantee program implemented by the government of Japan between 1998 and 2001 rendered only a temporary availability of funds for the intended program participants, and their ex post performance deteriorated relative to nonusers of the guarantee. Also, major banks often used the guarantee scheme to replace nonguarantee loans with guaranteed ones to minimize their exposure to risky assets (Uesugi, Sakai, and Yamashiro (2010). Another scheme set up by the Japanese government in October 2008, the Emergency Credit Guarantee Program, failed to translate a greater availability of funds into higher investment and employment among user firms and, in addition, deteriorated their creditworthiness (Ono, Uesugi, and Yasuda 2011).

The success of credit guarantees is tightly linked to the design of the scheme. The literature identifies and discusses a set of good practices that contribute to the successful implementation of a credit guarantee scheme (Beck and others 2010; Green 2003;

Honohan 2010). For instance, credit *risk assessment* practices should be outsourced to the private sector (rather than being conducted by the government) to improve the quality of risk decisions and to minimize loan losses. However, outsourcing risk management in the case of public guarantee schemes could potentially lead the lender to assign to the guarantee the worst eligible risks in the portfolio. This can be mitigated by penalizing lenders that have high claims and by imposing higher future premium payments. *Targeting* for the credit guarantee scheme should be broad (for example, specific sector and areas) if the focus remains on credit-constrained groups, whereas too-specific targeting may involve high bureaucratic costs that might distort lending decisions. The *coverage ratios* determined by the scheme should provide incentives for lenders to properly assess and monitor borrowers. Most practitioners argue that lenders should retain a significant part of the risk—for example, from 30 to 40 percent. However, in practice, 40 percent of the 76 credit guarantee schemes analyzed in Beck and others (2010) offer guarantees of up to 100 percent. The median coverage is 80 percent, which is certainly not in line with providing incentives for lenders to properly assess and monitor borrowers. Guarantee programs with coverage ratios between 90 and 100 percent have been shown to bring about large losses. For instance, the rural credit guarantee fund established by the Lithuanian government, which offered 100 percent coverage for loans aimed at financing the purchase of tractors and other agricultural equipment, brought about a large number of bad loans within three years of its starting date (Rute 2002).

Regarding the *pricing* of credit guarantees, the fees charged by the scheme should be high enough to ensure financial sustainability of the fund and low enough to secure adequate participation by lenders and borrowers. The *payout* of the guarantee should take place after the bank initiates legal action following default in order to reduce moral hazard on the side of the lender, who might be too quick to write off a loan after default.

However, there is a dearth of schemes that structure the payout so as to maximize incentives for lenders to minimize loan losses (Beck and others 2010). Finally, among *risk management* practices, guarantee schemes can reduce lenders' own ex post exposure to loan defaults through reinsurance, loan sales, or portfolio securitization. Risk diversification abilities are tied to the development of local capital markets and financial products. Beck and others (2010) find that 76 percent of guarantee schemes use risk management tools. This figure is encouraging since the authors also find that schemes that do not use risk management tools exhibit higher incidence of default losses.

Finally, recent research shows that 49 percent of the 76 credit-guaranteed schemes covered in Beck and others (2010) are funded by governments. The government has a much more limited role in management, risk assessment, and recovery: less than 20 percent of schemes are managed by governments, and credit risk assessment and recovery are conducted by governments in only approximately 10 percent of the schemes. Government-backed guarantee schemes with responsibilities in credit risk and recovery are typically older, are more prone to guarantee loan portfolios, pay out after the bank initiates recovery, and lack a risk management program. These results are consistent with the notion that guarantee schemes with greater government involvement are less likely to manage risk and losses. Consistent with these findings, Beck and others (2010) find that government involvement in credit decisions is associated with higher incidence of default losses.

Overall, although government-backed credit guarantee schemes might help jump-start lending to certain borrowers in certain sectors, these schemes are not likely to have large macroeconomic effects nor are they likely to work as truly countercyclical tools. Furthermore, they cannot substitute for reform of the underlying institutional requirements of an effective credit system and should not diminish the focus on these long-term reforms. For instance, improving collateral

laws and enforcement mechanisms is preferable to government interventions in addressing inadequacies of the legal framework associated with the credit system (Holden 1997; Vogel and Adams 1997). Although rigorous impact evaluations of their costs and benefits are still scarce, their performance hinges on good design, which is more challenging to get right in weak institutional environments. Best-practice lessons suggest that the most successful credit guarantee schemes are those that move to broad eligibility and other criteria, reduce subsidies, and make greater use of the portfolio and wholesaling approach in preference to case-by-case evaluation by the guarantor of retail loans.

Finally, deploying credit through state-owned banks and extending credit guarantees were not the only means used by governments to prop up financial conditions during the recent crisis.[25] Some countries implemented alternative strategies to offset the credit crunch using their central banks. In addition to traditional policies such as interest rate cuts to support aggregate demand, developed economies tried to revive the ailing financial markets by implementing unconventional monetary policies that led to the expansion and change in the composition of their central bank's balance sheets. The wide array of measures implemented include the U.S. Federal Reserve Board's purchase of long-term Treasury bills, the European Central Bank's purchase of covered bonds, relaxation of the collateral framework to access the discount window, changes in funding terms or auction schedules, support of money markets, and foreign currency swaps.[26]

Using the central bank as a countercyclical tool in times of crisis has its advantages. This type of intervention not only has smaller implementation lags but also is easier to unwind. Generating mechanisms to retrench lending activity by state-owned banks is more cumbersome, especially during the expansion that follows a crisis. However, legal constraints and credibility issues due to high inflation episodes may make it difficult for emerging markets to use a more unconventional approach to central banking and credit stabilization. Also, emerging market economies do not have an international reserve currency, so quantitative easing measures may jeopardize the stability and value of their currencies. Finally, the monetary authority in emerging markets can actively participate by setting up open bank assistance lines to the financial sector. However, as in the case of bank ownership, this approach also requires strong corporate governance so as to avoid political interference.

A comprehensive examination of the conduct of monetary policy, conventional or unconventional, during times of financial stress is beyond the scope of this report. A more detailed account of the response of the monetary authority during the recent crisis can be found in Aït-Sahalia and others (2010); Brave and Gesnay (2011); Giannone and others (2011); and Lenza, Pill, and Reichlin (2010).[27]

CONCLUSION

Governments actively responded to restore credit conditions during the recent global financial crisis. Emerging markets used their state-owned banks mainly to inject liquidity in their financial markets, while many developed economies effectively used their central bank to prop up the financial sector. Credit guarantees were also actively used to foster credit in some underserved segments of the economy.

Having state-owned banks may have facilitated the flow of credit in some countries during the recent global financial crisis. It helped stabilize aggregate credit in some emerging markets and restored credit conditions. State-owned banks partially compensated for the slowdown (and, in some cases, decline) in credit provided by (domestic and foreign) private banks. However, the evidence on the short-term benefits of government bank lending is far from conclusive. Some macrolevel evidence, including the recent as well as previous crises, shows that credit fluctuations are more volatile in countries with high participation of state-owned banks (as opposed to those with low participation) and

that the recovery of credit—although stronger because of a larger rebound effect—is slower. Microlevel evidence for the Latin America and the Caribbean and Central and Eastern Europe regions suggests that state-owned banks were not universally responsible for propping up credit during the recent crisis. Banks in Latin America and the Caribbean seem primarily to have played a countercyclical role.

Furthermore, the benefits of this short-term credit stabilization may come at a cost. From experience, the associated costs of the intervention are likely to be steep, with agency and political economy problems leading to credit misallocation and economic inefficiency. Lending and investment decisions by state-owned banks (typically motivated by political connections or allegiances) lead to a deterioration of the quality of loans and, hence, to a greater misallocation of resources. So far, the financial and economic costs of recent state interventions are difficult to ascertain since the overall effects are still unfolding. Hence, the potential benefits and costs require careful consideration by policy makers. The track record of state banks in credit allocation remains generally unimpressive, questioning the wisdom of using state banks as a countercyclical tool.

Ideally, the performance of state-owned banks can be improved by adopting a set of good practices in their institutional design. A clear and sustainable mandate is needed so that state-owned banks complement rather than substitute private efforts in the credit markets. An adequate risk management system is required to guarantee the financial sustainability of the institution. Finally, sound corporate governance—and, more specifically, the elaboration of an *ownership* policy—is also a key factor for the optimal function of these banks. Unfortunately, these design features are challenging to implement in weak institutional environments, precisely where state-owned banks can make the greatest contributions—but often fail to do so because of these design weaknesses.

Governments also devised strategies to prop up the financial sector that did not directly involve the use of state-owned banks. Both developing and developed countries actively used credit guarantees during the crisis to enhance credit to the sectors of the economy underserved by private financial intermediaries (for example, small and medium enterprises). Analogous to interventions through state-owned banks, credit guarantees may generate some short-term benefits, but they often come with fiscal and economic costs in the form of contingent government liabilities and misallocation of resources. The success of guarantee schemes hinges on their design features. Best practices include (a) leaving credit assessments and decision making to the private sector, (b) capping coverage ratios and delaying the payout of the guarantee until recovery actions are taken by the lender so as to minimize moral hazard problems, (c) pricing guarantees to take into account the need for financial sustainability and risk minimization, and (d) encouraging the use of risk management tools. However, as in the case of state banks, these best-practice design features are more challenging to get right in weak institutional environments.

Finally, the monetary authority in advanced countries provided unprecedented amounts of liquidity to the financial sector by expanding their balance sheets. Although easier to unwind than the expansion of the balance sheets of government banks, the method's successful implementation among emerging countries may be difficult because of legal obstacles and policy credibility issues.

NOTES

1. State-owned banks can also be deployed for populist reasons (Acharya 2011).
2. During the crisis, Germany's KfW introduced a "special countercyclical program" that provided lines of credit and loan guarantees to banks to keep credit to the economy flowing. For more details on the actions undertaken by governments in the financial markets, see Laeven and Valencia (2010, 2011), Rudolph (2010), among others.
3. For a more detailed look at the policy responses of advanced countries in terms of unconventional monetary and fiscal policies, see Aït-Sahalia and others (2010), Claessens and others (2011), and Lenza, Pill, and Reichlin (2010).
4. The main focus of this chapter is on direct interventions using state-owned banks rather than direct interventions in nonbank financial institutions (NBFIs) and markets. The choice to focus primarily on state-owned banks is driven by the wider evidence among developing economies and the greater availability of data on banking rather than on nonbanking institutions.
5. Laeven and Valencia (2010) document the increase in public debt and direct fiscal costs arising from the recent global financial crisis.
6. Financial additionality refers to whether the guarantee allows previous nonborrowers to access credit. Economic additionality refers to the real effects from a larger number of borrowers having access to credit as a result of guarantees (for example, more jobs created, firms being able to invest more).
7. Bonin, Hasan, and Wachtel (2005) provide a detailed examination of the trends and consequences of bank privatization in transition economies—namely, Bulgaria, Croatia, the Czech Republic, Hungary, Poland, and Romania).
8. The flagship report points out that the penetration of foreign banking in Africa witnessed another development over the past 15 years: a marked increase in the share of African banks among foreign banks, especially the expansion throughout the region of South African banks (for example, Absa and Standard Bank), West African banks (Bank of Africa and Ecobank), as well as Moroccan and Nigerian banks (Beck, Maimbo, and others 2011).
9. Clarke, Cull, and Megginson (2005) provide extensive evidence on the trends, determinants, and consequences of bank privatization both at the cross-country level and in country case studies.
10. Farazi, Feyen, and Rocha (2011) point out that there is a great deal of heterogeneity in terms of government ownership in the Europe and Central Asia region.
11. Recent evidence suggests that much of the decline in new lending reflects changes in the supply as opposed to the demand for credit (Huang and Stephens 2011; Ivashina and Scharfstein 2010).

12. Biggs, Mayer, and Pick (2010) argue that recoveries in the real sector typically come along with a recovery in the flow of credit. The authors build a model in which an upturn in real GDP coincide with a recovery in the flow of credit even as the stock of credit decreases. Data from developed economies and emerging market economies confirm that premise of their model.

13. Tier 2 credit operations refer to lending by state-owned banks through other private financial institutions to reach agents in the economy.

14. De la Torre, Gozzi, and Schmukler (2007) provide a good summary of the different views on the role of the state in the financial sector.

15. The development view is also referred to as "the interventionist view" (de la Torre, Gozzi, and Schmukler 2007).

16. The political view is included in what de la Torre, Gozzi, and Schmukler (2007) refer to as "the laissez faire" view.

17. IDB (2005) reviews the empirical evidence on the impact of government-owned banks and finds that, although the result that these banks have a negative impact is not as strong as previously thought, there is no indication that government ownership has a positive effect. It concludes that public banks, at best, do not play much of a role in financial development. Andrianova, Demetriades, and Shortland (2010) and Körner and Schnabel (2010) conducted cross-country analyses of the effects of government bank ownership on financial development and macroeconomic outcomes, which conclude that government bank ownership might not be as harmful to development as suggested by earlier studies. However, these studies cannot convincingly dispel concerns about omitted variables and reverse causality biases.

18. In contrast with the observed lower profitability and efficiency of government-owned commercial banks in developing economies, the empirical evidence suggests that in developed countries there are no significant differences in performance between public and private banks (see, for example, Altunbas, Evans, and Molyneux 2001; Micco, Panizza, and Yañez 2007).

19. For example, Levy Yeyati, Micco, and Panizza (2007) try to deal with the endogeneity problem by using panel data and by conducting GMM System estimations and find no impact of government bank ownership on private credit growth. Galindo and Micco (2004) try to address the problem of causality by analyzing within-country differences in industry growth. They find that the development of private financial intermediaries is associated with a higher growth rate of industries that rely more on external finance and have less collateral, while public bank ownership has no effect on the growth of these industries.

20. Dinç (2005) shows that increased lending by government-owned banks during election years is not specific to India but is also observed in a sample of 19 emerging markets (but not in developed economies). Micco, Panizza, and Yañez (2007) show that these results hold for a much larger sample of developing economies and that the increased lending by government-owned banks during election years is associated with a decrease in their interest rate margins and profitability.

21. Acharya (2011) shows that government policies in the housing market that enhanced the ability of the government-sponsored enterprises Fannie Mae and Freddie Mac to take riskier mortgages led to the deterioration of the quality of their assets and a competitive "race to the bottom" among financial intermediaries.

22. De la Torre, Gozzi, and Schmukler (2007) provide an extensive description of the different advances in the provision of noncredit services by Mexican state development banks. Other well-established state-owned banks include Japan Development Bank, Kreditanstalt fuer Wiederaufbau (KfW) in Germany, Kommunalbank in Norway, as well the multilateral development banks, all of which have remained profitable for decades.

23. Podpiera (2011) also documents the use of credit subsidies as a countercyclical crisis measure in Serbia.

24. This is what Anginer, de la Torre, and Ize (2011) call collective action frictions. Furthermore, they argue that in a world devoid of risk aversion and collective action frictions, agency frictions (such as informational asymmetries or adverse selection) cannot justify government guarantees. They argue that only partial equilibrium models that ignore the welfare effects of the taxes needed to finance the guarantees come to the flawed conclusion that guarantees are not justified by agency frictions.

25. It should be noted that though many countries did not have a significant presence of state-owned banks before the crisis, measures taken during the crisis, such as massive bailouts and nationalizations, amounted to the socialization of risks and losses that might also bring negative consequences to the economy down the line.

26. For instance, the Federal Reserve Board of the United States aggressively expanded its balance sheet in two different stages. First, it tried to contain the stress in financial markets by providing loans to financial institutions and injecting liquidity in key markets. Second, it launched a massive asset purchase program.

27. Countercyclical fiscal policy can complement the actions from the central bank and state-owned banks by containing the response of aggregate expenditure to changing financial conditions. However, discretionary countercyclical deployment of fiscal policy often faces considerable delays, which limit its ability to counteract a sudden crash in a timely manner. This limitation underscores the need to build up self-deploying automatic stabilizers, which are still weak in most developing economies, including Latin America (Claessens and others 2010; Debrun and Kapoor 2010).

5

The Role of the State in Financial Infrastructure

- *The global financial crisis has highlighted the importance of a resilient financial infrastructure and reignited the debate on what role the state should play in its development, particularly in (a) promoting the availability and exchange of reliable credit information and (b) supporting the development of institutions to better manage counterparty risk in interbank markets and securities transactions.*

- *Transparent credit information is a prerequisite for sound risk management and financial stability. However, due to the prevalence of monopoly rents in the market for credit information, information sharing among private lenders may not arise naturally. This creates an important rationale for the involvement of the state.*

- *Existing credit reporting systems contain extensive information on credit risks in the financial sector. There is significant potential for improving their use for risk management and prudential supervision.*

- *Many credit reporting systems cover only risks in the traditional financial sector. This limits their effectiveness in supporting credit market efficiency and stability. An important role of the state is to help extend the coverage of credit reporting systems to include nonregulated lenders, such as nonbank financial institutions and microfinance lenders, in existing credit reporting systems.*

- *The state can help establish market infrastructure that helps to manage and mitigate counterparty risk. This includes robust large-value payment systems and, potentially, support for the development of collateralized interbank markets.*

- *There is significant scope for state involvement in the development of a robust infrastructure for securities and derivatives settlements. The state can further reduce counterparty and settlement risks by monitoring these transactions and their clearing and settlement arrangements.*

The global financial crisis has highlighted the importance of a resilient financial infrastructure and reignited the debate on what role central banks and other state agencies should play in its development. *Financial infrastructure*, as defined in this report, consists of credit reporting institutions (credit registries and bureaus), payment and settlement systems, and the legal framework that governs financial transactions.[1] A well-developed financial infrastructure makes credit markets more efficient by reducing information asymmetries and legal uncertainties that may hamper the supply of new credit. This improves the *depth* of credit market transactions and broadens access to finance. The global financial crisis has also renewed interest in the role of financial infrastructure in supporting systemic *stability*. Financial infrastructure promotes financial stability in several ways. Transparent credit reporting can support the internal risk management of financial institutions and supply financial regulators with timely information on the risk profile of systemically important financial institutions. Similarly, well-designed payment and security settlement systems enhance financial stability by reducing counterparty risk in interbank markets and complex securities and derivatives transactions.

The role of the state in financial infrastructure has varied over time and across countries. This chapter examines how state agencies and central banks can operate, regulate, and oversee financial infrastructure. The focus is on two areas: first, the state's role in developing and using credit information systems, and second, the state's role in improving payment and securities settlement systems. The chapter does not examine, for example, retail payment systems or the legal framework that governs financial transactions. Reflecting the report's focus on the financial crisis, these areas will be explored in future editions.

The first part of the chapter focuses on the role of the state in credit reporting. It reviews the evidence on credit information and financial stability and the public good nature of information sharing. The chapter highlights the important role of the state in establishing a legal and regulatory framework that allows open and transparent credit reporting to emerge. The chapter emphasizes the challenges posed by market segmentation and the prevalence of monopolies in the market for credit information, which may provide a rationale for the measured involvement of the state. The chapter then turns to the lessons of the financial crisis for credit reporting and discusses how existing credit information systems can be used as a tool for prudential oversight and regulation.

The second part of the chapter discusses the role of the state in ensuring the stability of payment and securities settlement systems. The chapter argues that large-value payment systems around the world have demonstrated remarkable stability during the global financial crisis, thanks in large part to the widespread adoption of modern real-time settlement systems over the past two decades. The crisis nonetheless revealed several areas for policy improvements. In particular, the chapter argues that the state can further reduce counterparty risk by supporting the development of collateralized interbank markets and derivatives settlement systems, particularly in countries where the development of a modern settlement infrastructure has lagged the rapid growth of equity and securities markets.

CREDIT REPORTING

Introduction

Transparent credit information is a prerequisite for sound risk management and financial stability. Credit reporting institutions support financial stability and credit market efficiency and stability in two important ways. First, banks and nonbank financial institutions (NBFIs) draw on credit reporting systems to screen borrowers and monitor the risk profile of existing loan portfolios. Second, regulators rely on credit information to understand the interconnected credit risks faced by systemically important borrowers and financial institutions and to conduct essential oversight functions. Such efforts reduce default risk and improve the efficiency of financial intermediation. In a competitive credit market, these efforts ultimately benefit consumers through lower interest rates.

Effective credit reporting systems can mitigate a number of market failures that are common in financial markets around the world, and most severely apparent in less developed economies. The availability of high-quality credit information, for example, reduces problems of adverse selection and asymmetric information between borrowers and lenders (Stiglitz and Weiss 1981; Jappelli and Pagano 2002; Pagano and Jappelli 1993). This reduces default risk and improves the allocation of new credit. Information sharing can also promote a responsible "credit culture" by discouraging excessive debt and rewarding responsible borrowing and repayment (de Janvry, McIntosh, and Sadoulet 2010; Padilla and Pagano 2000).[2]

Perhaps most important, credit reporting allows borrowers to build a credit history and to use this "reputational collateral" to access formal credit outside established lending relationships. This is especially beneficial for small enterprises and new borrowers with limited access to physical collateral (Djankov, McLiesh, and Shleifer 2007; Love and Mylenko 2003; see also Padilla and Pagano 2000). Stylized evidence from the recent financial crisis also suggests that positive credit information helped to safeguard the financial access of creditworthy borrowers that would have otherwise been cut off from institutional credit (Simovic, Vaskovic, and Poznanovic 2009). This finding is consistent with evidence from the literature on relationship banking (Berger and others 2003; Petersen and Rajan 1995), which emphasizes how access to more detailed client information can facilitate profitable lending to informationally opaque borrowers, such as start-ups and small enterprises (Mian 2006).[3]

The World Bank Group has supported the development of credit reporting systems around the world for more than a decade. The International Finance Corporation's *Credit Bureau Knowledge Guide* (IFC 2006) provides an overview of experiences in developing the capabilities of private credit reporting institutions through public private partnerships and institutional innovation. The World Bank's *General Principles for Credit Reporting* (2011a) reviews best practices and makes policy recommendations for developing credit reporting systems.

Credit information as a public good

The open and transparent exchange of credit information has several characteristics of a public good that benefits both borrowers and lenders. However, because lenders can use the information advantage over their existing clients to extract monopoly rents, credit information sharing does not always arise naturally. The state therefore plays an important role in promoting the exchange of credit information and in protecting open and equal access to the market for credit information.

There are at least three areas in which a well-functioning credit reporting infrastructure performs the role of a public good. First, credit reporting benefits banks and nonbank lenders by mitigating problems of moral hazard and adverse selection. Detailed information on the credit history of individual borrowers allows banks to improve the ex ante screening of prospective clients as well as the ex post monitoring of credit risks in their existing loan portfolios. This, in turn, reduces the cost of financial intermediation and allows banks to price, target, and monitor loans more effectively.

Second, credit reporting supports financial stability by making it easier for financial regulators to assess and monitor systemic risks. Although traditional approaches to financial oversight have focused on risks at the level of individual financial institutions, a key advantage of comprehensive credit information systems is that they allow regulators to monitor the interconnected risks of systemically important financial institutions.

While the recent financial crisis has underscored this important function of credit reporting, it has also revealed a number of limitations of current credit information systems. In many countries, regulators have access to credit information only from regulated financial institutions but lack access to similarly comprehensive data on nonregulated lenders. Extending the reach of credit information systems to nonregulated lenders to better capture systemic risks outside the traditional banking sector is an important policy prescription that has emerged from the recent financial crisis. At the same time, the unfolding of the financial crisis in the United States and around the globe has shown that the availability of high-quality credit information is a necessary but not a sufficient condition to promote financial stability: even where a well-developed information infrastructure exists, it needs to be accompanied by regulatory incentives that reward the appropriate use of available information in the evaluation and management of credit risk.

Third, open and transparent credit reporting benefits bank customers by promoting credit market competition. The exchange of credit information enables customers to build reputational collateral and to access credit outside established lending relationships. This reduces the ability of established lenders to exploit their privileged knowledge of clients' credit histories. Because open access to credit information erodes the information monopoly of individual lenders, banks are often reluctant to share such information—especially positive information that may empower borrowers with good credit histories to seek credit elsewhere. Similarly, where credit reporting institutions exist, larger financial institutions often have an incentive to prevent equitable access to credit information through anticompetitive pricing or the formation of closed user groups, despite the positive efficiency implications that improved access to credit information would have on the financial system as a whole.

Taken together, the positive implications of credit reporting for financial stability and credit market efficiency create an important rationale for an active role of the state in promoting the development of an effective credit reporting infrastructure.

Public and private credit reporting around the world

The role of the state in credit reporting has varied widely across countries and over time. Two main types of credit reporting institutions can be found around the world: (a) credit registries, which are public entities that are managed by bank supervisors or central banks and typically collect information from supervised financial institutions, and (b) credit bureaus, which are privately owned enterprises that tend to cover smaller loans, often collect credit information from bank and nonbank lenders, and provide a range of value-added services, such as credit scores, to banks and nonbank lenders.

Historically, public and private credit reporting institutions have evolved to serve different purposes. Credit registries generally developed to support the state's role as a supervisor of financial institutions. Where credit registries exist, loans above a certain amount must, by law, be registered in the national credit registry. In some cases, credit registries have relatively high thresholds for loans that are included in their databases. Credit registries tend to monitor loans made by regulated financial institutions and usually do not offer value-added services, such as credit scores or collection services. Against the backdrop of the financial crisis, many countries have made efforts to optimize the use of credit registry data for prudential oversight and regulation.

Credit bureaus, by contrast, are privately owned commercial enterprises catering to the information requirements of commercial lenders. Though there is variation in the type and extent of information they collect, credit bureaus generally strive to collect very detailed data on individual clients. They therefore tend to cover smaller loans than registries and often collect information from a wide variety of financial and nonfinancial entities, including retailers, credit card companies, and microfinance institutions. As a result, data collected by credit bureaus are often more comprehensive and better geared to assess and monitor the creditworthiness of individual clients. Compared to credit registries, private credit bureaus are a relatively recent institution. Although credit bureaus have existed in Germany, Sweden, and the United States for nearly a century, they emerged in many other high-income countries, including France, Italy, and Spain, as recently as the 1990s.[4]

To provide an overview of the state of public and private credit reporting around the world, this section presents data on the ownership structure and extent of information collected by credit bureaus and registries. Map 5.1 shows the prevalence of credit reporting institutions around the world. The maps and summary statistics in table 5.1

MAP 5.1   Credit Information Systems around the World

a. Global distribution of credit registries

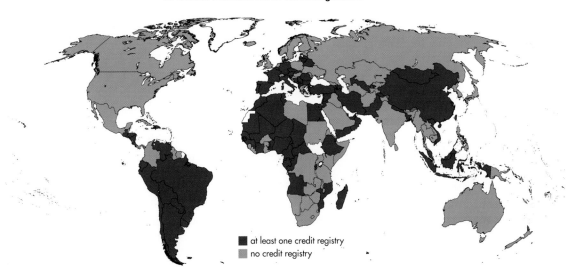

b. Global distribution of credit bureaus

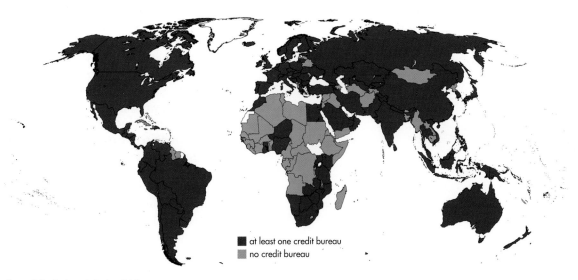

Source: Doing Business Indicators database.

TABLE 5.1   Credit Reporting, Coverage by Region

Region	Credit registry coverage		Credit bureau coverage	
	% of population	% of GDP	% of population	% of GDP
East Asia and Pacific	8.2	60.5	17.3	20.2
Eastern Europe and Central Asia	13.1	38.9	21.3	35.8
Latin America and the Caribbean	10.1	19.5	31.5	18.1
Middle East and North Africa	5.3	53.2	7.0	13.2
OECD	8.0	157.1	61.1	36.6
South Asia	0.8	46.2	3.8	108.4
Sub-Saharan Africa	2.7	16.6	4.9	7.9

Source: Calculations based on Doing Business Indicators database.
Note: GDP = gross domestic product.

show that there is some striking geographic variation in the existence of public and private credit reporting institutions. Overall, credit registries are more prevalent in countries with a French legal tradition, whereas private credit reporting is more widespread in countries of British legal origin. In a number of countries—primarily in Latin America—private and public credit reporting systems coexist, often catering to distinct segments of the credit market.

Figure 5.1 looks at the evolution of credit reporting institutions over time. As late as the early 1980s, few countries had a significant

credit information infrastructure in place. The first credit registries emerged in the United States in the 1830s in response to recurring episodes of defaults and financial instability, but credit reporting institutions did not arise in many other countries until much later. Especially in countries with a European common law tradition, legal barriers to disclosing credit information have often constrained the development of private credit reporting (Djankov, McLiesh, and Shleifer 2007; Olegario 2003). Despite these obstacles, which persist in many countries, credit information has expanded rapidly. The number of credit markets covered by either private or public credit reporting systems (or both) almost tripled over the past two decades.

The effectiveness of a credit reporting system is determined by the quality and depth of information it makes available to market participants. To assess the quality of information sharing, this report focuses on three important characteristics of a country's credit reporting system: (a) the coverage of the credit reporting system, measured by the number of borrowers or the volume of credit listed in the credit reporting system (see summary figures in table 5.1 and figure 5.2); (b) the extent of institutional participation (that is, which types of financial and nonfinancial institutions exchange information through the credit reporting system); and (c) the depth of credit information (that is, what kind of information on borrowers and credit risk is tracked).

FIGURE 5.1   The Development of Credit Reporting Institutions, 1980–2012

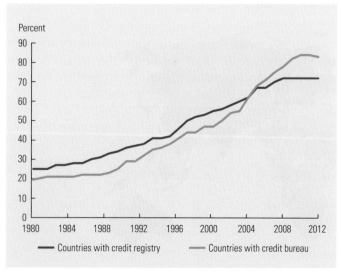

Source: Calculations based on Doing Business Indicators database.

FIGURE 5.2 **Prevalence of Credit Reporting by Income Group**

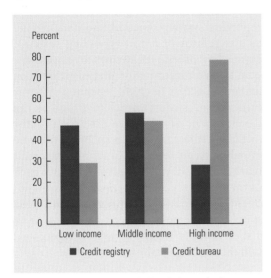

Source: Calculations based on Doing Business Indicators database.

Figure 5.3 presents evidence on the reach of credit reporting institutions by summarizing which types of financial institutions participate in the exchange of credit information. The figure shows that credit registries are less likely than credit bureaus to contain data from nonregulated financial institutions. Nearly all credit registries collect information from banks, whereas only 67 percent of registries contain information from any unregulated lender. Credit bureaus are more likely to cover NBFIs such as leasing and retail finance companies and microfinance lenders—and may therefore be better suited to promote financial access of new borrowers.

Turning to the *quality* and *depth* of available credit information, figure 5.4 compares the type of credit information collected by credit registries and credit bureaus, respectively. To do so, the figure presents four information indexes based on the Doing Business data. For each credit reporting institution, the data set provides information on the different types of information collected and reported by the credit registry or bureau. Examples of information items include customer age, total liabilities, or data on previous defaults or late

payments. Each information item can be classified as personal information, loan information, or information on a client's repayment history. Each index sums the range of information items contained in the credit registry or bureau and normalizes the resulting score so that the summary index lies between 0 (poor information content) and 1 (high information content).

Figure 5.4 reveals some striking differences in the *type* of information collected by credit bureaus and credit registries. On average, credit registries and credit bureaus collect approximately the same extent of information on the personal or identifying information of borrowers. In line with their historical role as a supporter of the state's supervisory function, registries tend to record more-detailed information about the type, terms, and structure of individual loans. The information collected by credit bureaus, on the other hand, is much more geared toward tracking the repayment history of individual borrowers in order to provide commercially viable data to market participants.

FIGURE 5.3 **The Reach of Credit Reporting: Who Contributes Information?**

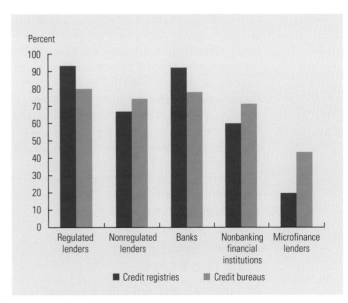

Source: Calculations based on Doing Business Indicators database.

FIGURE 5.4   **The Depth of Credit Reporting: What Information Is Collected?**

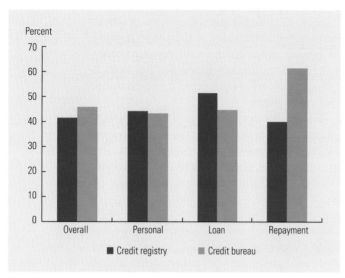

Source: Calculations based on Doing Business Indicators database.

Despite the growth of credit reporting institutions, their development has been highly uneven across and within regions. In many emerging credit markets, the development of credit reporting systems remains constrained by the lack of an appropriate legal infrastructure needed for the voluntary exchange of credit information. In many countries, privacy laws have no provision for credit reporting or, in some cases, prohibit the disclosure of vital information to third parties altogether. Finally, as the chapter discusses in greater detail in the following sections, the structure of competition in the banking sector can pose a significant obstacle to the emergence of comprehensive credit reporting systems. This creates an important role for the state in establishing an appropriate legal framework in which transparent credit reporting can evolve.

CREDIT REPORTING AND THE STATE

The state can play three main roles in supporting the development of a transparent credit reporting infrastructure. First, state actors, such as central banks and financial regulators, can both operate and use credit reporting systems. Second, the state can act as a regulator of credit reporting systems, compelling private lenders to exchange high-quality credit information and ensuring open and equal access to credit reporting systems. Finally, the state can act to promote the development of a private credit reporting infrastructure that can complement the role of public credit registries in supporting credit market efficiency. This section reviews each of these roles in turn and provides examples of the challenges and opportunities of the state's involvement in credit reporting, with a special focus on the state's changing role in light of the global financial crisis.

The state as a user of credit information: Risk management and supervision

The global financial crisis has generated renewed interest in the use of information from national credit registries for prudential oversight and regulation (Girault and Hwang 2010). Although many countries' registries collect detailed data on loans, the crisis has highlighted the need for improvements in the use of existing credit information for financial oversight and regulation. The new Basel III accords, which are being adopted around the world, present an important window of opportunity to improve the use of credit information for the purpose of identifying and managing threats to financial stability.

Currently, financial regulators use data from credit registries primarily for the off-site monitoring of credit risks. Credit registry data can support this task in several ways. First, they allow regulators to estimate the portfolio credit risk and calculate loan loss provisions for individual financial institutions. Second, they enable regulators to compare loan credit risk across banks, to conduct stress tests, and to detect anomalies in lending patterns, portfolio structure, and loan performance. Third, registries track and monitor the development of credit risk by type of borrower or type of credit. This allows regulators to detect credit risks concentrated in a specific sector, loan category, or region.

The Basel III accords represent a shift from a microprudential approach to financial regulation, centered on the risk of individual financial institutions, toward a macroprudential approach that is focused on systemically important financial institutions. Understanding and containing these threats requires detailed understanding of interconnected credit risks in the traditional financial system as well as risks outside it. There is much room to leverage data from credit registries for this purpose. Credit registry data can provide the basis for

- *Evaluating the systemic importance of financial institutions.* The Basel III accords require more stringent provisions for systemically important financial institutions. Comprehensive credit information is required to assess and monitor their interrelated exposures.
- *Informing countercyclical buffer decisions.* The countercyclical capital framework introduced by the Basel III accords tries to reduce the cyclicality of bank lending. It introduces a conservation buffer, set at 2.5 percent of banks' risk-weighted assets, and a countercyclical capital buffer to address potentially excessive risk-taking as a result of cyclical credit growth. Better credit information can increase the accuracy of risk weighting in banks' loan portfolios.
- *Building more reliable early warning systems.* Early warning systems used by bank regulators often only capture portfolio risk for individual financial institutions. Better use of credit registry data for offsite monitoring allows for more nuanced tracking of links in credit risk exposures across institutions.

Though some of these tasks can be accomplished with data from financial institutions themselves, credit registries can provide a wealth of data for this purpose (see box 5.1). Since credit registries generally contain information on all loans above a given threshold, making full use of this information allows regulators to obtain a more comprehensive picture of interconnected risks in the financial sector.

The main challenges to the use of existing credit registry data for prudential supervision are the limited coverage of unregulated financial institutions and the often high minimum loan sizes of existing credit registries, which further limit the range of loans captured by the registry. The unfolding of the financial crisis in Europe and the United States has shown that financial stability is increasingly affected by the risks taken on by nonregulated financial entities. In developed economies this market includes hedge funds, money market funds, and structured investment vehicles, sometimes referred to as the *shadow banking system*. In many emerging markets, nonbanking financial institutions play an important role in consumer credit, which has often remained outside the scope of information available to financial regulators.

In its role as a user and regulator of credit information, the state can therefore play an important role in extending the coverage of existing credit reporting systems to new and systemically important borrower groups, and in incentivizing regulators to make appropriate use of credit reporting systems for identifying and monitoring threats to systemic stability.

The state as a regulator of credit reporting: Removing barriers to information sharing

Another important role of the state is to ensure that the market for credit information remains transparent, open, and efficient. Because banks can extract information rents from proprietary credit information, lenders may try to retain monopolistic knowledge of their clients' creditworthiness by sharing only limited, inaccurate, or incomplete credit

BOX 5.1   Argentina: Using Credit Registry Information for Prudential Supervision

Argentina's central bank, the Banco Central de la República Argentina, has been operating a credit reporting system since 1991. The system is mostly focused on large loans and has been increasingly used for supervisory purposes. In 1995, the system was reformed, and access to data was granted to financial institutions. After Argentina's financial crisis in 2003, several reforms of Argentina's credit reporting system were undertaken to facilitate its use for prudential regulation and to support greater stability in the financial sector.

Currently, the Argentine credit reporting industry comprises a public credit registry and several private sector credit bureaus. The legal and regulatory framework covering credit reporting activities in Argentina is limited to data protection compliance, which places some limitations on the authorities' ability to adopt a holistic approach to credit reporting. The Argentine central bank currently acts as an operator of databases. Regulated entities are required to report their credit exposures to the central bank, which makes this information available to private credit reporting agencies.[a] Several private credit bureaus operate in Argentina, with the largest credit bureau, Veraz, holding data on approximately 90 percent of all credit lines in the market.

In the aftermath of the Argentine economic crisis, the central bank focused on a strategy to enhance the availability of credit information for risk management and prudential supervision. This strategy included extending the coverage of the system and the collection of new information. In addition to providing data useful for prudential oversight and regulation, these reforms also aimed to facilitate the restructuring of the banking sector. The aim of these reforms was to make it easier for banks and regulators to (a) iden-

tify and contain a deterioration in the quality of loan portfolios, (b) facilitate provisioning and supervision of provisioning requirements for credit risk, and (c) facilitate the debt refinancing process. Monitoring credit risk and informing banks of these risks remain primary objectives of the Argentine credit registry.

Initially, Argentina's public credit registry included only information on debts above US$200,000. As a means of broadening the coverage of the system, the minimum threshold was reduced to US$50,000 in 2002. To further improve the quality of recorded credit information, the central bank has taken important steps toward the establishment of a financial statements database and has begun to collect new information on loans already covered by the system (including credit lines, currency denomination, and maturity structure of outstanding liabilities). These improvements in data collection have been particularly helpful in facilitating the implementation of portfolio models of credit risk based on data from the registry. In particular, the expanded data can be used to check that provisions for credit risk properly cover banks' expected and unexpected losses and serve as the foundation of scenario analyses and stress tests. For example, credit registry data can be used for simulations to test for the effects of new internal ratings–based capital standards as envisaged in the Basel III accords.

Taken together, these changes have significantly enhanced the central bank's ability to leverage Argentina's existing credit reporting system for the purpose of prudential oversight and regulation. Some opportunities for improving the capabilities of the system nonetheless exist, for example, with regard to tracking the risk profile of securitized loans and monitoring loan portfolios after origination.

a. Initially, this arrangement came into existence because Argentina's leading banks failed to agree on a mechanism for the voluntary exchange of credit information (see Berger and others 2003). In response, the Argentine authorities required banks to share information and made the data available to private credit reporting agencies on an equal basis. Private credit reporting agencies may access data from the central bank's databases and offer value-added services.

information. The state can act to overcome such barriers to information sharing in a variety of ways, ranging from the establishment of an appropriate legal framework to direct interventions, mandating the exchange of credit information.

As a first step, the government can help lay the legal foundations for effective information sharing. This includes a sound legal framework that maintains consumer protection but at the same time permits banks and nonbank lenders to share relevant information with credit reporting institutions. The legal framework that governs the exchange of credit information should include provisions that limit the data that can be shared among lenders to just information that is relevant for the lending decision (for example, to prevent discrimination in lending).[5] It should also grant borrowers the right to appeal incorrect information. At the same time, government and regulators need to ensure that consumer protection laws are clear and that the administrative burden for compliance does not in fact reduce incentives for information sharing. Brazil's data protection law, the Consumer Protection and Defense Code, for example, requires lenders to notify consumers whenever their data are updated. It has been argued that this procedure is so costly that it prevents lenders from sharing positive credit information and constrains credit reporting more generally (OECD 2010).

In some countries, the existing legal framework may already balance the goals of protecting consumers while allowing for broad and comprehensive credit reporting. However, in many countries, the existing legal infrastructure may constrain the exchange of credit information. This was the case in Egypt (see box 5.2). Until recently, Egypt's existing banking and data protection laws were highly restrictive and did not allow lenders to disclose client information to the market. Amendments to the legal framework for credit information sharing had to be made to allow the exchange of information among lenders, credit bureaus, and the central bank without obtaining borrower consent for each report. The Central Bank of Egypt was instrumental in helping to bring about these changes and helped to create a framework conducive to the operation of a credit bureau covering both banks and nonbank lenders.

When considering whether any changes to existing laws are necessary, policy makers should keep in mind that information sharing may involve not only banks. Other lenders, such as mortgage finance, leasing, and credit card companies may also be included

in the information-sharing framework. In addition, capturing information from nonfinancial entities can provide information that gives greater insight into borrowers' payment behavior, for example, vis-à-vis utility companies and retailers. Enabling companies outside the traditional banking sector to share credit information is advantageous for borrowers because it facilitates the establishment of a credit history, but it may require additional changes to existing laws. The collection of such additional information may, however, also place greater consumer protection responsibilities on the regulator.

Although having a sound legal framework in place is crucial for allowing the market for credit information to develop, it may not be enough to ensure a level playing field for the exchange of credit information. As highlighted in this section and in Bruhn, Farazi, and Kanz (2012), market failures such as monopoly rents and coordination problems are prevalent in the market for credit information and can create important barriers to the development of a private credit reporting infrastructure.

Since credit information is a public good, it is most effective when contribution and access to credit reporting systems are widely shared. For an individual lender, the benefits of joining a credit bureau depend on the number of other members. Setting up a credit bureau thus requires extensive coordination and collaboration among lenders. In practice, this coordination may be difficult to achieve. In fact, experience has shown that commitment by lenders can be a major problem in establishing credit bureaus in developing economies. In addition, the private interests of banks and other information providers may also get in the way of sharing deep and comprehensive information among a large number of entities, since individual banks can capture monopoly rents by not sharing information. That is, lenders benefit from having information on borrowers from other lenders, but at the same time they can profit from not sharing their own information with other lenders. Large banks may therefore be particularly reluctant to share proprietary

BOX 5.2   **Egypt: Removing Regulatory Barriers to the Development of a Private Credit Bureau**

The first private credit bureau in Egypt—"I-Score"—was established in September 2005 and became operational in March 2008. I-Score's shareholders consist of 25 banks and Egypt's Social Fund for Development. In Egypt, data secrecy laws posed a major obstacle to the establishment of a private credit reporting infrastructure. The Central Bank of Egypt was highly instrumental in creating a legislative framework conducive to the operations of a private credit bureau.

The World Bank Group, through the International Finance Corporation, provided implementation support accompanying the launch of I-Score in 2008. On the legislative front, existing laws were amended to allow the exchange of information among banks, mortgage finance and financial leasing companies, credit bureaus, and the central bank *without* obtaining individual borrower consent. The new legislation also specifies which users— that is, subscribers of I-Score—have a legitimate purpose to inquire, obtain credit reports, and use the services provided by the bureau. In September 2006, I-Score contracted with an international partner, Dun & Bradstreet, to provide software solutions, enhance operational know-how, and build the technological capability for the management of its database.

Since the beginning of 2011, I-Score has been proactive in winning the confidence of microfinance institutions (MFIs) to participate in the Egyptian information-sharing scheme. Initially, Egypt's MFIs envisioned a separate credit bureau for microfinance clients. However, a pilot study highlighted how much relevant borrower information would remain invisible to MFIs in a segmented credit information system. This convinced the country's leading MFIs to defer their decision to establish a separate microfinance credit bureau and to join I-Score instead. Including MFI clients in the credit reporting system will prevent the negative effects of data fragmentation and enhance the use of credit bureau data for risk management and financial inclusion.

Since its inception, I-Score has managed to establish a transparent and advanced credit bureau that offers services in Arabic and English. I-Score's data center has been vastly expanded to include 9 million data records, a 13-fold increase from the baseline of 0.9 million facilities initially held by the Central Bank of Egypt's Public Credit Registry. The data pertain to over 4 million small and medium enterprises and consumer borrowers. I-Score currently services the credit information needs of 55 institutional subscribers, which include 41 banks, eight mortgage finance companies, four leasing companies, the Egyptian Social Fund for Development, and one retailer. All banking institutions and the Social Fund for Development have completed the credit data migration process to I-Score. Mortgage finance companies have submitted approximately 65 percent of their data records, and the four leasing companies have submitted 35 percent of their data. I-Score has devised a specific package for MFIs to help them join in the credit information–sharing scheme; that is, special prices have been agreed upon for MFI lenders, technical support is being offered, a free trial period for newcomers is being granted, and the development of ad hoc services is part of the package tailored to the specific needs of Egyptian MFIs.

The role of I-Score is to provide Egyptian facility grantors with accurate, factual information relevant to the history and payment habits of their existing or prospective clients, enabling them to better assess their clients' creditworthiness. To date, the effects on financial access and risk management have been very impressive. For example, since 2008 the consumer loans have been on an ascending scale while the nonperforming loans have decreased by significant percentages. I-Score also aims to educate the general public of the values, benefits, and consequences of owning a good credit file. Therefore, it plays a major role in changing and modifying the behavior and culture of borrowers in the Egyptian credit market. Reforms to the legal and regulatory framework governing the exchange of credit information were essential in removing barriers to the establishment of a well-functioning credit reporting system in Egypt and laid the foundation for I-Score's success.

credit information. Empirical evidence (see box 5.3) shows that credit bureaus are indeed less likely to emerge in markets where the banking sector is highly concentrated and dominated by a small number of lenders. This finding highlights that policies or regulatory interventions intended to support the development of a comprehensive credit reporting system need to be informed by an understanding of the underlying structure of credit market competition.

Where a well-functioning private credit reporting infrastructure is in place, the state plays an important role in safeguarding competition in the market for credit information. In doing so, the state as a regulator has to balance the need to counter monopolistic tendencies, while avoiding excessive market fragmentation. Although no consensus exists about the optimal degree of competition in credit reporting, there is agreement among regulators and policy makers that regulatory oversight should (a) ensure a level playing field for new entrants into the credit information market, (b) ensure open and equal access to credit information systems for regulated and unregulated lenders, (c) identify and eliminate anticompetitive

---

BOX 5.3   Monopoly Rents, Bank Concentration, and Private Credit Reporting

Although the existence of a comprehensive credit reporting system is beneficial for the financial market as a whole, individual lenders may profit from sharing only limited information with other market participants. If only one lender has credit information on firms or individuals, this lender faces less competition in lending to these borrowers because other institutions may be reluctant to offer them credit. In economic terms, a lender can capture monopoly rents from not sharing information. This issue may be particularly pronounced when the market for credit is dominated by a few large banks. These banks each have a broad customer base already and may try to maintain their large market share by holding onto information. Not making information available can also prevent entry from new banks.

Bruhn, Farazi, and Kanz (2012) study the relationship between bank concentration and the emergence of private credit reporting. Using data for close to 130 countries, the authors find that bank concentration is negatively associated with the probability that a credit bureau emerges. Table B5.3.1 illustrates that 80 percent of countries with low bank concentration have a credit bureau, whereas only 39 percent of countries with high bank concentration have a credit bureau. This difference is smaller for credit registries (56 percent versus 37 percent), which may reflect the fact that banks are required to report to a credit registry while participation in a credit bureau is often voluntary.

This result is robust for controlling for confounding factors that could bias the analysis. In addition, the data also show that higher bank concentration is associated with lower coverage and quality of information being distributed by credit bureaus. These findings suggest that market failures can prevent the development of effective credit-sharing systems, implying that the state may have to intervene to help overcome these obstacles.

TABLE B5.3.1   **Bank Concentration and Credit Reporting**

	Countries with low bank concentration	Countries with high bank concentration
Credit registry?	0.56	0.37
Credit bureau?	0.80	0.39
Credit bureau or registry?	0.92	0.53

Source: Bruhn, Farazi, and Kanz 2012.

pricing policies, and (d) prevent the formation of closed user groups.

If market failures prevent the development of a transparent credit reporting system altogether, the state can play a productive role by creating incentives for information sharing or—in extreme cases—by requiring banks to provide credit information to public or private providers of credit information.

There are several cases in which states have mandated information sharing among private lenders to overcome monopolies and coordination problems in the market for credit information. Argentina, as one example, managed to extend its credit reporting infrastructure in this manner, despite a backdrop of high and increasing bank concentration. Because banks were reluctant to share credit information directly, the central bank made information sharing mandatory for all loans above 50 pesos, which essentially meant that the national credit registry, the Central de Riesgo, covered all loans in the market. To promote the development of a private credit reporting infrastructure, the Argentine central bank then made these data available to private credit information providers, which provide client-level risk assessments and other value-added services (see Berger and others 2003).

Elsewhere, state interventions to overcome barriers to competition in credit reporting have met with greater challenges. Even after a private credit reporting infrastructure emerges, the information can be captured by closed user groups. As discussed in box 5.4, this has been a challenge in the case of Mexico, where credit information is fragmented among multiple credit bureaus, each controlled by a distinct subset of lenders that cover different segments of the market. Mexican regulators have made attempts to overcome these barriers to the emergence of a universal credit reporting system. These attempts have, however, been challenging because the fragmentation of the market for credit information reflects a similar underlying segmentation of the Mexican credit market.

Finally, the state also plays a role in monitoring the *quality* of credit information. This is important since lenders, when required to share information, may try to retain market power by reporting inaccurate, incomplete, or lower-quality information (Semenova 2008).

The state as a promoter of private credit reporting

Public and private credit reporting systems fulfill distinct and at times complementary roles. Aside from acting as an operator and regulator of credit reporting systems, the state can therefore enhance credit market efficiency by promoting the development of a private credit reporting infrastructure.

In many cases, the type of credit information required by private lenders differs significantly from that required by central banks and financial regulators. Regulators require information allowing them to monitor the loan portfolio of financial institutions and to estimate associated risks. Such information is often available from public credit registries. Private lenders, by contrast, have to assess the creditworthiness of individual borrowers. This assessment may require more detailed information on indebtedness and repayment behavior, including information on utility payments, debt with credit card companies and retailers, or individual credit scores. This generally goes beyond the information available from national credit registries and is more readily available from private credit bureaus that routinely provide such data through their value-added services. This functional differentiation explains why public and private credit information systems often coexist, and it makes a case for the role of the state in promoting the development of a private credit reporting infrastructure even where a credit registry is already in place.

Governments can promote private credit reporting by working closely with lenders to help them overcome the coordination failures discussed in the previous section and

BOX 5.4   Mexico: State Interventions to Prevent Market Fragmentation and Closed User Groups

Until the early 1990s, very little credit information was available and shared in Mexican credit markets. The only information-sharing mechanism available at that time was the National Banking Credit Information Service (*Servicio Nacional de Información de Crédito Bancario*), a public credit registry established by Banco de Mexico in 1964. In the mid-1990s, several segments of the Mexican credit markets were experiencing fast growth, particularly the consumer lending and residential mortgages sectors. The 1994 Tequila Crisis and ensuing large wave of defaults prompted lenders, as well as the Mexican regulators, to pay greater attention to background checks based on credit information to facilitate sound credit decisions.

In reaction to this situation, Mexico's largest private credit reporting agency, Buró de Crédito, was established in 1995, as a collaboration between TransUnion Mexico (covering consumer credit) and Dun & Bradstreet (covering SME lending). The Buró de Crédito includes information on loans from the banking sector, and commercial banks have been holding a stake of up to 70 percent in the credit bureau. At present, Buró de Crédito, with 2,800 users and 900 data contributors, contains information on 52 million individuals and 6 million firms. Two other credit bureaus existed in Mexico, but both have ceased operations: Experian failed to obtain sufficient data from the banking sector, and Equifax sold its database to TransUnion so that it was subsumed in Buró de Crédito in 2000.

To foster competition in the credit information industry, the Mexican authorities passed a new legal framework in 2002.[a] The framework mandated all regulated institutions to have access to a report as part of their underwriting practices, based on the data subject's consent. In addition, it allowed for credit reporting service providers to exchange databases between themselves on a for-profit basis.

During the early 2000s consumer credit from nonfinancial institutions grew significantly in Mexico and accounted for 40 percent of total credit to the private sector after 2000. Partly in response to this development, in 2005 a new credit bureau, Circulo de Crédito, was established, which covered primarily retail and mass-market loans. For example, Circulo de Crédito collects information from major microfinance institutions, credit cooperatives, savings and loans firms, retailers, grocery stores, and two banks that specialize in consumer credit to poorer segments of the population.

The Buró de Crédito and the Circulo de Crédito, however, did not exchange information, leading to data fragmentation within the credit reporting system, because each bureau filled a niche in the market for credit information. In an effort to address these issues, Mexican regulators amended the laws governing credit reporting in 2004, 2008, and more recently in 2010. One legal change introduced a new governance structure within the Buró de Crédito, limiting the extent to which users of the system could simultaneously act as owners of credit reporting service providers. The reforms also established new rules for the exchange of databases and created a mechanism to avoid exclusivity agreements between lenders and providers of credit information.

These legal changes have facilitated access to the Buró de Crédito by smaller banks, an important achievement in Mexico's concentrated banking market, where the five largest banks hold more than 80 percent of total assets. The Buró de Crédito and the Circulo de Crédito have also started exchanging some information, but this exchange remains limited because fragmentation of the market for credit information reflects a corresponding segmentation in the credit market (with banks serving higher-income clients and NBFIs catering to lower-income households).

a. The main components of this legislation were the Law to Regulate Credit Information Societies (*Ley para Regular las Sociedades de Información Crediticia*), the Operational Rules for the Functioning of Credit Reporting Systems (*Reglas a las que Deberán Sujetarán las Operaciones y Actividades de las SIC y Sus Usuarios*), and the Law to Regulate Financial Groups (*Ley de Grupos Financieros*).

to provide legislation that makes it easy for lenders to make credit information available to a credit bureau. Several successful country cases illustrate how public-private partnerships can be used to improve a country's credit reporting infrastructure. Box 5.5 describes the case of Morocco, where the central bank worked with lenders from different market segments to build a comprehensive information-sharing network.

An important point, highlighted by the case of Morocco, is that—where public and private credit reporting institutions coexist—the state needs to ensure that public credit registries and private credit bureaus do not duplicate services. After a well-functioning credit bureau is in place, the state may, for example, scale back the services provided by the credit registry.

Providing support for the development of a private credit reporting infrastructure can also allow central banks to focus on their core competencies of collecting credit information for the purpose of prudential oversight and regulation. In fact, there is no clear economic reason why the state should act as a distributor of comprehensive data on individual borrowers for commercial purposes or why it should provide value-added services, such as credit scores, if these can be provided by a private entity instead, after market failures have been addressed successfully. As the previous section has argued, a more productive role for the state is to establish the legal framework that allows for the transparent exchange of credit information, to forestall the formation of information monopolies and closed user groups, and to provide technical assistance for the establishment of private credit reporting institutions where such assistance is required.

To summarize, in addition to its supervisory and regulatory responsibilities, the most adequate role for the state may be to remove legal and institutional obstacles to the development of private credit reporting rather than to provide comprehensive and value-added credit information services to lenders where such information can be provided by the private sector.

CONSUMER CREDIT AND MICROFINANCE: EXTENDING THE REACH OF CREDIT REPORTING SYSTEMS

Credit reporting is most effective in supporting financial access, efficiency, and stability when participation in the exchange of credit information is as widely shared as possible. Nonetheless, many credit reporting systems cover only risks in the traditional banking sector. This limits their effectiveness in supporting market efficiency and creates an important rationale for an active role of the state in promoting the inclusion of nonregulated lenders (such as NBFIs and microfinance lenders) into existing credit reporting systems.

Over the past decade, many emerging markets have witnessed a dramatic growth in consumer and microfinance lending. In Indonesia, for example, consumer lending grew at an average of 36 percent annually between 2001 and 2007 (Santoso and Sukada 2009). In many countries, this expansion in consumer credit has been spearheaded by nonregulated lenders, such as microfinance institutions and NBFIs. Bringing information on this rapidly growing market segment into the fold of the credit reporting infrastructure is important not only for the risk management of individual financial institutions but also for systemic stability. Many regulators have begun to recognize this and have been proactive in extending the coverage of credit reporting systems to lenders outside the traditional banking sector.

The challenges of extending the reach of existing credit reporting systems to new borrower groups and lenders outside the traditional financial system are twofold: First, established lenders often view microfinance institutions and NBFIs as potential competitors and are therefore reluctant to grant them access to existing information-sharing arrangements. This gives rise to the well-documented concerns of data fragmentation and closed user groups highlighted in the previous section. Second, nonregulated financial institutions, such as NBFIs and microlenders,

BOX 5.5   Morocco: Public Support for the Development of a Private Credit Bureau

At the onset of 2005, Morocco was characterized by unfavorable credit market conditions[a] and an inadequate credit reporting system.[b] The country lacked a stable regulatory framework for credit reporting, and there was no cross-sector information sharing by key lenders (that is, banks, microfinance institutions, and nonbank institutions). Responding to these shortcomings, lenders were considering plans to create separate informational databases, one for each sector. This would have led to a fragmented, partial credit reporting system, which would not allow lenders to check the complete financial profile of credit applicants. Against this background, Morocco's central bank, the Bank of Morocco, decided to take a leadership role in introducing a best practice private credit reporting system in the country.

Initially, the Bank of Morocco planned to upgrade Morocco's existing public credit registry. However, in a successive stage, the Bank of Morocco was open to consider other viable credit reporting models, including the participation of private sector partners. Given the limited capabilities of Morocco's existing public credit reporting system, and drawing on the results of a market assessment study, the International Finance Corporation suggested a public-private partnership model similar to that operating in several Latin American countries (such as Bolivia, Ecuador, and Peru). In this model, the central bank first upgraded its technological capabilities necessary to receive and process credit information (positive and negative) from the entire universe of regulated lenders. Building on the trusted leadership of the central bank among financial institutions, the public credit registry would then consolidate this information and make it available to any private credit bureau established and licensed by the central bank. In September 2007, the central bank issued the first private credit bureau license to Experian Morocco, which provides both positive and negative credit reporting information.

So that overlap in the services provided by the public and private credit reporting systems could be prevented, lenders could no longer access the public credit registry once the first private credit bureau became operational. (Lenders were, however, still required to provide information.) To promote the use of available credit information, the system also required lenders to consult at least one credit bureau prior to making any credit decision. The central bank also introduced several innovative measures to achieve a more effective credit reporting infrastructure. Nonregulated lenders would be able to provide information directly to any private credit bureau on consumer consent. Nonregulated lenders that provided data to the credit bureau were then given the right to consult the bureau on the basis of reciprocity principles. This step ensured that participation in the private credit reporting system would gradually extend to nonregulated lenders outside the traditional banking system.

Finally, to provide the legal framework for the effective operation of private credit bureaus in the country, the government and central bank also undertook some reforms to the legal and regulatory framework governing the exchange of credit information. The current legislative and operational framework counteracts the creation of information monopolies and closed user groups, because all existing and future private credit bureaus will be supplied with the same information from the central bank. This, in return, will allow for competition on prices and service quality.

Through this initiative, Morocco's central bank has established a transparent, competitive, and advanced credit information sharing infrastructure that incorporates private credit bureaus to provide value-added services that are more effectively supplied by the private sector. At the same time, Morocco's central bank has been building a wealth of information that assists in its supervisory role as a regulator of the financial system, as well as the regulator of private credit reporting institutions.

a. Specifically, this included limited, collateralized, and selective credit access, elevated rejection rates, and extremely high debt rates.
b. Bank Al-Maghrib's public credit registry (established in 1978) was the only entity providing, albeit limited, credit information.

may also lack the technological capabilities necessary to participate in comprehensive information sharing.

In both instances, the state can support market efficiency through regulation and capacity-building initiatives that ensure that information on the rapidly growing market for microfinance and consumer credit is brought into the view of established credit reporting systems. There are several models of how this can be achieved. In China, where consumer lending has grown at double-digit rates since the deregulation of consumer credit in 1999, the state has taken an active role in the establishment of a comprehensive credit reporting infrastructure. The People's Bank of China is currently establishing the world's largest credit registry, covering more than 600 million consumers. Information sharing is mandatory, and the registry collects data from regulated as well as nonregulated lenders, so that it covers more than 90 percent of all consumer loans (Jentzsch 2008).

Attaining similarly high coverage rates for mass-market and microfinance loans has been more challenging elsewhere, despite regulatory interventions. In Latin America, the significant presence of microfinance lenders has required regulators to incorporate nonregulated lenders into credit reporting systems much earlier than in other world regions. However, both the involvement of the state and the success in creating a level playing field for the exchange of credit information have varied. In Guatemala, the state limited its intervention to the creation of a legal framework that allowed the country's leading microfinance lenders to form a private credit bureau. In Bolivia, by contrast, regulators responded to a large microfinance default crisis in the late 1990s by promoting the development of credit reporting institutions outside the traditional banking sector. Despite such reforms, many credit reporting systems in the region remain highly fragmented and characterized by closed user groups. As a result, these credit reporting systems have often lagged behind in their ability to incorporate new segments of the credit

market into a comprehensive credit information infrastructure.

Extending the reach of credit reporting to new client groups can also pose technological challenges. Participation in advanced credit reporting systems can be expensive and technologically complex, requiring lenders to adopt new data management and telecommunications solutions. In addition, for a credit reporting system to function effectively, it must be possible to identify borrowers with reasonable certainty. Many developing economies lack a national identification system, particularly for borrowers at the bottom of the financial pyramid. This constraint has given rise to some innovative solutions using, for example, biometric technology to uniquely identify borrowers (see, for example, Giné, Goldberg, and Yang 2011). Many initiatives in this area are state led, and the state can play an important role in supporting both the technological and regulatory infrastructure required to extend credit reporting to important new borrower groups, such as consumer finance clients and microfinance borrowers.

INTRODUCTION TO PAYMENT AND SECURITIES SETTLEMENT SYSTEMS

Payment and securities settlement systems are a key part of a country's financial infrastructure. They can also be a major transmission channel of shocks during times of crisis. The state can reduce potential threats to systemic stability through the regulation of payment and securities settlement systems or through direct interventions to reduce counterparty risk. State agencies and central banks can also support systemically important participants of payment and settlement systems in times of financial distress. This section explores the role that the state has played in the development and operation of payment and securities settlement infrastructure.

There are two ways in which state interventions before and during the financial crisis helped to promote the stability of payment and settlement systems. First, large-value payment systems survived the crisis relatively unaffected, in large part because of efforts by central banks to introduce robust payment systems (such as real-time gross settlement systems that reduce counterparty risk) well before the onset of the crisis. Second, once the crisis spread, many central banks acted decisively to step up liquidity provision to stabilize large-value payment systems and the markets that rely on this infrastructure, such as the interbank money market. Without support from central banks, the failure of one or more participants to settle their exposures in these markets could have created credit or liquidity problems for other participants and posed a systemic risk to the financial system. The timely provision of liquidity by and large mitigated these concerns about counterparty risk.

The global financial crisis did, nonetheless, reveal some limitations in existing payment and securities settlement systems. For instance, stress emerged in securities settlement systems, in particular for over-the-counter (OTC) derivatives markets. In this area, the crisis highlighted limitations in the transparency and legal framework governing securities settlement systems.[6] Building a stronger infrastructure for securities and derivatives settlement systems to minimize counterparty risk is an important concern for many emerging markets, where the development of robust securities settlement systems has sometimes lagged behind the rapid development of equity and derivatives markets.

The remainder of this section reviews the role that state agencies and central banks have played in supporting payment and settlement systems through the financial crisis. It also highlights some of the challenges to the development and operation of payment and securities settlement systems that have become apparent during the crisis. The chapter argues for an active role of the state in the development, regulation, and oversight of payment and securities settlement systems, particularly in (a) mitigating counterparty risk through interventions in interbank markets and (b) mitigating counterparty and settlement risks in securities transactions

through the development of a sound legal and regulatory framework.

Payment and securities settlement systems

Payment and securities settlement systems are the infrastructure that enables the transfer of monetary value between parties discharging mutual obligations (World Bank 2011b). This infrastructure consists of several components, which include the legal, regulatory, and oversight frameworks for payment transactions, large-value funds transfer systems, retail payment systems, foreign exchange settlement systems, and securities settlement systems.

Payment systems are a key part of a country's financial infrastructure. They can, however, also be a major transmission channel of shocks during times of financial crisis: large-value payment systems are particularly important for systemic stability because they have the potential to generate and transmit disruptions between the financial and the real sector of an economy. Since the current report focuses on financial stability and the role of the state, this chapter focuses on large-value payment systems and the steps that central banks have taken to strengthen these systems. The chapter also touches on securities settlement systems. In particular, it reviews the performance of OTC derivatives settlement systems, which is one of the areas in which the crisis highlighted the need for proactive oversight and development support.

Robust payment and security settlement systems promote economic activity by controlling the counterparty risk inherent in the transfer of high-value funds and by helping with the implementation of monetary policy. Payment systems are essential for financial sector development because they contribute to the innovation and development of new financial products and facilitate functioning of financial markets (Listfield and Montes-Negret 1994). The smooth functioning of payment systems can mitigate financial crises by reducing or eliminating counterparty risk related to financial market transactions and is therefore vital for ensuring financial stability

(Afonso and Shin 2009; Cirasino and García 2009; Flannery 1996). Finally, improvements in payment infrastructure can result in significant efficiency gains, reductions in transaction costs, and increased economies of scale in financial intermediation (Hasan, Schmiedel, and Song 2009; Humphrey and others 2006; Lindquist 2002). Greater efficiency of interbank payment systems can therefore have a wider positive impact on credit creation and financial development (Merrouche and Nier 2010).

The World Bank, through its Payment Systems Development Group, has been paying close attention to payment and securities settlement systems as a key component of the financial infrastructure of a country. For example, country assessments done by the World Bank and the IMF under the Financial Sector Assessment Program (FSAP) frequently include a component that assesses the design, safety, and efficiency of payment and securities settlement systems.[7] Some concrete recommendations on payment systems that have come out of recent FSAPs include (a) strengthening the overall legal framework for payment system oversight to ensure safety and soundness of the system, (b) linking large-value payment systems with securities depositories to address potential settlement risks for securities transactions, and (c) ensuring business continuity of payment systems by having backup servers to avoid any loss of transaction data. The World Bank also actively works with international standard-setting bodies to establish the set of standards and best practices.[8]

Large-value payment systems

Large-value payment systems are the financial infrastructure used to process time-sensitive high-value payments. Banks and other financial institutions use these systems to transfer funds to each other. They are also the platform on which the interbank money market operates. As such, stable and resilient large-value payment systems are an essential prerequisite for the efficient operation of a financial market.

Large-value payment systems are important for systemic stability because they are able to generate and transmit disturbances of a systemic nature to the financial sector. Bank-to-bank transactions in the interbank money market, in particular, depend strongly on large-value payment systems in two ways. First, the interbank money market, as the distributor of liquidity throughout the financial sector, relies heavily on payment systems to transmit funds across the financial system rapidly and safely. Second, the interbank money market is a key source of liquidity for the operation of payment and settlement systems. Because of their central role in allocating liquidity, efficient large-value payment systems are also indispensable for the swift implementation of monetary policy. Because of the significant amount of funds channeled through the system, large-value payment systems can also transmit and, where inefficiencies exist, amplify disturbances in the financial sector.

The turnover of large-value payment systems, as measured by the number of times an amount equivalent to the value of the GDP in each country is settled in a year, is typically several times a country's GDP. Figure 5.5 shows that the size of these flows, however, varies quite substantially across regions. It tends to be higher in countries with active securities markets that are supported by large-value payment systems, with several national payment systems handling transactions more than 30 to 40 times their country's GDP. These high turnover rates underscore the importance of well-functioning payments infrastructure for financial stability more broadly.[9]

The role of central banks in large-value payment systems

Central banks have historically performed the function of payment intermediaries and remain centrally important for the efficient operation of payment systems (Johnson and Steigerwald 2008; Millard and Saporta 2005). In particular, central banks provide banks with the physical infrastructure

FIGURE 5.5   GDP Turnover of Large-Value Payment Systems by Region, 2009

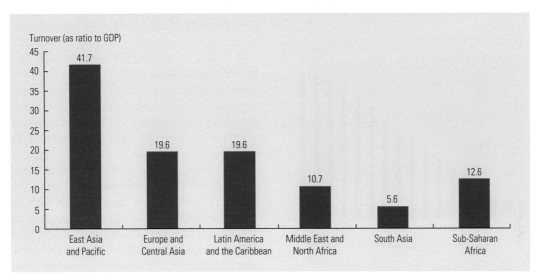

Sources: World Bank 2011b and Global Payment Systems Survey 2010.
Note: Weighted averages.

needed to make interbank payments, as well as overdraft and deposit facilities (central bank money[10]). Central banks have also been actively involved in promoting safety and efficiency of these systems to maintain financial stability (Bech, Preisig, and Soramäki 2008). The involvement of the central bank in payment systems can take several non–mutually exclusive forms:

- As an *operator of payment systems,* the central bank acts as the settlement and sometimes clearing agent in payment systems. In this role, the central bank also at times provides the technological infrastructure for settlement systems, as well as intraday and overnight credit (lender of last resort), to preserve liquidity in the system.
- As a *regulator of payment systems,* the central bank enforces regulatory rules and monitors safety and efficiency of transactions taking place through the system. It also safeguards the legal rules governing interactions in interbank money markets and other transactions using the large-value payment system.
- As a *promoter of the development,* it acts as a catalyst of innovation and supports

cooperation and coordination among payment system participants.

Instead of discussing each role separately, this chapter focuses on the recent contributions central banks have made to make large-value payment infrastructure more resilient and on the role payment systems can play in possible future crises.

Evolution of real-time gross settlement systems and the role of central banks

Around the world, large-value payment systems have rapidly evolved over the past two decades. Two key risks faced by such systems are liquidity and credit risk, and most countries have upgraded existing large-value payment systems to more effectively address these risks.[11] Over the past two decades, countries have largely moved away from deferred net settlement (DNS) systems to real-time gross settlement (RTGS) systems. The key advantage of RTGS is that each payment is settled immediately (in real time) and processed individually (on a gross basis). On the other hand, in a DNS system, processing of funds is delayed (usually at the end of the business day) and is done on net basis (see Martin

FIGURE 5.6   **The Adoption of Real-Time Gross Settlement Systems over Time, 1990–2010**

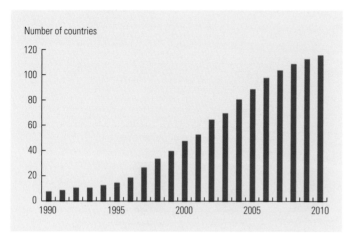

Sources: World Bank 2011b, Global Payment Systems Survey 2010, and Bech and Hobijn 2007.

2005 for more detail). The main drawback of conventional DNS systems is that they are vulnerable to counterparty credit risk: a payment system participant can become insolvent between the time a payment is made and the time it is settled. The credit risk in deferred settlement systems is thus generally borne by market participants.

Real-time gross settlement systems eliminate this risk, because all transactions are settled instantaneously on an individual basis. However, the central bank now has a greater responsibility in providing liquidity in the system. The flow of funds provided by central banks consists of both collateralized and uncollateralized current account overdrafts and central bank credit, either in the form of a loan or a repo. As the next section shows, the shift toward real-time gross settlement systems has increased the responsibilities of central banks in providing liquidity for better management of counterparty risks, particularly in times of crisis, when credit lines between banks may dry up.

Figure 5.6 traces the rapid adoption of real-time settlement systems around the world over the time period between 1990 and 2010. Developed economies were the early adopters; for example, most European countries adopted RTGS systems by the late 1990s (Bech and Hobijn 2007). Many developing

countries have followed suit and have shifted to real-time gross settlement systems in the past decade. More recent adopters include, for example, El Salvador and the West Bank and Gaza, where RTGS systems did not become operational until 2010, and Ethiopia and Rwanda, which established RTGS systems in 2011 (World Bank 2011b).[12] According to the World Bank's 2010 Global Payment Systems Survey, 116 out of 139 countries surveyed (83 percent) have RTGS systems (World Bank 2011b). In 112 of these countries, central banks act as the operator of the system (private entities operate the system in the remaining four countries). In virtually all of those countries (115), the central bank also acts as settlement agent for the system. The vast majority of RTGS participants are commercial banks: the payment systems survey shows that 95 percent of RTGS systems give access to only commercial banks, 60 percent give access to noncommercial banks, and 69 percent give access to NBFIs.

In addition to managing liquidity risk, central banks and regulators have also played an important role in reforming large-value payment systems to mitigate systemic risk. Before we turn to the role of central banks in managing liquidity risk, box 5.6 reviews country cases highlighting a number of reforms designed to make large-value payment systems more resilient to systemic financial risks.[13]

THE STATE'S ROLE IN PAYMENT AND SECURITIES SETTLEMENT SYSTEMS

At the peak of the financial crisis, large-value payment systems showed some signs of distress but generally proved to be resilient.[14] This resilience was mainly due to the swift and decisive action of central banks providing liquidity to the system. This section looks at the role of central banks in distributing liquidity in the system to address rising concerns about counterparty risk during the recent financial crisis. In particular, it considers the role of central banks in stabilizing interbank money markets and highlights some new measures that have been proposed to improve the management of liquidity risk.

BOX 5.6 Reforming Large-Value Payment Systems to Mitigate Systemic Risk

PAKISTAN

The national payment system (NPS) in Pakistan has undergone major reforms during the past five years under the strong leadership of the State Bank of Pakistan (SBP). This has been a complex project comprising the modernization of the infrastructure for wholesale and retail payments, the modernization of the legal and regulatory framework for payment systems and instruments, and the introduction of innovative solutions in the provision of payment services for the underserved banking population.

This box first describes the new features the SBP introduced in the large-value payment system as a result of the reform and then highlights various roles the SBP performs to ensure the smooth and secure functioning of the country's national payment system.

Launch of PRISM

In July 2008, the SBP launched the Pakistan Real Time Interbank Settlement Mechanism (PRISM) to better cope with systemic risk associated with large-value payment systems. PRISM is a real-time gross settlement (RTGS) system. Before the introduction of PRISM, financial market transactions and large-value government payments used to be processed through checks and settled on a multilateral net basis once a day. In such a system, if multilateral credit exposures are not managed properly, the system's participants can be exposed to considerable credit risk.

The shift from end-of-day to intraday settlement and the gradual introduction of time-critical payments has considerably increased liquidity needs in PRISM. Opening balances and funds received from other participants during the operational day are the main sources of liquidity for participants in PRISM. In addition, the participants can use the cash reserve requirements and statutory liquidity requirements they hold in accounts with the SBP to make payments during the day in the RTGS system. These funds are available free of charge.

Several mechanisms have been put in place to better manage liquidity risks in PRISM. The system offers centralized queuing whereby payments that cannot be settled immediately because of lack of sufficient funds in the settlement accounts of participants are placed in a central queue. A gridlock resolution mechanism is another tool used in the system to facilitate timely settlement of payments and

mitigate liquidity risk. In addition, PRISM generates and sends participants liquidity alerts, followed up by phone calls to the banks to arrange the required funds from the interbank market. In the second year of PRISM, the SBP introduced intraday liquidity facilities, a credit from the SBP to participants in PRISM for the settlement of payments. It is available only on a fully collateralized basis against approved government securities as specified by the SBP.

As an operator of the large-value system, the SBP, during the reform process, paid increasing attention to the operational reliability and security of PRISM, fixing the security policies and operational procedures in a number of normative documents and instructions. Business continuity–related activities for PRISM have been established and documented as well. Procedures are in place for periodic backing-up and storing of data. A secondary processing site has been established, and full system recovery is expected in 30 minutes to four hours with no data loss. In addition, the SBP has developed requirements and recommendations for system participants to have in place the necessary business resumption and recovery tools.

Various roles of the SBP

Clearly, the SBP played a vital role in reforming the national payment system and continues to play various roles to support the system's functioning. First, the SBP is the operator and owner of the RTGS system. It also operates the securities settlement system and the central depository for government securities (which is part of PRISM). Second, the SBP provides safe settlement assets for all interbank payments settled through the RTGS system by maintaining and managing settlement accounts for all participants in PRISM.

Third, the SBP is responsible for the regulation and oversight of all recognized payment systems and payment instruments in the country. As part of its oversight role, the SBP has been working continuously to ensure that the overseen systems comply with international standards and best practices, such as the Committee on Payment and Settlement Systems' "Core Principles for Systemically Important Payment Systems" and the Committee on Payment and Settlement Systems, and International Organization of Securities Commissions' "Recommendations for Securities Settlement Systems." In addition, the SBP supported the government in establishing the Pakistan Remittance Initiative, and played a

(Box continues next page)

BOX 5.6   Reforming Large-Value Payment Systems to Mitigate Systemic Risk   *(continued)*

catalyst role by encouraging the commercial banks to leverage the PRISM system to support faster processing of international remittances.

Fourth, the SBP has been playing a leading role in establishing a sound legal and regulatory framework for payments to reduce legal risk. The SBP had initiated the drafting of the Payment System and Electronic Fund Transfer Act (PSEFT Act), which was introduced in 2007 and deals with a broad range of risk-related issues such as irrevocability of payments and settlement finality, validity and enforceability of netting arrangements, and finality of settlement of government securities. The act empowers the SBP to issue rules, guidance, circulars, bylaws, standards, or directions with respect to such systems or instruments in pursuing its objectives to promote monetary stability and a sound financial structure.

BRAZIL

In 2002, the Banco Central do Brasil (BCB) launched the new Brazilian Payment System (*Sistema de Pagamento*). Brazil had a fairly sophisticated payment system even prior to the launching of the reform program. However, to better manage systemic risk, the Reserves Transfer System (*Sistema de Transferência de Reservas*—STR) was launched. With this system, interbank fund transfers can be settled irrevocably and unconditionally, that is, with finality, on a real-time basis. This allows for settlement risk reduction for interbank transactions and, consequently, systemic risk reduction. As of 2010, the STR had 151 participants, including the BCB, the National Treasury Secretariat, three clearinghouses, and 137 banks. In 2010, the STR processed 12.7 million transactions for a total value of R$132,318.9 billion.

With the launch of the new central bank payment system, a direct link was established between the STR and the central depository for federal public securities (*Sistema Especial de Liquidação e de Custódia*—SELIC). The link made it possible for SELIC to settle all transactions in real time on a

gross basis, that is, according to model 1 of delivery versus payment, with the STR processing the cash leg of the securities transactions. As defined by the Committee on Payment and Settlement Systems, delivery versus payment is a link between a securities transfer system and a funds transfer system that ensures that delivery occurs if, and only if, payment occurs. Currently, delivery versus payment is observed in all securities settlement systems,[a] and almost all securities are dematerialized.

The Brazilian payment system reform, however, went beyond the launch of the STR and the SELIC's modus operandi changes. To reduce the systemic risk and vulnerability to shocks, changes to the legal and regulatory framework were also necessary, in terms of clarifying the rights and obligations of participants in payment transactions. Prior to the reform, Brazil was lacking legal validation of multilateral netting, protection of assets pledged as collateral in case of failure of a participant, and a sound legal basis for the central bank's oversight function.

In this complex process of reform, the BCB assumed a leading role. In particular, the reform of the Brazilian payment system had three important outcomes: (a) the reduction of systemic risk in the settlement of financial transactions; (b) a more appropriate sharing of the risks associated with settlement of payment transactions between the central bank and private market players; and (c) the compliance of the systemically important payment systems of the country with international standards and best practices.

In particular, two elements of the Brazilian reform process have been notable, contributing to its breadth, scope, and complexity. First, the central bank conducted a comprehensive diagnostic study before defining the reform, which sought to identify all forms of risks present in the system. Second, the central bank consistently involved key stakeholders (banks, other financial institutions, clearinghouses, other regulators, and so forth) in the reform debate.

a. Federal government bonds are traded by telephone (in the traditional OTC market) or on a BM&FBOVESPA-operated electronic trading platform (SISBEX). In this market, repurchase agreements predominate over outright transactions. Traditional OTC is also the main trading method for corporate bonds, state government bonds, non-standard derivatives and most securities relating to the National Treasury's special responsibilities. Some of the National Treasury's securities can also be traded at organized OTC markets operated by CETIP and BM&FBOVESPA. Stocks, standardized derivatives, and commodities are traded at BM&FBOVESPA, the only Brazilian stock and derivatives exchange. Two electronic trading platforms are used: MEGABOLSA for equities and equity derivatives, and Global Trading System (GTS) for commodities and other derivatives.

The section then turns to the performance of securities settlement systems, an area in which the crisis highlighted a number of challenges and possibilities for reform and improvement.

Management of liquidity risk[15]

In most countries, the primary source of intraday liquidity for financial institutions having access to real-time gross settlement systems is funds received from other participating institutions (see figure 5.7).[16] However, during times of stress it can become difficult for banks to obtain sufficient funds from banks holding excess reserves. As market participants become more cautious, they tend to hold onto liquid assets or target them toward investments perceived to be less risky, rather than extending loans in the interbank market.[17] Significant shocks to the willingness of financial institutions to lend to each other—for example, in the form of a default or bank run—can result in a liquidity crunch in interbank markets that is potentially severe enough to trigger a payment system crisis. The collapse of Lehman Brothers in the United States is a prominent example of a recent event that triggered a liquidity crisis in interbank markets.[18]

To revive interbank markets and to stop a contagion spreading through the payment system,[19] central banks worldwide actively provided liquidity to interbank markets, for example, by extending access to their liquidity facilities to a wider set of payment system participants, by widening the range of collateral accepted in their operations (both the Federal Reserve and the Bank of England extended their list of eligible collateral), and by lending at longer maturities (the European Central Bank used the *open market operations*, and the Federal Reserve used the *term auction facility*). These proactive interventions in interbank markets were by and large successful, and they highlighted the important, and possibly increased, role of central banks in liquidity management.

Liquidity crises ensuing from deterioration in the perceived creditworthiness of counterparties in the interbank market generally

FIGURE 5.7   **Sources of Intraday Liquidity for Participants of Real-Time Gross Settlement Systems**

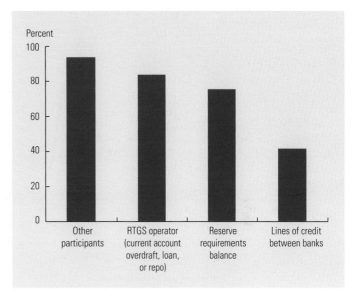

Sources: World Bank 2011b and Global Payment Systems Survey 2010.

have a stronger effect on the uncollateralized or unsecured segment of the money market. In secured (or repo) transactions, such concerns are mitigated to some extent by the presence of collateral.[20] Therefore, an important policy measure that has been proposed to stabilize interbank markets—especially in emerging economies—is to collateralize transactions in the interbank market.

To illustrate the rationale behind this proposition, figures 5.8 and 5.9 compare the volatility of interbank money market rates around the collapse of Lehman Brothers in economies with secured and unsecured interbank money markets. Figure 5.8 shows the high volatility of interbank money market rates in the United States and the United Kingdom, two of the economies most severely affected by the financial crisis that use an unsecured interbank market. Figure 5.9 compares the volatility of interbank money market rates in the Russian Federation and Ukraine,[21] where interbank money markets are largely unsecured, and Brazil and Mexico, where for historical reasons the interbank money market operates mainly on a secured basis. Although these economies

FIGURE 5.8   Interbank Money Market Rates in the United States and United Kingdom

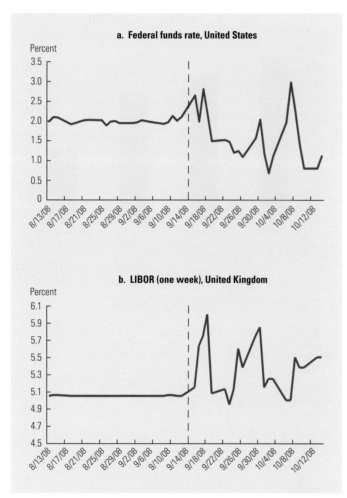

Sources: Federal Reserve Bank of New York and Bank of England.
Note: U.S. and U.K. interbank money market rates are shown for the periods August 13–September 12, 2008 (before failure of Lehman Brothers), and September 15–October 14, 2008 (increased volatility). LIBOR = London interbank offered rate

were arguably affected by different shocks, the stylized evidence suggests that collateralizing transactions in interbank markets can reduce volatility during times of financial crisis.

The potential benefits of encouraging collateralization in interbank markets can be illustrated by some recent country experiences. In Italy, for example, in an effort to help restart activity in the interbank market during the peak of the crisis, the Bank of Italy introduced an innovative collateralized interbank market (MIC) segment that

takes advantage of existing infrastructure, and proved to be successful in reviving Italy's interbank market. The case of Italy is reviewed in box 5.7.

Although collateralized interbank markets can improve financial stability, introducing collateralized transactions also comes with a number of legal and technological requirements, which can be challenging to achieve, particularly in low- and middle-income countries. In terms of legal requirements, the introduction of collateralized interbank market necessitates (a) a sound legal framework that ensures finality of funds and securities transfers; (b) the legal protection to pledged collateral from third-party claims; (c) the possibility of seizing the pledged collateral efficiently in case of a default by the debtor; and (d) reliable, universally accepted, and enforceable accounting standards for valuing collateral. In terms of technology, a collateralized interbank market relies on the existence of a large-value payment system that is fully integrated with an electronic book-entry system that enables the recording of pledges on securities and changes in their ownership.

Integrating payment systems and collateral registries and securities depositories can also make sense in view of some of the steps central banks took to stabilize the interbank markets during the recent financial crisis. For example, central banks began to accept a broader range of collateral in all classes of lending operations (accepting private sector collateral and allowing counterparties to economize on the use of government securities, which is often the only collateral that counterparties can still use in secured, or *repo*, markets). Expanding the pool of eligible collateral would generally mean that central banks are willing to accept securities other than those issued by the government or by itself as collateral in lending operations. In practice, this can be done quickly, safely, and efficiently only if the funds transfer system is interconnected with the securities depository that holds such other, newly eligible securities.

Although many RTGS systems have some interface with securities depositories and the related settlement systems, in many cases (especially in the case of private securities depositories) this interface is available solely for the final settlement of securities trades and is not operational for any other purpose, such as for collateralization in interbank markets (World Bank 2011b). Also, typically, though not in all cases, when an RTGS system is interconnected with a securities depository, the latter holds the records for government and central bank securities only. This type of securities depository is usually owned and operated by the central bank, just as in the case of RTGS systems. Central banks can therefore support better integration of funds transfer systems with securities settlement systems in their country.

Securities settlement systems

Financial transactions can take place either through organized exchanges or as "over-the-counter" (OTC) transactions. Exchanges, such as the stock market, offer a centralized way of transacting, where one party facilitates transactions by connecting buyers and sellers. They also offer greater regulatory oversight and transparency, since only members of the exchange can trade the products that are listed on the exchange. There is no counterparty risk in transactions settled through exchanges, because the exchange acts as the regulator and the counterparty to each transaction. By contrast, OTC markets are generally decentralized, with numerous mediators trying to connect buyers and sellers. Until recently, the majority of these markets remained largely unregulated and hence were not very transparent. OTC markets are prone to counterparty risk because there is no centralized exchange and the parties deal directly with each other.[22] As a result, the stability of OTC markets, especially in times of financial crisis, depends strongly on the legal and regulatory framework that governs their operation.

The global financial crisis emphasized the risks to financial stability that may arise from the lack of transparency and the significant counterparty risk that characterizes many OTC markets. The crisis made apparent that risks emanating from OTC transaction—the value of which dwarfs exchange

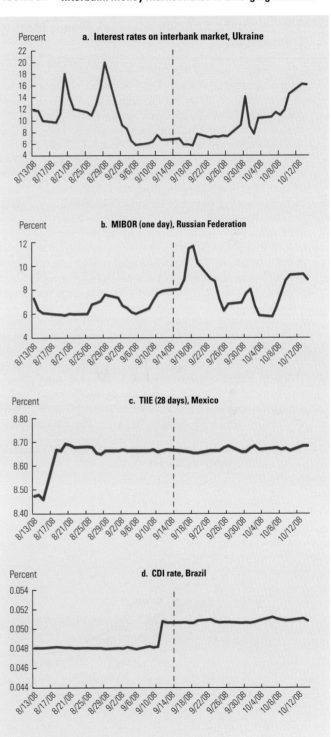

FIGURE 5.9   Interbank Money Market Rates in Emerging Markets

Sources: National Bank of Ukraine, Bank of Russia, Banco Central do Brasil, and Banco de Mexico.
Note: Interbank money market rates in emerging countries are shown for the periods August 13–September 12, 2008 (before failure of Lehman Brothers), and September 15–October 14, 2008 (increased volatility). Banco de Mexico increased its target interest rate to 25 basis points on August 18. MIBOR = Moscow interbank offered rate.

BOX 5.7 Italy: Reviving Interbank Money Markets through Collateralized Transactions

As a consequence of the Lehman Brothers collapse in September 2008, the Italian segment of the euro money market was particularly severely disrupted. Before the crisis the Italian market—an electronic market called the e-MID—accounted for 17 percent of interbank transactions within the euro area. Between August 2007 and October 2008, the daily volume of activity transiting from the e-MID almost halved, dropping from €24 billion to €14 billion.

The reason why the e-MID was more affected than other parts of the euro money market may be traced to a specificity whereby the e-MID offers a more transparent trading model than other parts of the euro money market. In the e-MID, bid and ask volumes are known by other participants in the market (Vento and La Ganga 2010). Indeed, in this market banks publish the liquidity amounts they want to lend or borrow, indicating different maturities and interest rates.

The move toward collateralized operations and less transparent transactions (OTC) has prompted the Bank of Italy to introduce a temporary innovation within the e-MID in order to meet this new demand and revive interbank activity. The MIC,

the collateralized interbank market segment of the e-MID, was started in February 2009.

The Bank of Italy has played a chief role in ensuring the success of this innovation. The trading on the MIC was characterized by a guarantee from the Bank of Italy on the obligations of market participants and by an active role of the central bank in the custody, administration, and evaluation of the collateral, as well as by complete anonymity of the participants and management of any payment failures.[a] Owing to the central guarantor and facilitator role played by the Bank of Italy, the MIC made it possible to eliminate the credit, liquidity, and reputational risks that caused the collapse of activity in the e-MID.

This innovation effectively allowed the system to overcome obstacles that hampered the smooth functioning of activity in the unsecured market, as reflected in a large increase in the volumes of activity migrating to the MIC and the narrow spreads relative to other segments of the euro market. Besides the recovery of market activity, the market witnessed a move toward greater diversification of contract maturities (figures B5.7.1 and B5.7.2).

FIGURE B5.7.1   Interbank Rates in the Italian Collateralized Money Market (MIC) and Other Segments of the Euro Money Market

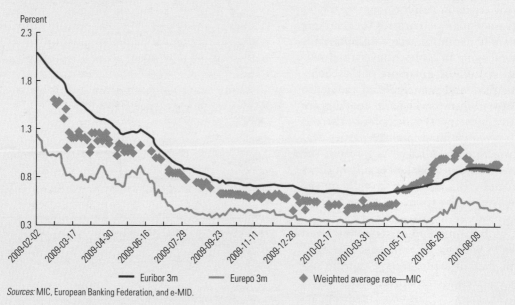

Sources: MIC, European Banking Federation, and e-MID.

BOX 5.7   **Italy: Reviving Interbank Money Markets through Collateralized Transactions**   *(continued)*

The Bank of Italy had set the expiration date of the MIC initiative on December 31, 2010. However, the MIC initiative proved to be so useful that before its expiration, banks ended up creating their own New MIC. On October 11, 2010, the New MIC started as the continuation of the MIC. It is a permanent market, fully based on private infrastructures.

FIGURE B5.7.2   **Outstanding Volumes and Average Maturity Trend on the MIC**

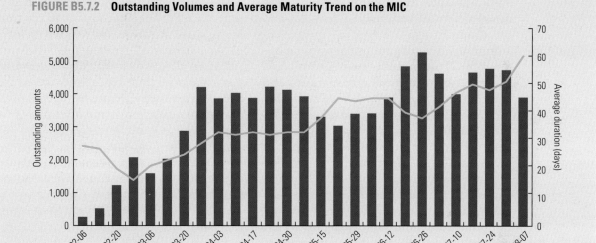

Legend: ■ Outstanding amount (euros million)   —— Average duration (days)

Sources: Vento and La Ganga 2010; e-MID.

a. Bank of Italy website http://www.bancaditalia.it/sispaga/MIC.

---

traded markets[23]—can create substantial systemic risks and can significantly exacerbate financial distress. The crisis highlighted that, in particular, OTC derivatives markets proved to be deficient in risk management and transparency. As the crisis unfolded, regulators became particularly concerned about the buildup of large nontransparent counterparty exposures that were not subject to appropriate risk management; contagion risk arising from the interconnectedness of market participants; and the limited transparency of overall counterparty exposures in OTC markets, which precipitated a loss of confidence and market liquidity in time of stress (FSB 2010c).

Several proposals have been made to better address the risks to financial stability arising in OTC derivatives markets. First, the G-20, in its September 2009 communiqué, proposed that all standardized OTC derivatives contracts should be centrally cleared and traded on exchanges or electronic platforms, where appropriate, by the end of 2012. In addition, transactions in OTC derivatives should be reported to trade repositories to enhance the transparency of the market.[24]

Another proposal for increasing stability in OTC derivatives transactions is to strengthen the role of so-called central counterparties (CCPs).[25] Clearing transactions through institutions acting as CCPs can contribute to financial stability and standardization of OTC derivatives contracts by mitigating counterparty risk, using multilateral netting, requiring daily or intraday margin calls and clearing fund contributions, and enhancing transparency. Should a counterparty of a CCP that is involved in OTC trading become insolvent, it would not create the chain reaction that, for example, the default of Lehman Brothers triggered, because a properly managed and supervised CCP should be able to act as a firewall between the defaulter and other counterparties.

Finally, promoting the use of trade repositories in OTC derivatives transactions could further enhance market transparency and reduce counterparty risks. A trade repository for OTC derivatives is a centralized registry that maintains an electronic database of open OTC derivatives transaction records. In the absence of a trade repository, transaction data are maintained by individual counterparties and possibly other institutions providing services to market participants (for example, prime brokers, CCPs, trading platforms, and custodians), often stored in proprietary systems in various formats with different data fields. An important benefit of a trade repository is that it helps promote standardization and provides a level of consistency in the quality of transaction data. Enhanced market transparency through trade repositories helps public authorities and market participants monitor the buildup of exposures in relevant markets, thereby supporting sound risk management; market discipline; and effective oversight, regulation, and supervision.

To better manage risks in the future, the state has to ensure regulatory reforms in OTC markets to increase transparency and encourage supervisors and overseers to effectively monitor the buildup of systemic risk. Moving toward increased use of CCPs and trade repositories for OTC derivatives markets is an important step in the right direction. However, despite the stated benefits, CCPs are no panacea for all products and all markets. A CCP is typically attractive for a market with highly liquid, standardized contracts.

Also, greater use of CCPs for OTC derivatives transactions and the conditions under which market participants can obtain access will increase their systemic importance (BIS 2011). Accordingly, it is critical that the risk management at these CCPs be robust and comprehensive. A CCP would need to comply with high risk management standards and require counterparties to post appropriate collateral in a timely manner. The state has to ensure supervision, oversight, and regulation of CCPs. The same applies to the trade repositories. An increased reliance of users, public authorities, interoperable infrastructures, service providers, and other market participants on trade repositories means that adequate measures are needed to ensure the availability, timeliness, and accuracy of the data stored in trade repositories. The new *Principles for Financial Market Infrastructures*, released by the Committee on Payment and Settlement Systems and the International Organization of Securities Commissions in April 2012, covers the CCPs and trade repository issues discussed above.

Finally, CCPs may not be a viable solution for all OTC derivatives markets, because their risk management systems are not necessarily equipped to clear all types of derivatives contracts. Given that, as a result, a certain share of OTC derivatives trades will remain bilaterally cleared, enhancing the safety and transparency of bilateral clearing also merits attention.[26] Given the international character of OTC derivatives markets, it will be critical to ensure consistency of initiatives to prevent regulatory arbitrage.

NOTES

1. This definition of financial infrastructure follows that in previous publications, such as World Bank (2009).
2. The introduction of credit information can have both screening and incentive effects. Luoto, McIntosh, and Wydick (2007) present a theoretical model that highlights this point.
3. The literature on relationship banking suggests that decentralized banks are better able to lend to informationally opaque borrowers,

because they can make better use of "soft" relationship-specific information. Better credit reporting can improve access to credit by making part of this proprietary information accessible to the market.

4. See Olegario (2003) for a detailed discussion of the historical development of credit reporting institutions.

5. Many countries have included anti-discrimination provisions in their data protection laws. In the United States, for example, the Equal Credit Opportunity Act prohibits using data on a borrower's gender, race, age, or marital status to determine creditworthiness. Many credit bureaus also refrain from using this data due to public relations concerns (Bostic and Calem 2003; OECD 2010).

6. Securities systems and large-value payment systems are mutually dependent. To achieve delivery versus payment, settlement of securities in the securities settlement system is conditional on settlement of cash, normally in a large-value payment system. In parallel, credit extensions in large-value payment systems are often dependent on the provision of collateral through a securities system.

7. In 2001, the Committee on Payment and Settlement Systems (CPSS) and the International Organization of Securities Commissions (IOSCO) published the "Core Principles for Systemically Important Payment Systems" (CPSIPS) and the "Recommendations for Securities Settlement Systems" (RSSS). In 2004, CPSS-IOSCO also published the "Recommendations for Central Counterparties" (RCCP). These documents are used as standards for assessment by the FSAP. The CPSS and IOSCO recently reviewed these standards and published in April 2012 the "Principles for Financial Market Infrastructures," which will replace the CPSIPS, RSSS, and RCCP.

8. In particular, the World Bank contributes to the work done by the CPSS and IOSCO.

9. CPSS (2005, 2006) provide information on new developments in large-value payment systems and general guidelines for payment system development, respectively.

10. Central bank money is issued in the form of banknotes and deposits held by commercial banks. The majority of payment systems, especially those transferring large-value funds, use central bank money, which greatly reduces credit and liquidity risks in payment and settlement systems (European Central Bank 2010b).

11. Credit risk is the risk that a participant will fail to meet an obligation when due or anytime thereafter. Liquidity risk is the risk that participant will fail to meet an obligation when due, but at an unspecified time thereafter. The European Central Bank (2010b) provides a discussion of risks associated with large-value payment systems.

12. The World Bank has supported several client countries with the adoption of RTGS systems (for example, the Dominican Republic). Since 2007, implementation of 19 new RTGS systems has taken place; such systems are currently being implemented in Honduras; Macao SAR, China; Papua New Guinea; and Paraguay (World Bank 2011b). According to the survey a relatively small number of countries indicate that large-value payments are being processed, exclusively or in parallel with the RTGS system, through check-clearing systems (23 percent) or other non-RTGS large-value systems (17 percent).

13. An additional case study on the West Bank and Gaza is available at http://worldbank.org/financialdevelopment.

14. Financial stability reports from the Bank of England (2010, 2011) provide evidence of the resilience of CHAPS and CREST, the United Kingdom's large-value and securities settlement systems.

15. This section draws on Cirasino, García, and Guadamillas (2009).

16. Banks typically hold low volumes of cash and reserves and rely on incoming funds to make payments. For example, before the financial crisis, many banks in the United States held cash and reserve holdings equivalent to only about 1 percent of their total daily payment volume (Afonso and Shin 2009).

17. Information asymmetries and adverse selection problems can explain why market participants prefer to hoard liquidity in times of stress. For further reading refer to Vento and La Ganga (2010).

18. There are similar examples from the past (for example, disruptions in payment systems after September 11, 2001). McAndrews and Potter (2002) examine the classic example of Herstatt Bank (in 1974) that resulted in payment system problems.

19. Davis (2009) gives an overview of the chronology of the crisis and the steps central banks took to revive the markets.

20. IMF (2010b) and Hördahl and King (2008) provide an overview of the impact of the financial crisis on various funding markets.

21. Ukraine had been facing severe difficulties in its banking sector for several months. This may explain why the money market was highly volatile even before the aggravation of the global financial crisis in mid-September 2008. However, the volatility of interest rates kept on increasing for the rest of 2008 (with standard deviation increasing to approximately 10.6 for the period from September 15 to December 31, 2008).

22. The upside of OTC derivatives markets is that they can improve the pricing of risk, add to liquidity in the market, and help market participants manage their respective risks (FSB 2010c).

23. According to BIS estimates, the notional value of outstanding OTC contracts exceeded the staggering amount of US$700 trillion in June 2011.

24. In line with the G-20 requests, the Committee on Payment and Settlement Systems and the International Organization of Securities Commissions have initiated a review of their existing principles and recommendations in order to address issues specific to OTC derivatives (see, for example CPSS-IOSCO 2010a, 2010b). In addition, various attempts have been made by individual country legislators to meet the obligations, for example, by the United States and the European Union.

25. A CCP is an entity that interposes itself between counterparties to contracts traded in one or more financial markets, becoming the buyer to every seller and the seller to every buyer.

26. In October 2011, the Financial Stability Board (FSB) noted delays in the implementation of OTC derivatives reforms, urged jurisdictions to achieve the end-2012 deadline, and stressed the importance of coordination between national supervisors and regulators.

Statistical Appendix

TABLE A.1   **Countries and Their Financial System Characteristics, Averages, 2008–2010**

	Financial institutions				Financial markets			
	Private credit to GDP (%)	Accounts per thousand adults, commercial banks	Lending-deposit spread (%)	Z-score–weighted average, commercial banks	(Stock market capitalization + outstanding domestic private debt securities)/ GDP (%)	Market capital-ization out of the top 10 largest companies (%)	Stock market turnover ratio (%)	Asset price volatility
Afghanistan	7.9	71.1		9.7				
Albania	33.8		6.2	22.4				
Algeria	13.7	343.3	6.3	15.5				
Andorra				21.7				
Angola	15.0	114.5	8.0	12.0				
Antigua and Barbuda	70.8			7.0				
Argentina	12.3	667.2	4.6	5.3	20.5	27.8	13.5	43.0
Armenia	19.8	524.1	10.3	16.3	1.3		0.4	
Aruba	57.1			7.7				
Australia	124.4		3.4	34.7	172.6	56.9	97.5	38.6
Austria	120.5	1,401.2		12.8	79.5	36.1	68.0	
Azerbaijan	16.0	38.0	8.1	10.0				
Bahamas, The	82.2		1.8	23.6				
Bahrain	74.0		6.3	48.6	97.7		6.6	11.7
Bangladesh	38.3	365.5	6.3	8.3	9.1		216.1	
Barbados	96.0		6.0	37.8	127.7		1.7	
Belarus	29.8		0.4	30.7				
Belgium	94.4			6.7	100.1		63.6	34.8
Belize	62.8	995.6	5.8	20.4				
Benin	20.8			20.5				
Bermuda				11.1				
Bhutan	30.8			17.8				
Bolivia	32.0		9.0	24.0	15.7		1.6	
Bosnia and Herzegovina	56.1	911.2	4.2	17.3				22.1
Botswana	22.0	477.2	6.7	10.0	32.2		4.4	16.4
Brazil	45.6		34.0	15.9	82.5	45.8	83.0	49.1
Brunei Darussalam	39.8		4.8	5.9				
Bulgaria	63.7	1,988.7	6.2	12.3	20.9		7.9	33.1
Burkina Faso	17.0			7.5				
Burundi	18.5			13.0				
Cambodia	23.3	91.6		15.2				
Cameroon	10.4	58.4		19.3				

(appendix continues on next page)

TABLE A.1   **Countries and Their Financial System Characteristics, Averages, 2008–2010** *(continued)*

	Financial institutions				Financial markets			
	Private credit to GDP (%)	Accounts per thousand adults, commercial banks	Lending-deposit spread (%)	Z-score—weighted average, commercial banks	(Stock market capitalization + outstanding domestic private debt securities)/GDP (%)	Market capitalization out of the top 10 largest companies (%)	Stock market turnover ratio (%)	Asset price volatility
Canada	126.6		2.7	19.3	139.1	74.2	97.0	35.0
Cape Verde	57.0		7.4	38.1				
Cayman Islands				28.8				
Central African Republic	6.9	2.4		7.7				
Chad	4.1	19.0		10.0				
Chile	75.9	2,015.2	4.7	8.9	125.5	53.7	20.9	30.0
China	111.1		3.1	34.8	109.9	71.6	187.8	41.3
Colombia	31.1		6.7	15.2	49.9	24.6	15.2	31.7
Comoros	10.8	61.8	8.5					
Congo, Dem. Rep.	4.9		41.5	9.7				
Congo, Rep.	3.2	16.1		4.4				
Costa Rica	46.0		12.1	20.7	5.4		3.5	21.8
Côte d'Ivoire	16.4			10.7	30.4		3.0	
Croatia	65.6		8.1	39.8	51.0		6.3	36.0
Cuba				8.0				
Cyprus	265.6			7.7	47.3	21.3	13.9	45.3
Czech Republic	50.2		4.7	27.1	38.2		50.3	39.8
Denmark	208.1			15.1	229.1		95.2	33.2
Djibouti	24.2	77.4	9.5	11.6				
Dominica	50.2		6.3	9.2				
Dominican Republic	19.9		9.1	23.6				
Ecuador	25.7			22.8	8.3		9.2	
Egypt, Arab Rep.	37.2		5.3	23.1	54.4	56.0	81.4	32.0
El Salvador	41.6			31.8	23.2		0.7	
Equatorial Guinea	3.3	121.8		16.3				
Eritrea				9.2				
Estonia	101.8	1,925.4	4.7	5.7	14.2		19.9	29.1
Ethiopia	17.2	91.7	3.3	10.3				
Fiji	46.9		3.4		32.7		0.8	
Finland	89.6			18.9	90.4		114.5	38.6
France	109.7			14.4	126.4		107.7	34.4
Gabon	9.3	91.1		14.8				
Gambia, The	16.8		12.7	7.4				
Georgia	30.5	653.1	13.7	6.7	6.6		0.7	
Germany	109.1			10.5	75.4	51.7	142.9	33.3
Ghana	14.0	298.8		15.4	9.8		5.9	

TABLE A.1   **Countries and Their Financial System Characteristics, Averages, 2008–2010** *(continued)*

	Financial institutions				Financial markets			
	Private credit to GDP (%)	Accounts per thousand adults, commercial banks	Lending-deposit spread (%)	Z-score—weighted average, commercial banks	(Stock market capitalization + outstanding domestic private debt securities)/GDP (%)	Market capitalization out of the top 10 largest companies (%)	Stock market turnover ratio (%)	Asset price volatility
Greece	98.6	3,799.7		12.0	48.6	39.8	64.0	41.7
Grenada	75.6		7.2	12.0				
Guatemala	24.9		8.2	27.6				
Guinea				2.8				
Guinea-Bissau	4.9							
Guyana	27.2		12.2	18.9	14.3		0.3	
Haiti	12.8	329.4	16.2	20.5				
Honduras	49.8		8.7	29.8				
Hong Kong SAR, China	152.9		4.8	33.1	532.5	58.1	155.8	30.6
Hungary	65.2	1,027.5	2.7	14.4	27.8	4.4	123.8	51.0
Iceland	137.5			9.1	152.8		46.6	67.3
India	44.1	747.3		27.8	84.7	72.1	131.4	39.8
Indonesia	23.8		5.5	18.3	33.1	53.2	93.7	39.4
Iran, Islamic Rep.	33.9		0.1		15.3	54.0	55.6	
Iraq	5.5			21.9				
Ireland	228.2			3.7	129.6	21.3	50.6	46.0
Israel	93.9	1,055.7	2.8	26.3	91.1	42.6	65.4	20.9
Italy	108.9	1,221.2		27.3	73.5	38.9	133.0	34.9
Jamaica	26.3		10.9	23.5	56.4		4.8	15.0
Japan	103.7	7,185.2	1.2	32.9	114.3	60.7	124.9	28.6
Jordan	71.8		4.5	48.2	148.3	30.6	60.3	22.8
Kazakhstan	45.8	902.7		4.3	34.7		11.3	44.2
Kenya	29.0	328.4	9.1	19.2	38.1		13.9	26.9
Korea, Rep.	101.6	4,374.1	1.7	13.4	147.8	67.1	229.4	42.2
Kosovo	30.3	728.9						
Kuwait	65.6		2.9	24.6	98.2		92.8	15.4
Kyrgyz Republic		162.5	20.8	17.2	1.8		100.8	
Lao PDR	10.4	44.3	20.2	11.2				
Latvia	88.1	1,230.7	7.1	3.0	6.9		2.1	31.5
Lebanon	66.7	873.0	2.2	33.0	32.1		12.5	20.5
Lesotho	11.2	245.3	8.1	19.4				
Liberia	12.3		10.2	7.2				
Libya	8.0		3.5	77.3				
Lithuania	66.4		2.2	4.3	13.5		8.4	29.7
Luxembourg	184.0			24.6	189.6	3.7	0.7	35.0
Macao SAR, China	51.7		4.9	22.6				

(appendix continues on next page)

TABLE A.1   **Countries and Their Financial System Characteristics, Averages, 2008–2010** *(continued)*

	Financial institutions				Financial markets			
	Private credit to GDP (%)	Accounts per thousand adults, commercial banks	Lending-deposit spread (%)	Z-score–weighted average, commercial banks	(Stock market capitalization + outstanding domestic private debt securities)/GDP (%)	Market capital-ization out of the top 10 largest companies (%)	Stock market turnover ratio (%)	Asset price volatility
Macedonia, FYR	41.1		3.1	10.8	15.9		6.6	34.3
Madagascar	10.7	36.1	35.2	19.1				
Malawi	11.7		21.5	18.9	29.7		2.1	
Malaysia	106.3	1,570.3	2.8	19.6	173.2	62.5	34.4	21.1
Maldives	66.1	1,130.0	6.4	7.8				
Mali	17.1			12.0				
Malta	127.6	3,561.8		12.6	50.1	5.8	1.3	17.4
Mauritania	25.5		10.9	23.1				
Mauritius	80.8		11.0	23.5	51.4	41.8	10.1	28.1
Mexico	17.5	1,161.2	4.9	9.9	48.0	33.8	35.6	36.9
Micronesia, Fed. Sts.			13.4	24.9				
Moldova	34.3	1,132.0	5.8	16.1				
Mongolia	38.8	1,283.3	8.6	24.4	10.3		10.1	35.0
Montenegro	77.5			5.5	84.9		5.3	
Morocco	71.8	584.2		33.0	74.6	26.8	34.1	21.0
Mozambique	19.5		6.7	22.5				
Myanmar	3.3		5.0	3.2				
Namibia	44.5	635.3	5.0	41.1	8.2		3.4	48.1
Nepal	44.7		5.2	16.3	37.2		6.2	
Netherlands	201.9	1,762.5	0.2	12.2	146.0		138.7	32.8
New Zealand	145.0		1.9	19.3	35.1	43.9	60.0	30.9
Nicaragua	34.4		8.3	17.9				
Niger	10.9			30.0				
Nigeria	31.1		6.5	13.3	26.1		24.3	24.6
Norway		513.6	1.9	22.4	81.8	32.2	138.9	48.0
Oman	38.4	1,011.5	3.1	23.3	33.2		49.7	25.1
Pakistan	24.3	219.5	5.9	10.7	22.1		121.3	31.5
Panama	78.7		4.7	22.6	31.4		2.6	11.3
Papua New Guinea	24.5	176.4	8.2	37.2	136.5		0.4	
Paraguay	27.0		24.8	19.8				
Peru	23.0	395.8	18.6	14.2	61.4	36.2	5.8	43.7
Philippines	27.2	431.6	4.8	36.8	49.7	51.2	28.8	31.3
Poland	43.2			24.4	31.5	43.8	52.9	44.2
Portugal	179.0	2,774.9		29.9	89.8		61.0	29.6
Qatar		725.3	3.7	32.4				31.4
Romania	37.7		5.8	10.3	16.6		10.5	45.1

TABLE A.1   Countries and Their Financial System Characteristics, Averages, 2008–2010 *(continued)*

	Financial institutions				Financial markets			
	Private credit to GDP (%)	Accounts per thousand adults, commercial banks	Lending-deposit spread (%)	Z-score–weighted average, commercial banks	(Stock market capitalization + outstanding domestic private debt securities)/GDP (%)	Market capitalization out of the top 10 largest companies (%)	Stock market turnover ratio (%)	Asset price volatility
Russian Federation	41.3		6.0	18.1	58.2	34.3	129.0	52.8
Rwanda		204.2	9.7	8.9				
Samoa	42.7		7.3	54.9				
San Marino	361.7			24.6				
São Tomé and Príncipe	29.5		18.9					
Saudi Arabia	45.3	744.6		17.2	77.6	39.6	126.8	30.5
Senegal	23.6			20.2				
Serbia	41.5		7.2	10.2	31.1		6.6	28.8
Seychelles	23.6	1,132.0	7.8	19.6				
Sierra Leone	7.6	131.1	13.4	7.9				
Singapore	97.4	2,070.3	5.1	46.4	169.9	65.0	104.2	30.8
Slovak Republic	44.7		2.0	9.7	10.9		3.1	23.3
Slovenia	88.6		3.6	15.8	34.0	23.7	6.8	28.1
Solomon Islands	23.7		11.9					
South Africa	75.8	882.9	3.4	27.1	245.6	67.6	69.9	39.5
Spain	203.7	801.1		57.3	144.8	59.7	159.1	36.2
Sri Lanka	26.2		5.5	19.3	19.4	55.3	29.8	25.3
St. Kitts and Nevis	64.0		4.1	18.8	83.5		1.4	
St. Lucia	112.0		7.1	24.3				
St. Vincent and the Grenadines	48.9		6.4	10.2				
Sudan	11.0			16.8				
Suriname	24.9		5.5	16.5				
Swaziland	22.8	443.1	6.2	11.9				
Sweden	124.3			19.6	149.6		124.8	41.7
Switzerland	169.6		2.8	15.4	244.0	35.5	100.0	26.3
Syrian Arab Republic	17.4	190.3	3.1	13.6				
Tajikistan			17.2	13.0				
Tanzania	14.4	126.6	7.3	19.9				27.0
Thailand	93.7	1,082.7	4.8	4.5	75.2	52.4	109.1	33.4
Timor-Leste	17.8		11.0					
Togo	18.8	175.5		7.9				
Tonga	49.2		6.9					
Trinidad and Tobago	29.7		7.1	29.6	55.9		2.6	
Tunisia	56.5			29.2	17.3		23.3	13.4
Turkey	34.0	1,263.1		32.4	30.7	49.0	201.9	46.6
Turkmenistan				8.0				

(appendix continues on next page)

TABLE A.1   **Countries and Their Financial System Characteristics, Averages, 2008–2010** *(continued)*

	Financial institutions				Financial markets			
	Private credit to GDP (%)	Accounts per thousand adults, commercial banks	Lending-deposit spread (%)	Z-score–weighted average, commercial banks	(Stock market capitalization + outstanding domestic private debt securities)/ GDP (%)	Market capitalization out of the top 10 largest companies (%)	Stock market turnover ratio (%)	Asset price volatility
Tuvalu				21.0				
Uganda	12.3	169.5	11.2	10.6	18.0		0.5	
Ukraine	66.0	3,176.4	6.7	6.3	25.0		8.8	58.8
United Arab Emirates				21.4				35.5
United Kingdom	205.3			18.1	126.6	62.2	183.1	33.1
United States	60.0			24.0	219.7	72.6	342.7	28.8
Uruguay	22.9	551.0	8.8	4.7	0.4		4.8	
Uzbekistan		909.2		65.8				
Vanuatu	56.6		4.1	39.2				
Venezuela, RB	18.2		4.4	8.4	1.7		1.4	57.0
Vietnam	96.8		2.4	23.2	17.1		141.6	43.7
West Bank and Gaza		543.3	6.1					
Yemen, Rep.	7.1	89.9	5.8	18.0				
Zambia	11.8		13.7	7.6	17.9		14.8	

Source: Data from and calculations based on the Global Financial Development Database.
Note: The four blue bars summarize where the country's observation is vis-à-vis the global statistical distribution of the variable in the Global Financial Development Database. Each blue bar corresponds to one quartile of the statistical distribution. So, values below the 25th percentile show only one full bar, values equal or greater than the 25th and less than the 50th percentile show two full bars, values equal or greater than the 50th and less than the 75th percentile show three full bars, and values greater than the 75th percentile show four full bars. The blue bars on the far left are based on a simple (unweighted) average of the eight financial characteristics, each converted to a 0–100 scale. For details, see Čihák, Demirgüç-Kunt, Feyen, and Levine (2012).

MAP A.1 DEPTH—FINANCIAL INSTITUTIONS

To approximate financial institutions' depth, this map uses domestic private credit to the real sector by deposit money banks as a percentage of local currency GDP. Data on domestic private credit to the real sector by deposit money banks are from the International Financial Statistics (IFS), line 22D, published by the International Monetary Fund (IMF). Local currency GDP is also from IFS. Missing observations are imputed by using GDP growth rates from World Development Indicators (WDI), instead of substituting the levels. This approach ensures a smoother GDP series. The four shades of blue in the map are based on the average value of the variable in 2008–10: the darker the blue, the higher the quartile of the statistical distribution of the variable.

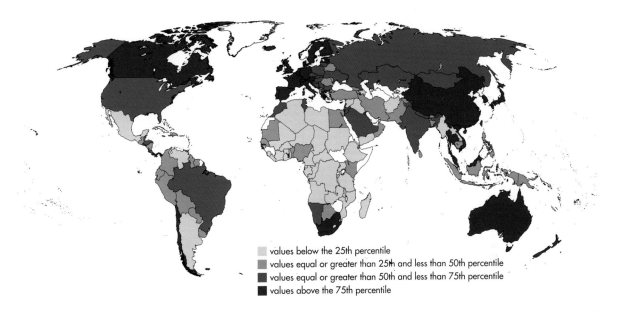

- values below the 25th percentile
- values equal or greater than 25th and less than 50th percentile
- values equal or greater than 50th and less than 75th percentile
- values above the 75th percentile

Private credit to GDP (%)		Number of countries	Average	Median	Standard deviation	Minimum	Maximum	Weighted average[a]
	World	173	56.3	38.8	54.6	3.2	361.7	89.9
By developed/developing economies								
	Developed economies	48	113.3	100.1	68.6	3.3	361.7	103.0
	Developing economies	125	34.5	26.3	24.9	3.2	112.0	60.5
By income level								
	High income	48	113.3	100.1	68.6	3.3	361.7	103.0
	Upper middle income	49	48.6	44.5	28.0	8.0	112.0	67.8
	Lower middle income	49	30.8	27.0	18.7	3.2	96.8	36.6
	Low income	27	15.4	12.8	9.8	3.3	44.7	24.9
By region								
	High income: OECD	30	124.0	109.4	52.2	43.2	228.2	103.7
	High income: non-OECD	17	97.3	65.6	90.7	3.3	361.7	80.7
	East Asia & Pacific	17	46.8	38.8	34.6	3.3	111.1	100.1
	Europe & Central Asia	19	44.9	41.1	19.6	16.0	88.1	40.4
	Latin America & Caribbean	29	41.5	32.0	24.2	12.3	112.0	33.4
	Middle East & North Africa	12	34.5	29.1	26.0	5.5	71.8	32.1
	South Asia	8	35.3	34.6	17.3	7.9	66.1	41.1
	Sub-Saharan Africa	41	20.1	16.4	16.9	3.2	80.8	38.7

Source: Global Financial Development Database, 2008–10 data.
Note: OECD = Organisation for Economic Co-operation and Development.
a. Weighted average by current GDP.

MAP A.2 ACCESS—FINANCIAL INSTITUTIONS

To approximate access to financial institutions, this map uses the number of depositors with commercial banks per 1,000 adults. For each type of institution the calculation follows: (reported number of depositors)*1,000/adult population in the reporting country. Number of depositors from commercial banks is from the Financial Access Survey reported by the IMF. Adult population data are from WDI. The four shades of blue in the map are based on the average value of the variable in 2008–10: the darker the blue, the higher the quartile of the statistical distribution of the variable.

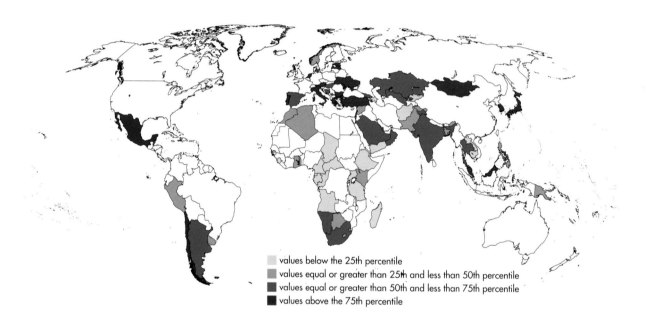

values below the 25th percentile
values equal or greater than 25th and less than 50th percentile
values equal or greater than 50th and less than 75th percentile
values above the 75th percentile

Accounts per thousand adults from commercial banks		Number of countries	Average	Median	Standard deviation	Minimum	Maximum	Weighted average[a]
	World	79	904.7	584.2	1,147.3	2.4	7,185.2	1,339.0
By developed/developing economies								
	Developed economies	18	2,004.3	1,311.2	1,766.1	121.8	7,185.2	3,761.8
	Developing economies	61	580.2	395.8	598.2	2.4	3,176.4	691.5
By income level								
	High income	18	2,004.3	1,311.2	1,766.1	121.8	7,185.2	3,761.8
	Upper middle income	21	921.1	902.7	534.1	38.0	2,015.2	997.9
	Lower middle income	24	570.1	437.3	664.1	16.1	3,176.4	725.9
	Low income	16	147.9	128.9	112.0	2.4	365.5	222.5
By region								
	High income: OECD	12	2,320.2	1,581.8	1,945.7	513.6	7,185.2	3,933.9
	High income: non-OECD	6	1,372.5	878.1	1,248.0	121.8	3,561.8	1,082.9
	East Asia & Pacific	7	668.6	431.6	630.3	44.3	1,570.3	799.3
	Europe & Central Asia	13	1,047.8	909.2	811.2	38.0	3,176.4	1,645.5
	Latin America & Caribbean	7	873.6	667.2	587.6	329.4	2,015.2	967.0
	Middle East & North Africa	7	385.9	343.3	295.6	77.4	873.0	384.7
	South Asia	5	506.7	365.5	429.7	71.1	1,130.0	531.7
	Sub-Saharan Africa	22	261.0	150.3	294.5	2.4	1,132.0	281.1

Source: Global Financial Development Database, 2008–10 data.
Note: OECD = Organisation for Economic Co-operation and Development.
a. Weighted average by total adult population.

MAP A.3 EFFICIENCY—FINANCIAL INSTITUTIONS

To approximate efficiency of financial institutions, this map uses the spread (difference) between lending rate and deposit rate. Lending rate is the rate charged by banks on loans to the private sector, and deposit interest rate is the rate offered by commercial or similar banks on three-month deposits. The lending and deposit rates are from IFS line 60P and 60L, respectively. The four shades of blue in the map are based on the average value of the variable in 2008–10: the darker the blue, the higher the quartile of the statistical distribution of the variable.

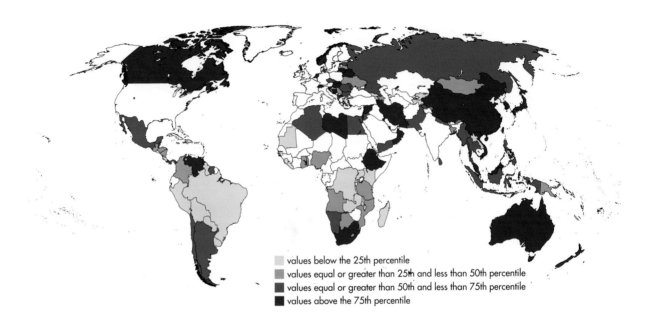

values below the 25th percentile
values equal or greater than 25th and less than 50th percentile
values equal or greater than 50th and less than 75th percentile
values above the 75th percentile

Lending-deposit spread (%)		Number of countries	Average	Median	Standard deviation	Minimum	Maximum	Weighted average[a]
	World	129	7.7	6.3	6.4	0.1	41.5	6.9
By developed/developing economies								
	Developed economies	28	3.8	3.5	2.0	0.2	8.1	2.2
	Developing economies	101	8.8	6.9	6.7	0.1	41.5	7.3
By income level								
	High income	28	3.8	3.5	2.0	0.2	8.1	2.2
	Upper middle income	43	6.7	6.2	5.3	0.1	34.0	6.5
	Lower middle income	39	8.8	8.0	4.7	2.4	24.8	6.0
	Low income	19	13.7	10.2	10.1	3.3	41.5	13.0
By region								
	High income: OECD	14	2.6	2.7	1.2	0.2	4.7	1.9
	High income: non-OECD	13	5.1	4.9	1.9	1.8	8.1	5.1
	East Asia & Pacific	17	7.3	5.5	4.7	2.4	20.2	3.6
	Europe & Central Asia	17	7.7	6.2	5.2	0.4	20.8	6.7
	Latin America & Caribbean	27	9.6	7.2	6.8	4.1	34.0	16.9
	Middle East & North Africa	10	4.6	4.9	2.6	0.1	9.5	4.6
	South Asia	5	5.9	5.9	0.5	5.2	6.4	6.0
	Sub-Saharan Africa	26	11.7	8.8	8.9	3.3	41.5	12.8

Source: Global Financial Development Database, 2008–10 data.
Note: OECD = Organisation for Economic Co-operation and Development.
a. Weighted average by total population.

MAP A.4 STABILITY—FINANCIAL INSTITUTIONS

To approximate stability of financial institutions, this map uses the average weighted z-score for commercial banks. The indicator for each commercial bank is estimated as follows: (ROA + Equity / Assets)/ (Standard Deviation of ROA). Return on assets (ROA), equity, and assets are from Bankscope. Market share in terms of total assets is used to calculate the country aggregate. The four shades of blue in the map are based on the average value of the variable in 2008–10: the darker the blue, the higher the quartile of the statistical distribution of the variable.

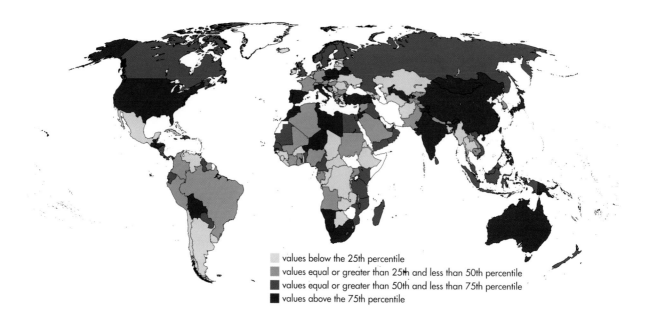

values below the 25th percentile
values equal or greater than 25th and less than 50th percentile
values equal or greater than 50th and less than 75th percentile
values above the 75th percentile

Z-score weighted average from commercial banks		Number of countries	Average	Median	Standard deviation	Minimum	Maximum	Weighted average[a]
	World	178	19.2	17.9	11.8	2.8	77.3	23.4
By developed/developing economies								
	Developed economies	53	21.6	19.6	11.2	3.7	57.3	23.4
	Developing economies	125	18.1	16.3	11.9	2.8	77.3	23.4
By income level								
	High income	53	21.6	19.6	11.2	3.7	57.3	23.4
	Upper middle income	48	18.2	15.3	13.5	3.0	77.3	26.8
	Lower middle income	47	21.5	19.3	12.0	4.4	65.8	23.6
	Low income	30	12.8	10.5	6.3	2.8	30.0	12.1
By region								
	High income: OECD	31	19.3	18.1	10.6	3.7	57.3	23.3
	High income: non-OECD	21	25.2	23.6	11.7	5.9	48.6	25.0
	East Asia & Pacific	15	24.6	23.2	14.0	3.2	54.9	30.0
	Europe & Central Asia	22	15.5	11.5	13.7	3.0	65.8	20.9
	Latin America & Caribbean	29	17.4	18.8	7.3	4.7	31.8	14.5
	Middle East & North Africa	11	29.5	23.1	19.1	11.6	77.3	24.3
	South Asia	8	14.7	13.5	6.9	7.8	27.8	23.5
	Sub-Saharan Africa	41	15.4	13.0	8.4	2.8	41.1	14.9

Source: Global Financial Development Database, 2008–10 data.
Note: OECD = Organisation for Economic Co-operation and Development.
a. Weighted average by total population.

MAP A.5 DEPTH—FINANCIAL MARKETS

To approximate depth of financial markets, this map uses market capitalization plus the amount of outstanding domestic private debt securities as percentage of GDP. Market capitalization (also known as market value) is the share price times the number of shares outstanding. Listed domestic companies are the domestically incorporated companies listed on the country's stock exchanges at the end of the year. Listed companies do not include investment companies, mutual funds, or other collective investment vehicles. Data are from Standard & Poor's Global

Stock Markets Factbook and supplemental S&P data, and are compiled and reported by the WDI. Amount of outstanding domestic private debt securities is from table 16A (domestic debt amount) of the Securities Statistics by the Bank for International Settlements. The amount includes all issuers except governments. The four shades of blue in the map are based on the average value of the variable in 2008–10: the darker the blue, the higher the quartile of the statistical distribution of the variable.

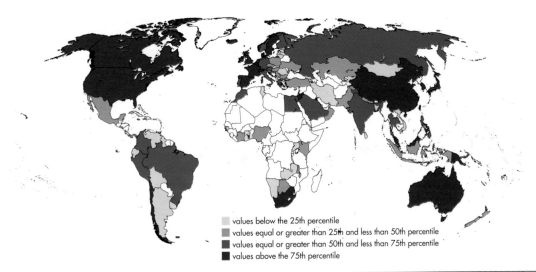

□ values below the 25th percentile
▨ values equal or greater than 25th and less than 50th percentile
▩ values equal or greater than 50th and less than 75th percentile
■ values above the 75th percentile

Stock market capitalization plus outstanding domestic private debt securities to GDP (%)		Number of countries	Average	Median	Standard deviation	Minimum	Maximum	Weighted average[a]
	World	103	71.2	48.6	74.7	0.4	532.5	130.6
By developed/developing economies								
	Developed economies	43	111.1	91.1	88.0	10.9	532.5	152.1
	Developing economies	60	42.5	30.0	46.1	0.4	245.6	76.4
By income level								
	High income	43	111.1	91.1	88.0	10.9	532.5	152.1
	Upper middle income	33	51.9	32.1	55.1	0.4	245.6	82.0
	Lower middle income	21	33.6	23.2	31.8	1.3	136.5	56.7
	Low income	6	22.3	23.9	15.1	1.8	38.1	18.4
By region								
	High income: OECD	31	108.2	100.1	63.6	10.9	244.0	151.3
	High income: non-OECD	11	121.9	77.6	142.1	33.2	532.5	180.4
	East Asia & Pacific	9	70.9	49.7	57.2	10.3	173.2	100.0
	Europe & Central Asia	14	24.9	18.8	23.1	1.3	84.9	43.7
	Latin America & Caribbean	16	39.3	27.3	35.7	0.4	125.5	59.6
	Middle East & North Africa	6	57.0	43.3	50.2	15.3	148.3	42.3
	South Asia	5	34.5	22.1	29.8	9.1	84.7	72.6
	Sub-Saharan Africa	11	46.1	29.7	67.3	8.2	245.6	133.7

Source: Global Financial Development Database, 2008–10 data.
Note: OECD = Organisation for Economic Co-operation and Development.
a. Weighted average by current GDP.

MAP A.6 ACCESS—FINANCIAL MARKETS

To approximate access to financial markets, this map uses the ratio of market capitalization outside of the top 10 largest companies to total market capitalization. The World Federation of Exchanges provides data on the exchange level. This variable is aggregated up to the country level by taking a simple average over exchanges. The four shades of blue in the map are based on the average value of the variable in 2008–10: the darker the blue, the higher the quartile of the statistical distribution of the variable.

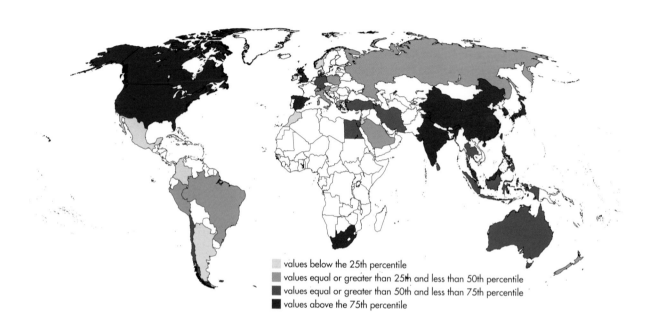

values below the 25th percentile
values equal or greater than 25th and less than 50th percentile
values equal or greater than 50th and less than 75th percentile
values above the 75th percentile

Market capitalization out of top 10 largest companies (%)		Number of countries	Average	Median	Standard deviation	Minimum	Maximum	Weighted average[a]
	World	46	44.8	44.8	18.2	3.7	74.2	63.6
By developed/developing economies								
	Developed economies	25	42.4	42.6	20.8	3.7	74.2	64.4
	Developing economies	21	47.6	51.2	14.6	24.6	72.1	60.9
By income level								
	High income	25	42.4	42.6	20.8	3.7	74.2	64.4
	Upper middle income	15	45.7	45.8	14.6	24.6	71.6	59.9
	Lower middle income	6	52.4	54.3	14.6	26.8	72.1	66.7
	Low income	0						
By region								
	High income: OECD	20	43.5	43.2	20.2	3.7	74.2	64.9
	High income: non-OECD	5	38.0	39.6	24.8	5.8	65.0	55.2
	East Asia & Pacific	5	58.2	53.2	8.8	51.2	71.6	69.6
	Europe & Central Asia	2	41.6	41.6	10.4	34.3	49.0	37.4
	Latin America & Caribbean	6	37.0	35.0	11.0	24.6	53.7	42.1
	Middle East & North Africa	4	41.8	42.3	15.3	26.8	56.0	44.8
	South Asia	2	63.7	63.7	11.9	55.3	72.1	72.2
	Sub-Saharan Africa	2	54.7	54.7	18.3	41.8	67.6	68.4

Source: Global Financial Development Database, 2008–10 data.
Note: OECD = Organisation for Economic Co-operation and Development.
a. Weighted average by stock market capitalization.

MAP A.7 EFFICIENCY—FINANCIAL MARKETS

To approximate efficiency of financial markets, this map uses the total value of shares traded during the period divided by the average market capitalization for the period. Average market capitalization is calculated as the average of the end-of-period values for the current period and the previous period. Data are from Standard & Poor's Global Stock Markets Factbook and supplemental Standard & Poor's data, and are compiled and reported by the WDI. The four shades of blue in the map are based on the average value of the variable in 2008–10: the darker the blue, the higher the quartile of the statistical distribution of the variable.

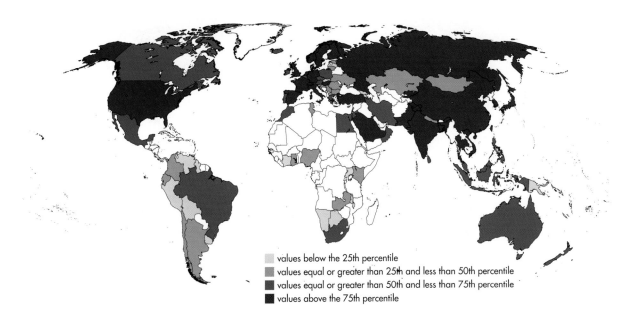

values below the 25th percentile
values equal or greater than 25th and less than 50th percentile
values equal or greater than 50th and less than 75th percentile
values above the 75th percentile

Stock market turnover ratio (%)		Number of countries	Average	Median	Standard deviation	Minimum	Maximum	Weighted average[a]
	World	103	56.9	28.8	65.3	0.3	342.7	197.5
By developed/developing economies								
	Developed economies	43	84.4	68.0	70.0	0.7	342.7	218.5
	Developing economies	60	37.2	10.3	54.2	0.3	216.1	127.0
By income level								
	High income	43	84.4	68.0	70.0	0.7	342.7	218.5
	Upper middle income	33	35.2	10.5	52.2	1.4	201.9	131.8
	Lower middle income	21	35.0	10.1	47.8	0.3	141.6	103.6
	Low income	6	56.6	10.1	87.0	0.5	216.1	69.5
By region								
	High income: OECD	31	98.9	97.0	69.9	0.7	342.7	223.4
	High income: non-OECD	11	51.1	13.9	58.2	1.3	155.8	131.9
	East Asia & Pacific	9	67.4	34.4	68.2	0.4	187.8	166.6
	Europe & Central Asia	14	35.7	8.2	62.2	0.4	201.9	121.5
	Latin America & Caribbean	16	12.8	4.8	21.0	0.3	83.0	56.9
	Middle East & North Africa	6	44.6	44.9	25.7	12.5	81.4	58.6
	South Asia	5	101.0	121.3	84.6	6.2	216.1	126.4
	Sub-Saharan Africa	11	13.9	5.9	19.9	0.5	69.9	62.1

Source: Global Financial Development Database, 2008–10 data.
Note: OECD = Organisation for Economic Co-operation and Development.
a. Weighted average by stock market capitalization.

MAP A.8 STABILITY—FINANCIAL MARKETS

To approximate stability of financial markets, this map uses the annual standard deviation of the price of a 1-year sovereign bond divided by the annual average price of the 1-year sovereign bond (both based on month-end data). The underlying data are based on Bloomberg. The four shades of blue in the map are based on the average value of the variable in 2008–10: the darker the blue, the higher the quartile of the statistical distribution of the variable.

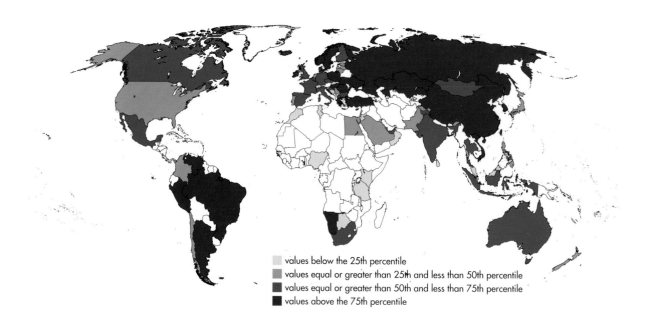

values below the 25th percentile
values equal or greater than 25th and less than 50th percentile
values equal or greater than 50th and less than 75th percentile
values above the 75th percentile

Asset price volatility		Number of countries	Average	Median	Standard deviation	Minimum	Maximum	Weighted average[a]
	World	84	33.6	33.1	10.8	11.3	67.3	38.0
By developed/developing economies								
	Developed economies	41	34.1	33.3	10.0	11.7	67.3	32.8
	Developing economies	43	33.2	31.7	11.6	11.3	58.8	39.3
By income level								
	High income	41	34.1	33.3	10.0	11.7	67.3	32.8
	Upper middle income	30	33.1	32.4	12.3	11.3	57.0	41.5
	Lower middle income	11	34.8	32.0	10.6	21.0	58.8	37.3
	Low income	2	26.9	26.9	0.1	26.9	27.0	27.1
By region								
	High income: OECD	30	36.3	34.9	9.2	20.9	67.3	33.0
	High income: non-OECD	11	28.2	30.6	10.0	11.7	45.3	30.5
	East Asia & Pacific	7	35.0	35.0	7.6	21.1	43.7	40.1
	Europe & Central Asia	11	38.8	34.3	11.4	22.1	58.8	49.0
	Latin America & Caribbean	10	34.0	34.3	14.9	11.3	57.0	42.3
	Middle East & North Africa	5	21.9	21.0	6.7	13.4	32.0	27.1
	South Asia	3	32.2	31.5	7.3	25.3	39.8	38.6
	Sub-Saharan Africa	7	30.1	27.0	10.5	16.4	48.1	28.0

Source: Global Financial Development Database, 2008–10 data.
Note: OECD = Organisation for Economic Co-operation and Development.
a. Weighted average by total population.

References

Abiad, Abdul, Giovanni Dell'Ariccia, and Bin Li. 2011. "Creditless Recoveries." Working Paper 11/58, International Monetary Fund, Washington, DC.

Acharya, Viral V. 2011. "Government as Shadow Banks: The Looming Threat to Financial Stability." Paper prepared for the Federal Reserve Board of Governors Conference on "Regulation of Systemic Risk," Washington, DC, September 15.

Acharya, Viral V., and Nirupama Kulkarni. 2010. "State Ownership and Systemic Risk: Evidence from the Indian Financial Sector during 2007–09." Unpublished paper, NYU–Stern, New York.

Acharya, Viral V., and Nada Mora. 2012. "Are Banks Passive Liquidity Backstops? Deposit Rates and Flows During the 2007–2009 Crisis." NBER Working Paper 17838, National Bureau of Economic Research, Cambridge, MA.

Admati, Anat, and Martin Hellwig. 2012. "Good Banking Regulation Needs Clear Focus, Sensible Tools, and Political Will." International Centre for Financial Regulation, London.

Afonso, António, Davide Furceri, and Pedro Gomes. 2011. "Sovereign Credit Ratings and Financial Markets Linkages: Application to European Data." Working Paper 1347, European Central Bank, Frankfurt, Germany.

Afonso, Gara Minguez, and Hyun Song Shin. 2009. "Systematic Risk Liquidity in Payment Systems." Staff Report No. 352, Federal Reserve Bank of New York.

Aisen, Ari, and Michael Franken. 2010. "Bank Credit during the 2008 Financial Crisis: A Cross-Country Comparison." Working Paper 10/47, International Monetary Fund, Washington, DC.

Aït-Sahalia, Yacine, Jochen Andritzky, Andreas Jobst, Sylwia Nowak, and Natalia Tamirisa. 2010. "Market Response to Policy Initiatives during the Global Financial Crisis." NBER Working Paper 15809, National Bureau of Economic Research, Cambridge, MA.

All About Finance (blog). 2011. "Can State-Owned Banks Play an Important Role in Promoting Financial Stability and Access?" Responses to the virtual debate question, Charles Calomiris and Franklin Allen. February 11. http://blogs.worldbank .org/allaboutfinance/the-question-can-state -owned-banks-play-an-important-role-in -promoting-financial-stability-and-acces.

Allen, Franklin, and Douglas Gale. 2000. *Comparing Financial Systems*. Cambridge, MA: MIT Press.

———. 2004. "Competition and Financial Stability." *Journal of Money, Credit and Banking* 36 (3, pt. 2): 453–80.

Altunbas, Yener, Lynne Evans, and Philip Moly-neux. 2001. "Bank Ownership and Efficiency." *Journal of Money, Credit and Banking* 33 (4): 926–54.

Andrianova, Svetlana, Panicos Demetriades, and Anja Shortland. 2008. "Government Ownership of Banks, Institutions, and Financial Development." *Journal of Development Economics* 85: 218–52.

———. 2010. "Government Ownership of Banks, Institutions, and Economic Growth." Working Paper 11/01, University of Leicester Department of Economics, Leicester, UK.

Angelidis, Dimitrios, and Katerina Lyroudi. 2006. "Efficiency in the Italian Banking Industry: Data Envelopment Analysis and Neural Networks." *International Research Journal of Finance and Economics* 5: 155–65.

Anginer, Deniz, Augusto De La Torre, and Alain Ize. 2011. "Risk Absorption by the State: When Is It a Good Public Policy?" Policy Research Working Paper 5893, World Bank, Washington, DC.

Anginer, Deniz, and Aslı Demirgüç-Kunt. 2011. "Has the Global Banking System Become More Fragile over Time?" Policy Research Working Paper 5849, World Bank, Washington, DC.

Anginer, Deniz, Aslı Demirgüç-Kunt, and Min Zhu. 2012. "How Does Bank Competition Affect Systemic Stability?" Policy Research Working Paper 5981, World Bank, Washington, DC.

Anzoategui, Diego, Maria Soledad Martínez Pería, and Martin Melecky. 2010. "Banking Sector Competition in Russia." Policy Research Working Paper 5449, World Bank, Washington, DC.

Anzoategui, Diego, Maria Soledad Martínez Pería, and Roberto Rocha. 2010. "Bank Competition in the Middle East and Northern Africa Region." Policy Research Working Paper 5363, World Bank, Washington, DC.

Arcand, Jean-Luis, Enrico Berkes, and Ugo Panizza. 2011. "Too Much Finance?" VoxEU. http://www.voxeu.org/index.php?q=node/6328.

Arezki, Rabah, Bertrand Candelon, and Amadou Sy. 2011. "Sovereign Rating News and Financial Markets Spillovers: Evidence from the European Debt Crisis." Working Paper 11/68, International Monetary Fund, Washington, DC.

Armendáriz de Aghion, Beatriz. 1999. "Development Banking." *Journal of Development Economics* 58: 83–100.

Arping, Stefan, Gyöngyi Lóránth, and Alan Morrison. 2010. "Public Initiatives to Support Entrepreneurs: Credit Guarantees Versus Co-funding." *Journal of Financial Stability* 6 (17): 26–35.

Ashcroft, Adam, and Donald Morgan. 2003. "Using Loan Rates to Measure and Regulate Bank Loan Risk." *Journal of Financial Services Research* 24: 181–200.

Ayyagari, Meghana, Aslı Demirgüç-Kunt, and Vojislav Maksimovic. 2011a. "Do Phoenix Miracles Exist? Firm-Level Evidence from Financial Crises." Policy Research Working Paper 5799, World Bank, Washington, DC.

———. 2011b. "Small vs. Young Firms across the World: Contribution to Employment, Job Creation, and Growth." Policy Research Working Paper 5631, World Bank, Washington, DC.

Bagehot, Walter. 1873. *Lombard Street*. Homewood, IL: Richard D. Irwin.

Bank of England. 2010. *Financial Stability Report* 28 (December). http://www.bankofengland.co.uk/publications/Pages/fsr/default.aspx.

Bank of England. 2011. "Payment Systems Oversight Report 2010." Bank of England, London.

Bank Regulation and Supervision Survey 2007 (database), World Bank, Washington, DC. http://econ.worldbank.org/WBSITE/EXTERNAL/EXTDEC/EXTRESEARCH/0,,contentMDK:20345037~pagePK:64214825~piPK:64214943~theSitePK:469382,00.html.

Bankscope (database). Bureau van Dijk. http://www.bvdinfo.com/Products/Company-Information/International/BANKSCOPE.aspx.

Barron, John M., and Michael Staten. 2003. "The Value of Comprehensive Credit Reports: Lessons from U.S. Experience, Credit Reporting Systems and the International Economy." MIT Press, Cambridge, MA.

Barth, James R., Gerard Caprio Jr., and Ross Levine. 2001. "The Regulation and Supervision of Banks around the World: A New Database." Policy Research Working Paper 2588, World Bank, Washington, DC.

———. 2004. "Bank Regulation and Supervision: What Works Best?" *Journal of Financial Intermediation* 13 (2): 205–48.

———. 2006. *Rethinking Bank Regulation: Till Angels Govern.* New York: Cambridge University Press.

———. 2008. "Bank Regulations Are Changing: For Better or Worse?" *Comparative Economic Studies* 50: 537–63.

———. 2012a. "Bank Regulations Around the World from 1999–2011: Evolution and Impact?" Policy Research Working Paper, World Bank, Washington, DC.

———. 2012b. *Guardians of Finance: Making Regulators Work for Us.* Cambridge, MA: MIT Press.

Bartlett, Robert. 2012. "Making Banks Transparent." *Vanderbilt Law Review* 65 (2).

BCBS (Basel Committee on Banking Supervision). 2005. *Basel II: International Convergence of Capital Measurement and Capital Standards: A Revised Framework—Comprehensive Version.* Basel, Switzerland: Bank for International Settlements. http://www.bis.org/publ/bcbs128.pdf.

———. 2006. "Core Principles for Effective Banking Supervision." Bank for International Settlements, Basel, Switzerland. http://www.bis.org/publ/bcbs129.html.

———. 2011. *Basel III: A Global Regulatory Framework for More Resilient Banks and Banking Systems.* Basel, Switzerland: Bank for International Settlements. http://www.bis.org/publ/bcbs189.pdf.

———. 2011. "Global Systemically Important Banks: Assessment Methodology and the Additional Loss Absorbency Requirement." Bank for International Settlements, Basel, Switzerland. http://www.bis.org/publ/bcbs201.pdf.

Bebczuk, Ricardo. 2003. *Asymmetric Information in Financial Markets: Introduction and Applications.* Cambridge, U.K.: Cambridge University Press.

Bech, Morten, and Bart Hobijn. 2007. "Technology Diffusion within Central Banking: The Case of Real-Time Gross Settlement." *International Journal of Central Banking* 3 (3): 147–81.

Bech, Morten, Christine Preisig, and Kimmo Soramäki. 2008. "Global Trends in Large-Value Payments." Federal Reserve Bank of New York, *Economic Policy Review* 14 (2): 59–81.

Beck, Thorsten. 2008. "Bank Competition and Financial Stability: Friends or Foes?" Policy Research Working Paper 4656, World Bank, Washington, DC.

———, ed. 2011. *The Future of Banking.* London: Center for Economic and Policy Research (CEPR).

Beck, Thorsten, Diane Coyle, Mathias Dewatripont, and Xavier Freixas. 2010. *Bailing Out the Banks: Reconciling Stability and Competition.* London: CEPR.

Beck, Thorsten, Olivier De Jonghe, and Glenn Schepens. 2011. "Bank Competition and Stability: Cross-Country Heterogeneity." Discussion Paper No. 2011–019, European Banking Center, Tilburg, Netherlands.

Beck, Thorsten, Aslı Demirgüç-Kunt, and Ross Levine. 2000. "A New Database on the Structure and Development of the Financial Sector." *World Bank Economic Review* 14 (3): 597–605.

———. 2006. "Bank Concentration, Competition and Crises: First Results." *Journal of Banking & Finance* 30: 1581–1603.

———. 2007a. "Bank Concentration and Fragility. Impact and Mechanics." In *The Risks of Financial Institutions*, edited by Mark Casey and Rene M. Stulz, 193–231. Chicago, IL: University of Chicago Press.

———. 2007b. "Finance, Inequality and the Poor." *Journal of Economic Growth* 12 (1): 27–49.

———. 2010. "Financial Institutions and Markets across Countries and over Time." *World Bank Economic Review* 24 (1): 77–92.

Beck, Thorsten, Aslı Demirgüç-Kunt, and Vojislav Maksimovic. 2004. "Bank Competition and Access to Finance: International Evidence." *Journal of Money, Credit and Banking* 36 (3): 627–48.

Beck, Thorsten, Aslı Demirgüç-Kunt, and Maria Soledad Martínez Pería. 2007. "Reaching Out: Access to and Use of Banking Services Across Countries." *Journal of Financial Economics* 85 (1): 234–66.

———. 2008. "Banking Services for Everyone? Barriers to Bank Access and Use Around the

World." *World Bank Economic Review* 22 (3): 397–430.

Beck, Thorsten, Erik Feyen, Alain Ize, and Florencia Moizeszowicz. 2006. "Benchmarking Financial Development." Policy Research Working Paper 4638, World Bank, Washington, DC.

Beck, Thorsten, and Michael Fuchs. 2004. "Structural Issues in the Kenyan Financial System: Improving Competition and Access." Policy Research Working Paper 3363, World Bank, Washington, DC.

Beck, Thorsten, Leora F. Klapper, and Juan Carlos Mendoza. 2010. "The Typology of Partial Credit Guarantee Funds Around the World." *Journal of Financial Stability* 6: 10–25.

Beck, Thorsten, and Ross Levine. 2004. "Stock Markets, Banks and Growth: Panel Evidence." *Journal of Banking & Finance* 28 (3): 423–42.

———. 2005. "Legal Institutions and Financial Development." In *Handbook of New Institutional Economics*, edited by C. Ménard and M. M. Shirley, 251–78. Dordrecht, Netherlands: Springer.

Beck, Thorsten, Ross Levine, and Alexey Levkov. 2010. "Big Bad Banks? The Winners and Losers from Bank Deregulation in the United States." *Journal of Finance* 65 (5): 1637–67.

Beck, Thorsten, Samuel Munzele Maimbo, Issa Faye, and Thouraya Triki. 2011. *Financing Africa: Through the Crisis and Beyond*. Washington, DC: World Bank.

Belley, Philippe, and Lance Lochner. 2007. "The Changing Role of Family Income and Ability in Determining Educational Achievement." NBER Working Paper 13527, National Bureau of Economic Research, Cambridge, MA.

Benavente José Miguel, Alexander Galetovic, and Ricardo Sanhueza. 2006. "FOGAPE: An Economic Analysis." Working Paper 222, University of Chile, Department of Economics, Santiago.

Bennardo, Alberto, Marco Pagano, and Salvatore Piccolo. 2009. "Multiple-Bank Lending, Creditor Rights and Information Sharing." Working Paper 211, Centre for Studies in Economics and Finance Cranfield, U.K.

Berger, Allen N. 1995. "The Profit Structure Relationship in Banking: Tests of Market-Power

and Efficient-Structure Hypotheses." *Journal of Money, Credit and Banking* 27: 404–31.

Berger, Allen N., Christa H. S. Bouwman, Thomas Kick, and Klaus Schaeck. 2010. "Bank Liquidity Creation and Risk Taking during Distress." Discussion Paper 2, No. 05/2010, Deutsche Bundesbank, Frankfurt, Germany.

Berger, Allen N., Aslı Demirgüç-Kunt, Ross Levine, and Joseph G. Haubrich. 2004. "Bank Concentration and Competition: An Evolution in the Making." *Journal of Money, Credit and Banking* 36 (3, part 2): 433–51.

Berger, Allen N., and Timothy Hannan. 1998. "The Price-Concentration Relationship in Banking." *Review of Economics and Statistics* 80: 454–65.

Berger, Allen N., Iftekhar Hasan, and Mingming Zhou. 2009. "Bank Ownership and Efficiency in China: What Will Happen in the World's Largest Nation?" *Journal of Banking & Finance* 33 (1): 113–30.

Berger, Allen N., Leora F. Klapper, Maria Soledad Martínez Pería, and Rida Zaidi. 2008. "Bank Ownership Type and Banking Relationships." *Journal of Financial Intermediation* 17 (1): 37–62.

Berger, Allen N., Leora Klapper, Margaret Miller, and Gregory F. Udell. 2003. "Relationship Lending in the Argentine Small Business Credit Market." In *Credit Reporting Systems and the International Economy*, edited by Margaret Miller, Cambridge, MA: MIT Press.

Berger, Allen N., Leora. F. Klapper, and Rima Turk-Ariss. 2009. "Bank Competition and Financial Stability." *Journal of Financial Services Research* 35 (2): 99–118.

Bertay, Ata Can, Aslı Demirgüç-Kunt, and Harry Huizinga. 2012. "Bank Ownership and Credit over the Business Cycle: Is Lending by State Banks Less Procyclical?" Policy Research Working Paper 6110, World Bank, Washington, DC.

Besley, Timothy J., and Stephen Coate. 1995. "Group Lending Repayment Incentives and Social Collateral." *Journal of Development Economics* 46 (1): 1–18.

Biggs, Michael Thomas Mayer, and Andreas Pick. 2010. "Credit and Economic Recovery: Demystifying Phoenix Miracles." Manuscript, Erasmus University Rotterdam.

Bijsterbosch, M., and Tatjana Dahlhaus. 2011. "Determinants of Credit-less Recoveries." Working Paper 1358, European Central Bank, Frankfurt, Germany.

Bikker, Jacob Antoon, and Laura Spierdijk. 2008. "How Banking Competition Changed over Time." Working Paper 167, De Nederlandsche Bank, Amsterdam.

BIS (Bank of International Settlements). 2011. "The Macrofinancial Implications of Alternative Configurations for Access to Central Counterparties in OTC Derivatives Markets." CGFS Publication 46, BIS, Basel, Switzerland.

Bonin, John P., Iftekhar Hasan, and Paul Wachtel. 2005. "Privatization Matters: Bank Efficiency in Transition Countries." *Journal of Banking & Finance* 29 (8–9): 2155–78.

Boone, Jan. 2001. "Intensity of Competition and the Incentive to Innovate." *International Journal of Industrial Organization* 19: 705–26.

Boone, Jan, Rachel Griffith, and Rupert Harrison. 2005. "Measuring Competition." Research Paper 022, Advanced Institute of Management Research, Cranfield, U.K.

Boot, Arnoud W. A., and Stuart I. Greenbaum. 1993. "Bank-Regulation, Reputation and Rents: Theory and Policy Implications." In *Capital Markets and Financial Intermediation*, edited by C. Mayer and X. Vives. Cambridge, U.K.: Cambridge University Press.

Boot, Arnoud W. A., and Anjan Thakor. 2000. "Can Relationship Banking Survive Competition?" *Journal of Finance* 55: 679–713.

Bostic, Raphael, and Paul Calem. 2003. "Privacy Restrictions and the Use of Data at Credit Repositories." In *Credit Reporting Systems and the International Economy*, edited by Margaret J. Miller. Cambridge, MA: MIT Press.

Boyd, John H., and Gianni De Nicoló. 2005. "The Theory of Bank Risk-Taking and Competition Revisited." *Journal of Finance* 60: 1329–43.

Boyd, John H., and Stanley L. Graham. 1991. "Investigating the Banking Consolidation Trend." *Quarterly Review*, Federal Reserve Bank of Minneapolis, Spring, 1–15.

Boyd, John H., and Stanley L. Graham. 1996. "Consolidation in U.S. Banking: Implications for Efficiency and Risk." Working Paper 572, Federal Reserve Bank of Minneapolis Research Department, MN.

Boyd, John H., and David E. Runkle. 1993. "Size and Performance of Banking Firms: Testing the Predictions of Theory." *Journal of Monetary Economics* 31 (1): 47–67.

Brave, Scott A., and Hesna Gesnay. 2011. "Federal Reserve Policies and Financial Market Conditions during the Crisis." Working Paper 2011–04, Federal Reserve Bank of Chicago, IL.

Brown, Martin, and Christian Zehnder. 2010. "The Emergence of Information Sharing in Credit Markets." *Journal of Financial Intermediation* 19: 255–78.

Bruck, Nicholas. 1998. "The Role of Development Banks in the Twenty-First Century." *Journal of Emerging Markets* 3 (3): 39–67.

Bruhn, Miriam, Subika Farazi, and Martin Kanz. 2012. "Bank Concentration and Credit Reporting." Policy Research Working Paper, World Bank, Washington, DC.

Brunnemeier, Markus, Andrew Crocket, Charles Goodhart, Avinash D. Persaud, and Hyun Shin. 2009. "The Fundamental Principles of Financial Regulation." Centre for Economic Policy Research, London. http://www.cepr.org/pubs/books/P197.asp.

Calderón, Cesar. 2012. "Credit Fluctuations and State Ownership: Evidence at the Macroeconomic Level." Manuscript, World Bank, Washington, DC.

Calderón, Cesar, and Klaus Schaeck. 2012. "Bank Bailouts, Competitive Distortions, and Consumer Welfare." Policy Research Working Paper, World Bank, Washington, DC.

Calomiris, Charles. 2011. "An Incentive-Robust Programme for Financial Reform." *Manchester School* 79: 39–72.

Calomiris, Charles, and Richard Herring. 2011. "Why and How to Design a Contingent Convertible Debt Requirement." http://www.economics21.org/commentary/contingent-capital-requirement-banks.

Calvo, Guillermo A., Alejandro Izquierdo, and Ernesto Talvi. 2006a. "Phoenix Miracles in Emerging Markets: Recovering without Credit from Systemic Financial Crises." NBER Working Paper 12101, National Bureau of Economic Research, Cambridge, MA.

————. 2006b. "Sudden Stops and Phoenix Miracles in Emerging Markets." *American Economic Review* 96 (2): 405–10.

Campion, Anita. 2001. "Client Information-Sharing in Bolivia." *Journal of Microfinance* 3 (1): 45–64.

Campion, Anita, and Liza Valenzuela. 2001. "Credit Bureaus: A Necessity for Microfinance?" Microenterprise Best Practices, Development Alternatives, Inc., Bethesda, MD.

Caprio, Gerard, Aslı Demirgüç-Kunt, and Edward J. Kane. 2010. "The 2007 Meltdown in Structured Securitization: Searching for Lessons, not Scapegoats." *World Bank Research Observer* 25 (1): 125–55.

Caprio, Gerard, and Maria Soledad Martínez Pería. 2002. "Avoiding Disaster: Policies to Reduce the Risk of Banking Crisis." In *Monetary Policy and Exchange Rate Regimes: Options for the Middle East*, edited by E. Cardoso and A. Galal, 193–230. Cairo: Egyptian Center for Economic Studies.

Carbó-Valverde, Santiago, Francisco Rodríguez-Fernández, and Gregory F. Udell. 2009. "Bank Market Power and SME Financing Constraints." *Review of Finance* 13: 309–40.

Carmichael, Jeffrey, Alexander Fleming, and David T. Llewellyn. 2004. *Aligning Financial Supervisory Structures with Country Needs*. Washington, DC: World Bank.

Carmichael, Jeffrey, and Michael Pomerleano. 2002. *The Development and Regulation of Non-Bank Financial Institutions*. Washington, DC: World Bank.

Carvalho, Daniel R. 2010. "The Real Effects of Government-Owned Banks: Evidence from an Emerging Market." Manuscript, Marshall Business School, University of Southern California, Los Angeles.

Casu, Barbara, and Claudia Girardone. 2009. "Testing the Relationship between Competition and Efficiency in Banking: A Panel Data Analysis." *Economic Letters* 105: 134–37.

Cecchetti, Stephen, and Enisse Kharroubi. 2012. "Reassessing the Impact of Finance on Growth." BIS Working Paper 381, Bank for International Settlements, Basel, Switzerland.

Cetorelli, Nicola. 1999. "Competitive Analysis in Banking: Appraisal of the Methodologies." *Economic Perspectives*, Federal Reserve Bank of Chicago, First Quarter, 2–15.

Chan, Yuk-Shee, Stuart Greenbaum, and Anjan V. Thakor, 1986. "Information Reusability, Competition, and Bank Asset Quality." *Journal of Banking & Finance* 10: 255–276.

Chong, Terence T. L., Liping Lu, and Steven Ongena. 2012. "Does Banking Competition Alleviate or Worsen Credit Constraints Faced by Small and Medium Enterprises? Evidence from China." Discussion Paper 2012-007, European Banking Center, Tilburg, Netherlands.

Čihák, Martin, Aslı Demirgüç-Kunt, Erik Feyen, and Ross Levine. 2012. "Benchmarking Financial Development Around the World." Policy Research Working Paper 6175, World Bank, Washington, DC.

Čihák, Martin, Aslı Demirgüç-Kunt, and Robert Barry Johnston. 2012a. "Good Regulation Needs to Fix the Broken Incentives." Working Paper, World Bank, Washington, DC. http://www.icffr.org/assets/pdfs/February-2012/ICFR---Financial-Times-Research-Prize-2011/Highly-Commended-Papers/M-Cihak-A-Demirguc-Kunt-and-R-B-Johnston---Good-Re.aspx.

————. 2012b. "Incentive Audits: A New Approach to Financial Regulation." Policy Research Working Paper, World Bank, Washington, DC.

Čihák, Martin, Aslı Demirgüç-Kunt, Maria Soledad Martínez Pería, and Amin Mohseni. 2012. "Banking Regulation and Supervision around the World: A Crisis Update." Policy Research Working Paper, World Bank, Washington, DC.

Čihák, Martin, Sonia Muñoz, and Ryan Scuzzarella. 2011. "The Bright and the Dark Side of Cross-Border Banking Linkages." Working Paper 11/186, International Monetary Fund, Washington, DC.

Čihák, Martin, Sonia Muñoz, Shakira Teh Sharifuddin, and Kalin Tintchev. 2012. "Financial Stability Reports: What Are They Good For?" Working Paper 12/1, International Monetary Fund, Washington, DC.

Čihák, Martin, and Li L. Ong. 2010. "Of Runes and Sagas: Perspectives on Liquidity Stress Testing Using an Iceland Example." Working

Paper 10/156, International Monetary Fund, Washington, DC.

Čihák, Martin, and Richard Podpiera. 2008. "Integrated Financial Supervision: Which Model?" *North American Journal of Economics and Finance* 19: 135–52.

Čihák, Martin, and Klaus Schaeck. 2010. "How Well Do Aggregate Prudential Ratios Identify Banking System Problems?" *Journal of Financial Stability* 6 (3): 130–44.

Čihák, Martin, and Alexander Tieman. 2011. "Quality of Financial Sector Regulation and Supervision Around the World." In *Handbook of Central Banking, Financial Regulation and Supervision*, edited by S. Eijffinger and D. Masciandaro. Cheltenham, U.K.: Edward Elgar.

Cirasino, Massimo, and José Antonio Garcia. 2009. "Measuring Payment System Development." Financial Infrastructure Series Working Paper, World Bank, Washington, DC.

Cirasino, Massimo, José Antonio Garcia, and Mario Guadamillas. 2009. "A Case for Collateralized Interbank Money Markets." Unpublished paper, World Bank, Washington, DC.

Claessens, Stijn. 2006. "Access to Financial Services: A Review of the Issues and Public Policy Objectives." *World Bank Research Observer* 21 (2): 207–40.

Claessens, Stijn. 2009. "Competition in the Financial Sector: Overview of Competition Policies." *World Bank Research Observer* 24 (1): 83–118.

Claessens, Stijn, Giovanni Dell'Ariccia, Deniz Igan, and Luc Laeven. 2010. "Lessons and Policy Implications from the Global Financial Crisis." Working Paper 10/44, International Monetary Fund, Washington, DC.

Claessens, Stijn, Aslı Demirgüç-Kunt, and Harry Huizinga. 2001. "How Does Foreign Entry Affect Domestic Banking Markets?" *Journal of Banking & Finance* 25: 891–911.

Claessens, Stijn, Douglas D. Evanoff, George G. Kaufman, and Laura Kodres, eds. 2012. *Macro-prudential Regulatory Policies: The New Road to Financial Stability* (World Scientific Studies in International Economics). London: World Scientific.

Claessens, Stijn, Erik Feyen, and Luc Laeven. 2008. "Political Connections and Preferential Access to Finance: The Role of Campaign Contributions." *Journal of Financial Economics* 88: 554–80.

Claessens, Stijn, and Daniela Klingebiel. 2001. "Competition and Scope for Financial Services." *World Bank Research Observer* 16 (1): 18–40.

Claessens, Stijn, and Luc Laeven. 2003. "Financial Development, Property Rights and Growth." *Journal of Finance* 58 (6): 2401–36.

———. 2004. "What Drives Bank Competition? Some International Evidence." *Journal of Money, Credit and Banking* 36 (3, pt. 2): 563–83.

———. 2005. "Financial Dependence, Banking Sector Competition, and Economic Growth." *Journal of the European Economic Association* 3 (1): 179–207.

Claessens, Stijn, Ceyla Pazarbasioglu, Luc Laeven, Mark Dobler, Fabian Valencia, Oana Nedelescu, and Katharine Seal. 2011. "Crisis Management and Resolution: Early Lessons from the Financial Crisis." IMF Discussion Note SDN/11/05, International Monetary Fund, Washington, DC.

Claessens, Stijn, and Enrico Perotti. 2007. "Finance and Inequality: Channels and Evidence." *Journal of Comparative Economics* 35 (4): 748–73.

Claessens, Stijn, Geoffrey R. D. Underhill, and Xiaoke Zhang. 2008. "Basle II Capital Requirements and Developing Countries: A Political Economy Perspective." *World Economy* 31 (3): 313–44.

Claessens, Stijn, and Neeltje van Horen. 2010. "Being a Foreigner among Domestic Banks: Asset or Liability?" Working Paper 09/273, International Monetary Fund, Washington, DC.

Claessens, Stijn, and Neeltje van Horen. 2011. "Foreign Banks: Trends, Impact and Financial Stability." Working Paper 12/10, International Monetary Fund, Washington, DC.

Clarke, George R. G., Robert Cull, and William Megginson. 2005. "Introduction to the Special Issue on Bank Privatization." *Journal of Banking & Finance* 29 (8–9): 1903–04.

Cole, Shawn A. 2009a. "Financial Development, Bank Ownership, and Growth: or, Does

Quantity Imply Quality?" *Review of Economics and Statistics* 91 (1): 33–51.

———. 2009b. "Fixing Market Failures or Fixing Elections? Elections, Banks, and Agricultural Lending in India." *American Economic Journal Applied Economics* 1 (1): 219–50.

Competition Commission of South Africa. 2006. "The National Payment System and Competition in the Banking Sector." Report prepared by Feasibility Ltd., Johannesburg, South Africa.

Courtis, John K. 1998. "Annual Report Readability Variability: Tests of the Obfuscation Hypothesis." *Accounting, Auditing and Accountability Journal* 11 (4): 459–71.

Cowan, Kevin, Alejandro Drexler, and Alvaro Yañez. 2009. "The Effect of Partial Credit Guarantees on the Credit Market for Small Businesses." Working Paper 524, Central Bank of Chile, Santiago.

CPSS (Committee on Payment and Settlement Systems). 2001. "Core Principles for Systemically Important Payment Systems." CPSS Publication No. 43, Bank for International Settlements, Basel, Switzerland.

———. 2005. *New Developments in Large-Value Payment Systems*. Bank for International Settlements, Basel, Switzerland.

———. 2006. "General Guidance for National Payment System Development." CPSS Publication No. 70. Bank for International Settlements, Basel, Switzerland.

CPSS (Committee on Payment and Settlement Systems) and IOSCO (International Organization of Securities Commissions). 2001. "Recommendations for Securities Settlements Systems." Bank for International Settlements, Basel, Switzerland.

———. 2004. "Recommendations for Central Counterparties." Basel, Switzerland: Bank for International Settlements.

———. 2010a. "Guidance on the Application of the 2004 CPSS-IOSCO Recommendations for Central Counterparties to OTC Derivatives CCPs–Consultative Report." Bank for International Settlements, Basel, Switzerland.

———. 2010b. "Considerations for Trade Repositories in OTC Derivatives Markets." CPSS Publication No. 90, Bank for International Settlements, Basel, Switzerland.

———. 2012. "Principles for Financial Market Infrastructures." CPSS Publication No. 94, Bank for International Settlements, Basel, Switzerland.

Craig, Ben. R., William E. Jackson III, and James B. Thompson. 2007. "On Government Intervention in the Small-firm Credit Market and Its Effect on Economic Performance." Working Paper 07–02, Federal Reserve Bank of Cleveland, OH.

Cull, Robert, and Maria Soledad Martínez Pería. 2012. "Bank Ownership and Lending Patterns during the 2008–2009 Financial Crisis: Evidence from Eastern Europe and Latin America." Unpublished paper, World Bank, Washington, DC.

Das, Udaibir S., Marc Quintyn, and Kina Chenard. 2004. "Does Regulatory Governance Matter for Financial System Stability? An Empirical Analysis." Working Paper 04/89, International Monetary Fund, Washington, DC.

Davis, Philip. 2009. "The Lender of Last Resort and Liquidity Provision—How Much of a Departure Is the Subprime Crisis?" Paper presented at the conference "Regulatory Response to the Financial Crisis," London School of Economics, January 19.

Debrun, Xavier, and Radhicka Kapoor. 2010. "Fiscal Policy and Macroeconomic Stability: Automatic Stabilizers Work, Always and Everywhere." Working Paper 10/111, International Monetary Fund, Washington, DC.

De Haas, Ralph, Yevgeniya Korniyenko, Elena Loukoianova, and Alexander Pivovarsky. 2012. "Foreign Banks and the Vienna Initiative: Turning Sinners into Saints?" Working Paper 12/117, International Monetary Fund, Washington, DC.

de Janvry, Alain, Craig McIntosh, and Elisabeth Sadoulet. 2010. "The Supply- and Demand-side Impacts of Credit Market Information." *Journal of Development Economics* 93: 173–88.

de la Torre, Augusto, Erik Feyen, and Alain Ize. 2011. "Financial Development: Structure and Dynamics." Policy Research Working Paper 5854, World Bank, Washington, DC.

de la Torre, Augusto, Juan Carlos Gozzi, and Sergio L. Schmukler. 2007. "Innovative Experiences in Access to Finance: Market Friendly Roles for the Visible Hand?" Policy Research

Working Paper 4326, World Bank, Washington, DC.

de la Torre, Augusto, and Alain Ize. 2011. "Containing Systemic Risk: Paradigm-Based Perspectives on Regulatory Reform." *Economia* 11 (1): 25–64.

de la Torre, Augusto, Alain Ize, Sergio L. Schmukler, eds. 2011. *Financial Development in Latin America and the Caribbean: The Road Ahead.* Washington, DC: World Bank.

Delis, Manthos D. 2012. "Bank Competition, Financial Reform, and Institutions: The Importance of Being Developed." *Journal of Development Economics* 97 (2): 450–65.

Delis, Manthos D., and Efthymios G. Tsionas. 2009. "The Joint Estimation of Bank-level Market Power and Efficiency." *Journal of Banking & Finance* 3: 1842–50.

De Luna-Martínez, José, and Carlos L. Vicente. 2012. "Global Survey of Development Banks." Policy Research Working Paper 5969, World Bank, Washington, DC.

Dell'Ariccia, Giovanni, Ezra Friedman, and Robert Marquez. 1999. "Adverse Selection as a Barrier to Entry in the Banking Industry." *RAND Journal of Economics* 30 (3): 515–34.

Dell'Ariccia, Giovanni, Deniz Igan, and Luc Laeven. 2012. "Credit Booms and Lending Standards: Evidence from the Subprime Mortgage Market." *Journal of Money, Credit and Banking* 44: 367–84.

Demirgüç-Kunt, Aslı. 2011. "Do We Need Deposit Insurance for Large Banks?" http://blogs.worldbank.org/allaboutfinance/do-we-need-deposit-insurance-for-large-banks.

Demirgüç-Kunt, Aslı, Thorsten Beck, and Patrick Honohan. 2008. *Finance for All? Policies and Pitfalls in Expanding Access.* Washington, DC: World Bank.

Demirgüç-Kunt, Aslı, and Enrica Detragiache. 1997. "The Determinants of Banking Crises in Developing and Developed Countries." *IMF Staff Papers* 45: 81–109.

Demirgüç-Kunt, Aslı, and Enrica Detragiache. 2002. "Does Deposit Insurance Increase Banking System Stability? An Empirical Investigation." *Journal of Monetary Economics* 49 (7): 1373–1406.

Demirgüç-Kunt, Aslı, and Enrica Detragiache. 2011. "Basel Core Principles and Bank Soundness: Does Compliance Matter?" *Journal of Financial Stability* 7 (4): 179–90.

Demirgüç-Kunt, Aslı, Enrica Detragiache, and Poonam Gupta. 2006. "Inside the Crisis: An Empirical Analysis of Banking Systems in Distress." *Journal of International Money and Finance* 25: 702–18.

Demirgüç-Kunt, Aslı, Enrica Detragiache, and Ouarda Merrouche. 2012. "Bank Capital: Lessons from the Financial Crisis." *Journal of Money, Credit and Banking.*

Demirgüç-Kunt, Aslı, Enrica Detragiache, and Thierry Tressel. 2008. "Banking on the Principles: Compliance with Basel Core Principles and Bank Soundness." *Journal of Financial Intermediation* 17 (4): 511–42.

Demirgüç-Kunt, Aslı, Erik Feyen, and Ross Levine. 2012. "The Evolving Importance of Banks and Securities Markets." *World Bank Economic Review.*

Demirgüç-Kunt, Aslı, and Harry Huizinga. 1999. "Determinants of Commercial Bank Interest Margins and Profitability: Some International Evidence." *World Bank Economic Review* 13 (2): 379–408.

———. 2004. "Market Discipline and Deposit Insurance." *Journal of Monetary Economics* 51 (2): 375–399.

———. 2011. "Do We Need Big Banks? Evidence on Performance, Strategy and Market." Policy Research Working Paper 5576, World Bank, Washington, DC.

Demirgüç-Kunt, Aslı, Ed Kane, and Luc Laeven. 2008. "Deposit Insurance Around the World: Issues of Design and Implementation." Cambridge, MA: MIT Press.

Demirgüç-Kunt, Aslı, and Leora Klapper. 2012. "Measuring Financial Inclusion: The Global Findex." Policy Research Working Paper, 6025, World Bank, Washington, DC.

Demirgüç-Kunt, Aslı, Luc Laeven, and Ross Levine. 2004. "Regulations, Market Structure, Institutions and the Cost of Financial Intermediation." *Journal of Money, Credit and Banking* 36: 593–622.

Demirgüç-Kunt, Aslı, and Ross Levine. 2008. "Finance, Financial Sector Policies, and Long-Run Growth." M. Spence Growth Commission Background Paper 11, World Bank, Washington, DC.

———. 2009. "Finance and Inequality: Theory and Evidence." *Annual Review of Financial Economics* 1: 287–318.

Demirgüç-Kunt, Aslı, and Maria Soledad Martínez Pería. 2010. "A Framework for Analyzing Competition in the Banking Sector: An Application to the Case of Jordan." Policy Research Working Paper 5499, World Bank, Washington, DC.

Demirgüç-Kunt, Aslı, and Luis Servén. 2010. "Are All the Sacred Cows Dead? Implications of the Financial Crisis for Macro and Financial Policies." *World Bank Research Observer* 25(1): 91–124.

Demsetz, Harold. 1973. "Industry Structure, Market Rivalry, and Public Policy." *Journal of Law and Economics* 16: 1–9.

De Nicoló, Gianni. 2000. "Size, Charter Value and Risk in Banking: An International Perspective." International Finance Discussion Paper 689, Board of Governors of the Federal Reserve System, Washington, DC.

Dewatripont, Mathias, and Jean Tirole. 1994. *The Prudential Regulation of Banks*. Cambrige, MA: MIT Press.

DeYoung, Robert, Iftekhar Hasan, and Bruce Kirchhoff. 1998. "The Impact of Out-of-State Entry on the Cost Efficiency of Local Banks." *Journal of Economics and Business* 50: 191–203.

D'Hulster, Katia. 2011. "Cross Border Banking Supervision: Incentive Conflicts in Supervisory Information Sharing between Home and Host Supervisors." Policy Research Working Paper 5871, World Bank, Washington, DC.

Dick, Astrid. 2006. "Nationwide Branching and Its Impact on Market Structure, Quality and Bank Performance." *Journal of Business* 79: 567–92.

Dinç, I. Serdar. 2005. "Politicians and Banks: Political Influences on Government-Owned Banks in Emerging Markets." *Journal of Financial Economics* 77: 453–79.

Djankov, Simeon, Caralee McLiesh, Andrei Shleifer. 2007. "Private Credit in 129 Countries." *Journal of Financial Economics* 84 (2): 299–329.

Doing Business Indicators (database). World Bank, Washington, DC. http://www.doing business.org.

Drehmann, Mathias, Claudio Borio, and Kostas Tsatsaronis. 2011. "Anchoring Countercyclical Capital Buffers: The Role of Credit Aggregates." BIS Working Paper No. 355, Bank for International Settlements, Basel, Switzerland.

Duchin, Ran, and Denis Sosyura. 2011. "Safer Ratios, Riskier Portfolios: Banks' Response to Government Aid." Ross School of Business Paper No. 1165, University of Michigan, Ann Arbor.

Economist. 2012. "Economist Debates: Opening Statements: Franklin Allen and Thorsten Beck." June 1. http://www.economist.com/ debate/days/view/706/.

Ellul, Andrew, and Vijay Yerramilli. 2010. "Stronger Risk Controls, Lower Risk: Evidence from U.S. Bank Holding Companies." AFA 2011 Denver Meetings Paper, American Finance Association, Berkeley, CA.

Enriquez, Luca, and Gerard Hertig. 2010. "The Governance of Financial Supervisors: Improving Responsiveness to Market Developments." Paper presented at the 5th International Conference on Financial Regulation and Supervision, Universita Bocconi, Milan, June 24–25.

European Central Bank. 2010a. "Euro Money Market Study." European Central Bank, Frankfurt, Germany.

———. 2010b. *The Payment System: Payments, Securities and Derivatives and the Role of the Eurosystem.* Frankfurt, Germany: European Central Bank.

Falkena, Hans, Gabriel Davel, Penelope Hawkins, David Llewellyn, Christo Luus, Elias Masilela, Geoff Parr, Johnny Pienaar, and Henry Shaw. 2004. "Competition in South African Banking." Task Group Report for the National Treasury and the South African Reserve Bank, Pretoria.

Farazi, Subika, Erik Feyen, and Roberto Rocha. 2011. "Bank Ownership and Performance in the Middle East and North Africa Region." Policy Research Working Paper 5620, World Bank, Washington, DC.

Farhi, Emmanuel, and Jean Tirole. 2012. "Collective Moral Hazard, Maturity Mismatch and Systemic Bailouts." *American Economic Review* 102 (1): 63–90.

Flannery, Mark J. 1996. "Financial Crises, Payment System Problems, and Discount Window

Lending. *Journal of Money, Credit and Banking* 28 (4): 804–24.

FSA (Financial Services Authority). 2009. "The Turner Review." U.K. Financial Services Authority, London, U.K.

FSB (Financial Stability Board). 2009a. "Improving Financial Regulation." FSB, Basel, Switzerland. http://www.financialstabilityboard.org/publications/r_090925b.pdf.

———. 2009b. "FSB Principles for Sound Compensation Practice." FSB, Basel, Switzerland.

———. 2009c. "FSB Principles for Sound Compensation Practices: Implementation Standards." FSB, Basel, Switzerland. http://www.financialstabilityboard.org/publications/r_090925c.pdf.

———. 2010a. "Ongoing and Recent Work Relevant to Sound Financial Systems." FSB, Basel, Switzerland. http://www.financialstabilityboard.org/publications/on_1006.pdf.

———. 2010b. "Principles for Reducing Reliance on CRA Ratings." FSB, Basel, Switzerland. http://www.financialstabilityboard.org/publications/r_101027.pdf.

———. 2010c. "Implementing OTC Derivatives Market Reforms." FSB, Basel, Switzerland. http://www.financialstabilityboard.org/publications/r_101025.pdf

———. 2011a. "Key Attributes of Effective Resolution Regimes for Financial Institutions." FSB, Basel, Switzerland.

———. 2011b. "Intensity and Effectiveness of SIFI Supervision." FSB, Basel, Switzerland.

———. 2012. "Strengthening the Oversight and Regulation of Shadow Banking." Progress Report to G20 Ministers and Governors. FSB, Basel, Switzerland.

FSB (Financial Stability Board) Secretariat and IMF (International Monetary Fund). 2009. "The Financial Crisis and Information Gaps." FSB, Basel, Switzerland.

———. 2010. "The Financial Crisis and Information Gaps: Progress Report." FSB, Basel, Switzerland. http://www.financialstabilityboard.org/publications/r_100510.pdf.

FSB, IMF, and World Bank. 2011. "Financial Stability Issues in Emerging Market and Developing Economies." Report to the G-20 Finance Ministers and Central Bank Governors Prepared by a Task Force of the Financial Stability Board and Staff of the International Monetary Fund and the World Bank, October. http://siteresources.worldbank.org/EXTFINANCIALSECTOR/Resources/G20_Report_Financial_Stability_Issues_EMDEs.pdf.

Financial Stability Institute. 2004. "Implementation of the New Capital Adequacy Framework in Non-Basel Committee Member Countries, Summary of Responses to the 2004 Basel II Implementation Assistance Questionnaire." Occasional Paper No. 4, July. http://www.bis.org/fsi/fsipapers04.htm.

G-20 Leaders. 2009. "Leaders' Statement: The Pittsburgh Summit." September 24–25.

Galindo, Arturo José, and Alejandro Micco. 2004. "Do State Owned Banks Promote Growth? Cross-Country Evidence for Manufacturing Industries." *Economics Letters* 84: 371–76.

Galindo, Arturo José, and Margaret Miller. 2001. "Can Credit Registries Reduce Credit Constraints? Empirical Evidence on the Role of Credit Registries in Firm Investment Decisions." IDB-IIC 42nd Annual Meeting, Santiago, Chile.

Gerschenkron, Alexander. 1962. *Economic Backwardness in Historical Perspective.* Cambridge, MA: Harvard University Press.

Ghatak, Maitreesh, and Timothy W. Guinnane. 1999. "The Economics of Lending with Joint Liability: A Review of Theory and Practice." *Journal of Development Economics* 60 (1): 195–228.

Giannone, Domenico, Michele Lenza, Huw Pill, and Lucrezia Reichlin. 2011. "Non-Standard Monetary Policy Measures and Monetary Developments." CEPR Discussion Papers 8125, Center for Economic and Policy Research, London.

Giné, Xavier, Jessica Goldberg, and Dean Yang. 2011. "Credit Market Consequences of Improved Personal Identification: Field Experimental Evidence from Malawi." NBER Working Paper 17449, National Bureau of Economic Research, Cambridge, MA.

Giné, Xavier, and Dean Karlan. 2006. "Group versus Individual Liability: A Field Experiment in the Philippines." Policy Research working Paper 4008, World Bank, Washington, DC.

Girault, Matias Gutierrez, and Jane Hwang. 2010. "Public Credit Registries as a Tool for

Bank Regulation and Supervision." Policy Research Working Paper 5489, World Bank, Washington, DC.

Goldberg, Lawrence G., and Anoop Rai. 1996. "The Structure-Performance Relationship in European Banking." *Journal of Banking and Finance* 20: 745–71.

Goldstein, Morris, and Nicolas Véron. 2011. "Too Big to Fail: The Transatlantic Debate." Peterson Institute for International Economics Working Paper 11–2, PIIE, Washington, DC.

Goodhart, Charles. 2008. "The Regulatory Response to the Financial Crisis." London School of Economics Financial Markets Group Paper Series, London.

Green, Anke 2003. "Credit Guarantee Schemes for Small Enterprises: An Effective Instrument to Promote Private Sector-Led Growth?" UNIDO SME Technical Working Paper Series 10, United Nations Industrial Development Organization, Vienna.

Greenberg, Joshua B., and Witness Simbanegavi. 2009. "Testing for Competition in the South African Banking Sector." Unpublished paper, University of Cape Town, Faculty of Commerce, Cape Town.

Greenspan, Alan. 2005. "Economic Flexibility." Remarks to the National Association for Business Economics Annual Meeting, Chicago, September 27.

Gropp, Reint, Hendrik Hakenes, and Isabel Schnabel. 2011. "Competition, Risk-Shifting, and Public Bail-Out Policies." *Review of Financial Studies* 24 (6): 2084–2120.

Gutiérrez, Eva, Heinz P. Rudolph, Theodore Homa, and Enrique Blanco Beneit. 2011. "Development Banks: Role and Mechanisms to Increase Their Efficiency." Policy Research Working Paper 5729, World Bank, Washington, DC.

Hakenes, Hendrik, and Isabel Schnabel. 2010. "Banks Without Parachutes: Competitive Effects of Government Bail-Out Policies." *Journal of Financial Stability* 6: 156–68.

Haldane, Andrew G. 2011. "Capital Discipline." Speech at the American Economic Association, Denver, CO, January 9.

Haldane, Andrew, Simon Brennan, and Vasileios Madouros. 2010. "What Is the Contribution of the Financial System: Miracle or Mirage?"

In *The Future of Finance: The LSE Report*, ed. Adair Turner and others, 87–120. London: London School of Economics and Political Science.

Hancock, Diana, Joe Peek, and James A. Wilcox. 2007. "The Repercussions on Small Banks and Small Businesses of Bank Capital and Loan Guarantees." Working Paper 07–22, University of Pennsylvania, Wharton School, Financial Institutions Center.

Hasan, Iftekhar, Heiko Schmiedel, and Liang Song. 2009. "Return to Retail Banking and Payments." Working Paper 1135, European Central Bank, Frankfurt, Germany.

Hay, Donald, and Guy S. Liu. 1997. "The Efficiency of Firms: What Difference Does Competition Make?" *Economic Journal* 107: 597–617.

Hellwig, Martin. 2010. "Capital Regulation after the Crisis: Business as Usual?" Working Paper 2010_31, Max Planck Institute for Research on Collective Goods, Bonn, Germany.

Hicks, J. 1935. "The Theory of Monopoly." *Econometrica* 3: 1–20.

Holden, Paul. 1997. "Collateral Without Consequences: Some Causes and Effects of Financial Underdevelopment in Latin America." *The Financier–Analyses of Capital and Money Market Transactions* 4: 12–21.

Honohan, Patrick. 2010. "Partial Credit Guarantees: Principles and Practice." *Journal of Financial Stability* 6 (1): 1–9.

Hördahl, Peter, Michael R. King. 2008. "Developments in Repo Markets during the Financial Turmoil." *BIS Quarterly Review* (December).

Hoshi, Takeo, and Anil K. Kashyap. 2010. "Will the U.S. Bank Recapitalization Succeed? Eight Lessons from Japan." *Journal of Financial Economics* 97: 398–417.

Houston, Joel F., Chen Lin, Ping Lin, and Yue Ma. 2010. "Creditor Rights, Information Sharing, and Bank Risk Taking." *Journal of Financial Economics* 96: 485–512.

Hovakimian, Armen, and Edward J. Kane. 2000. "Effectiveness of Capital Regulation at U.S. Commercial Banks, 1985–1994." *Journal of Finance* 55: 451–68.

Huang, Haifang, and Eric Stephens. 2011. "From Housing Bust to Credit Crunch: Evidence from Small Business Loans." Economics

Working Paper 2011–15, University of Alberta, Edmonton.

Humphrey, David, Magnus Willesson, Goran Bergendahl, and Ted Lindblom. 2006. "Benefits from a Changing Payment Technology in European Banking." *Journal of Banking and Finance* 30 (6): 1631–52.

Iannotta, Giuliano, Giacomo Nocera, and Andrea Sironi. 2007. "Ownership Structure, Risk and Performance in the European Banking Industry." *Journal of Banking and Finance* 31: 2127–49.

Iannotta, Giuliano, Giacomo Nocera, and Andrea Sironi. 2011. "The Impact of Government Ownership on Bank Risk and Lending Behavior." Carefin Working Paper, Bocconi University, Milan, Italy.

IDB (Inter-American Development Bank). 2005. *Unlocking Credit: The Quest for Deep and Stable Bank Lending.* Washington, DC: Inter-American Development Bank.

IFC (International Finance Corporation). 2006. *Credit Bureau Knowledge Guide.* Washington, DC: IFC.

———. 2010. *Access to Finance Annual Review Report 2010.* IFC Advisory Services.

———. 2012. *Global Credit Bureau Program.* Washington, DC: IFC Advisory Services.

IFC (International Finance Corporation) and World Bank 2012. *Doing Business in the Arab World 2012.* Washington, DC: IFC and World Bank.

IMF (International Monetary Fund). 2004. "Are Credit Booms in Emerging Markets a Concern?" In *World Economic Outlook.* Washington, DC: IMF. http://www.imf.org/external/pubs/ft/weo/2004/01/pdf/chapter4.pdf.

———. 2009. "Romania: Financial Sector Stability Assessment." IMF Country Report No. 10/47, International Monetary Fund, Washington, DC.

———. 2010a. "Malaysia: 2010 Article IV Consultation." Staff Report, IMF Country Report No. 10/265, IMF, Washington, DC.

———. 2010b. "Sovereigns, Funding, and Systemic Liquidity." In *Global Financial Stability Report.* Washington, DC: IMF.

———. 2010c. "A Fair and Substantial Contribution by the Financial Sector." Final Report

for the G-20. http://www.imf.org/external/np/g20/pdf/062710b.pdf.

———. 2012. "Peru: 2011 Article IV Consultation." IMF Country Report No. 12/26, IMF, Washington, DC.

Ivashina, Victoria, and David S. Scharfstein. 2010. "Bank Lending During the Financial Crisis of 2008." *Journal of Financial Economics* 97 (3): 319–38.

Jappelli, Tullio and Marco Pagano. 2002. "Information Sharing, Lending and Defaults: Cross-Country Evidence." *Journal of Banking and Finance* 26 (10): 2017–45.

———. 2003. "Public Credit Information: A European Perspective." In *Credit Reporting Systems and the International Economy,* edited by Margaret J. Miller, 81–114. Cambridge, MA: MIT Press.

———. 2005. "Role and Effects of Credit Information Sharing." Working Paper 136, Centre for Studies in Economics and Finance, University of Salerno, Italy.

Jayaratne, Jith, and Philip E. Strahan. 1996. "The Finance-Growth Nexus: Evidence from Bank Branch Deregulation." *Quarterly Journal of Economics* 111 (3): 639–70.

Jentzsch, Nicola. 2008. "An Economic Analysis of China's Credit Information Monopoly." *China Economic Review* 19 (4): 537–50.

Jiménez, Gabriel, Jose A. Lopez, and Jesús Saurina. 2007. "How Does Competition Impact Bank Risk Taking?" Working Paper 2007–23, Federal Reserve Bank of San Francisco.

Johnson, Christian A., and Robert S. Steigerwald. 2008. "The Central Bank's Role in the Payment System: Legal and Policy Aspects." In *Current Developments in Monetary and Financial Law,* 445–70. Frankfurt, Germany: European Central Bank.

Johnson, Simon, and James Kwak. 2010. *13 Bankers: The Wall Street Takeover and the Next Financial Meltdown.* New York: Pantheon Books.

Johnston, R. Barry, Jingquing Chai, and Liliana Schumacher. 2000. "Assessing Financial System Vulnerabilities." Working Paper 00/76, International Monetary Fund, Washington, DC.

Kallberg, Jarl G., and Gregory F. Udell. 2003. "The Value of Private Sector Credit

Information." *Journal of Banking and Finance* 27: 449–469.

Kaminsky, Graciela, and Carmen Reinhart. 1999. "The Twin Crises: The Causes of Banking and Balance of Payments Problems." *American Economic Review* 89 (3): 473–500.

Kane, Edward J. 1989. *The S&L Insurance Mess: How Did It Happen?* Washington, DC: Urban Institute Press.

Kane, Edward J. 2000. "Designing Financial Safety Nets to Fit Country Circumstances." Policy Research Working Paper 2453, World Bank, Washington, DC.

———. 2007. "Basel II: A Contracting Perspective." *Journal of Financial Services Research* 32 (1): 39–53.

Kane, Edward J., and Tara Rice. 2001. "Bank Runs and Banking Policies: Lessons for African Policy Makers." *Journal of African Economies* 10: 36–71.

Kang, Jae Won, and Almas Heshmati. 2008. "Effect of Credit Guarantee Policy on Survival and Performance of SMEs in the Republic of Korea." *Small Business Economics* 31 (4): 445–62.

Kaufmann, Daniel, Aart Kraay, and Massimo Mastruzzi. 2009. "Governance Matters VIII: Aggregate and Individual Governance Indicators, 1996–2008." Policy Research Working Paper 4978, World Bank, Washington, DC.

Keeley, Michael C. 1990. "Deposit Insurance, Risk, and Market Power in Banking." *American Economic Review* 80 (5): 1183–1200.

Keen, Michael. 2011. "Rethinking the Taxation of the Financial Sector." *CESifo Economic Studies* 57 (1): 1–24.

Kerr, William R., and Ramana Nanda. 2009. "Democratizing Entry: Banking Deregulations, Financing Constraints, and Entrepreneurship." *Journal of Financial Economics* 94 (1): 124–49.

Keys, Benjamin J., Tanmoy K. Mukherjee, Amit Seru, and Vikrant Vig. 2010. "Did Securitization Lead to Lax Screening? Evidence from Subprime Loans." *Quarterly Journal of Economics* 125 (1): 307–62.

Khwaja, Asim Ijaz, and Atif Mian. 2005. "Do Lenders Favor Politically Connected Firms? Rent Provision in an Emerging Financial Market." *Quarterly Journal of Economics* 120 (4): 1371–1411.

Klapper, Leora. 2006. "The Role of Factoring for Financing Small and Medium Enterprises." *Journal of Banking & Finance* 30 (11): 3111–31.

Klapper, Leora, Luc Laeven, and Raghuram Rajan. 2006. "Entry Regulation as a Barrier to Entrepreneurship." *Journal of Financial Economics* 82 (3): 591–629.

Kornai, János. 1979. "Resource-Constrained Versus Demand-Constrained Systems." *Econometrica* 47 (4): 801–19.

Körner, Tobias, and Isabel Schnabel. 2010. "Public Ownership of Banks and Economic Growth: The Role of Heterogeneity." CEPR Discussion Paper 8138, Center for Economic and Policy Research, London.

Kremers, J., and D. Schoenmaker. 2008. "Paulson's Welcome Strategy." Financial *Regulator* 13 (1): 46–52.

———. 2010. "Twin Peaks: Experiences in the Netherlands." Special Paper 196, LSE Financial Markets Group, London.

Laeven, Luc, and Fabián Valencia. 2010. "Resolution of Banking Crisis: The Good, the Bad, and the Ugly." Working Paper 10/146, International Monetary Fund, Washington, DC.

———. 2011. "The Real Effects of Financial Sector Interventions during Crises." Working Paper 11/45, International Monetary Fund, Washington, DC.

———. 2012. "Systemic Banking Crisis Database: An Update." Working Paper 08/224, International Monetary Fund, Washington, DC.

Laffont, Jean-Jacques, and Jean Tirole. 1993. "A Theory of Incentives in Procurement and Regulation." Cambridge, MA: MIT Press.

La Porta, Rafael, Florencio López-de-Silanes, and Andrei Shleifer. 2002. "Government Ownership of Banks." *Journal of Finance* 57 (1): 265–301.

Larraín, Christian, and Jorge Quiroz. 2006. "Estudio Para El Fondo de Garantía de Pequeños Empresarios." Working paper, Banco Estado, Santiago, Chile.

Lazzarini, Sergio G., Aldo Musacchio, Rodrigo Bandeira-de-Mello, and Rosilene Marcon. 2011. "What Do Development Banks Do? Evidence from Brazil, 2002–2009." Working Paper 12–047, Harvard Business School, Cambridge, MA.

Lenza, Michelle, Huw Pill, and Lucrezia Reichlin. 2010. "Monetary Policy in Exceptional Times." *Economic Policy* 25 (4): 295–339.

Lerner, Abba Ptachya. 1934. "The Concept of Monopoly and the Measurement of Monopoly Power." *Review of Economic Studies* 1: 157–75.

Levine, Ross. 2005. "Finance and Growth: Theory and Evidence." In *Handbook of Economic Growth*, ed. Philippe Aghion and Steven Durlauf, 865–934.

———. 2011. "Regulating Finance and Regulators to Promote Growth." Paper prepared for the Federal Reserve Bank of Kansas City's Jackson Hole Symposium, August 25–27.

Levine, Ross, and Sara Zervos. 1998. "Stock Markets, Banks, and Economic Growth." *American Economic Review* 88 (3): 537–58.

Levy Yeyati, Eduardo, Alejandro Micco, and Ugo Panizza. 2005. "State-Owned Banks: Do They Promote or Depress Financial Development and Economic Growth?" Background paper prepared for the conference on Public Banks in Latin America: Myths and Reality, Inter-American Development Bank, February 25.

———. 2007. "A Reappraisal of State-Owned Banks." *Economia* 7 (2): 209–47.

Lin, Chen, Yue Ma, and Frank M. Song. 2010. "Bank Competition, Credit Information Sharing and Banking Efficiency." City University of Hong Kong, Hong Kong SAR, China.

Lindquist, Kjersti-Gro. 2002. "The Effect of New Technology in Payment Services on Banks' Intermediation." Norges Bank Working Paper ANO 2002/6, Oslo, Norway.

Listfield, Robert, and Fernando Montes-Negret, 1994. "Modernizing Payment Systems in Emerging Economies." Policy Research Working Paper No. 1336, World Bank, Washington, DC.

Loayza, Norman, and Romain Ranciere. 2006. "Financial Development, Financial Fragility, and Growth." *Journal of Money, Credit and Banking* 38 (4): 1051–76.

London School of Economics. 2010. *The Future of Finance: The LSE Report*. London: LSE.

Love, Inessa, and Nataliya Mylenko. 2003. "Credit Reporting and Financing Constraints." Policy Research Working Paper 3142, World Bank, Washington, DC.

Lucas, Robert E. 1988. "On the Mechanics of Economic Development." *Journal of Monetary Economics* 22: 3–42.

Luoto, Jill, Craig McIntosh, and Bruce Wydick. 2007. "Credit Information Systems in Less Developed Countries: A Test with Microfinance in Guatemala." *Economic Development and Cultural Change* 55 (2): 313–34.

Majnoni, Giovanni. 2012. "Basel III and Macro Prudential Policies in Developing Countries: A New Framework or a Familiar Agenda?" http://idbdocs.iadb.org/wsdocs/get document.aspx?docnum=36209155.

Marcus, Alan J. 1984. "Deregulation and Bank Financial Policy." *Journal of Banking and Finance* 8: 557–65.

Marquez, Robert. 2002. "Competition, Adverse Selection and Information Dispersion in the Banking Industry." *Review of Financial Studies* 15: 901–26.

Martin, Antoine. 2005. "Recent Evolution of Large-Value Payment Systems: Balancing Liquidity and Risk." *Economic Review*, Federal Reserve Bank of Kansas City, First Quarter, 33–58.

Masciandaro, Donato, Rosaria Vega Pansini, and Marc Quintyn. 2011. "The Economic Crisis: Did Financial Supervision Matter?" Working Paper 11/261, International Monetary Fund, Washington, DC.

McAndrews, James, and Simon Potter. 2002. "Liquidity Effects of the Events of September 11, 2001." *Economic Review*, Federal Reserve Bank of New York, 8 (2) (November).

Melecky, Martin, and Anca Podpiera. 2012. "Institutional Structures of Financial Sector Supervision, Their Drivers, and Emerging Benchmark Models." MPRA Paper 37059, University of Munich, Germany.

Merrouche, Ouarda, and Erlend Nier. 2010. "Payment Systems, Inside Money and Financial Intermediation." Policy Research Working Paper 5445, World Bank, Washington, DC.

Mersch, Yves. 2007. "AmCham—Principles versus Rules." Speech at a conference of ALFI and the American Chamber of Commerce, Luxembourg, June 14. BIS Review 79/2007.

Merton, Robert. 1974. "On the Pricing of Corporate Debt: The Risk Structure of Interest Rates," *Journal of Finance* 29: 449–70.

———. 1992. "Financial Innovation and Economic Performance." *Journal of Applied Corporate Finance* 4: 12–22.

Merton, Robert, and Zvi Bodie. 2004. "The Design of Financial Systems: Towards a Synthesis of Function and Structure." NBER Working Paper Number 10620, National Bureau of Economic Research, Cambridge, MA.

Mian, Atif. 2006. "The Supply and Demand Side Impacts of Credit Market Information—Comments." *Proceedings*, Federal Reserve Bank of San Francisco, November.

Micco, Alejandro, and Ugo Panizza. 2006. "Bank Ownership and Lending Behavior." *Economics Letters* 93: 248–54.

Micco, Alejandro, Ugo Panizza, and Mónica Yañez. 2007. "Bank Ownership and Performance. Does Politics Matter?" *Journal of Banking and Finance* 31: 219–41.

Michalopoulos, Stelios, Luc Laeven, and Ross Levine. 2009. "Financial Innovation and Endogenous Growth." NBER Working Paper 15356, National Bureau of Economic Research, Cambridge, MA.

Millard, Stephen, and Victoria Saporta. 2005. "Central Banks and Payment Systems: Past, Present and Future." Background paper for the Bank of England conference "The Future of Payments," London, May 19–20.

Miller, Margaret J. 2003. "Credit Reporting Systems around the Globe: The State of the Art in Public Credit Registries and Private Credit Reporting Firms." In *Credit Reporting Systems and the International Economy*, edited by Margaret J. Miller, 25–79. Cambridge, MA: MIT Press.

Miller, Merton. 1998. "Financial Markets and Economic Growth." *Journal of Applied Corporate Finance* 11: 8–14.

Mlambo, Kupukile, and Mthuli Ncube. 2011. "Competition and Efficiency in the Banking Sector in South Africa." *African Development Review* 23 (1): 4–15.

Motta, Massimo. 2004. *Competition Policy: Theory and Practice*. Cambridge, U.K.: Cambridge University Press.

Narain, Aditya, Inci Ötker, and Ceyla Pazarbasioglu. 2012. *Building a More Resilient Financial Sector: Reforms in the Wake of the Global Crisis*. Washington, DC: International Monetary Fund.

Newson, Roger. 2002. "Parameters Behind 'Nonparametric' Statistics: Kendall's Tau, Somers' D and Median Differences." *Stata Journal* 2 (1): 45–64.

Nier, Erlend W., Jacek Osiński, Luis I. Jácome, and Pamela Madrid. 2011. "Institutional Models for Macroprudential Policy." IMF Staff Discussion Note 11/18, IMF, Washington, DC.

Nier, Erland, Jing Yang, Tanjo Yorulmazer, and Amadeo Alentorn. 2007. "Network Models and Financial Stability." *Journal of Economic Dynamics and Controls* 31 (6): 2033–60.

OECD (Organisation for Economic Co-operation and Development). 2008. *Competition Issues in the Financial Sector—Key Findings*. Paris: OECD.

———. 2009. "Facilitating Access to Finance." Discussion paper, OECD, Paris.

———. 2010. "Roundtable on Competition, Concentration and Stability in the Banking Sector." Paris: OECD Policy Roundtables. http://www.oecd.org/dataoecd/52/46/46040053.pdf.

———. 2011. *Competition Issues in the Financial Sector—Key Findings*. Paris: OECD.

Olegario, Rowena. 2003. "Credit Reporting Agencies: A Historical Perspective." In *Credit Reporting and the International Economy*, edited by Margaret J. Miller. Cambridge, MA: MIT Press.

Oliver, Richard, and Stuart Weiner. 2009. "The Role of Central Banks in Retail Payments: The Central Bank as Operator." Presented at the conference "The Changing Retail Payments Landscape: What Role for Central Banks?" Federal Reserve Bank of Kansas City, Kansas City, MO, November 9–10.

Ongena, Steven, José Luis Peydró, and Neeltje van Horen. 2012. "Shocks Abroad, Pain at Home? Bank-Firm Level Evidence on Financial Contagion during the Recent Financial Crisis." Paper presented at the "Workshop on Financial Globalization, Financial Crises and the (Re-) Regulation of Banking: Macroeconomic Implications," University of Zurich, May 15–16.

Ongena, Steven, and Ilkay Sendeniz-Yuncu. 2011. "Which Firms Engage Small, Foreign or State Banks? And Who Goes Islamic? Evidence from Turkey." *Journal of Banking & Finance* 35 (12): 3215–24.

Ono, Arito, Iichiro Uesugi, and Yukihiro Yasuda. 2011. "Are Lending Relationships Beneficial or Harmful for Public Credit Guarantees? Evidence from Japan's Emergency Credit Guarantee Program." RIETI Discussion Paper 11–E–035, March.

Ötker-Robe, İnci, Aditya Narain, Anna Ilyina, and Jay Surti. 2011. "The Too-Important-to-Fail Conundrum: Impossible to Ignore and Difficult to Resolve." IMF Staff Discussion Note SDN/11/12, IMF, Washington, DC.

Ötker-Robe, İnci, and Ceyla Pazarbasioglu, with Alberto Buffa di Perrero, Silvia Iorgova, Turgut Kışınbay, Vanessa Le Leslé, Fabiano Melo, Jiří Podpiera, Noel Sacasa, and André Santos. 2010. "Impact of Regulatory Reforms on Large Complex Financial Institutions." IMF Staff Position Note 10/16, IMF, Washington, DC.

Padilla, A. Jorge, and Marco Pagano. 2000. "Sharing Default Information as a Borrower Discipline Device." *European Economic Review* 44 (10): 1951–80.

Pagano, Marco, and Tullio Jappelli. 1993. "Information Sharing in Credit Markets." *Journal of Finance* 48 (5): 1693–1718.

Palmer, John, and Caroline Cerruti. 2009. "Is There a Need to Rethink the Supervisory Process?" Paper presented at the international conference on "Reforming Financial Regulation and Supervision: Going Back to Basics," Madrid, June 15.

Panzar, John C., and James Nelson Rosse. 1982. "Structure, Conduct and Comparative Statistics." Bell Laboratories Economic Discussion Paper No. 248, Bell Labs Statistics Research Department, Murray Hill, NJ.

———. 1987. "Testing for 'Monopoly' Equilibrium." *Journal of Industrial Economics* 35: 443–56.

Petersen, Mitchell A., and Raghuram Rajan. 1995. "The Effect of Credit Market Competition on Lending Relationships." *Quarterly Journal of Economics* 110: 407–43.

Philippon, Thomas, and Ariell Reshef. 2009. "Wages and Human Capital in the U.S. Financial Industry 1909–2006." NBER Working Paper 14644, National Bureau of Economic Research, Cambridge, MA.

Piatkowski, Marcin. 2012. "PKO Bank Polski in Poland." World Bank, ECSPF, Washington, DC.

Podpiera, Jiří. 2011. "Credit Subsidy as a Countercyclical Crisis Measure: Evidence from Serbia." Working Paper, International Monetary Fund, Washington, DC.

Powell, Andrew, Nataliya Mylenko, Margaret J. Miller, and Giovanni Majnoni. 2004. "Improving Credit Information, Bank Regulation and Supervision: On the Role and Design of Public Credit Registries." Policy Research Working Paper 3443, World Bank, Washington, DC.

Rajan, Raghuram. 2010. *Fault Lines: How Hidden Fractures Still Threaten the World Economy.* Princeton, NJ: Princeton University Press.

Rajan, Raghuram G., and Luigi Zingales. 1998. "Financial Dependence and Growth." *American Economic Review* 88 (3): 559–86.

Ranciere, Romain, Aaron Tornell, and Frank Westermann. 2008. "Systemic Crises and Growth." *Quarterly Journal of Economics* 123 (1): 359–406.

Ravallion, Martin. 2011. "On Multidimensional Indices of Poverty." Policy Research Working Paper 5580, World Bank, Washington, DC.

Richardson, Gary, and William Troost. 2009. "Monetary Intervention Mitigated Banking Panics during the Great Depression: Quasi-Experimental Evidence from a Federal Reserve District Border, 1929–1933." *Journal of Political Economy* 117: 1031–73.

Riding, Allan, Judith Madill, and George Haines Jr. 2007. "Incrementality of SME Loan Guarantees." *Small Business Economics* 29: 47–61.

Rioja, Felix, and Neven Valev. 2004. "Finance and the Sources of Growth at Various Stages of Economic Development." *Economic Inquiry* 42 (1): 127–40.

Robinson, Joan. 1952. "The Generalization of the General Theory." In *The Rate of Interest and Other Essays.* London: Macmillan.

Rocha, Roberto, Zsofia Arvai, and Subika Farazi. 2011. *Financial Access and Stability: A Road Map for the Middle East and North Africa.* Washington, DC: World Bank.

Roper, Stephen. 2009. "Credit Guarantee Schemes: A Tool to Promote SME Growth and Innovation in the MENA Region." Paper prepared for the 3rd meeting of the Working Group on SME Policy, Entrepreneurship and Human Capital Development, "Fostering Entrepreneurship and Enhancing Access to Finance," Warwick Business School, U.K., October 26.

Rudolph, Heinz P. 2009. "State Financial Institutions: Mandates, Governance, and Beyond." Policy Research Working Paper 5141, World Bank, Washington, DC.

———. 2010. "State Financial Institutions: Can They Be Relied on to Kick-Start Lending?" Crisis Response Note 12, Financial and Private Sector Development Vice Presidency, World Bank, Washington, DC.

Rute, Maive. 2002. "The Role of Credit Guarantees in Improving the Availability of Financing." Speech at the Committee for Enterprise Development, Moscow, January 22.

Saldaña, Cesar G. 2000. "Assessing the Economic Value of Credit Guarantees." *Journal of Philippine Development* 27 (1): 27–68.

Santoso, Wimboh, and Made Sukada. 2009. "Risk Profile of Households and the Impact on Financial Stability." BIS Working Paper No. 46, Bank for International Settlements, Basel, Switzerland.

Sapienza, Paola. 2004. "The Effects of Government Ownership on Bank Lending." *Journal of Financial Economics* 72: 357–84.

Schaeck, Klaus, and Martin Čihák. 2008. "How Does Competition Affect Efficiency and Soundness in Banking? New Empirical Evidence." ECB Working Paper 932, European Central Bank, Frankfurt, Germany.

———. 2010a. "Competition, Efficiency, and Soundness in Banking: An Industrial Organization Perspective." Discussion Paper 2010–20S, European Banking Center, Tilburg, Netherlands.

———. 2010b. "Banking Competition and Capital Ratios." *European Financial Management*, June 15. doi:10.1111/j.1468-036X.2010.00551.

Schaeck, Klaus, Martin Čihák, Andrea Maechler, and Stephanie Stolz. 2011. "Who Disciplines Bank Managers?" *Review of Finance* 16: 197–243.

Schaeck, Klaus, Martin Čihák, and Simon Wolfe. 2009. "Are Competitive Banking Systems More Stable?" *Journal of Money, Credit, and Banking* 41 (4): 711–34.

Scott, David H. 2007. "Strengthening the Governance and Performance of State-Owned Financial Institutions." Policy Research Working Paper 4321, World Bank, Washington, DC.

Semenova, Maria. 2008. "Information Sharing in Credit Markets: Incentives for Incorrect Information Reporting." *Comparative Economic Studies* 50 (3): 381–415.

Shadow Regulatory Financial Committee. 2011. "The Basel Proposed Rules on Liquidity Regulation and a Suggestion for a Better Approach." Statement No. 317, American Enterprise Institute, Washington, DC.

Shleifer, Andre, and Robert Vishny. 1998. *The Grabbing Hand: Government Pathologies and Their Cures.* Cambridge, MA: Harvard University Press.

Simovic, Vladimir, Vojkan Vaskovic, and Dusan Poznanovic. 2009. "A Model of Credit Bureau in Serbia: Instrument for Preserving Stability of the Banking Sector in Conditions of the Global Economic Crisis." *Journal of Applied Quantitative Methods* 4 (4): 429–39.

Smith, Adam. 1776. *An Inquiry into the Nature and Causes of the Wealth of Nations.* London: Strahan and Cadell.

Special Investigation Commission. 2010. "Report on the Collapse of the Three Main Banks in Iceland." Icelandic Parliament, April 12.

Squam Lake Group. 2010. "The Squam Lake Report: Fixing the Financial System." Princeton University Press, Princeton, NJ.

Stigler, George. 1971. "The Economic Theory of Regulation." *Bell Journal of Economics* 2: 3–21.

Stiglitz, Joseph E., and Michael E. Rothschild. 1976. "Equilibrium in Competitive Insurance Markets." *Quarterly Journal of Economics* 90: 629–49.

Stiglitz, Joseph E., and Andrew Murray Weiss, 1981. "Credit Rationing in Markets with

Imperfect Information." *American Economic Review* 71 (3): 393–410.

Sun, Yu. 2011. "Recent Developments in European Bank Competition." Working Paper 11/146, International Monetary Fund, Washington, DC.

Turk-Ariss, Rima. 2010. "On the Implications of Market Power in Banking: Evidence from Developing Countries." *Journal of Banking & Finance 34*: 765–75.

UBS AG. 2008. "Shareholder Report on UBS's Write-Downs." UBS AG, Zurich.

Uesugi, Iichiro, Koji Sakai, and Guy Yamashiro. 2010. "The Effectiveness of Public Credit Guarantees in the Japanese Loan Market." *Journal of the Japanese and International Economies* 24: 457–80.

Urdapilleta, Eduardo, and Constantinos Stephanou. 2009. "Banking in Brazil: Structure, Performance, Drivers, and Policy Implications." Policy Research Working Paper 4809, World Bank, Washington, DC.

Vento, Gianfranco Antonio, and Pasquale La Ganga. 2010. "Interbank Market and Liquidity Distribution during the Great Financial Crisis: The e-Mid Case." *Journal of Money, Investment and Banking*, 18: 68–94.

Vercammen, James A. 1995. "Credit Bureau Policy and Sustainable Reputation Effects in Credit Markets." *Economica* 62: 461–78.

Véron, Nicolas and Guntram B. Wolff. 2012. "Rating Agencies and Sovereign Credit Risk Assessment." Bruegel 2011/17. http://www .bruegel.org.

Viñals, José, and Jonathan Fiechter, with Aditya Narain, Jennifer Elliott, Ian Tower, Pierluigi Bologna, and Michael Hsu. 2010. "The Making of Good Supervision: Learning to Say 'No.'" IMF Staff Position Note SPN/10/08, IMF, Washington, DC.

Vives, Xavier. 2011. "Competition Policy in Banking." *Oxford Review of Economic Policy* 27 (3): 479–97.

Vogel, Robert C., and Dale W. Adams. 1997. "Costs and Benefits of Loan Guarantee Programs." *The Financier–Analyses of Capital and Money Market Transactions* 4: 22–29.

Wall Street Journal. 2011. "BOE's King 'Baffled' by Logic of EU Capital Directive." November 3.

Wallison, Peter J., and Charles W. Calomiris. 2009. "The Last Trillion-Dollar Commitment: The Destruction of Fannie Mae and Freddie Mac." *Journal of Structured Finance* Spring: 71–80.

Weder di Mauro, Beatrice. 2009. The Dog That Didn't Bark. *Economist*, October 1. http:// www.economist.com/node/14539774.

Wellink, Nout. 2011. "Remarks at the High Level Meeting on Better Supervision and Better Banking in a Post-crisis Era." Kuala Lumpur, Malaysia, January 17.

Wilcox, James, and Yukihiro Yasuda. 2008. "Do Government Loan Guarantees Lower, or Raise, Banks' Non-Guaranteed Lending? Evidence from Japanese Banks." Haas School of Business, UC Berkeley; Faculty of Business Administration, Tokyo Keizai University; World Bank Workshop on Partial Credit Guarantees, March 13–14, Washington, DC.

World Bank. 2001. Public Credit Registries Survey dataset. http://go.worldbank .org/ PQW3K8Z0O0.

———. 2006. "Financial Sector Development Indicators." Project description, World Bank, Washington, DC. http://siteresources.world-bank.org/INTTOPACCFINSER/Resources /Webintro.pdf.

———. 2009. "Financial Infrastructure: Building Access through Transparent and Stable Financial Systems." World Bank and International Finance Corporation, Washington, DC.

———. 2010. "A New Database on Financial Development and Structure." World Bank, Washington, DC. http://go.worldbank.org/ X23UD9QUX0.

———. 2011a. *General Principles for Credit Reporting.* Washington, DC: World Bank.

———. 2011b. *Payment Systems Worldwide: a Snapshot. Outcomes of the Global Payment Systems Survey 2010.* Washington, DC: World Bank. http://siteresources.world-bank.org/FINANCIALSECTOR/Resources /282044-1323805522895/121534_text_ corrections_3-15.pdf.

———. 2011c. "China: Financial Sector Assessment." FSAP Report No. SecM2011-0492.

———. 2012. "African Financial Sectors and the European Debt Crisis: Will Trouble Blow across the Sahara?" Africa Financial Sector Policy Note, World Bank, Washington, DC.

Zarutskie, Rebecca. 2006. "Evidence on the Effects of Bank Competition on Firm Borrowing and Investment." *Journal of Financial Economics* 81: 503–37.

Zecchini, Salvatore, and Marco Ventura. 2006. "Public Credit Guarantees and SME Finance."

ISAE Working Paper 73, Institute for Economic Studies and Analyses, Rome.

Zia, Bilal H. 2008. "Export Incentives, Financial Constraints, and the (Mis)Allocation of Credit: Micro-Level Evidence from Subsidized Export Loans." *Journal of Financial Economics, Elsevier* 87 (2): 498–527.